T0382340

A Liberal Education

Enlisting a natural experiment, global surveys, and historical data, this book examines the university's evolution and its contemporary impact. Its authors conduct an unprecedented big-data comparative study of the consequences of higher education. They conclude that university education has a profound effect on social and political attitudes across the world, greater than that registered by social class, gender, or age. A university education enhances political trust and participation, reduces propensities to crime and corruption, and builds support for democracy. It generates more tolerant attitudes toward social deviance, enhances respect for rationalist inquiry and scientific authority, and usually encourages support for leftist parties and movements. It does not nurture support for taxation, redistribution, or the welfare state, and may stimulate opposition to these policies. These effects are summarized by the coauthors as *liberal*, understood in its classic, nineteenth-century meaning.

Brendan Apfeld is a lead data scientist for CVS Health. He holds a PhD in Political Science from the University of Texas at Austin. His research on comparative politics and the politics of education has appeared in journals such as *The Journal of Politics* and *Political Science Research and Methods*.

Emanuel Coman is an assistant professor in the Department of Political Science at Trinity College Dublin, where he teaches and researches party politics, elections, and local politics. His work has been featured in journals such as *Comparative Political Studies*, *The Journal of Politics*, *European Journal of Political Research*, *West European Politics*, and *Electoral Studies*.

John Gerring is Professor of Government at the University of Texas at Austin. His teaching and research center on methodology and comparative politics. He is coeditor of the Cambridge University Press series Strategies for Social Inquiry and serves as co-principal investigator of Varieties of Democracy (V-Dem) and the Global Leadership Project (GLP).

Stephen Jessee is Professor of Government at the University of Texas at Austin. His research studies political ideology and other latent traits, as well as voting behavior, legislative politics, and the Supreme Court. He is the author of *Ideology and Spatial Voting in American Elections* (2012).

The Comparative Politics of Education

Editor

Terry M. Moe, Stanford University

Education and its reform are matters of great political salience throughout the world. Yet as Gift and Wibbels observed, "It is hard to identify a community of political scientists who are dedicated to the comparative study of education." This series is an effort to change that. The goal is to encourage a vigorous line of scholarship that focuses squarely on the politics of education across nations, advances theoretical thinking, includes a broad swath of educational terrain – from elementary and secondary education to vocational education to higher education – and explores the impacts of education on key aspects of society. The series welcomes books of very different types. Some may be grounded in sophisticated quantitative analysis, but qualitative work is welcome as well, as are big-think extended essays that develop agenda-setting ideas. Work is encouraged that takes on big, important, inherently messy topics, however difficult they may be to study. Work is also encouraged that shows how the politics of education is shaped by power, special interests, parties, bureaucracies, and other fundamentals of the political system. And finally, this series is not just about the developed nations, but encourages new work on developing nations and the special challenges that education faces in those contexts.

Books in the series

A Liberal Education

The Social and Political Impact of the Modern University

BRENDAN APFELD
CVS Health

EMANUEL COMAN
Trinity College Dublin

JOHN GERRING
University of Texas at Austin

STEPHEN JESSEE
University of Texas at Austin

CAMBRIDGE
UNIVERSITY PRESS

CAMBRIDGE
UNIVERSITY PRESS

Shaftesbury Road, Cambridge CB2 8EA, United Kingdom

One Liberty Plaza, 20th Floor, New York, NY 10006, USA

477 Williamstown Road, Port Melbourne, VIC 3207, Australia

314–321, 3rd Floor, Plot 3, Splendor Forum, Jasola District Centre,
New Delhi – 110025, India

103 Penang Road, #05–06/07, Visioncrest Commercial, Singapore 238467

Cambridge University Press is part of Cambridge University Press & Assessment,
a department of the University of Cambridge.

We share the University's mission to contribute to society through the pursuit of
education, learning and research at the highest international levels of excellence.

www.cambridge.org
Information on this title: www.cambridge.org/9781009424776

DOI: 10.1017/9781009424783

© Brendan Apfeld, Emanuel Coman, John Gerring, and Stephen Jessee 2024

This publication is in copyright. Subject to statutory exception and to the provisions
of relevant collective licensing agreements, no reproduction of any part may take
place without the written permission of Cambridge University Press & Assessment.

First published 2024

A catalogue record for this publication is available from the British Library

A Cataloging-in-Publication data record for this book is available from the Library
of Congress

ISBN 978-1-009-42477-6 Hardback
ISBN 978-1-009-42473-8 Paperback

Cambridge University Press & Assessment has no responsibility for the persistence
or accuracy of URLs for external or third-party internet websites referred to in this
publication and does not guarantee that any content on such websites is, or will
remain, accurate or appropriate.

To Leah (BA)
To Veronica, Gael, and Luca (EC)
To Asli, Ozzie, and Oreo (JG)
To Nalinda, Max, and Ellie (SJ)

Contents

Figures

Tables

Acknowledgments

This book grew out of four studies based on a natural experiment in Romania, several of which are published separately (Apfeld et al. 2022a, 2022b, 2023). We are grateful to the editors and anonymous reviewers who offered feedback and to the journals (*Journal of Experimental Political Science*, *The Journal of Politics*, and *Political Science Research and Methods*) for permission to reprint portions of these publications. A fourth study is posted on the Social Science Research Network (SSRN) as a working paper (Apfeld et al. 2022c).

The project received financial support from Trinity College Dublin and the Center for European Studies at the University of Texas at Austin.

We are grateful to Lee Cojocaru and Shengqiao Lin, who painstakingly gathered and analyzed data and conducted original coding – work that was essential to the analyses that appear throughout the book.

We thank the participants in our book conference, including Steven Brint, Roger Geiger, Neil Gross, John Holbein, and Evan Schofer. This was an invaluable experience and we have endeavored to integrate their insights and suggestions into the final draft.

Finally, we thank all the scholars who answered our queries, shared their data, or read portions of the manuscript. This includes Andrew Abbott, Elizabeth Armstrong, Alejandro Avenburg, Richard Bensel, David Bills, Adam Bonica, Barry Burden, Larry Ceplair, Jack Citrin, Rodolfo Disi, Danny Dorling, Mike Findley, Julian Garritzmann, Miriam Golden, Dominik Hangartner, Richard Hardack, Dave Hart, Erin Hartman, John Henderson, Mike Hout, Martin Jay, Michael Johnston, Paul Kingston, Daniel Klein, Charlie Kurzman, Mitchell Langbert, Karl-Oskar Lindgren, Bob Luskin, Raul Madrid, Bob Maranto, Pat McDonald, John Meyer, Jeff Miron, Dan Nielsen, Sven

Oskarsson, Charles Pattie, Mikael Persson, Christopher Rootes, Sheldon Rothblatt, Eric Schickler, Peter Schochet, Rich Snyder, Arthur Spirling, Laura Stoker, Chandler Stolp, Devin Stauffer, Sid Tarrow, Rocio Titiunik, Stephen Turner, Nella Van Dyke, David Voas, Chris Welzel, and Josh Yesnowitz.

PART I

BACKGROUND

I

Introduction

Coming of age as an affluent citizen of the twenty-first century involves matriculation at a university almost as a matter of course. While elites used to receive their education from private tutors, this form of higher education has all but disappeared. Nowadays, children of the well-to-do, along with high-achievers from modest backgrounds, attend university.

Many students regard the experience as transformative. College degrees and college networks guide the search for employment. Beyond that, there are social and affective ties. Lifelong memories are associated with particular classes, friendship circles, college organizations, and events. College graduates frequently retain connections to their old school. Universities provide a modern-day rite of passage that structures the lives and livelihoods of those who pass through.

Those who do not attend college generally lead quite different lives. Indeed, one of the most consequential divides in the twenty-first century is that which separates those with university degrees from those without. Higher education is correlated with income, consumption habits, political affiliation, family structure, entertainment, and many other aspects of modern life. Everywhere, education appears to be a differentiating characteristic, displacing older cleavages based on social class, region, language, race, and religion.[1]

Of course, many of these differences may be driven by selection. Those who are interested in pursuing a college education, qualified to gain entrance to an institution of higher education, and capable of paying for it may be quite

---

[1] For work focused on this new cleavage, see Bell (1973), Brint (1984), Brint and colleagues (2022), and Gouldner (1979). For recent work on the alignment between education and lifestyle, see Baldassarri and Gelman (2008), Bovens and Wille (2017), Brooks (2010), Currid-Halkett (2017), DellaPosta, Shi, and Macy (2015), and Hunter (1991). Work on education and party ideology is reviewed in Duch and Taylor (1993), Gethin, Martínez-Toledano, and Piketty (2021, 2022), Stubager (2008, 2013), and van der Waal and colleagues (2007).

different from those who are not. From this perspective, higher education serves as a marker of identity and status, akin to a PBS tote bag, but not a cause.

This brings us to the central question of this book. Does university affect the social and political attitudes and behavior of those who attend? If so, how?

A MULTIMETHOD APPROACH

This is not the first book to address the question of university effects on social and political attitudes. After all, debates on these topics extend back to antiquity. However, the din of controversy has grown louder in recent years, creating an ongoing fracas between those who defend and critique the university for its role in educating the youth.

Many of these pronouncements are discursive in nature, intended to present a broad argument but not to wrestle with problems of causal inference. Other work is more focused but nonetheless limited by the data at hand. Because those who attend university are different from those who do not, it is difficult to tease apart the effect of education on social and political attitudes, net everything else. Another problem with the literature on this subject is its obsessive focus on the present. Studies published in the 1960s were focused on the 1960s, just as studies published in the 2020s are focused on the 2020s. There is little attempt to track the history of this evolving subject. Finally, most of the work on higher education's impact on social attitudes is focused on a single country – the United States. Accordingly, our understanding of higher education is embarrassingly parochial.

In this study, we also rely on country-specific data. However, the chosen country – Romania – is a long way from the US, literally and figuratively. Considering such metrics as educational attainment, educational performance, per-capita GDP, partisan cleavages, and other factors that might affect the relationship of theoretical interest, Romania is also more globally representative than the US.

In any case, the main reason for choosing Romania as a site of investigation is that it offers a unique opportunity for a natural experiment – which we refer to henceforth as the Romanian Natural Experiment (RNE). In Romania, admission to universities (private and public) is regulated by a national baccalaureate exam (the *bac*) taken by virtually all students graduating from high school. A score of 6.0 (out of 10.0) is required for entrance to university, meaning that those whose scores fall just above and below the cutoff are likely to be similar on background factors that might otherwise serve as confounders, but quite different in their likelihood of attending university. If we assume that those whose scores fall just above and below the passage threshold are similar, on average, the *bac* offers an opportunity for a (fuzzy) regression discontinuity design.

While the RNE offers strong internal validity, its external validity is uncertain. To provide a broader view of our question, we enlist data from the latest round of the World Values Survey (WVS), conducted in tandem with the European Values Survey (EVS). Most of the questions on this long-running global survey reflect on social and political attitudes. There is also a question about educational attainment from which we code a binary measure of university education, and there are questions eliciting pretreatment factors that might serve as confounders such as parents' education and occupation.

With this data, we construct a regression-based analysis that includes over 120,000 respondents across 79 countries, representing two-thirds of the world's population. It is as close to a global sample as one can get and thus well suited to the task of building general theory. Although causal inference in this setting involves untestable assumptions, one may compare effect estimates across various outcomes. We can see where a university education seems to matter most and where it matters least, or perhaps in theoretically unexpected ways.

These comparisons complement the narrow, but inferentially strong, RNE. Together, these two research designs offer a strong empirical basis for generalizing about the impact of college education on social and political attitudes throughout the world.

Complementing these analyses of the university's contemporary impact, we also investigate its history. To track the university's intellectual trajectory across several centuries, we focus on the views of students, former students, faculty, and intellectuals, as recorded in a variety of sources. Although this historical reconstruction remains speculative, it adds an important, and largely ignored, dimension to our subject.

Finally, it seems appropriate to draw attention to our own personal experiences. As students, researchers, and professors, we have spent most of our lives within the ambit of a university. We have fully participated in the experiences that we study. Although we did not take fieldnotes and do not introduce personal anecdotes into the text, these experiences cannot help but inform our intuitions and judgments. In these respects, ethnography should be acknowledged as a behind-the-scenes methodology.

THESIS

Having outlined our approach, we come to the argument.

The evidence presented in this book suggests that tertiary education has a profound impact on social and political attitudes in the twenty-first century. It is not merely a proxy for other factors. Moreover, the university effect is greater, overall, than that registered by other widely studied factors such as social class, gender, or age.

What is this "university effect"?

We argue that a college education promotes citizenship, enhancing political trust and participation, reducing propensities to crime and corruption, and building support for democracy. It generates more tolerant attitudes toward forms of social deviance that do not directly impact others (and thus may be regarded as matters of personal choice or identity) – for example, premarital sex, abortion, divorce, prostitution, and recreational drug use – forms of sexuality that depart from the heterosexual norm, and forms of gender identity that depart from the male/female norm. It undermines traditional modes of authority and identity such as the family, patriarchy, religion, race, ethnicity, and ethnonationalism. It favors a more inclusive perspective toward outgroups such as immigrants, minorities, and women, a softer, ameliorative approach to criminal justice, and a cosmopolitan perspective on the world. It enhances respect for rationalist inquiry and scientific authority. It usually encourages support for leftish parties and movements. It does *not* enhance support for taxation, redistribution, or the welfare state, and may, in fact, stimulate opposition to these policies.

One might regard this lengthy list as a smorgasbord of independent outcomes. However, we believe that there is some coherence to the university effect. To express this coherence, and to simplify the exposition, we adopt the term *liberalism*.

Liberalism's most distinctive feature is its embrace of freedom and liberty, from which the term derives. Beyond this, there is a commitment to the rule of law (also known as constitutionalism), law-abidingness (e.g., opposition to corruption), democracy, citizenship, progress, education, individualism, tolerance, openness to new ideas, rationalism, secularism, cosmopolitanism, and equality with respect to rights, duties, and dignity – but not redistribution or the welfare state.

These values are associated with the concept of liberalism in what is variously referred to as its original, classic, nineteenth-century, or European incarnation. Our use of the term thus differs from everyday usage in the US, where liberalism has come to be associated with the ideology of the Democratic Party and with what would be called the left elsewhere in the world. Readers will need to bear this in mind. Liberals (as we use the term) generally support parties on the left, but they are leery of the redistributive aspects of this agenda.

Because liberalism encompasses a wide-ranging set of attributes, there is no obvious antonym. We employ *conservatism, traditionalism, parochialism, the right*, or *anti-liberal*, as appropriate. *Leftism* is understood as an ideology that is liberal with respect to most policies except those with a libertarian or redistributive objective. Leftists, unlike liberals, embrace taxes, spending, regulation, and the welfare state.

In the following sections, we offer further thoughts on the meaning of this vexed concept, which we consider first as an *ideology*, then as a *philosophy*, and finally – our preferred usage – as a *worldview*. Despite its diffuse meaning and diverse interpretations, we shall insist that there are some widely recognized principles that qualify liberalism as more than an empty vessel.[2]

Ideology

The concept of liberalism, as we use the term, maps fairly neatly onto the agendas of parties in the liberal family such as the British Liberals (now the Liberal Democrats) and the German Free Democratic Party (FDP). Liberal parties, in the words of one recent study, "tend to promote right-wing economic policies (lower taxes, free-market economy, etc.) while being on the centre-left or progressive side of sociocultural policies (e.g., permissive or libertarian positions on moral issues such as euthanasia, same sex marriage; as well as quite positive stances on multiculturalism)" (Close 2019: 327).

Of course, many polities do not have any party that could be clearly identified as liberal, or that party is trivially small. This does not necessarily mean that the culture of liberalism is weak. In the US, for example, it is sometimes argued that *both* major parties subscribe, at least in their official pronouncements, to the values of liberalism (Hartz 1955).

To complicate matters further, many radical movements identify "liberalism" with mainstream politics and the status quo, their sworn enemy. Yet, these same radical movements often embrace ideals that we classify as liberal. Socialist movements, for example, were liberal insofar as they supported self-determination and independence for European colonies and full citizenship rights for minorities (African-Americans in the US, Jews in Europe, outcastes in India, and so forth). They were also generally at the forefront of campaigns for female suffrage. Indeed, in some respects socialist movements were more liberal (in our sense) than the mainstream ("Liberal") governments they opposed.

All of this is to say that our use of the term liberal encompasses the ideology of liberalism but should not be equated with the latter. It is, in fact, much broader insofar as it embraces some aspects of movements on the left as well as beliefs, values, and opinions that are not explicitly ideological at all. Trust, political participation, and democracy, for example, are consensual values that all parties and movements ought to be able to agree upon. They are not partisan, or at least not typically.

---

[2] Formulations of liberalism that overlap with our own can be found in Freeden (2003: 81–82) and Gray (1995: xii). For additional work on this much-studied topic, see Bell (2014), de Ruggiero (1927), Fawcett (2018), Freeden, Fernández-Sebastián, and Leonhard (2019), Fukuyama (2022), Katznelson (2021), McCloskey (2019), and Starr (2007). Our characterization of the academy as a liberal institution is in sync with Adcock's (2014) interpretation of American political science.

Philosophy

Our vision of liberalism resembles a *philosophy* in its breadth and abstraction.

Conveniently, there is a liberal philosophical tradition. One strand extends back to Enlightenment figures in the social contract tradition such as Hobbes, Kant, Locke, Rousseau, and Smith. Another strand is linked to the history of utilitarian thought as articulated by Bentham, the Mills, and Sidgwick.[3] A third strand is libertarian, with a lineage that includes von Mises, Hayek, and Nozick.

What all strands share, according to a common interpretation, is a commitment to the sanctity and separateness of persons. This individualistic philosophical tradition is entirely consistent with our interpretation of liberalism. However, it is misleading to call our vision of liberalism a philosophy.

First, it glosses over the many differences within the liberal tradition – not only across the three strands just referenced but also within each strand. Some utilitarians find the idea of a minimal state congenial; others are convinced that utilitarian principles require a far-reaching global redistribution of wealth (Singer 1972). Some interpretations of libertarianism assume considerable inequality; others are egalitarian (Otsuka 2003). Evidently, a commitment to the moral importance of the individual does not resolve many crucial social and political issues.

Second, treating liberalism as a philosophy suggests that there is a core value – for example, individualism – around which all subsidiary values and issue-positions revolve. A philosophy must be logically consistent. However, this is not how most people think about the world. Mass attitudes are not philosophies; they do not cohere in neat, tidy bundles and they are not derived logically from first principles (Converse 1964). Since our goal is to understand popular attitudes rather than the attitudes of philosophers, it would be misleading to approach the topic of liberalism from a philosophical perspective. There is no point in trying to recover a hidden logic from the jumble of attitudes that most people hold.

Worldview

To summarize, liberalism as we use the term is consistent with the ideology of liberal parties but is not limited to that particular ideology and is in any case broader than an ideology. It is also consistent with the philosophical tradition known as liberalism. However, since this is a vague designation, we cannot say that our use of the term is consistent with every philosopher's view of that tradition, and we certainly do not assume that mass attitudes cohere in a logical fashion around a single idea.

---

[3] J. S. Mill is an especially influential figure insofar as he provides a link between liberalism as a political philosophy and as a political ideology (Hamburger 1965).

Given these considerations, our conception of liberalism is best described as a *worldview* or *sensibility*. The values implied by liberalism (listed earlier) are closely related. They tend to travel together. But they also contain contradictions. There is, for example, the oft-noted conflict between liberty and equality (Narveson and Sterba 2010), as well as "negative" and "positive" visions of liberty/freedom (Berlin 1969), which echo in "classical" and "social" versions of liberalism (Freeden 1986).

There is also a conflict between activism and tolerance. Integral to liberalism is the injunction to be engaged in politics, to participate, and in doing so to defend and expand substantive goals such as the inclusion of outgroups. Also integral to liberalism is the injunction to tolerate differences, to respect free speech, to consider alternate points of view, and to deliberate in a rational and open-minded fashion. These two commitments exist in tension with each other. Passionate advocacy of a (liberal) point of view may be viewed as intimidating, unthinking, or disrespectful (and hence illiberal) by those who disagree. This is implied by charges of "PC," "cancel culture," and "woke-ness" that have been leveled against liberal activists (Holmes 2016; Rauch 2021). It is often difficult to find the right balance between speaking out and shouting down.

These exceptions notwithstanding, we believe that the commitments that define liberalism have more synergies than contradictions. Liberalism is not a random collection of values, and these values are fairly constant through time if interpreted in a general fashion.

Of course, the particular *issues* that define the liberal worldview have changed substantially over the years. In J. S. Mill's lifetime, liberals were beginning to appreciate the equality of women and their claim to basic civil and political rights. Now, liberals struggle with multiculturalism and LGBTQ rights, issues that Mill and his contemporaries would have had difficulty wrapping their minds around. Societies in the twenty-first century are considerably more liberal than they were in the nineteenth century. However, one can interpret these transformations as part of an ongoing commitment to the liberal principle of equality, which now embraces topics that were previously taboo.

On economic issues, one might say that liberals have ceded a lot of ground since the nineteenth century. Governments tax and regulate to a much greater extent today than they did in Mill's lifetime. The twenty-first-century welfare state would be virtually unrecognizable to a citizen of the nineteenth century. To the extent that the welfare state has gained general acceptance, societies have moved in a socialist (anti-liberal) direction. For our purposes, what is important is that those with a university education are less enamored of these statist features than those without a university education. In this respect, Mill's legacy persists.

Readers should bear in mind that when we invoke the term it is sometimes in an *ideal* sense (as a set of values toward which liberals strive) and sometimes in a *relative* sense (relative to the views of a particular society at a particular point in time). Mill was an outstanding liberal during his lifetime, though he would probably fall into the conservative camp today. We trust these nuances are clear from the context.

Readers should also bear in mind that Part IV of the book, centered on the history of the university, highlights the partisan elements of liberalism over the other elements. This is because we have historical evidence about the partisan identity of university faculty, students, and former students, while we have very little evidence of their views on other subjects prior to the late twentieth century. Accordingly, our treatment of liberalism is truncated in that part of the book.

WHAT LIES AHEAD

Having introduced our general approach and our argument, let us take a peek at what lies ahead.

Chapter 2 surveys extant work on the topic, beginning with a discursive view of the material and continuing with a systematic survey focused on journal articles that estimate a causal effect. Most of these studies indicate that university education has a liberal effect on students. However, a closer look at this literature reveals a more complex picture.

The second part of the book is focused on trying to estimate the causal effect of the university on social and political attitudes.

Chapter 3 introduces our data and methods of analysis. (Those uninterested in methodological issues may skip this chapter without losing the thread of the argument.) We begin by laying out the research design employed for the RNE. In the second section of the chapter we discuss problems of generalizability and how they might be overcome. In the third section, we introduce the WVS/EVS and our empirical strategy for analyzing that data, along with important caveats. In the final section, we address a potential problem of measurement in the RNE and WVS/EVS surveys, both of which are subject to social desirability bias.

Chapter 4 presents the main results from the RNE and WVS/EVS analyses. Outcomes are divided into seven general topics: (a) social capital, (b) democracy, (c) law-abidingness, (d) culture, (e) cosmopolitanism, (f) economics, and (g) overall ideology. In each case, we show that university attendance exerts a liberal effect on social and political attitudes.

The third part of the book pursues various extensions of these findings. Because the nature of the evidence is weaker, readers should be aware that this part of the book is more speculative.

Chapter 5 explores nuances – for example, the size of the causal effects; heterogeneous effects across different research designs, specifications, and samples; potential moderators; the effect of university attendance on partisan identity; and the aggregation of individual-level effects to societal levels.

Chapter 6 focuses on causal mechanisms. What aspects of the university experience generate liberalizing effects? We begin by introducing three mechanisms that seem to promise broad applicability: economics, empowerment, and socialization. We argue that the latter offers the most compelling explanation. However, this is a difficult claim to establish empirically. In the concluding section, we discuss the difficulty of reaching a determination on the question of mechanisms, noting the many methodological obstacles that stand in the way.

The fourth part of the book addresses historical issues. How did we get here? This part of the book highlights the partisan-ideological components of liberalism, as noted.

Chapter 7 begins with a thumbnail sketch of the history of universities. The rest of the chapter focuses on the modern era, where we home in on particular aspects of our topic: intellectuals, university faculty, student activism, university communities, and university graduates. In each section we try to ascertain historical patterns. When did universities become more liberal than the societies they are situated within, and how much more liberal are they today?

Chapter 8 focuses on differences across disciplines. We investigate patterns over time as well as ideological differences at the present time. Since data is most plentiful for the US, this chapter focuses primarily on a single country.

Chapter 9 explores various explanations for this liberal shift in the academy. We begin by reviewing six common explanations: dislocation between cultural and economic capital, public sector employment, genetics, intellectual activity, the opening of higher education in the postwar era, and self-selection. Next, we introduce a functionalist approach that focuses on the long-term consequences of an institution with a high degree of organizational autonomy whose purpose is to pursue general truths about nature and society that can be grounded in reason.

The final part of the book offers concluding thoughts.

Chapter 10 is our attempt to put the previous chapters together in a coherent fashion, recapitulating the main arguments and surveying the findings. (Readers looking for punchlines, reflections, and takeaways will find them here.) We begin by delving into the history of the university. Next, we examine evidence pertaining to the university's effect on social and political attitudes, revisiting Part II of the book. In the third section, we address some of the nuances connected to those findings as well as the mechanisms at work, presented in Part III of the book. The final section takes a wide-angle view of our subject, speculating on the overall impact of universities on societies in the modern era, which we characterize as "soft power."

A short Afterword focuses on the American university, which has become an epicenter of partisan combat in recent years. We show that although a university education may have greater impact on social and political attitudes in the US than in other countries, that impact does not conform to the expectations of conservative critics.

CONCLUSIONS

By way of conclusion, let us consider the sensitive nature of the subject before us. Much of what is written about the modern university has a tendentious tone. Some authors defend the honor of the university as they might a religion, while others attack it as a cult. There is something cultish about the whole enterprise. You are either on the inside, in which case you find yourself on the defensive. Or you are on the outside, in which case your instinct may be to knock down the ivory tower, or at least bring it down a few pegs. (*Who do they think they are?*)

We are on the inside, and we presume that most of our readers are university students or graduates, if not employees of the academy. As such, this book may appear didactic and self-congratulatory. *Well done!*, we seem to be saying to ourselves and our readers – and, by implication, *What fine fellows we are*. A moralizing, Whiggish tone is difficult to avoid.

It should be clear that although we are generally bullish on higher education, we do not see the impact of the modern university as an unadulterated triumph of reason and humanity over the forces of darkness. There are certainly things to celebrate. But there are also things to decry in the university's growing role in society. Where one stands on this question depends upon where one stands on the issues at hand.

Those on the free-market (neoliberal) right will be relieved to learn that a university education does not foster statism or socialism, and will see these results as a commitment to individual liberty.

Those on the left may view the same finding as an example of extreme hypocrisy. University graduates are apparently attracted by the egalitarian ideal except when it adversely affects their pocketbooks. They wear their hearts on the left and their wallets on the right.

We shall not weigh in on the rightness or wrongness of various policy positions and social values. Of course, we have our own views, but this does not seem an appropriate platform for ventilating them. Suffice to say that "liberalism" is understood as a description – not a commendation, and certainly not a condemnation.

2

Previous Work

What is education designed to achieve? What is its purpose? And what is its effect?

Work on the philosophy of education reaches back to classical writers such as Plato, Aristotle, and Quintilian, Renaissance writers such as Baldassare Castiglione and Erasmus, Enlightenment writers such as John Locke, Charles Rollin, George Turnbull, Jean-Jacques Rousseau, and Immanuel Kant, and modern writers such as William Whewell, James Mill, John Henry (Cardinal) Newman, Matthew Arnold, Émile Durkheim, and John Dewey.[1]

Throughout this long intellectual journey one may discern three sorts of questions. The first concerns the influence of education on the development of the self. The second concerns the influence of education on civic virtues. The third concerns the impact of education on actions and attitudes that one might call ideological (by virtue of the fact that commentators disagree violently on their rightness and goodness). Along each of these dimensions, one finds a lively intellectual debate. After presenting these debates, we proceed to a more focused survey of recent studies that attempt to estimate the causal effect of university education on social and political attitudes.

SELF-DEVELOPMENT

Some view education conservatively – as a mode of preserving ancient wisdom and imprinting valued traditions on feckless youth. Here, education serves to guide wayward children into adulthood, exemplifying an ideal variously

---

[1] For work by the aforementioned writers, see Plato (1992 [ca. 375 BCE]), Aristotle (1987, 1988), Quintilian (1892 [ca. 95 CE]), Castiglione (2003 [1528]), Erasmus (1998 [1516]), Locke (1887 [1693]), Rollin (1872 [1731]), Turnbull (1742), Rousseau (2007 [1762]), Kant (1960 [1803]), Whewell (1838), Mill (1969), Newman (1976 [1852]), Arnold (2006 [1869]), Durkheim (1973 [1903]), and Dewey (1897, 2013 [1899], 1923). For general discussion, see Gordon and Lawton (2002) and Rorty (1998).

described as gentlemanly, noble, Christian, or civilized. College should develop *character* (Eddy 1959), which one might interpret as conformity to established values and social roles.

Others view education as a mode of liberation, freeing students from the shackles of the past and from customary modes of thinking and behavior. Here, education serves as a mechanism of discovery and creativity. Individuality, rather than conformity to an established social role, is the goal. We are familiar with the slogans: "The truth will set you free," "Think critically," and "Speak truth to power."

The ancients and our contemporaries are united on at least one point: the role of higher education in cultivating a love of learning and of its product – knowledge or wisdom (the original meaning of "philosophy"). Those who are truly well educated should be inured to lowbrow attacks on science (Jewett 2020). They should be less susceptible to advertising, tweetstorms, and YouTube videos and more reflective in their consumption of news. They should consider themselves engaged in a lifelong quest for knowledge – of themselves and of the world.

In this spirit, those in the higher education business often defend the value of their product. William Bowen and Derek Bok (1998: xxii) insist: "Education is a special, deeply political, almost sacred civic activity. It is not merely a technical enterprise – providing facts to the untutored. Inescapably, it is a moral and aesthetic enterprise – expressing to impressionable minds a set of convictions about how most nobly to live in the world." Every commencement ceremony touches upon the ideal of a university education – what it is, what it could be, or what it should be. Presumably, every college president has written a speech, paper, or book on the subject. It is a well-worn genre.[2]

However, there is considerable skepticism about whether contemporary universities are delivering on their lofty promises. On the left, many writers bemoan the capitalistic orientation of the modern university: its capitulation to corporate sponsors and neoliberalism and its management by Philistine technocrats.[3] According to Roy Chan (2016: 2):

colleges and universities have begun to operate as a corporate industry with predominant economic goals and market-oriented values, which has reduced higher education to a transactional process rather than maintaining its transformative potential. This dual role has resulted in the rise of the new industrial model of privatization, commercialization,

[2] See Axtell (1998), Bok (1982), Dearden (2011), Freedman (2001), Gibbs (2017), Henry and Beaty (2007), Hirst (2010), Hutchins (1936), Jaspers (1960 [1923]), Kass (1981), Keohane (2006), Levinson (1999), McDonough and Feinberg (2003), Meiklejohn (1920), Nussbaum (1998), Oakeshott (1989), Peters (1968), Shapiro (2009), Thompson (2014), Whitehead (1967), Wolff (1969), and Wren and Riggio (2009). Variations on this theme emphasize the importance of learning from the classics (Bloom 1987; Strauss 2004 [1959]) and defending the humanities (Babbitt 1986 [1908]; Bennett 1984; Bod 2013; Donoghue 2008; Nussbaum 2010).
[3] See Cote and Allahar (2011), Donoghue (2008), Giroux (2014), Kronman (2007), Marsden (1994), Ohmann (2003), Reuben (1996), Shumar (1997), Slaughter (2014), and Washburn (2005).

and corporatization and has altered higher education's traditional mission, and has also increased the mission differentiation in higher education systems in preparing all graduates for democratic participation, active citizenship, and personal development.

Although the vocabulary is recognizably leftist, the themes articulated in this passage are not alien to those on the right, many of whom are also concerned with the increasing commercialization of a college degree. Indeed, one finds a good deal of consensus on these points across the usual ideological divide. Those on the liberal left (including Bowen, Bok, and most of those cited in the previous paragraph) and the conservative right (e.g., William Bennett, Alan Bloom, Michael Oakeshott, and Leo Strauss) can unite in defending crucial elements of the liberal arts curriculum while doubting their realization in the increasingly technocratic curriculum of the "multiversity."

Between the optimists and the pessimists there is an empirical abyss. We simply do not know very much about the university's ability to foster a distinctive *Bildung* or, to the extent that it is successful, what that *Bildung* consists of. Most of the writers just cited do not present evidence for their case, which rests at a hortatory or philosophical level.

"To effectively defend education," Bryan Caplan (2018: 19) writes, "you need to do more than appeal to humanistic ideals. You need to ask: How often do academics successfully broaden students' horizons?" His answer is bleak. "While great teachers can turn students into Shakespeare fans, Civil War buffs, avant-garde artists, and devoted violinists, such transformations are rare. Despite teachers' best efforts, most youths find high culture boring – and few change their minds in adulthood." In Caplan's view, the liberal arts mantra fails to broaden horizons because most students can't be bothered. The ideal is noble, but our ability to inspire is meager.

CIVIC VIRTUES

A second, closely connected objective of a college education is to train the citizens and leaders of a democratically governed society. Again, there is an ancient lineage to mine.

The connection between democracy and education goes back at least as far as the ancient Greeks (Heater 2003). In American history, the first touchstones are Noah Webster, the creator of the first American English dictionary (1787); Thomas Jefferson, the founder of the University of Virginia (Cremin 1961; Hellenbrand 1990; Honeywell 2011); and Horace Mann, the founder of the common school movement (Cremin 1957).

In more recent times, John Dewey is regarded as a foremost authority. His best-known work, *Democracy and Education*, includes the following thought-provoking passage:

The devotion of democracy to education is a familiar fact. The superficial explanation is that a government resting upon popular suffrage cannot be successful unless those who elect and who obey their governors are educated. Since a democratic society repudiates the principle of external authority, it must find a substitute in voluntary disposition and interest; these can be created only by education. But there is a deeper explanation. A democracy is more than a form of government; it is primarily a mode of associated living, of conjoint communicated experience. The extension in space of the number of individuals who participate in an interest so that each has to refer his own action to that of others, and to consider the action of others to give point and direction to his own, is equivalent to the breaking down of those barriers of class, race, and national territory which kept men from perceiving the full import of their activity. These more numerous and more varied points of contact denote a greater diversity of stimuli to which an individual has to respond; they consequently put a premium on variation in this action. They secure a liberation of powers which remain suppressed as long as the incitations to action are partial, as they must be in a group which in its exclusiveness shuts out many interests. (Dewey 1923: 93)

Our reading of this passage is that education matters for a democratic citizenry not simply because they must select their own leaders but also because they must live together, managing their affairs in a consensual fashion without the heavy hand of an autocrat telling them what to think and what to do. In these respects, education is essential to a democracy.

University life may also provide direct models for electoral democracy, for participation in voluntary associations, and for civic life more generally. The university is, after all, a voluntary association and there one may find an experience of fellowship, common purpose, and sacrifice for the common good. Universities are rife with student activities, so there are many opportunities to join in and to gain experience, both as a leader and a follower. Many of these activities are organized in a democratic fashion, and universities themselves embody a democratic ethic and usually include a variety of elective offices (though not the top offices).[4]

Not surprisingly, the topic of democracy and education has received a good deal of attention from political theorists, philosophers, and public intellectuals. Some of this work focuses explicitly on civic education, where the goal of the class or program is to foster community engagement. The conventional wisdom from this body of work is that education fosters political knowledge, trust, efficacy, participation, and other attributes associated with good citizenship. Diane Ravitch (2001: 28) concludes, "The best protection for a democratic society is well-educated citizens."[5]

---

[4] See Blessinger and Anchan (2015), Goodman (1962), Gutmann (1987: 185–193), and Wolff (1969).
[5] See Arthur, Davies, and Hahn (2008), Barber (1992), Bridges (1997), Callan (1997), Campbell, Levinson, and Hess (2012), Colby and colleagues (2003), Daniels and colleagues (2021), Gutmann (1987), Macedo (2009), Meiklejohn (1920), Nussbaum (2010), Ravitch and Viteritti (2001), and Sullivan (2020).

Early empirical studies of the question confirm the conventional wisdom. Philip Converse (1972: 324) concludes:

Whether one is dealing with cognitive matters such as level of factual information about politics or conceptual sophistication in its assessment; or such motivational matters as degree of attention paid to politics and emotional involvement in political affairs; or questions of actual behavior, such as engagement in any of a variety of political activities from party work to vote turnout itself: education is everywhere the universal solvent.

A couple of decades later, Putnam (1995: 672) affirms that "education is by far the strongest correlate that I have discovered of civic engagement in all its forms." Nie and Hillygus (2001: 30) concur: "formal education is almost without exception the strongest factor in explaining what citizens do in politics and how they think about politics."[6]

Recent work regards the connection between education and civic virtues more skeptically. One article, based on a study of twins, concludes that "when controlling for such familial factors the estimated effects of education on social trust are close to zero" (Oskarsson et al. 2017: 515). Another study uses propensity score matching to balance on various pretreatment characteristics and finds that there is little or no relationship between higher education and political participation (Kam and Palmer 2008). A third study leverages a natural experiment provided by draft lotteries to examine the connection between higher education and participation, finding no relationship (Berinsky and Lenz 2011). Some argue that native intelligence explains both education and political participation (Cassel and Lo 1997; Luskin 1990). Accordingly, there is now considerable doubt about whether university education fosters civic virtues.

IDEOLOGY

Thus far, we have explored university outputs that most commentators approve of; that is, personal development and civic virtues. Now, we turn to outputs that commentators often disagree on, which we shall refer to as *ideology*.

Complaints about teachers corrupting the youth are as old as written history. Socrates was famously accused of indoctrinating young and impressionable minds in ancient Athens (Euben 1997). Although modern readers may chortle, this antique conflict is by no means antiquated. Anyone who believes that education matters must take a lively interest in the content of that education. Ravitch (2001: 16) notes, "those who have a vision of schooling usually have a vision ... of a particular kind of social order." It is difficult to imagine one without the other. Since visions of justice vary, we should not be surprised that visions of education vary. Nor should we be surprised that these

---

[6] See also Almond and Verba (1963), Campbell and colleagues (1960: 252), Dahl (1961: 316), Key (1961: 329), Lazarsfeld and colleagues (1944), Stouffer (1955), Verba, Schlozman, and Brady (1995), and Wolfinger and Rosenstone (1980: 102).

visions often revolve around larger ideologies that may be framed schematically as liberal left or conservative right.

Leftists worry that universities indoctrinate students with mainstream, establishment views that inhibit free thinking. A century ago, Upton Sinclair's muckraking exposé *Goose-Step* (1923) exposed connections between the university and corporations (and capitalism more generally) – a concern that persists to this day. Universities are thought to be beholden to a military-industrial complex and prey to anti-left witch hunts.[7] Although some of these worries may seem to lie more in the past than in the present, talk of removing tenure from appointments to state-sponsored university systems has revived the threat of political interference in academic research and teaching. One recent article concludes that the institution of tenure in the US is more imperiled today than at any time in the past seven decades (Gardner 2018). Indeed, threats to academic freedom, often launched from populists on the right, are legion (Douglass 2021). An ongoing concern is the structure of governance, with wealthy individuals (often chief executive officers of corporations) holding positions on boards of trustees or influencing college policy via their contributions (Gerber 2014).

Conservatives see things differently. They note that the tertiary sector in most countries is a haven for leftists, where professors with strong political commitments color the minds of those they are tasked with educating. Together with activist students, this may tilt the university experience toward left-wing social views, left parties, and a secular culture devoid of traditional values, one that prioritizes egalitarian values over the free exchange of ideas. Lest one imagine that this issue is limited to the US, one observer noted several decades ago: "The greatest and most permanent politicization has occurred in Latin America, Italy, Japan, and in scattered places elsewhere. This politicization consists of attempts by radical groups in the universities to enforce certain political views by more or less open discrimination and pressures (frequently including violence) against recalcitrants, particularly in politically sensitive fields" (Ben-David 1977: 130; see also Albornoz 1967). The terms "politically correct," "woke," "cancel culture," "identity politics," "microaggression," "safe spaces," "institutional racism," "cultural appropriation," "White privilege," "male privilege," "trigger warnings," and "victimhood" are often cited as examples of left-wing campus politics that inhibit free speech and rational deliberation and contribute to an ongoing culture war.[8]

[7] See Aufderheide (1992), Barrow (1990), Feldman (1989), Giroux (2015), Heller (2016), Leslie (1993), Schrecker (1986, 2010), Scott (2019), and Wallerstein and Starr (1971).
[8] See al-Gharbi (2019), Black (2004), Bloom (1987), Buckley (1951), Campbell and Manning (2014, 2018), D'Souza (1991), Ellis (2020), Greer (2017), Horowitz (2009), Horowitz and Laksin (2009), Kimball (1990), Kors and Silverglate (1999), Lukianoff (2014), Lukianoff and Haidt (2019), Maranto, Hess, and Redding (2009), and Shapiro (2004). Responses to these conservative attacks are also legion (e.g., Bérubé 2006; Smith, Mayer, and Fritschler 2008; Wilson 1995).

In the US, conservatives see a closing of the American mind (Bloom 1987), while liberals see an opening (Levine 1996). A signal of this divide can be found in popular views of the university. When asked whether colleges and universities have a positive effect on the way things are going in the country, 67 percent of Democrats, but only 33 percent of Republicans, answered in the affirmative. This may have something to do with the perception of universities as liberal redoubts. At the present time, 79 percent of Republicans, but only 17 percent of Democrats, believe that professors bring their political and social views into the classroom (Parker 2019).

In many countries, education appears to be displacing social class, religion, and urbanization as a basis for partisanship. The new cleavage is variously described as liberal versus authoritarian (Kitschelt 1994), new politics versus old politics (Franklin 1992), integration versus demarcation (Kriesi et al. 2006), green/alternative/libertarian versus traditional/authoritarian/nationalist (Hooghe et al. 2002), social left versus social right (Coman 2017), and materialist versus post-materialist (Inglehart 2018).[9] Some research suggests that those without advanced degrees form the principal support base of populist parties (Spruyt 2014). In this light, the case for college as a polarizing institution seems plausible.[10]

Not surprisingly, the modern university finds itself at the center of an ideological war in which partisans battle for control over appointments and curricula (Berman 2011; Gless and Smith 2020). Both sides invoke the mantra of academic freedom, seeing their side as the victim in a war over freedom of speech. Leftists worry about pressures emanating from trustees, alumni, corporate sponsors, and government. Rightists worry about pressures emanating from faculty and students (the "PC police").

In the US, there is pressure to discipline faculty who are perceived to have surpassed the realm of acceptable speech (Graff 1993; Horowitz 2013). In other countries, the war over the university plays by harsher rules. In Hungary, the Central European University was forced to relocate because of its presumed anti-regime sympathies (Bárd 2020). In Turkey, many academics have been fired, exiled, or incarcerated because of perceived disloyalty to the regime (Aydin, Mak, and Andrews 2021). In China, academics have even less scope to voice opposition (Hao and Zabielskis 2020).

Amid this tumult, it is surprising how little we know about the actual impact of university education on the ideological proclivities of students. It cannot be denied that many college students hold views that are to the left of the average citizen. But this could be a product of selection. People

---

[9] See Duch and Taylor (1993), Ford and Jennings (2020: 302), Gethin, Martínez-Toledano, and Piketty (2021, 2022), Ivarsflaten and Stubager (2013), Stubager (2008, 2013), and van der Waal and colleagues (2007).

[10] See Abramowitz and Saunders (2008), Baldassarri and Gellman (2008), Bunch (2022), Henry and Napier (2017), and Kaslovsky (2015).

from left-wing backgrounds may be more inclined to attend university and to pursue careers in higher education, becoming college faculty, administrators, and staff.

Likewise, it could be that most professors do not try to indoctrinate their students, or that students are resistant to their doctrine (Caplan 2018; Gross 2013). Perhaps they even react against it. It is sometimes said that a religious education is the best antidote to religion; conceivably, the same boomerang effect applies to liberal arts colleges in the grip of the PC police. In a recent study, Binder and Wood (2012) show how the college experiences of some students nourish a conservative worldview. The available evidence is hard to parse.

It is important to appreciate that social scientists have been banging their heads against this problem for quite a while. Back in the Jazz Age, a spate of studies sought to understand the attitudes and behavior of American youth, and in particular college-bound youth (Fass 1977). In 1922, Manly Harper (1927) developed a set of survey questions intended to compose a liberalism–conservatism scale to describe the views of nearly 3,000 educators nationwide. This study showed, among other things, an association between liberalism and educational attainment, suggesting a causal relationship. At around the same time, Symonds (1925) administered a similar test to students of varying ages and educational levels in Hawaii, finding no relationship between attainment and liberalism.

By mid-century, a sizeable literature had accumulated. Attempting to summarize this set of findings, Philip Jacob (1957: 52) writes: "When all is said and done, the value changes which seem to occur in college and set the college alumnus apart from others are not very great, at least for most students at most institutions. They certainly do not support the widely held assumption that a college education has an important, general, almost certain 'liberalizing' effect."

Shortly thereafter, Allen Barton, a member of Columbia's Bureau of Applied Social Research, wrote a lengthy critique focused on the methodological shortcomings of Jacob's study. Barton's (1959) conclusion, in blunt terms, is that we do not know much at all about how college impacts the social and political attitudes of students. Much of the critique centers on problems of bias stemming from self-selection. In the book's foreword, Paul Lazarsfeld (1959: 9) notes, "the people who go to college are clearly different kinds of people ... from those who do not go, and those who choose one kind of college and within it one program of studies are likely to be different in the first place from those who choose another kind of college and another program."

In other words, it is difficult to draw causal conclusions from correlative evidence. The point would scarcely warrant attention were it not for the fact that it was made in 1959 – decades prior to the causal-inference revolution in social science.

SURVEY OF RECENT STUDIES

Having examined the debates over higher education's influence in a general fashion – summarized under the rubrics of self-development, civic virtues, and ideology – we now turn to recent studies that attempt to estimate a precise causal effect.[11]

The purview of our review is limited to articles and books published after 1995 (inclusive) – with a few exceptions for earlier studies that are especially influential. This is an arbitrary date, to be sure. However, the quality of work has probably increased over time and our primary theoretical interest lies in the twenty-first century. From both perspectives it seems appropriate to give preference to more recent work.

To be included, education must be a topic of theoretical interest to the author. We do not include studies where an indicator of educational attainment serves merely as a background covariate, as the chosen specification and research design may not be appropriate for estimating that parameter.

We focus on tertiary education rather than primary or secondary education (for reasons explained in Chapter 3). Studies that measure educational attainment or multiple levels of education are included so long as university is one of the levels under consideration.

We include studies where individuals are the units of analysis, excluding those where larger communities – regions, territories, or countries – are the units of analysis. (The latter genre is reviewed briefly at the end of Chapter 5.)

Since our theoretical interest is in the overall effect of college, we exclude studies focused on variation across institutions of higher education (e.g., secular vs. nonsecular, two-year vs. four-year), across areas of study (e.g., humanities, social sciences, natural sciences), or across particular aspects of the student experience (e.g., peer effects, faculty effects), unless they also render an estimate of the overall impact of higher education. (These more focused studies inform our discussion of causal mechanisms and moderators in Chapters 5 to 6.)

We ignore work that is not published in peer-review venues. Exceptions are made for a few studies that are well constructed and very recent, as we assume they will eventually appear in a peer-reviewed journal or press.

We leave aside qualitative work because it is difficult to summarize along standard dimensions and does not provide precise causal estimates. (Qualitative work nonetheless informs our theorizing in Chapter 6.)

To be considered, the outcome of a study must pertain to some aspect of social and political attitudes or behavior. We are not interested in studies focused on the economic or demographic impact of a college education, for example.

---

[11] Previous surveys of the subject (not as extensive as our own) show mixed results. See Emler and Frazer (1999), Feldman and Newcomb (1969), Hastie (2007), and Pascarella and Terenzini (2005).

If a single study examines multiple outcomes that reveal different relationships to higher education, each is represented separately. In defining outcomes, we generally rely on the author's judgment. If several variables are grouped together as part of a larger concept, we list that concept as the outcome. If they are distinguished – and especially if their relationship to education varies – we list them separately. Thus, the unit of analysis is a particular outcome explored in a particular study, for which we employ the term *analysis*.

The resulting compendium, contained in the Appendix at the end of this chapter, includes 89 studies and 146 analyses. For each analysis, Tables 2a.1–3 note the outcome, the outcome type, the location of the study, the treatment, the subjects (units of analysis), the research design (characterized in broad terms), the period of study, the number of waves (observations through time), the number of observations, and the finding.

General Characteristics

The general characteristics of this sample, summarized in Table 2.1, may be quickly reviewed.

First, there is the *venue* of publication. The vast majority of studies under review are published as articles in scholarly journals. Only a few are books or book chapters. This is to be expected since journals are the most likely venue for work of a quantitative nature. Books tend to be more discursive. Of course, books may republish or discuss quantitative analysis published elsewhere, but in this capacity they are redundant.

Second, there is the *field*. Each study is classified into a field according to the discipline of the journal or, if a book, the disciplinary home of the first author. Among disciplines, political science and sociology are well represented, while a smaller number of studies appear in economics and education venues. Two studies are published in psychology journals and the remainder do not fit neatly into a single discipline.

Third, there is the *treatment*. Usually, this is conceptualized as educational attainment (an interval scale) or education level (an ordinal scale). Occasionally, university education is the sole focus. As discussed in Chapter 3, the tendency to treat education as a single, relatively coherent phenomenon – an educational *system* – may be justified. But it could also be the case that the impact of tertiary education differs from the impact of primary and secondary education. If so, there is very little evidence speaking directly to our question as only twelve studies focus narrowly on university education.

Fourth, there is the *outcome*. Most studies focus on a single outcome. A much smaller number of studies embrace two to five outcomes and two studies encompass six to ten outcomes. None embrace a larger range of topics.

Fifth, there is the *sample size*. It will be seen that N varies considerably. However, most studies enlist between 100 and 100,000 subjects.

TABLE 2.1 *Characteristics of studies under review*

	N		N
Venue		**Sample size**	
Article	84	−100	0
Book chapter	3	100+	10
Book	2	1,000+	36
		10,000+	32
Field		100,000+	7
Economics	7	Unreported	4
Education	12		
Political science	34	**Subjects**	
Psychology	2	Citizens	83
Sociology	20	Students	6
Other, unclassifiable	15		
		Countries	
Treatment		1	67
Educational attainment (interval scale)	45	2–10	3
Education level (nominal scale)	33	>10	19
University (usually a dummy)	12		
		Region	
Outcomes		US	39
1	68	Europe	36
2–5	19	Asia and Oceania	4
6–10	2	Latin America	4
>10	0	Global	8

Characteristics of studies in Tables 2a.1–3 (N=89).

Sixth, there are the *subjects* under study. The overwhelming majority of studies focus on lay citizens, though a few are limited to students.

Seventh, there is the geographical *scope*. Two-thirds of these studies focus on a single country, while a few encompass a handful of countries (two to ten) and nineteen extend to more than ten countries.

Eighth, there is the *region* of focus. Four-fifths of all studies focus on the US or Europe. Other regions of the world are weakly represented and no study of our topic has been conducted in Africa. The "Western" orientation of scholarship presents a serious problem of external validity. This region of the world is rich and shares a common culture and history, especially as pertains to higher education. It is not clear, therefore, that one can generalize from the West to the rest.

Nearly half of all studies focus on the US,[12] posing an even greater problem of generalizability. Note that the tertiary education sector in the US is highly fragmented, ideologically diverse, and includes a large number of small private universities, many of them denominational (Bok 2013; Koblik and Graubard 2000). Politics in the US is the exclusive property of two political parties, generating one of the purest two-party monopolies in the world (Gerring 2005).[13] The political terrain in the US has become highly polarized over the past several decades (Sides and Hopkins 2015), a fact that may affect the relationship between universities and politics. Finally, there are unique features of history and political culture in the US that stretch back to the founding era (Lipset and Marks 2000). Although every country is exceptional, the US may be more exceptional than most, especially as relates to our topic. Again, one must wonder about generalizability.

Findings

The finding from each analysis is indicated by an arrow in the final column of Tables 2a.1–3. An up arrow (↑) indicates that higher education is associated with more liberal social and political attitudes or behaviors. A down arrow (↓) reflects a negative association between education and liberalism. A null sign (∅) indicates that education is uncorrelated with liberalism in the benchmark model (at least not at traditional levels of statistical significance) or that the relationship is mixed or non-robust. Where there is doubt about how to interpret findings, we rely on the author's interpretation of the evidence.

Readers will recall from Chapter 1 that liberalism encompasses the ideals of freedom, democratic citizenship, secularism, tolerance, cosmopolitanism, and equality – the latter understood as equal rights and equal dignity but not equal income. A "liberal" outcome is thus opposed to government-sponsored redistribution, taxation, regulation, and the welfare state more generally.

The main results from this comprehensive review of the literature are summarized in Table 2.2. Most analyses, and most studies, indicate that university education has a liberal effect on students. Only five analyses find effects in the opposite direction, as indicated on the bottom row.

Looking across various outcomes, we find that the most popular topics overall are ideology, family, ethnicity, participation, and democracy. Less

---

[12] This may reflect the extraordinarily large sector of researchers in the US (located mostly in sociology departments and schools of education), the ubiquity of universities across the country (see Figure 7.4), and perpetual dissatisfaction with the American system of higher education (Grant and Riesman 1978).

[13] Analyzing partisanship is different in a two-party system than in a multiparty system, where "exit" is easier and there is a greater diversity of ideologies and often more than one dimension of conflict.

TABLE 2.2 *Findings*

	Studies	Analyses		
		↓	Ø	↑
1. **Overall ideology:** left, liberal	9	0	1	8
2. **Family:** gender, sexuality, domestic violence	12	0	0	13
3. **Ethnicity:** race, immigration, xenophobia	20	1	3	24
4. **Other social issues:** death penalty, recreational drugs, abortion	1	0	0	2
5. **Religiosity:** religious adherence, belief in God	4	0	2	3
6. **Economics:** redistribution, welfare state, social policies	5	3	1	3
7. **Cosmopolitanism:** internationalism, anti-nationalism, pro-European Union, individualism	4	0	0	4
8. **Law-abidingness:** intolerance for corruption, crime, vote-buying	7	0	1	6
9. **Participation:** civic and political engagement, interest, knowledge	22	1	7	31
10. **Trust:** generalized, political	7	0	0	10
11. **Democracy:** civil liberty, moderation, stability, anti-authoritarian	16	0	2	15
12. **Post-materialism:** environmentalism	4	0	0	5
All		5	17	124

Studies and analyses in Tables 2a.1–3 classified by outcome type. Higher education is reported to have a liberalizing influence (↑), an anti-liberal influence (↓), or no demonstrable influence (Ø).

attention has been given to other social issues, religiosity, economics, cosmopolitanism, law-abidingness, trust, and post-materialism.

Although analyses of these various topics generally indicate that education exerts a liberalizing influence on political and social attitudes, there is some variability across outcomes. Findings are mixed for religiosity. And among outcomes classified as economic, analyses show a balance of positive and negative findings. Analyses focused on participation also report a substantial minority of null or negative results. On these subjects, scholarly consensus is not apparent.

RESEARCH DESIGNS

In Table 2.3, we disaggregate our sample of causal-effect studies by method. These are sorted into eight bins: cross-sectional or multilevel, matching, longitudinal, siblings, twins, instrumental variable, regression discontinuity, and experiment. For each method, Table 2.3 shows the number of studies that employ that method and the pattern of results across all the analyses employing

TABLE 2.3 *Findings by method*

Method	Studies (N)	Analyses ↓	Ø	↑
Cross-sectional or multilevel	66	3	5	89
Matching	3	0	1	2
Longitudinal (within-group)	8	2	3	16
Siblings	3	0	4	7
Twins	5	0	2	4
Instrumental variable	3	0	1	4
Regression discontinuity	1	0	1	2
Experiment	0			
All	89	5	17	124

Classification of studies and analyses in Tables 2a.1–3 by method. Education has a liberalizing influence (↑), an anti-liberal influence (↓), or no demonstrable influence (Ø).

that method. (Because many studies employ more than one analysis, the latter is often larger than the former.)

Now, let us delve into these subjects in greater detail.

Cross-Sectional and Matching Designs

The most common methodology applied to our topic relies on surveys of the general public. Here, the attitudes of those with a college education are compared to those without, relying on regression adjustments to reach causal inference. The resulting model must be correctly specified, including all pretreatment background conditions that are correlated with the treatment and excluding all post-treatment background factors.

An alternative to regression is a matching estimator (employed by three studies in our sample), where the analysis rests on those cases most closely matched on relevant background characteristics. In a notable study, Kam and Palmer (2008) use propensity score matching to balance on various pretreatment characteristics, finding that there is little or no relationship between higher education attainment and political participation. They interpret these findings as showing that education serves as a proxy for other characteristics that are related to participation.

Kam and Palmer's findings were later critiqued by Henderson and Chatfield (2011) and Mayer (2011), who maintain that pretreatment covariate imbalance remains (and perhaps even worsens) after Kam and Palmer's matching. They argue that as covariate imbalance is ameliorated, estimates of the impact of education on participation converge to positive values rather than the null effect estimated by Kam and Palmer.

The indeterminacy of this debate hinges on the nature of the data itself, which no estimator can solve. Obtaining a valid causal estimate with survey samples involves a great many assumptions that are virtually impossible to test. As usual, threats to inference arise primarily from selection effects. These may be based on family, peer groups, social class, urbanization, intelligence, or core personality attributes – all of which may affect social attitudes and thus constitute prima facie confounders. Some of these factors are fairly easy to measure and condition in a regression or matching framework. Others such as those rooted in genetics, core personality traits, or parental or family characteristics, such as care for children's education, are ineffable. And for those attributes that are measurable, one faces the usual difficulty of deciding which are pre- and post-treatment.[14]

Selection effects are especially invidious in this instance since the decision to attend university may be influenced by the outcome of theoretical interest, introducing circularity between cause and effect. If universities are bastions of progressivism, those who share this worldview are likely to be highly motivated to obtain a university education, while those holding more traditional views may be ambivalent and perhaps even repelled by the notion of attending college.

Knowledge of the destination may affect behavior all along the educational journey. Conservatives may be less motivated to achieve good grades in secondary school and to prepare for national exams that regulate admittance to university. When it is time to apply, they may be loath to postpone gainful employment and take on debt in order to attend an institution that challenges their deeply held views of the world and where they may be subject to social stigma.

Leaving home and attending college, which may be located far from home, requires courage. For some, this leap is easier than for others. The problem is that these selection effects generate biases in the data, leading to potentially spurious correlations. Causal inferences based on observational data in a cross-sectional format are notoriously unreliable, and in this case the biases seem to run in a liberal direction. Young people with liberal sympathies may be more likely to attend college.

Longitudinal (Within-Group) Designs

One approach to the problem of bias is to focus on longitudinal comparisons in which a group of individuals are surveyed iteratively over time as they pass

---

[14] Intelligence is an especially recalcitrant confounder as it is hard to measure and of questionable exogeneity. Nonetheless, a plausible case has been made for intelligence as a prior cause of political attitudes (e.g., Carl 2015) and of genetics as a factor in participation (Fowler and Dawes 2008). For a more general treatment, see Fowler and Dawes (2013). It is potentially significant that a number of genes have been shown to be correlated with educational attainment (Okbay et al. 2016).

through the educational system. Sometimes the analysis is limited to college students, whose attitudes are compared at the beginning and end of their educational journey or at various points in their journey through life.

This is the approach taken by a long-running and enormously influential series of studies focused on students at Bennington College, Vermont, who entered college in 1935 (Newcomb 1943) and were resurveyed twenty-five years later (Newcomb 1967) and again fifty years later (Alwin et al. 1991). Sometimes, longitudinal studies extend to those who do not attend college, allowing comparisons between treatment and control groups (e.g., Jennings and Stoker 2008).

Eight studies in our sample take this approach to causal inference, with mixed results. Thirteen analyses show a liberal effect, three analyses show a null effect, and two show an effect that runs counter to expectations.

Longitudinal studies offer some advantages over a cross-sectional design. In particular, one can include subject-specific fixed effects so that individuals are compared to themselves over time. Even so, obstacles to causal inference remain. Jennings and Stoker (2008: 6) identify five common weaknesses: "a critical lack of non-college control groups, time frames that terminate with graduation, attrition bias, localized samples, and different measures than those commonly found in the political science literature."

Jennings and Stoker (2008) is the only longitudinal study we are aware of that solves these problems. However, this study, like all others in the genre, runs into the usual problem of non-random assignment. Note that the factors that might sort individuals into college or non-college – family, class, genetics, personality, and so forth – could also affect their maturation through adulthood, and ultimately their social and political attitudes. It could be that those who end up in college would adopt liberal views even if they did not enter college.

Simply observing subjects over time does not necessarily provide sufficient evidence for causal inference, especially when the onset of treatment is not sharp. (University may be viewed by students as a continuation of their ongoing education, not a radical break.)

Moreover, since the causal counterfactual (a hypothetical reassignment of those in the treatment group to the control group) cannot be estimated, causal effects estimated for the treated group cannot be generalized to the untreated group except under very strong assumptions. That is, even if the causal effect for those attending university is correctly estimated, we cannot assume that the same effect would be realized by those who chose not to attend university (had they made a different choice).

Siblings and Twins

To overcome family-based confounders, one may focus on members of the same family, some of whom attend college and others of whom do not. As early as the

1930s, social scientists were enlisting twin studies to assess the independent impact of education on social attitudes (Kulp and Davidson 1933).

In our sample of studies there are three sibling studies and five twin studies. The latter match subjects on family and also on genetics, neutralizing another potential confounder. Based on this (admittedly small) sample, we can see that sibling and twin studies are twice as likely to find a liberal effect than a null effect.

While the methodology of comparing across family members (and even within genetically identical siblings in some cases) solves some problems, it encounters others. Consider the situation. If one sibling attends college while another does not, there is presumably an explanation for this divergence. Perhaps one was encouraged to develop their intellectual capacities, while the other was not. Perhaps one was the parental favorite. Perhaps one was naturally curious, while the other was not. Perhaps one experienced some childhood trauma. Perhaps one was optimistic and extroverted, while the other was not. Whatever the explanation, these factors could also lead siblings to adopt different social and political outlooks. Again, the confounder is obdurate.

Another problem encountered by research designs centered on members of the same family is posed by interference across units (a violation of the stable unit treatment assumption [SUTVA]). Since siblings are likely to be in close contact with one another, they are not truly independent research subjects and are likely to influence each other's social views. As such, treatment and control conditions are contaminated. From this perspective, the true causal effect may be underestimated.[15]

Instrumental Variables

Another approach to causal inference focuses on exogenous shocks that increase the supply of higher education, or in other ways encourage individuals to obtain higher education, but do not have a direct impact on the outcome of interest. These shocks may be used as instruments in a two-stage analysis, which in principle overcomes the threat from selection effects that mar other studies.

As instruments, recent studies have focused on eligibility for the GI Bill (Kaslovsky 2015), draft lotteries in the Vietnam War (Berinsky and Lenz 2011), a graduation quota program in South Korea (Jung and Gil 2019), the availability of junior and community colleges (Dee 2004), and changes in teen

---

[15] Methodological issues arising from studies of twins are discussed by Amin and colleagues (2015), Boardman and Fletcher (2015), Bound and Solon (1999), and Frisell and colleagues (2012). Some ambiguity is removed if one is confident about the specific genetic material causing the effect, as claimed by Dawes and colleagues (2021). For additional work in this vein, see Aarøe and colleagues (2021).

exposure to child labor laws (Dee 2004). Four analyses from these studies suggest that college has a liberal effect, while one suggests the effect is null or very minimal.

Instrumental variable (IV) analyses are subject to assumptions about the chosen instrument. In the first place, the instrument must influence the outcome only through the chosen variable of theoretical interest. This criterion is not generally testable and thus rests as an assumption.

Often, the assumption is questionable. It may be difficult to justify, for example, why a given factor affects people's decisions to attend university but does not otherwise affect their social or political behaviors or attitudes. It is also typically assumed that the instrument is independent of both potential outcomes and potential treatments. Both parts of this assumption may be difficult to justify in applications where the instrument is not assigned randomly or as-if randomly.

Another potential problem with IV analyses is that the population affected by the treatment is not very clearly defined. The estimator is vaguely described as a "local average treatment effect" (LATE), which means that it pertains to subjects whose selection into the treatment condition is determined by the instrument – so-called compliers. In many situations, we do not have a good sense of who the compliers are. When instruments are weak, as they often are, the question is even more open-ended and the resulting estimates may be severely biased.

Regression Discontinuity

Still another approach to causal inference leverages situations where assignment to treatment rests on a graduated scale with a sharp cutoff, creating an opportunity for a regression discontinuity (RD) design.

RD designs are not uncommon in studies focused on the economic returns of education. For example, Canaan and Mouganie (2018) compare students who barely pass, and barely fail, the first round of the French baccalaureate (*bac*) exam, administered annually to graduating high school students. Although failers are likely to continue their education (they have a second chance to pass the *bac*), the quality of the education they receive is likely to be lower on account of having failed on the first round. Accordingly, the authors can compare the impact of the quality of education on employment in subsequent years for these two closely matched groups.

When evaluating the impact of higher education on social and political attitudes, the quality of education is probably less important than the quantity. (One would not expect a slightly more exclusive educational experience to translate into vastly different outlooks on society and politics.) Accordingly, one must locate situations where a national exam regulates access to the higher education system as a whole such that it separates those who matriculate from those who do not.

Only one such RD design can be found in our review of the literature, which speaks to the rarity of this circumstance. Hangartner and colleagues (2020) employ an RD design focused on political participation in Switzerland, where the discontinuity centers on national exam scores with a cutoff for entry to a university track. The authors find that university education has a positive effect on voting and low-cost non-electoral avenues of participation. However, it has no effect on forms of participation that impose a higher cost on citizens such as collecting signatures for a referendum or joining a community organization or political party. It is a mixed result, partially validating the optimistic view of college as a socialization instrument for active citizenship.

RD designs are widely regarded as stronger than other observational methods insofar as they require fewer assumptions in order to reach causal inference and these assumptions are testable, at least to some degree, with observed data.[16] Like IV designs, they estimate a LATE. However, it is often easier to characterize this subpopulation and hence to generalize from the results.

We are fans of this research design, as will become apparent in the next chapter. When experiments are impossible, discontinuities in a background variable that determine exposure to a treatment are often the next best thing.

Experiments

Notably absent from our review of the literature is a study in which the treatment is randomized by the researcher. Although experiments have been employed on a few occasions with respect to primary and secondary education (e.g., Sondheimer and Green 2010), they have not been applied at the tertiary level.

We suspect that this absence is not coincidental. Higher education is expensive, so assembling a large sample requires a large investment, one that lies beyond the reach of most private donors and foundations. Governments have the resources to conduct experiments but are unlikely to view the prospect of randomizing access to higher education as politically palatable. Naturally, there are also ethical concerns. For these reasons, it is understandable that the vast majority of work on our topic is observational.

Nonetheless, there are some opportunities for experimental research that have been exploited for other purposes. One such approach is an encouragement design that nudges students to apply to college by informing them of financial aid packages they might not be aware of (Bird et al. 2021). The treatment is relatively cheap and can be randomized, though a good deal of non-compliance can be expected – leading to inferential problems associated with weak instruments and the necessity of very large samples.

In any case, it is important to note that the gold standard of research design, the classical experiment, has never been applied to our question of theoretical interest.

---

[16] See Cattaneo and colleagues (2020) for an excellent overview of RD designs.

CONCLUSIONS

Wherever a treatment is not randomly assigned, causal inferences are prone to confounding. This has become a truism of social science, and the problem seems especially acute with respect to the present question.

In Table 2.3, we classified extant research designs as cross-sectional or multilevel, matching, longitudinal, siblings, twins, instrumental variable, and regression discontinuity. Most of the cross-sectional studies show a strong association between university education and liberal social and political attitudes. By contrast, findings based on other research designs, which probably do a better job of controlling confounders, are less consistent. This may be a clue that the apparent consensus in the literature on our subject (see Table 2.2) does not rest on strong foundations.

Of course, this pattern could also reflect researcher bias and/or publication bias. Those who spend their time pursuing recondite research designs may be motivated by a sense that the positive findings obtained from cross-sectional designs are too good to be true. They may therefore be primed to discover null effects. Likewise, journals may be loath to publish null effects unless the research design is very strong. Both of these biases could generate the pattern of results displayed in Table 2.3.

Among extant studies, we find striking imbalances in the amount of attention devoted to various outcomes. Attitudes toward outgroups and political participation are a frequent focus of study. Other outcomes such as religiosity, economic values, cosmopolitanism, and post-materialism are rarely studied. And others are entirely neglected, as shown in Table 2.2.

We also raised issues about external validity due to the underrepresentation of regions outside Europe and North America and the concentration of studies focused on the possibly idiosyncratic case of the US. Relatedly, we pointed out that most studies examine educational systems as a whole – on the assumption that primary, secondary, and tertiary sectors have similar effects – an assumption that may, or may not, hold.

On a more general note, we observe that narrowly focused studies such as those reviewed in the previous section are at pains to address large research questions. To be sure, the author may invoke a capacious theory to explain a given outcome; however, the latter offers only a very small – and possibly misleading – test of the former. The shoe is much bigger than the foot.

Narrowly focused studies are prone to stochastic error associated with the author's choice of input and output variables, model specification, estimator, and research site. Even if internal validity is strong, external validity is often problematic. We do not know whether a study conducted in one context will be reproducible in another context or with another research design. The problem of generalizability looms (Findley et al. 2021).

For all these reasons, there are many ways to interpret the footprint left by published literature. These uncertainties set the stage for the rest of the book, where we present new evidence on the time-honored question of university effects.

APPENDIX: REVIEW OF CAUSAL-EFFECT STUDIES

Tables 2a.1–3 contain the findings of an extensive review of studies seeking to estimate the causal effect of higher education on social and political attitudes, as described in the text.

TABLE 2A *Causal-effect studies*

Study	Outcome	Type	Location	Treatment	Subjects	Design	Period	Waves	Obs	Finding
Berinsky and Lenz 2011	Participation	9	US	Attainment	Citizens	IV	1972–2000		250,000	Ø
Bobo and Licari 1989	Tolerance	11	US	Attainment	Citizens	Cross-section	1984	1	1,473	↑
Borgonovi 2012	Interpersonal trust	10	Europe	Attainment	Citizens	Cross-section	2002, 2007	2	88,813	↑
	Immigration	3	Europe	Attainment	Citizens	Cross-section	2002, 2007	2	88,813	↑
Brand 2010	Volunteer work	9	US	University	Citizens	Longitudinal	1979–2006		12,686	↑
Brehm and Rahn 1997	Civic engagement	9	US	Attainment	Citizens	Cross-section	1972–1994		32,380	↑
Brusco et al. 2004	Vote-buying	8	Argentina	Level	Citizens	Cross-section	2001	1	1,920	Ø
Buerkle Guseva 2002	Social capital	9	Czechia, Poland	Attainment	Citizens	Cross-section	1992–1993	1	4,766	↑
Burden 2009	Turnout	9	US	Attainment	Citizens	Cross-section	1952–2004	14	21,306	↑
Burden et al. 2020	Turnout	9	US	Attainment	Citizens	Siblings	1957–2011		3,784	↑
Campbell and Horowitz 2016	Ideology	1	US	University	Citizens	Siblings	1994	1	2,310	↑
	Civil liberty	11	US	University	Citizens	Siblings	1994	1	2,310	↑
	Gender	2	US	University	Citizens	Siblings	1994	1	2,310	↑
Chong and Gradstein 2015	Democratic preference	11	Global	Attainment	Citizens	Cross-section	1994–2008	3	240,000	↑

(continued)

Study	Concept	Count	Region	Measure	Sample	Method	Years	N studies	N	Effect
Coenders and Scheepers 2003	Chauvinism	2	Global	Attainment	Citizens	Cross-section	1995	1	23,000	↑
	Patriotism	7	Global	Attainment	Citizens	Cross-section	1995	1	23,000	↑
	Immigration	3	Global	Attainment	Citizens	Cross-section	1995	1	23,000	↑
	Refugees	3	Global	Attainment	Citizens	Cross-section	1995	1	23,000	↑
	Inclusion/exclusion	3	Global	Attainment	Citizens	Cross-section	1995	1	23,000	↑
Dee 2004	Turnout	9	US	Attainment	Citizens	IV	1984–1992	2	11,366	↑
	Civic behavior	9	US	Attainment	Citizens	IV	1984–1992	2	11,366	↑
	Right–left	1	US	Attainment	Citizens	IV	1984–1992	2	11,366	↑
de Witte 1999	Ethnicity	3	Belgium	Level	Citizens	Cross-section	1989	1	1,600	↑
Dinesen et al. 2016	Participation	9	US, Demark	Attainment, level	Citizens	Twins	2008–2010	4	3,096	↑
	Participation	9	Sweden	Attainment, level	Citizens	Twins	2008–2010	4	3,096	Ø
Duch and Taylor 1993	Post-materialism	12	Europe	Level	Citizens	Cross-section	1973–1984	1	13,000	↑
Dunn 2011	Right–left	1	Global	Attainment	Citizens	Cross-section	2001–2006	3	110,052	↑
Eftedal et al. 2020	Right-authoritarian	11	Norway	Level	Citizens	Twins	2016	1	1,987	↑
Elchardus and Spruyt 2010	Extreme right	1	Belgium	Level	Citizens	Cross-section	1991–2001	4	7,450	↑

(continued)

TABLE 2A (continued)

Study	Outcome	Type	Location	Treatment	Subjects	Design	Period	Waves	Obs	Finding
Farnworth et al. 1998	Death penalty	4	US	University	Students	Cross-section	1992	1	683	↑
	Recreational drugs	4	US	University	Students	Cross-section	1992	1	683	↑
Gaasholt and Togeby 1995	Ethnicity	3	Denmark	Attainment	Citizens	Cross-section	1988	1	2,855	↑
Ganzach 2020	Right–left	1	US	Attainment	Citizens	Cross-section	1972–2016	20	32,871	↑
Gelepithis and Giani 2020	Redistribution	6	Europe	University	Citizens	Cross-section	2002–2016	8	194,916	↑
	Xenophobia	3	Europe	University	Citizens	Cross-section	2002–2016	8	194,916	↑
	Race	3	Europe	University	Citizens	Cross-section	2002–2016	8	194,916	↑
	Social trust	10	Europe	University	Citizens	Cross-section	2002–2016	8	194,916	↑
	Political trust	10	Europe	University	Citizens	Cross-section	2002–2016	8	194,916	↑
Gesthuizen et al. 2008	Social capital	9	Europe	Attainment	Citizens	Cross-section	2004	1	27,000	↑
Gibson 2001	Volunteer work	9	New Zealand	Attainment	Citizens	Twins	1994	1	253	↑
Gidengil et al. 2019	Turnout	9	Finland	Level	Citizens	Cross-section	1999	1	78,937	↑

(continued)

Study	Topic		Country	Level/Attainment	Population	Design	Years		N	
Glaser 2001	Race	3	US	Level	Citizens	Cross-section	1998	1	770	↑
	Affirmative action	3	US	Level	Citizens	Cross-section	1998	1	770	→
Golebiowska 1995	Political tolerance	11	US	Attainment	Citizens	Cross-section	1988	1		↑
Haegel 1999	Ethnicity	3	France	Level	Citizens	Cross-section	1997	1	3,010	↑
Hainmuller and Hiscox 2007	Immigration	3	Europe	Attainment	Citizens	Cross-section	2003	1	28,878	↑
Hakhverdian et al. 2013	Euroscepticism	7	Europe	Attainment	Citizens	Cross-section	1973–2010	81	813,199	↑
Hangartner et al. 2020	Electoral participation	9	Switzerland	Attainment	Students	RD	2011–2014	1	4,373	↑
	Low-cost participation	9	Switzerland	Attainment	Students	RD	2011–2014	1	4,373	↑
	High-cost participation	9	Switzerland	Attainment	Students	RD	2011–2014	1	4,373	Ø
Hauser 2000	Civic participation	9	US	Attainment	Citizens	Cross-section	1974–1990	1	13,615	Ø
Heerwig and McCabe 2009	Race	3	US	Level	Citizens	Cross-section	2007	1	1,560	↑
Helliwell and Putnam 2007	Social trust	10	US	Attainment	Citizens	Cross-section	1972–1997		98,601	↑

(continued)

TABLE 2A (continued)

Study	Outcome	Type	Location	Treatment	Subjects	Design	Period	Waves	Obs	Finding
	Social engagement	9	US	Attainment	Citizens	Cross-section	1972–1997		98,601	↑
	Participation	9	US	Attainment	Citizens	Cross-section	1972–1997		98,601	↑
Hello et al. 2002	Ethnicity	3	Europe	Level	Citizens	Cross-section	1998	1	11,904	↑
Hello et al. 2004	Ethnicity	3	Netherlands	Attainment	Citizens	Longitudinal	1990–2000	3	1,225	↑
Henderson and Chatfield 2011	Participation	9	US	Attainment	Citizens	Matching	1965–1973	1	15,558	↑
Henry and Napier 2017	Ethnicity	3	US	Level	Citizens	Cross-section	1964–2012		24,232	↑
Highton 2009	Political sophistication	9	US	University	Citizens	Longitudinal	1965–1973	4	4,360	Ø
Hooghe and de Vroome 2015	Immigration	3	Europe	Level	Citizens	Cross-section	2010–2011	1	32,806	↑
	Political trust	10	Europe	Level	Citizens	Cross-section	2010–2011	1	32,806	↑
	Government satisfaction	10	Europe	Level	Citizens	Cross-section	2010–2011	1	32,806	↑
Jasinska-Kania 1999	Ethnicity	3	Poland	Level	Citizens	Cross-section	1988–1990	2	907	↑
Jennings and Stoker 2008	Political knowledge	9	US	University	Students	Longitudinal	935	4	935	↑

(continued)

Study	Variable		Country			Method			N	
	Political interest	9	US	University	Students	Longitudinal	935	4	935	↑
	Political efficacy	9	US	University	Students	Longitudinal	935	4	935	↑
	Civic participation	9	US	University	Students	Longitudinal	935	4	935	↑
	Cosmopolitan	7	US	University	Students	Longitudinal	935	4	935	↑
	Ideology, sophistication	9	US	University	Students	Longitudinal	935	4	935	↑
	Political trust	9	US	University	Students	Longitudinal	935	4	935	↑
	Civic tolerance	11	US	University	Students	Longitudinal	935	4	935	↑
	Labor	6	US	University	Students	Longitudinal	935	4	935	→
Jenssen and Engesbak 1994	Ethnicity	3	Norway	Level	Citizens	Cross-section	1988	1	2,048	Ø
Jung and Gil 2019	Right–left	1	South Korea	University	Students	IV	2003–2013	1	1,463	↑
Kam and Palmer 2008	Participation	9	US	Attainment	Citizens	Matching	1965–1973	1	15,558	Ø
Kane 1995	Gender	2	US	Level	Citizens	Cross-section	1990–1991	1	1,750	↑
Kingston et al. 2003	Civil liberty	11	US	Attainment	Citizens	Cross-section	1991–1998	5	2,825	↑
	Gender	2	US	Attainment	Citizens	Cross-section	1991–1998	5	2,825	↑
	Social capital	9	US	Attainment	Citizens	Cross-section	1991–1998	5	2,825	↑
	Civic knowledge	9	US	Attainment	Citizens	Cross-section	1991–1998	5	2,825	↑

(continued)

TABLE 2A (continued)

Study	Outcome	Type	Location	Treatment	Subjects	Design	Period	Waves	Obs	Finding
Lambert et al. 2006	Homosexuality	2	US	University	Students	Cross-section	2002	1	364	↑
Lancee and Sarrasin 2015	Immigration	3	Switzerland	Attainment	Citizens	Longitudinal	1999–2011	4	16,751	∅
La Roi and Mandemakers 2018	Homosexuality	2	UK	Level	Citizens	Longitudinal	1991–2008	6	18,571	↑
Loftus 2001	Homosexuality	2	US	Level	Citizens	Cross-section	1973–1998		19,413	↑
Makowsky and Miller 2014	Extremism	11	US	Attainment	Citizens	Cross-section	1972–2010		2,303	↑
Marquart-Pyatt and Paxton 2007	Political tolerance	11	US, Europe	Attainment	Citizens	Cross-section	1995–1997	1	11,060	↑
Mayer 2011	Participation	9	US	Level	Citizens	Matching	1965–1973	1	999	↑
Mayrl and Uecker 2011	Religiosity	5	US	University	Citizens	Longitudinal	2002–2008	2	5,064	↑
Meeusen et al. 2013	Ethnocentrism	3	Netherlands	Level	Citizens	Cross-section	2009	1	1,910	↑
Mocan 2008	Corruption	8	Global	Attainment	Citizens	Cross-section	1995–1996	1	55,107	↑

(continued)

Study	Outcome		Country	Measure	Population	Design	Years		N	Direction
Nie et al. 1996	Civic engagement	9	US	Attainment	Citizens	Cross-section				↑
	Civic enlightenment	11	US	Attainment	Citizens	Cross-section				↑
Ocantos et al. 2014	Vote-buying	8	Latin America	Level	Citizens	Cross-section	2009–2011	1	14,673	↑
Ohlander et al. 2005	Homosexuality	2	US	Level	Citizens	Cross-section	1988–1994		2,733	↑
Oskarsson et al. 2017	Social trust	10	Sweden	Attainment	Citizens	Twins	2010		11,578	↑
Peri 1999	Ethnicity	3	Italy	Attainment	Citizens	Cross-section	1994	1		↑
Phelan et al. 1995	Homelessness	6	US	Attainment	Citizens	Cross-section	1990	1	1,507	→
	Homeless assistance	6	US	Attainment	Citizens	Cross-section	1990	1	1,507	→
	Civil liberty	11	US	Attainment	Citizens	Cross-section	1990	1	1,507	Ø
Pradhanawati et al. 2019	Vote-buying	8	Indonesia	Level	Citizens	Cross-section	1990	1	1,005	↑
Reimer 2010	Theology	5	US	Level	Students	Cross-section	2004–2006	1	700	↑
Ruiter and van Tubergen 2009	Religiosity	5	Global	Attainment	Citizens	Cross-section	1990–2001	3	136,611	↑

(continued)

TABLE 2A (*continued*)

Study	Outcome	Type	Location	Treatment	Subjects	Design	Period	Waves	Obs	Finding
Scheepers et al. 2002	Moral attitudes/family	2	Global	Level	Citizens	Cross-section	1991	1	16,604	↑
Schnabel 2018	Violence	11	US	Level	Citizens	Cross-section	2010–2014	1	2,147	↑
Schnittker and Behrman 2012	Civic engagement	9	US	Attainment	Citizens	Twins	1995–1996	1	1,908	Ø
Schoon et al. 2010	Political trust	10	UK	Attainment	Citizens	Cross-section	1958	1	8,804	↑
	Liberalism	1	UK	Attainment	Citizens	Cross-section	1958	1	8,804	↑
Schuller et al. 2004	Race	3	US	Attainment	Citizens	Cross-section	2001	1	10,000	↑
	Political cynicism	10	US	Attainment	Citizens	Cross-section	2002	1	10,000	↑
	Authoritarian–liberal	11	US	Attainment	Citizens	Cross-section	2003	1	10,000	↑
	Political interest	9	US	Attainment	Citizens	Cross-section	2004	1	10,000	↑
	Civil society organization membership	9	US	Attainment	Citizens	Cross-section	2005	1	10,000	↑
	Turnout	9	US	Attainment	Citizens	Cross-section	2006	1	10,000	↑
Schwadel and Garneau 2017	Political tolerance	11	US	University	Citizens	Cross-section	1976–2014	1	21,681	↑

(*continued*)

Study	Variable		Country	Education	Sample	Design	Years		N	Effect
Scott 2022	Racism	3	UK	University	Citizens	Longitudinal	1970–1981	7	1,520	↑
	Authoritarianism	11	UK	University	Citizens	Longitudinal	1970–1981	7	1,520	↑
	Economics	6	UK	University	Citizens	Longitudinal	1970–1981	7	1,520	↑
Sieben and de Graaf 2004	Religiosity	5	Netherlands	Attainment	Citizens	Siblings	1992–1998	1	2,396	∅
	Church attendance	5	Netherlands	Attainment	Citizens	Siblings	1992–1998	1	2,396	∅
	Party ideology	1	Netherlands	Attainment	Citizens	Siblings	1992–1998	1	2,396	∅
	Economic conservatism	6	Netherlands	Attainment	Citizens	Siblings	1992–1998	1	2,396	∅
	Participation	9	Netherlands	Attainment	Citizens	Siblings	1992–1998	1	2,396	↑
	Post-materialism	12	Netherlands	Attainment	Citizens	Siblings	1992–1998	1	2,396	↑
	Gender	2	Netherlands	Attainment	Citizens	Siblings	1992–1998	1	2,396	↑
Stubager 2008	Authoritarian–liberal	11	Denmark	Level	Citizens	Cross-section	2004	1	1,192	↑
Stubager 2010	Authoritarian–liberal	12	Denmark	Attainment	Citizens	Cross-section	1979–2005	9		↑
Stubager 2013	Party ideology	12	Denmark	Attainment	Citizens	Cross-section	1979–2005	9	1,192	↑
	Authoritarian–liberal	12	Denmark	Level	Citizens	Cross-section	2004	1	1,192	↑
	Redistribution	6	Denmark	Level	Citizens	Cross-section	2004	1	1,192	↑

(continued)

TABLE 2A (*continued*)

Study	Outcome	Type	Location	Treatment	Subjects	Design	Period	Waves	Obs	Finding
Surridge 2016	Social liberalism	1	UK	Level	Citizens	Cross-section	2000	1	10,217	↑
Treas 2002	Homosexuality	2	US	Level	Citizens	Cross-section	1972–1998	1	10,101	↑
Truex 2011	Corruption tolerance	8	Nepal	Level	Citizens	Cross-section	2009	1	853	↑
van de Werfhorst and de Graaf 2004	Gender	2	Netherlands	Level	Citizens	Cross-section	1992–2000	1	2,974	↑
	Civil society organization membership	9	Netherlands	Level	Citizens	Cross-section	1992–2000	2	3,010	↑
Wagner and Zick 1995	Ethnicity	3	Europe	Level	Citizens	Cross-section	1988	1	3,788	↑
Walton and Peiffer 2017	Corruption reporting	8	Papua New Guinea	Attainment	Citizens	Cross-section	2010–2011	1	1,825	↑
Weakliem 2002	Individualism	7	Global	Attainment	Citizens	Cross-section	1989–1993	1	40,000	↑
Weitz-Shapiro and Winters 2017	Corruption discerning	8	Brazil	Attainment	Citizens	Cross-section	2013	1	2,002	↑

(*continued*)

Study	Topic		Place	Level	Sample	Type	Years		N	Finding
Wodtke 2012	Minorities	3	US	Attainment	Citizens	Cross-section	1990–2010		29,660	↑
	Race	3	US	Attainment	Citizens	Cross-section	1990–2010		29,660	Ø
	Race, affirmative action	3	US	Attainment	Citizens	Cross-section	1990–2010		29,660	↑
Yang and Hoskins 2020	Turnout	9	England	University	Citizens	Longitudinal	2009–2014	5	966	↑
	Civic engagement	9	England	University	Citizens	Longitudinal	2009–2014	5	966	↓
	Protest activity	9	England	University	Citizens	Longitudinal	2009–2014	5	966	Ø
Zhang and Brym 2019	Homosexuality	2	Global	Level	Citizens	Cross-section	1981–2014		344,255	↑

Type: see Table 2.2. IV: instrumental variable. Finding: education has a liberalizing influence (↑), an anti-liberal influence (↓), or no demonstrable influence (Ø). Empty cells: impossible to determine or not applicable.

Type: see Table 2.2. Finding: education has a liberalizing influence (↑), an anti-liberal influence (↓), or no demonstrable influence (Ø).

PART II

FOREGROUND

3

Methods

In the previous chapter, we reviewed the literature on our subject – first in a discursive fashion and then in a more structured fashion with a focus on recent studies that attempt to estimate a causal effect. Although most studies under review point in the direction of a liberalizing effect, there are numerous cracks in this apparent consensus.

Perhaps the most important feature distinguishing this study from previous studies is the breadth of our investigation, which encompasses nearly one hundred outcomes and two quite different research designs. In one setting, we capitalize on a regression discontinuity design situated in Romania – the Romanian Natural Experiment (RNE). To generalize from these results, we enlist data from the World Values Survey (WVS) and the European Values Survey (EVS), which together recruit subjects from seventy-nine countries around the world. Our hope is that by combining these approaches we can get closer to the elusive goal of generalizable knowledge.

This chapter lays out the methodological details. We begin by clarifying the treatment of theoretical interest – university education. Next, we introduce the RNE, followed by a discussion of its generalizability. In the fourth section, we discuss the WVS/EVS data that forms the basis of our global analyses. The final section discusses potential problems emanating from social desirability bias.

These issues will be of intense interest to some readers. For that reason, we have gone to considerable length to provide all the relevant details, bringing together matters discussed fleetingly in our published papers. Readers less interested in methodological nuances may skip to the findings, presented in the next chapter.

UNIVERSITIES

For present purposes, universities are defined as permanent institutions of higher learning that grant at least a bachelor's degree or its equivalent and offer instruction in the professions and the liberal arts. Cognate terms – college, university, the academy, tertiary education, higher education, and so forth – will be employed interchangeably.

This definition, consonant with the International Standard Classification of Education levels 6–8 (UNESCO Institute for Statistics 2012), excludes vocational schools, arts schools, theological seminaries, technical schools, military schools, police academies, yoga schools, two-year ("junior") colleges, and universities that grant only associates' degrees.

We might have chosen to broaden our purview so as to examine educational systems as a whole. However, there are important differences across levels, and especially between school (i.e., primary and secondary education) and university. School is designed for children while university is designed for adults, and this affects the nature of the curriculum, which is more specialized and demanding at higher levels. Children may be more prone to propaganda than adults, even though they may not be able to comprehend more complex ideas, which in turn limits the sorts of things teachers can talk about. Institutions of higher education generally enjoy greater autonomy from government and are more likely to be privately run, which may affect their mission. While primary and secondary education is usually mandatory, higher education is voluntary – a privilege rather than a requirement – which affects its constituency. These myriad differences make it problematic to generalize across levels or to assume that all educational levels can be arrayed on a unidimensional scale, for example as "number of years of schooling."

Why do we choose to focus on tertiary education rather than primary or secondary education? Five considerations come into play.

First, universities have become hotbeds of ideological contention, as discussed in Chapter 2. Primary and secondary schools were once at the forefront of similar debates, especially in countries with marked religious/ secular divides such as France (Ansell and Lindvall 2013). However, these debates seem to have cooled in many countries. Now, one might argue, it is university education that arouses the greatest passion.

Second, universities are situated at the apex of the educational system. School teachers are generally trained in universities or by university graduates, and primary and secondary education curricula are grounded in knowledge and perspectives validated by university faculty. In this respect, lower education follows trends in higher education.

Third, universities embody a fairly uniform treatment internationally. Note that primary and secondary education is imbued with national objectives, which differ from country to country. Patriotism is generic, but the content of patriotism – for example, the values and attitudes injected into high school textbooks – is diverse.[1] The language of instruction in primary and secondary schools is also local, which amplifies its parochialism. And in the developing world the curricula may extend to practical advice on all aspects of life – hygiene, health, comportment, and so forth. Accordingly, primary and secondary education is a diverse assortment of experiences and instructional materials that is difficult to compare cross-nationally.

By contrast, university education strives for international standards. Frequently, professors are graduates of universities abroad and they are in any case cognizant of international journals, textbooks, methods, and other standard-setting criteria. They are likely to identify as members of an international profession, may regularly attend international meetings, and probably have regular interactions with colleagues across the world. Instruction is often in English, which has become the recognized language of communication in most fields. Moreover, the student body is increasingly international. While most students receive primary and secondary instruction close to home, many students receive tertiary instruction abroad. Schofer, Ramirez, and Meyer (2020: 5) comment: "The organizational structures of higher education are diverse, but the character and categories of knowledge have important homogeneities: reciprocally recognized fields, courses of study, and degrees." This internationalization of higher education makes it plausible to talk about a "university effect" that is similar across countries.[2]

Fourth, there is considerable variability in higher education attainment. By contrast, primary and secondary education is nearly universal in many countries, so there is little treatment variation to leverage. We can ask whether having a high school degree affects social and political attitudes in Sweden but it would be difficult to provide an answer as there are so few people in the control group. Nor would it be policy-relevant.

This brings us to a final point. While the principle of universal primary and secondary education is well established, the wisdom of expanding university education is hotly contested. Article 26 of the Universal Declaration of Human Rights declares that "education shall be free, at least in the elementary and fundamental stages." By contrast, "higher education shall be equally accessible to all on the basis of merit," leaving open the question of supply.

Some believe that a university education should be offered at nominal charge to all who care to attend. Others feel that the tertiary sector is already overextended and does not merit additional public investment.[3] To reach

---

[1] Studies of political socialization/indoctrination are more likely to focus on primary and secondary schooling than universities, perhaps because the former are more firmly under government control and children are more susceptible than young adults. See, for example, Bowles and Gintis (1976), Lott (1990), and Pritchett (2013).

[2] See Altbach (2013), Frank and Gabler (2006), and Frank and Meyer (2020).

[3] For discussion of the pros and cons of higher education expansion, see Owen and Sawhill (2013). For work on the politics and policy of higher education, see Ansell (2008), Busemeyer, Garritzmann, and Neimanns (2020), and Garritzmann (2017).

a determination on this important matter of public policy, we need to know as much as possible about the impact of higher education on students – not just their job prospects but also their outlook on society and politics.

But how?

A NATURAL EXPERIMENT IN ROMANIA

In most countries, tertiary education is a decentralized good, allocated in a variety of unstandardized ways. There are many ways to get into college and thus many characteristics that might distinguish university students (or former students) from those who do not matriculate. This makes it difficult to estimate the causal effect of a college education. Even in those rare cases where random or as-if random treatments are discovered, the subpopulations exposed to these treatments are often small and idiosyncratic, and therefore difficult to generalize upon.

In Romania, we discovered a unique opportunity to explore the impact of university education on social and political attitudes in a fashion that promises strong causal identification. The baccalaureate (*bac*) exam, taken by the vast majority of students in their last year of high school, strongly predicts university attendance. Specifically, students who achieve a score of at least 6.0, even those who score at or narrowly above this mark, are quite likely to attend university. Conversely, those scoring less than 6.0, even those scoring very narrowly below this value, are very unlikely to attend university. Therefore, we can think of students who score 6.0 or above (passing the *bac*) as getting a push toward university attendance, while those who score narrowly below 6.0 (failing the exam) get a nudge away from university attendance. Yet, if we compare students with very similar exam scores, we would expect them to be similar on background characteristics upon graduation from high school.

We can think of this situation as a natural experiment in which, among *bac* takers who score very close to 6.0, passage is as-if randomly assigned. Looking within a narrow range around this passage threshold, it may be reasonable to assume that differences in exam scores are driven primarily by one or two lucky (or unlucky) guesses on exam questions. If this is the case, we can consider exam passage, and hence university attendance, as if it were randomly assigned among these observations near the threshold, interpreting any differences that arise in subsequent years between narrow passers and narrow failers as a product of their attendance (or non-attendance) at university.

Our strategy here differs from research designs in which control variables are adjusted for in regression models, as discussed in the latter part of this chapter. In the RNE, we rely instead on the assumption that narrow failers of the *bac* can tell us what narrow passers would have looked like if they had actually failed, and vice versa. In other words, these two groups should be the same on average except for the fact that one group is much more likely to be treated than the other.

This setup is referred to as a *regression discontinuity* (RD) design. In the standard RD setup, there exists some score variable and a threshold such that all observations whose score variable value is at or above the threshold qualify the subject for the treatment, while all those below the threshold are untreated. In our case, the treatment of university attendance is not deterministically assigned to anyone who scores at least 6.0 on the *bac*. Some students who pass the *bac* may decide not to attend university and it is still possible that students scoring below 6.0 end up attending university. But *bac* passage strongly increases the likelihood of university attendance. For example, among respondents in our survey who scored 5.98, which is the highest non-passing score, only 17 percent attended university. But among those scoring 6.0, the lowest passing score, 84 percent attended university. The differences between these two groups are likely to be minimal given that they received almost exactly the same score on the exam. But the narrow failers typically do not attend university while the narrow passers do.

This setup provides us with a unique opportunity to gain causal leverage on questions about university attendance's impact. Realizing this, and realizing that we would not be able to return to this site to conduct further studies (because of the limited number of subjects falling just above and below the cutoff), we determined to make the most of the opportunity. That meant conducting studies on several related topics simultaneously with a single survey.

Following protocol, we preregistered four studies – on social capital, law-abidingness (originally, corruption tolerance), cultural values, and party ideology – along with detailed pre-analysis plans. (Several of these studies are published separately.) The main analyses introduced next follow our pre-analysis plans closely with two potentially significant deviations that merit mention here. First, a reduction in sample size was necessitated because of the onset of the COVID-19 pandemic, which shuttered universities in Romania and thus modified the treatment of theoretical interest, forcing premature closure of our survey. This issue is discussed at length later. Second, although our preregistered analysis plans state that we will use a continuity-based RD framework, in this book we present results based on a local randomization framework, in which we consider treatment as if it were randomly assigned for those near the threshold. The local randomization approach is preferred because of its simplicity. Importantly, continuity-based results are presented in our published articles, and are generally quite similar, so this methodological issue has little impact on our results.

Because Romania is not a well-studied case, we begin with a review of some of the characteristics of this country that might affect the interpretation of our findings and their external validity. Next, we describe the *bac*, the process of university admissions, potential problems of noncompliance, and our recruitment of subjects. In the final section, we outline our procedure for the main RD analysis.

Bear in mind that the key feature of an RD design is that subjects who fall just above and below the cutoff are similar to each other in all pretreatment respects (other than their scores, which are nearly identical). Under this circumstance we can regard treatment assignment as *as-if random* – a natural experiment. Another key feature is *compliance* – that subjects who pass the threshold are more likely to attend university than those who do not. Because these features are so critical, we spend a good deal of time obsessing about details.

Setting

The country of Romania was chosen as the site for this study in an opportunistic fashion. To our knowledge, the design sketched out in this chapter could not have been conducted anywhere else – at least, not without the direct participation of government officials.

This, by itself, might engender skepticism. A study that can be conducted in only one location may also be *sui generis* for the same reasons. We think not. In fact, we shall argue that this is a fairly "typical" case, as cases go.

Romania is a middle-income country in Central Europe with a legacy of communist rule. Early in the democratic transition Romania struggled with reforms and the implementation of the rule of law. However, by the mid-2000s it had made significant progress, paving the way for its accession to the European Union (EU) in 2007. This progress has been documented in various European Commission reports (European Commission 2006), as well as cross-national measures such as the Liberal Democracy Index from the Varieties of Democracy project (Coppedge et al. 2020). Recent populist surges in nearby Poland and Hungary have so far had only a faint echo in Romania. This contrast emerged recently in the 2020 fight over the EU budget, where Romania was the only Eastern European member to strongly support tying EU funds to respect for the rule of law.[4]

Within the context of the Organisation for Economic Co-operation and Development (OECD), Romania's electoral system, party system size, methods of internal party governance, party finance, media, campaign finance, turnout, and level of partisanship are also unremarkable (Dalton, Farrell, and McAllister 2011). As in any newly democratized country, parties are fairly new and volatility is moderately high (though not extreme). Party identification is certainly not as entrenched as in the US or UK, and less likely to be perceived along a single left–right spectrum than in most other OECD countries.[5] Nonetheless, parties occupy identifiable ideological niches across

---

[4] See "Romanian PM berates Poland and Hungary over EU budget veto," *Financial Times*, November 23, 2020, www.ft.com/content/ed141f4f-24b4-4173-a739-f4686bc55a57.

[5] Insofar as left–right placement is consequential, surveys suggest that Romanian citizens situate themselves further to the right than citizens in most other OECD countries, on par with the US (Dalton, Farrell, and McAllister 2011: 90).

several dimensions, as suggested by coding provided by the Chapel Hill expert survey (see Chapter 4).

Citizens of Romania fall near the global mean in educational attainment (see Figure 7.3). Since countries omitted from this dataset are mostly poor and probably not well educated, we estimate that educational attainment in Romania is probably at or near the upper third of the world's countries. Counting universities per capita, Romania also falls well above the median – in 71st place out of 177 countries (Apfeld 2019).

There are few recognized measures of educational *quality* at the university level. As a proxy, one may focus on the quality of primary and secondary education, measured by the annual Programme for International Student Assessment (PISA). PISA includes seventy-seven countries around the world, including the richest and most developed along with some middle-income countries such as Romania. In 2018, Romania placed forty-seventh in reading and similarly in math and science.[6] If we assume that countries excluded from PISA have lower scores (a fairly safe assumption), we could conclude that the quality of Romanian primary and secondary education is in the top third globally.

A related issue concerns the *content* of higher education. Romania is one of the original joiners (1999) of the European Higher Education Area (the "Bologna Process"), which ensured comparability in standards and quality of higher education among EU states.[7] As a part of the Bologna Process, Romania undertook reforms to align its education system with EU requirements, and by 2015 (the earliest year our respondents could start university) we expect that universities in Romania were comparable to those in other European countries. Beyond Europe, it is more difficult to say. However, many studies emphasize the convergence of curricula in university faculties across the world during the postwar era, where lectures, textbooks, and faculty training are increasingly governed by international norms (Frank and Meyer 2007).

We return to questions of generalizability later. For the moment, suffice to say that Romania's status as a representative case is strongest with respect to neighboring countries in Eastern Europe that share a communist past, and perhaps almost as strong with respect to other countries within the EU. Outside the EU, it may be classified as an "upper-middle" country with respect to levels of education and economic development.

The *Bac*

One of the legacies of the Soviet era in Romania is an education system run largely by the state, access to which rests on a nationwide high school exit exam, the *bac*. The *bac* is the final assessment that high school students in Romania

---

[6] See www.oecd.org/pisa/PISA-results_ENGLISH.png.
[7] See Amaral and colleagues (2009) and www.ehea.info.

take at graduation. The results of the exam determine eligibility for college education as well as chances of admission to a student's university and major of choice. Accordingly, any student with any ambition – however vague – to enter college is likely to take the *bac*. This ambition is fairly widespread in Romania, as suggested by the roughly two-thirds of high school graduates who regularly sit for these exams.[8]

Two exams are administered each year, in June/July and August/September, respectively. The second session is only for students who did *not* pass or did not qualify to sit for the *bac* in the first session. High school graduates are entitled to take the *bac* free of charge twice. If the student does not pass either of the two attempts, they can continue to sit the exam but must pay a fee. All high school students in good standing are automatically registered for the first session of the *bac*, and students have nothing to lose by taking the *bac*, even if they fail. We assume that those who decline to take the exam are unlikely to reach the threshold for passage, and thus would not be in our bandwidth. Of course, some may have dropped out prior to completing high school. However, attrition rates are fairly low in Romania.[9]

Most *bac* takers sit for three different subjects, which determine the final average and the student's qualifications to progress to university. Each part of the exams is marked from 1.0 to 10.0. Most importantly for the purposes of our study, a grade of at least 5.0 on each of the three subjects and an overall average of at least 6.0 are required to pass. Graduates of high schools where the language of instruction is in an ethnic-minority language (Hungarian or German) must pass an additional exam in their mother language and literature. We exclude these students (of whom 1,133 in the population fulfill our other criteria), restricting our sample to those whose schooling is conducted in Romanian.

Written exams are administered in large centers incorporating 250–450 students and led by an examination commission composed of teachers and university professors. The location is heavily monitored with security cameras. To further ensure the integrity of the process, the content of each exam is randomly extracted on the day of the exam on national television. Completed exams are sent to forty-one centers (one center per county) across the country to be graded. Exams are anonymized, and the allocation of exams to examiners is randomized.

Any student who is unhappy with the results can challenge grades assigned to individual exams. (One may not challenge the overall grade.) In the first session

[8] In 2016, 36 percent of students who finished high school chose not to take the *bac*. See analysis by "Romania Curata" ("Clean Romania"), a well-known Romanian non-governmental organization focusing on corruption: www.romaniacurata.ro/evolutia-unei-generatii-o-alta-discutie-despre-bac.

[9] According to Eurostat, in 2019 83.4 percent of Romanians aged twenty to twenty-four had completed an upper-secondary degree, a number close to the EU average (83.5). See https://ec.europa.eu/eurostat/databrowser/view/tps00186/default/table?lang=en.

of 2017 roughly 22 percent of *bac* sitters challenged their grades on at least one of the subjects. In this instance, the exam is regraded by a county-level committee. In order to avoid complications due to challenges, we define our score variable based on the initial (pre-challenge) overall exam average received by each student their first time taking the *bac*.

Cheating and Other Possible Manipulations

Cheating on the *bac* might pose a challenge to the assumption of as-if random assignment across the cutoff. If those who barely pass did so by cheating, and those who barely fail did not cheat, then the treatment and control groups identified by the RD design would not be similar on background characteristics.

While cheating has historically been a problem in the administration of the *bac* (Borcan et al. 2017), the practice appears to have largely ended by 2015. Two major events account for this change.

First, a new law in 2011 introduced the use of large exam centers, supervised by cameras, for written exams. Prior to that, examinations took place in high schools across the country with no centralized system of supervision. The impact of this reform can be seen in the national success rate of *bac* takers, which dropped from 67.4 percent in 2010 (Neagu 2010) to 44.5 percent in 2011 (BAC 2011). Most observers believe that the reform had its intended effect, making cheating much more difficult (Borcan et al. 2017: 182).

Second, the Romanian anti-corruption agency investigated the problem in 2012–13, leading to a criminal investigation of hundreds of collaborators, most of whom were teachers (Craciun 2013). The importance of these criminal investigations in altering behavior was emphasized in discussions with Valentina Dimulescu of the Romanian Academic Society, the most important non-governmental organization monitoring corruption in Romania (Dimulescu 2018).

There are good reasons to believe that cheating is now rare. Even so, we must be concerned if any remaining cheating allows students to sort themselves on either side of the cutoff for our treatment variable, which measures a student's score on their first attempt (prior to any challenges they might make). If some set of students is able to recognize that they would narrowly fail the *bac* without cheating, and if these students are able to cheat so as to improve their score to a narrowly passing one, then we would be comparing narrow failers who are generally honest (non-cheaters) with narrow passers who are a mix of honest students and cheaters.

Fortunately, most methods of cheating would not have this effect. *In*-exam cheating (e.g., with "cheat sheets" or students copying from each other) is not limited to students who fall just below the cutoff for the simple reason that students do not know, a priori, whether they will fall into that category. In-exam cheating, if effective, is likely to result in a higher score but would not allow students to narrowly sort themselves above the passage threshold.

Post-exam cheating is potentially more threatening to our design because in this situation students know their score, which means that those who barely fail have a greater incentive to cheat than those who barely pass. However, this sort of cheating is very difficult to accomplish under the current system. If it does occur, it will likely occur after the first round of testing, perhaps even after a second or third round of testing, when students discover that their opportunities for college are foreclosed. Our analysis rests on the first *bac* exam, ignoring subsequent exams (if any). This ensures that anything occurring after the first exam will not introduce systematic bias.

Relatedly, one might worry if students were able to manipulate their scores through means other than cheating. The most obvious method is to study for the exam, which presumably most *bac* takers do. However, satisficing students are unable to foresee exactly how much effort might be needed to sort themselves into the "barely pass" category. Moreover, the payoff is not simply to pass but to get a strong score, as this determines the sort of program one is eligible for. Accordingly, we do not anticipate that many students are motivated simply to pass the exam.

In any case, studying does not threaten the as-if random assumption of the RD design because students are unable to sort themselves around the cutoff. Studying is likely to improve scores, but one cannot predict the score one will get, especially on the first round. This brings us to a key feature of our design – which sets it apart from some other RD designs – namely, the narrowness of the band that forms the basis for our analysis. We focus on students whose first test scores fall between 5.8 and 6.2; that is, 0.2 points above and below the threshold (6.0) on a ten-point scale.

Ex Ante Evaluations of Threats to As-If Random Assignment

Before collecting our survey data, the unique nature of our exam score data and research design allowed us to conduct a more general, albeit less direct, test of possible manipulation of exam scores around the cutoff. Using the Romanian government's public website, we have obtained the publicly available *bac* scores for all students who took the exam between 2004 and 2019. If sorting is occurring around the cutoff, it seems likely that it is primarily in the direction of passing. In this scenario, we ought to observe a break in the density of observed exam scores. By contrast, a more encouraging pattern would be a histogram of exam scores that is smoothly distributed around this threshold.

Figure 3.1 presents histograms of students' overall *bac* scores, separated into the periods before (2004–2014) and after (2015–2019) anti-cheating measures were fully in place. Informally, we should focus on whether there is a notable difference in the height of the histogram bars immediately above and below the passage threshold of 6.0. In particular, we can ask whether the difference in these adjacent bins is much larger than is typical between the other adjacent bins away from the passage threshold.

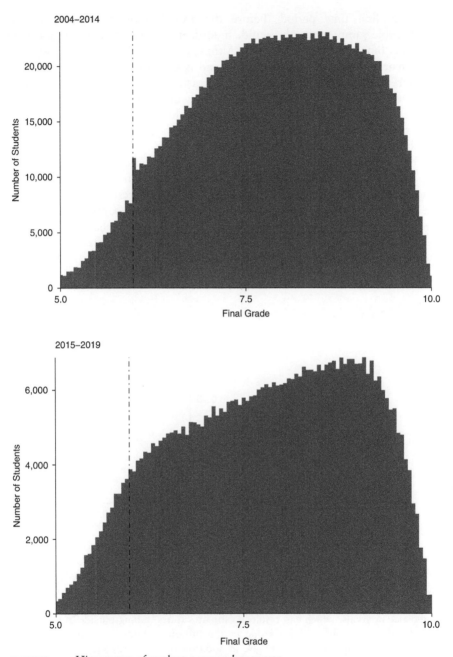

FIGURE 3.1 Histograms of student average *bac* scores
Histograms of overall bac scores among students taking the exam from 2004–2014 (top) and 2015–2019 (bottom). Vertical dashed line indicates 6.0 threshold for passage.

In the first time period (before the anti-cheating measures) there is a noticeable jump at the threshold. Indeed, it is the largest jump across all adjacent bins in the histogram. Although not definitive, this suggests problematic sorting around the cutoff and is consistent with descriptions of widespread cheating prior to 2015. By contrast, the second histogram, showing the time period after anti-cheating measures were in place, shows a difference between the height of the two bins around the threshold that is fairly typical of those throughout the rest of the histogram. This suggests that sorting across the threshold after 2014 was minimal.

The histograms presented in Figure 3.1 offer an informal diagnostic with respect to possible sorting. As a complement, we conduct manipulation tests following Cattaneo, Jansson, and Ma (2018). These tests estimate the density of the score variable in a neighborhood below and, separately, above the threshold, providing a formal test of the hypothesis that the densities immediately to the right and left of the threshold are different. Figure 3.2 shows the results of this analysis. The left pane includes tests for the period

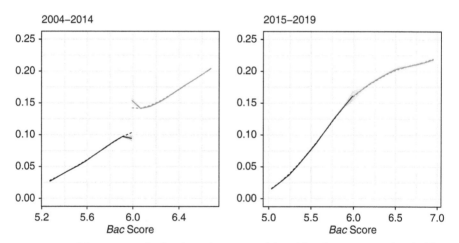

FIGURE 3.2 Nonparametric density estimates on either side of exam score threshold
Left (right) pane shows estimated density with 95 percent confidence interval for individual student *bac* scores from 2004–2014 (2015–2019), estimated separately above and below passage threshold using approach introduced by Cattaneo, Jansson, and Ma (2018). Note that their approach uses different methods for point estimates and confidence intervals, which can result in estimates (lines) falling outside of confidence bounds (shaded regions). This is due to the differing optimality criteria for point estimation and inference. Accordingly, in addition to this mean square error (MSE) optimal point estimate (dashed line), we also plot an estimate constructed simply by taking the average of the upper and lower bounds for the confidence interval at each point (solid line). Our ultimate inferences about possible sorting, which are based on the confidence interval rather than point estimates, however, are unaffected by this decision.

2004–2014. The right pane shows tests for the period 2015–2019. As is evident from these results, data from the earlier period shows evidence that is strongly consistent with manipulation around the threshold of 6.00. The t-statistic for the null hypothesis of no jump in the density is 17.2 (p<.0001) in the earlier period. By contrast, data from 2015–2019 shows only a small jump in the density at this threshold – one that does not reach the standard 0.05 significance level. This does not prove that there was no sorting around this cutoff in the later period, and it should be noted that the p-value for our test here is 0.15, which provides at most weak evidence of a small jump. However, it seems unlikely that there are very many rule-breakers in this more recent time period (2015–2019) from which we draw our sample.

Admission to University

The process of admission to university occurs in two rounds, in July and September, respectively. As such, *bac* takers from both the June/July and August/September sessions may be eligible for university admission. However, the September round of university admissions is meant to fill the allotted spots unoccupied after the July round, making it more difficult for the *bac* takers from the August/September session to be admitted to university. The admissions process is strict and explicit, as each course of study in each university has a precise formula for admission. Most majors in most universities use the final grade from the *bac* as the sole entrance criterion; some adopt additional criteria.

While the exam strongly affects students' college attendance, obtaining an average of at least 6.0 on the *bac* is neither a strictly necessary nor sufficient condition for a candidate to be admitted to their university of choice. Students who pass the exam could decide against attending university, perhaps because they did not get into their most preferred school or because of events in their personal lives. Conversely, a student who failed the *bac* on their first attempt could retake it and ultimately pass, subsequently matriculating to university. Alternatively, because our score variable is the initial exam average, students could improve their initial score by challenging the results of one or more of their subject exams, which may result in a recomputed average that surpasses the 6.0 threshold.[10]

The formulas for admission (i.e., how much weight the *bac* and the special exam have in the final decision) are known in advance, and admission results are public. Tuition is waived for candidates with the best test scores; the rest must

---

[10] We use initial scores on the first attempt taking the *bac*, not including any possible changes in score for students who challenge their scores. This is because the decision to challenge a score is likely related to relevant pretreatment characteristics for exam takers. Because narrow failers will be much more likely to challenge their scores than narrow passers, using post-challenge scores may render these two groups incomparable in terms of whichever characteristics predict challenging one's scores.

pay. However, tuition fees are rather low and not prohibitive for most families. In 2017–2018, yearly tuition at the University of Bucharest – the country's top university, by most accounts – ranged between 2,500 ($614) and 4,000 lei ($980) (Dumitru 2017). This was less than the average monthly salary in that year (Calculator salarii 2019).

Students who do not pass the *bac* can still enroll in vocational schools (*scoala postliceala*) where they learn skills that prepare them for blue-collar jobs. These vocational programs are shorter (one to three years) than university programs and are usually organized within high schools. The curricula include narrow subjects related to specific skills that require less intellectual ability than university courses. Subjects are taught by high school teachers. In the nomenclature of the Ministry of Education of Romania (Ministerul Educației Național), this form of education is considered pre-university; that is, part of secondary education. A few Romanians are privileged to attend school outside the country; however, they are unlikely to secure a place in foreign universities – where standards are generally stricter – unless they also pass the *bac*.

Noncompliance, Cutoff, Bandwidth

In summary, two problems of compliance arise in this RD design. Recall that the cutoff is defined by a student's score on their first exam. Some students challenge their scores or retake the exam, eventually managing to obtain a passing score, and then matriculate to university, thus receiving the treatment of theoretical interest. Likewise, not everyone who passes the exam chooses to continue their education at the university level. Those who pass the exam are not formally guaranteed a position at a university, but in practice there are typically enough spaces for all passers who want to attend, though not necessarily their university or faculty of preference. Although tuition costs are minimal, there are opportunity costs to pursuing a university education.

Evidently, the treatment of theoretical interest is not assigned perfectly based on a student's *bac* score as it would be in a sharp RD. Prior to collecting our survey data it would have been difficult to say how large these compliance problems might be; that is, how much slippage there would be on either side of the cutoff. However, it is clear that it is much easier for students to attend university if they pass the *bac* on their first try than if they do not. Hence, we expected a large jump (discontinuity) in the probability of attending university between those who barely fail and those who barely pass, which creates an occasion for a "fuzzy" RD design. Our causal estimand is therefore the effect of treatment (college attendance) among compliers, where a complier is understood as someone who would have gone to college if they passed the *bac* and would not have gone to college if they failed.

As mentioned earlier, passing the *bac* requires obtaining at least a 5.0 on each part of the exam and at least a 6.0 for the average of all parts. This creates multiple thresholds for passage, complicating the RD design – one for scores on each of three exam parts at 5.0 and one at 6.0 for the overall exam average. We therefore include in our sample only students scoring above 5.0 for all individual parts of the exam, as well as obtaining an overall average score between 5.8 and 6.2. Within this group, there is a single cutoff (at 6.00) for exam passage, facilitating a straightforward RD setup in which overall *bac* average is the score (or running) variable and university attendance is the treatment variable. The bandwidth for our score variable (overall exam average) is defined narrowly as scores falling within 0.2 of the cutoff, meaning that all observations in our sample scored relatively similarly on the *bac* overall.

Between 2015 and 2019, 462,943 students took the *bac* for the first time and graduated from Romanian (non-minority) high schools. Of these, 19,402 obtained scores that fell between 5.8 and 6.2 and scored at least 5.0 on each part of the exam. This is the population of immediate interest.

As discussed earlier, a key requirement of the RD design is that the probability of being treated (here attending university) is discontinuous at the score variable threshold. In other words, for the RD setup to be appropriate for analyzing the RNE, it must be the case that those narrowly passing the *bac* are more likely, ideally much more likely, to attend university than those narrowly failing.

To gauge compliance, Figure 3.3 displays a plot of the proportion of students in our sample attending university for respondents at each possible *bac* score in

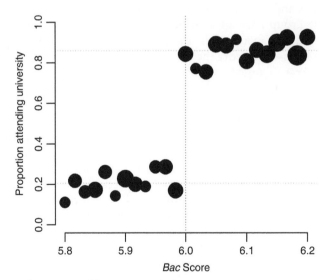

FIGURE 3.3 Relationship of *bac* score with the treatment
The proportion attending university among respondents having each unique value of *bac* score. Vertical line denotes (fuzzy) treatment threshold of 6. Horizontal lines show averages for all respondents above/below threshold. The size of each point is proportional to the number of observations at that *bac* score value.

our bandwidth. Note that these overall *bac* scores are the average of three parts, each scored in increments of 0.05. This means that there are twenty-five possible scores in our range between 5.8 and 6.2, with each possible score separated by 0.05/3 = 0.01666 .... It is obvious from Figure 3.3 that there is a sharp increase in the probability of attending university at the threshold (6.0), indicating that those who narrowly pass the *bac* are significantly more likely to attend university than those who narrowly fail. Just under 21 percent of *bac* failers in our sample attended university, as compared with 86 percent of *bac* passers, a difference of 65 percent in the probability of treatment. This difference is highly statistically significant. Moreover, we observe a similarly large difference and strong statistical significance when narrowing our bandwidth to include only those who fail or pass by the narrowest margins (i.e., those scoring 5.98 or 6.0). In other words, these two groups, who performed almost identically on the exam, had dramatically different likelihoods of receiving our treatment variable of interest.

This large difference in the likelihood of university attendance between two groups who seem likely to be otherwise quite similar is consistent with the requirements of an RD design. Narrow *bac* passers are much more likely to attend university than are narrow *bac* failers, meaning that by comparing the behaviors and attitudes of these two groups in an RD design, we can learn about the effect of university attendance. Our design relies on the natural experiment that occurs when comparing these two groups. In particular, we would expect narrow passers and narrow failers to be quite similar on average except for the fact that one group receives a strong nudge toward attending university by virtue of passing the exam, while the other group does not. This provides the key leverage for us to identify the effect of university attendance.

Recruitment

Until 2020, the Romanian Ministry of Education posted all *bac* exam results online complete with each exam taker's name, score, and high school.[11] Graduates of high schools where the language of instruction is in an ethnic-minority language (Hungarian or German) are eliminated, as they must pass an additional exam in their mother language and literature, introducing a potential confounder. The remaining population consists of those whose schooling is conducted in Romanian (designated as non-minorities in Figure 3.4).

Of these, we are able to identify 19,402 students high school students who fall within our population, as explained earlier. From this sampling frame, recruitment into the survey involved several steps.

---

[11] Data for exam takers from 2004–2019 was collected from a website devoted to the *bac* in July 2019. In 2020, the website removed older results (2004–2018) and anonymized newer results. The current website is located at http://static.bacalaureat.edu.ro/2020.

First, we identify those high schools with at least one student in our target population (N=1,321), randomly assigning them a number (from 1 to 1,321). This determines the order in which high schools are contacted. Second, we search for students in these high schools through Facebook (FB). Third, we invite these individuals to be FB friends with one of our online accounts (labeled "Social Attitudes in Romania"). The invitation mentions that they are invited as graduates of their high school, which was randomly selected for our study. Fourth, we send messages to each of the graduates from their high school FB account inviting them to participate in the survey.

This procedure requires identifying the correct individuals from each high school, a bit of a challenge given that some names are likely to be identical. To alleviate this problem, we ask respondents to name the high school from which they graduated and their year of graduation. If students do not respond, or these responses do not match records drawn from the government website, the survey is removed. Likewise, if a survey is begun but not completed, it is removed. Slightly over one hundred surveys (N=102) are eliminated on this basis.

Recruiting subjects through FB would be problematic in some countries. However, FB usage is extremely high in Romania, especially among our target population. An analysis conducted in January 2017 found that 93.2 percent of Romanians between the ages of fifteen and twenty-four use FB.[12]

One might also worry that participation in FB is post-treatment, a product of entering university. To address this potential bias, we calculate the percentage of those sampled whom we were able to locate on FB, above and below the cutoff. The two statistics are extremely close: 86.75 percent above the threshold and 86.80 percent below the threshold. Accordingly, there is no indication that attending a university affects one's propensity to engage on FB.[13]

Of 13,173 individuals in 893 randomly chosen high schools, we were able to identify the vast majority of people sampled (86.8 percent). Of these, 1,515 were correctly identified and completed the survey (13.3 percent), generating an overall response rate of 11.5 percent.

To make the comparison between treated and untreated groups as clear as possible, our main sample excludes respondents who graduated from high school in 2019 (N=280), some of whom received little or no university education at the time they were surveyed.[14] The latter serves as an auxiliary sample for several tests reported in Chapter 5.

The main sample is somewhat smaller than the target of 2–3,000 envisioned in our pre-analysis plan. The reason for the shortfall is twofold. First, the process of recruitment was slower than anticipated. This, by itself, would not have been an obstacle under normal circumstances, as we could have continued

[12] See www.facebrands.ro/demografice.html.
[13] We also tried to retrieve information about the date that each FB account was opened (as per our pre-analysis plan, registered at E-Gap) but were unable to do so.
[14] This follows our pre-analysis plan.

to recruit subjects indefinitely. However, the arrival of COVID-19 and subsequent shuttering of universities across Romania in March 2020 meant that the treatment of theoretical interest was altered – from in-person to online instruction and from on-campus to at-home residence. Although we continued recruitment for several months, we ultimately decided that it would be injudicious to continue, as there was no sign of university life returning to normal. As such, the treatment was altered – and presumably attenuated. During the final months of recruitment, most students were living off-campus and many had returned to their families. Classes continued online but the setting was changed. As it happens, we do not find attenuation in the treatment effect after the closing of universities. However, continuing to collect data might have fundamentally changed the composition of our research and the interpretation of findings. So, we broke off recruitment in October 2020, prior to the start of the fall term (when all instruction occurred online).

In any case, the resulting sample is entirely adequate for analyzing the main hypotheses, which were preregistered and are presented in Chapter 4. It is less adequate for analyzing subsidiary hypotheses having to do with moderators, as these analyses require sub-setting the full sample. These findings, presented in Chapter 5, are more susceptible to stochastic error, and we therefore regard them as exploratory.

To summarize the complex data-gathering process described in the previous sections, we construct a tree diagram in Figure 3.4 that includes each step of the journey, marking the number of subjects who fall within each category.

The final rows of Figure 3.4 indicate how many members of our main sample failed (553) and passed (677) the *bac* on their first attempt. They also indicate, among each group, how many matriculated at a university. For those who failed the *bac* on their first attempt but eventually managed to gain entry to university, we show how many were successful in challenging their initial scores (eighty-seven) and how many retook the *bac* and eventually achieved a passing score (sixteen). We are not sure how the remaining nine reached university, or if they in fact did so. (They may have incorrectly answered that question.)

Sample

Having discussed the data-generating process, let us turn to the composition of the main sample, as reflected in post-survey questions asked of each respondent. Summary statistics are displayed in Table 3.1. For comparison, we also show general-population characteristics wherever possible and pertinent.

By design, most of our respondents are between the ages of nineteen and twenty-three. As befits a young population in a fairly developed society, most are unmarried (77 percent) and nearly all are childless (94 percent). About half are currently employed. These features are similar to population characteristics for the same age group.

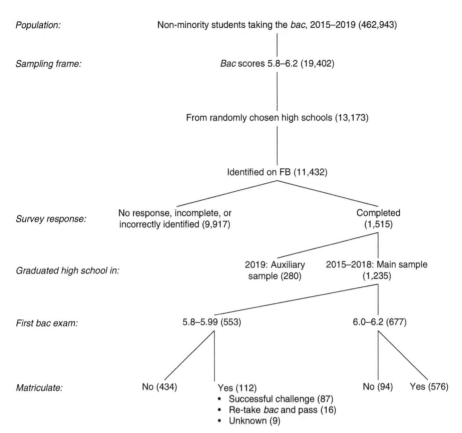

FIGURE 3.4 Summary of the data-generating process
Tree diagram describing the construction of the RNE sample. Note that among *bac* passers and failers there are seven missing values for our survey question about matriculation, which accounts for the slight discrepancy in these totals.

A wide range of social-class backgrounds are represented in our sample, as reflected in father's education, childhood socioeconomic status, and current status. Here, too, we find a fairly close correspondence to general-population statistics. Over 90 percent of our respondents are ethnically Romanian, which is very close to the national population.

The sample is 43 percent female. This might be a cause for concern if women are harder to identify through our recruitment protocol, which one might anticipate as they are likely to change their last name after marriage. As it turns out, FB has mechanisms for identifying women who may have changed their last names, which meant that we were able to contact women at roughly the same rate as men. Response rates were also similar – 10.2 percent for women and 12.2 percent for men.

TABLE 3.1 Main RNE sample

Attribute	Sample	Pop	Pop<24	Attribute	Sample	Pop	Pop<24	Attribute	Sample
Misc.				**Childhood SES**				**Age**	
Female	43	51	49	Lower class	10			18	2
Single (never married)	77	21	83	Working class	34			19	12
One or more children	6	74	6	Lower middle class	31			20	27
Employed	52	42	42	Upper middle class	21			21	15
Ethnically Romanian	91	85	84	Upper class	5			22	21
Father's education				**Current SES**				23	18
Vocational school	11			Lower class	10	7	5	24	4
				Working class	33	38	33	25+	2
Some university	17			Lower middle class	30	25	20		
Completed university	48			Upper middle class	23	26	36		
More than university	23			Upper class	5	4	5		

Descriptive statistics (%) for our sample (N=1,492). SES = socioeconomic status. Where available and relevant, we show parallel statistics for the general population of Romania, as reflected in WVS wave 7 (current SES and children) or 2011 census data (all other indicators).

The main reason we have fewer women in our sample is that there are fewer women in our sampling frame (47 percent). This, in turn, is a product of a phenomenon found nearly everywhere in the twenty-first century: women outperform men in secondary school. Consequently, they are overrepresented at higher *bac* scores and underrepresented within our bandwidth, which falls well below the mean (see Figure 3.3). With 47 percent women in our sampling frame and a 2 percent lower response rate, 43 percent is exactly the proportion of women we would expect to find in our sample.

Analysis

In Romania, private and public universities apply the same criteria for admission – passage of the nationwide *bac* – and there are few alternate paths to higher education. Accordingly, we are able to compare those who receive a university education with those who, in most cases, receive no university education at all. Our study therefore features a strong treatment. We are not measuring *degrees* of higher education (as in most other studies) but rather whether university education per se affects social and political attitudes.

Crucially, the treatment variable, university attendance, is assigned in an *as-if random* fashion. This is what qualifies it as a *natural* experiment – as contrasted with a normal experiment, where treatment assignment is randomized by the researcher.

Specifically, we leverage a discontinuity in the probability of attending university between those scoring just below the passage threshold and those scoring at, or just above, the threshold. Under a set of plausible and straightforward assumptions, this RD design allows us to identify the effect of university attendance on social and political attitudes.

As discussed earlier, any RD features a *score* variable, which in our case is a student's grade on the *bac* exam. In the simplest setup, there is a cutoff or threshold below which all observations are untreated (i.e., not attending university) and above which all observations are treated (i.e., attending university). This is known as a *sharp* RD design.

In this case, *bac* scores do not perfectly determine treatment assignment. Some students scoring below the threshold will attend university, perhaps because they retake the exam and subsequently pass it or for some other reason. Conversely, some students who score above the passage threshold will decide not to attend university. However, we expect that those who pass the exam are much more likely to attend university than those who do not. This establishes the framework for a *fuzzy* RD design.

Unlike a normal experiment, where treatment assignment is controlled and monitored by the researcher, a natural experiment rests on assumptions about a process that occurs "naturally" but is thought to follow a random pattern. Fortunately, our data offers a lot of information relevant to assessing this assumption.

As Figure 3.3 demonstrates, just over 20 percent of respondents with *bac* scores below 6.0 attended university, while 86 percent of those with scores of 6.0 or greater attended university. This represents a difference in treatment probability of 65 percent between those who narrowly passed and those who narrowly failed. By contrast, we see little difference in the probability of attending university when we compare those with similar exam scores below the threshold (e.g., those with scores just above versus just below 5.9) or above the threshold. To put it differently, we observe a similar proportion of respondents attending university among those scoring between 5.8 and 5.99, and we observe a similar proportion of respondents attending university among those between 6.0 and 6.2. But we see a large difference when comparing those narrowly below and above the threshold. This is what we would expect if the cutoff is serving its function – discouraging those below the cutoff from attending university and encouraging those above the cutoff to attend.

Even more important, those who fall just above and below the cutoff should be similar in all respects except their treatment status (and any features that are post-treatment; i.e., affected by the treatment). That is, *bac* takers with scores from 5.8 to 5.99 should be similar to *bac* takers with scores from 6.0 to 6.2 with respect to pretreatment factors such as gender, age, childhood socioeconomic status (SES), father's education, academic concentration (determined before the exam based on what subjects they took in the *bac*), and whether they attended high school in an urban environment.

If narrow passers are different from narrow failers, then we must worry that confounders are present; treatment is not as-if random, and these factors will inhibit our ability to identify the true relationship between university attendance and social-political attitudes. It could be that university students have different attitudes not because they attend university but because they have different backgrounds.

To test this assumption, Figure 3.5 plots the relationship between *bac* score and several background variables that might be expected to confound the relationship of interest (affecting both university attendance and social and political attitudes). Although there is some variability in all of these outcomes across *bac* scores, we do not observe any dramatic jumps as we did for the probability of treatment in Figure 3.3. This suggests that while narrow passers and narrow failers of the *bac* differ dramatically in their likelihood of attending university, they do not show dramatic differences in these important social and demographic characteristics.

The results in Figure 3.5, however, are somewhat informal. Although they seem to rule out any large differences in these relevant variables between those below and above the threshold, this does not imply that these two groups are exactly the same on average. We can also conduct formal statistical tests comparing these characteristics between *bac* passers and failers. Table 3.2 shows these results, first using the entire sample (bandwidth of 0.2 on either side of the threshold, going from 5.8 to 6.2) and then for narrower bandwidths.

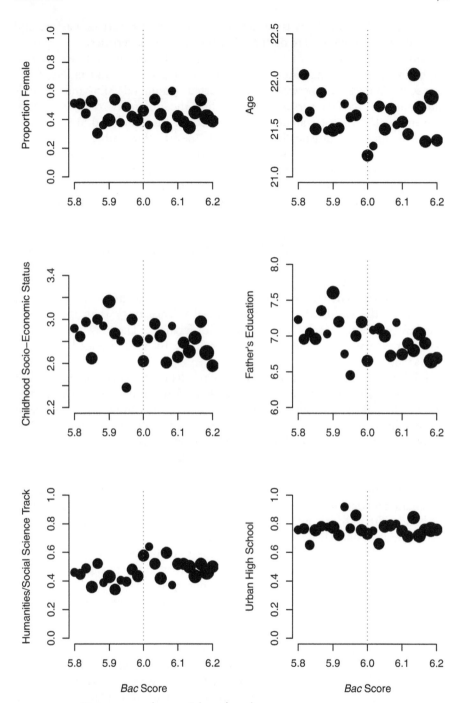

FIGURE 3.5 *Bac* scores and potential confounders
Points plot average value of each potential confounder among respondents having each unique value of *bac* score. Vertical line denotes (fuzzy) treatment threshold of 6.

The goal of these analyses is to determine how similar narrow passers and narrow failers of the *bac* are on these background characteristics.

Looking first at the leftmost column of results (bandwidth 0.2), we see that although gender and age are quite similar among passers and failers, there are some differences between the reported childhood SES and father's education for passers versus failers. While the difference does not reach conventional levels for statistical significance for the childhood SES variable, the difference is statistically significant (p=.01) for father's education. Surprisingly, narrow failers of the *bac* reported having *more* educated fathers on average than narrow failers. This is unexpected given that people with more advantaged upbringings generally perform better academically. We are not sure how to account for such differences and are inclined to regard them as stochastic.

In any case, the differences are not large in magnitude. The average difference for childhood SES is one-tenth of a point for a variable that runs from 1 to 5. Father's education, a variable that ranges from 1 to 11, shows a difference in means of only -0.22.

We also see that narrow passers of the exam are slightly more likely to have taken the *bac* in the humanities/social science track than the natural science/engineering track (an 8 percent difference). There is no evidence that narrow passers or failers were more likely to have attended an urban high school.

Subsequent columns of Table 3.2 show results of the same comparisons of means, but using only respondents with *bac* scores in narrower bandwidths around the passage threshold. In general, these results show less evidence of statistically significant differences. Of course, reducing the bandwidth, while likely reducing the potential for important differences between narrow passers and narrow failers, also reduces the number of observations in the analysis, thus reducing the statistical power of these tests.

Overall, these results suggest that there are only minor differences in the characteristics of those who passed and those who failed the *bac* within the bandwidth of scores included in our sample. This, in turn, suggests that the assumptions of our RD design are plausible.

Importantly, RD analyses that include these covariates as control variables show broadly similar results. Moreover, sensitivity analyses suggest that any potential confounders (observed or unobserved) would have to have implausibly large relationships with both exam passage and our dependent variables in order to explain away our central findings.

Of course, we cannot test every possible confounder. But the evidence presented here is encouraging, as it includes many of the characteristics that are most likely to relate to both treatment assignment and the outcomes of interest. We find few significant differences and when we do they tend to be quite small in magnitude and – in one case – hard to explain as anything but stochastic. Accordingly, it is reasonable to interpret the jump in university

TABLE 3.2 *Pretreatment covariates of narrow passers and failers of the bac*

DV	.2	.15	.1	.05	minimum
				Bandwidth	
Female	-.01	.01	.01	.02	.07
	[-.06, .05]	[-.05, .08]	[.04]	[-.08, .13]	[-.13, .26]
	(.81)	(.67)	(.76)	(.66)	(.50)
Age	-.08	-.06	-.11	-.25	-.60
	[-.24, .08]	[-.26, .13]	[-.33, .11]	[-.55, .04]	[-1.11, -.09]
	(.32)	(.53)	(.33)	(.09)	(.02)
Childhood SES	-.10	-.12	-.09	.07	-.18
	[-.22, .02]	[-.26, .03]	[-.25, .08]	[-.16, .29]	[-.60, .23]
	(.10)	(.11)	(.30)	(.57)	(.38)
Father's education	-.22	-.22	-.17	.04	-.54
	[-.39, -.05]	[-.42, -.01]	[-.41, .07]	[-.29, .37]	[-1.15, .07]
	(.01)	(.04)	(.16)	(.82)	(.08)
Humanities/social science track	.08	.09	.11	.09	.14
	[.02, .13]	[.02, .16]	[.03, .18]	[-.02, .20]	[-.05, .34]
	(.01)	(.01)	(.01)	(.10)	(.15)
Urban high school	-.02	-.03	-.04	-.06	-.02
	[-.07, .03]	[-.09, .02]	[-.11, .02]	[-.16, .03]	[-.19, .15]
	(.48)	(.26)	(.20)	(.17)	(.78)
N	1,230	815	623	339	106
(N_below, N_above)	(553, 677)	(373, 442)	(291, 332)	(146, 193)	(53, 52)

Estimates (with 95 percent confidence intervals and p-values underneath) from linear regressions predicting specified covariate with exam passage (i.e., having average *bac* score of at least 6), using data within specified bandwidth. The "minimum" bandwidth uses only observations with either the highest possible failing score (0.5983333) or the lowest possible passing score (6). Sample sizes listed are the number of *bac* scores in each bandwidth (including those below and above the cutoff). Number of responses to father's education and childhood SES questions are slightly different because of a small number of missing values (less than 5 percent for each variable). DV = dependent variable; SES = socioeconomic status.

attendance shown in Figure 3.3 as the product of slightly higher or lower exam scores rather than of other factors. Those who scored 5.8–5.99 appear similar to those who scored 6.0–6.2. Passing the exam may therefore be regarded as if it were a random event – akin to a true experiment with a manipulated treatment – among those falling within our narrow bandwidth.

Test Effects

The treatment of theoretical interest, university education, is empirically entangled with another feature of our design – passage (or failure) of the *bac*. One can imagine that students who fail the *bac*, scoring below 6.0, might feel discouraged about their future prospects, while those who pass might feel emboldened. This might lead to different perspectives on society and politics, and different behavioral patterns.

In this respect, analyses based on the RNE may reflect a compound treatment, composed of the assignment mechanism (passage of the *bac*) and the treatment of theoretical interest (university education). This poses a potential problem of interpretation. However, for a variety of reasons we do not believe that passing/failing the *bac*, *by itself*, is likely to affect the outcomes of concern in this study.

First, the Romanian educational system is exam-driven, so students are accustomed to the experience of passing and failing. The *bac* is not their first high-pressure exam. Nor is information from previous exams withheld. Indeed, exam scores are publicly posted and the ranking of candidates is a feature present in all school examinations as well as in interviews for public sector jobs. It is an integral part of Romanian life, imposed from an early age. Arguably, the most important exam is the *Evaluare Nationala*, administered at age fourteen, which decides a student's future career path as well as the quality of the high school they will attend. Accordingly, the emotional impact of passing or failing the *bac* at age eighteen is probably attenuated relative to what it might be for populations unaccustomed to high-stakes examinations.

Second, passing the *bac* is not very useful in and of itself. It is not a high school diploma and is of little consequence in applying for jobs. In this respect the *bac* is like the SAT and ACT exams that serve as filters for college applicants in the US. Its sole purpose is to facilitate entrance to university. That is the prize. Thus, although students who pass the *bac* are generally happy, while those who fail are deflated, their emotional state hinges on its implications for university education. Those who have passed can anticipate matriculating at a university in the fall, earning a bachelor's (or equivalent) degree, and eventually obtaining a white-collar job. Of course, this route to success is not assured; but it is a reasonable expectation. Those who have failed have less enticing career prospects.

If student views on society and politics change after learning test scores, this is not really a test effect but rather the anticipated effect of that test on university education, and by extension on their future career and earnings potential. In other words, the reason that the results of the *bac* may engender such responses, particularly for those who narrowly fail or pass, is precisely because it assigns the treatment of university attendance. Bear in mind that our understanding of the treatment – university education – is not limited to coursework and curriculum. It extends to all aspects of the college experience, including being accepted to college and coming to think of oneself as a college student.

In summary, the *bac* matters – a lot – but its impact is inseparable from the treatment of theoretical interest, namely university education. For this reason, we do not anticipate compound-treatment confounding.

Evidence for this conclusion may be drawn from our analysis of the WVS and EVS, described in the next section. There, the treatment is not limited to high school graduates who barely pass or fail a nationwide exam. All persons are included in this sample, most of whom do not fall into this narrow bandwidth and therefore would presumably not be subject to a large test effect. This global sample also includes many countries like the US, where entrance to university does not depend upon a single exam, further reducing test effects. Since estimated treatment effects are very similar in the RNE and WVS/EVS analyses, it seems unlikely that the former are driven by test effects.

GENERALIZABILITY

The natural experiment presented in the previous section focuses on a tiny slice of humanity: Romanian students who score just above or below the threshold required for entry into university. How generalizable are results from the RNE?

The first question is whether we can generalize to subjects within Romania beyond the narrow bandwidth of our RD design. The second question is whether results are generalizable beyond Romania.

Beyond the RD Bandwidth

For purposes of causal inference, the RNE focuses on a very narrow range of subjects: students whose *bac* scores fall 0.2 points above or below the threshold for passing the exam (6.0 on a ten-point scale). Estimated treatment effects apply to this subpopulation.

This subpopulation is apt to be quite different from those with much lower, or higher, scores. Consequently, we cannot infer that university education would have the same impact across the entire population of Romanian students who take the *bac*. For example, we have little to say directly about how an honor roll student would be affected if they had not attended university or, conversely, how a student who barely graduated high school would have done had they attended university.

One can speculate that those further above the threshold are likely to be less affected by the university experience because they are already well educated and probably living in a highly educated milieu. What they learn or experience in college is unlikely to be very novel. By contrast, those well below the threshold may be more affected by the university experience because they are even further removed from that milieu. As it happens, we find little evidence of this moderating effect (or others) in tests discussed in Chapter 5. However, these tests are underpowered and therefore inconclusive. The short answer is that we have scant grounds for generalizing beyond the narrow bandwidth of our RD design.

It is worth pointing out that students at the threshold are the most *policy-relevant* subgroup. Consider that when enrollment in higher education expands or contracts (because of family decisions, changes in the tertiary sector, government-initiated policy changes, or economic fluctuations), those on the threshold of viability are those most likely to enter, or exit, the university system. When supply expands, marginal students are likely to enter; when supply contracts, they are likely to exit. By contrast, those with very low scores are unlikely to attend university under any circumstances (never-takers) and those with very high scores are likely to attend university under all circumstances (always-takers).

Never-takers and always-takers are not very relevant when one is considering the effects of policy changes. To be sure, knowing the impact of university education on the always-takers would be helpful in understanding the impact of university on society at large. But this is not a question that is easily answered, precisely because – absent extreme and unethical constraints – there can be no control group.

The RNE therefore speaks to a question that is answerable and that lies before policymakers everywhere. What is the likely impact on society if the supply of college education expands or contracts?

Beyond Romania

Having discussed the problem of generalizing beyond the RD threshold, let us now consider the generalizability of our results outside Romania (for students who fall near a similar threshold of qualification in other countries). In doing so, we must consider the setting. How representative is the country of Romania with respect to our question of theoretical interest? And of what broader population is it representative?

Previously, we compared Romania to other countries in Europe and beyond. By a number of standards Romania exemplifies an "upper-middle" country. The quality of democracy is better than most but not at the very top. Party politics is similar to many countries with parliamentary executives and multiparty systems. Per-capita GDP is in the upper third, and educational attainment is above average but not in the top tier.

We can also get some purchase on this question by looking directly at social and political attitudes, the outcomes of theoretical interest. In Chapter 7, we compare responses from the RNE survey to responses obtained from a sample of nineteen- to twenty-three-year-olds across Romania, a sample of adults (all ages) across Romania, and samples of adults from across the world (gathered from the WVS and EVS). By all of these metrics of comparison, the RNE sample is quite close (see Table 7.4), suggesting that there is nothing unusual about our sample of participants.

The Prospect of Replication

To be sure, the only way to answer the question of generalizability definitively is to replicate our RD design across diverse settings. In practical terms, this means identifying countries where access to higher education is allocated by a nationwide test with a specified cutoff, where test takers cannot precisely sort themselves on either side of the threshold, where the identity of test takers falling on either side of the threshold is known, and where there is a mechanism for contacting those individuals and thereby inviting them to a survey.

Romania is quite possibly the only country in the world in which all of these criteria are satisfied – or were satisfied (until several years ago)[15] – on the basis of public records. Most countries have varying thresholds for admission to university; if a student misses one threshold, they are likely to qualify for another. Consequently, it is difficult to obtain an unbiased estimate of the treatment of theoretical interest, defined here as university/no university.

In several countries, a national exam determines eligibility for all (or most) universities and the cutoff is strictly enforced (no cheating). However, exam results along with the names of students are not publicly available. Departments of education in those countries have access to the names, scores, and addresses (or emails) of all individuals who take the test. With official assistance, the RD design sketched in this chapter could be replicated.

We recommend this avenue to researchers and policymakers interested in exploring social and political attitudes (as in this study) or any other outcome that might be affected by higher education. However, it is unclear whether government officials are willing to explore such sensitive subjects. The absence of such studies, to date, bespeaks uneasiness in official quarters. They have the data, but evidently choose not to exploit it (or such studies are kept secret).

---

[15] The education department in Romania has recently changed its policies and no longer posts the names of students next to their exam scores. Accordingly, it is no longer possible to replicate our study in Romania.

Field Experiments

One might imagine that our question could be explored with field experiments. A straightforward experiment in which students are granted admission to college in a random fashion is possible in a country where higher education is a state monopoly. However, such an approach requires government implementation and would likely meet with opposition from government officials. And for good reason, as it is probably unethical to deny someone an education because they landed, by chance, in the control group.

One could construct "encouragement" experiments in which high school students are randomly chosen as beneficiaries of a college scholarship covering tuition and/or a stipend. This would presumably incentivize those in the treatment group to attend university.

However, compliance is likely to be weak. Some in the treatment group would not matriculate, or would quickly attrit; some in the control group would attend. We suspect that noncompliance would be quite a bit higher than it is in our RD design. This means that a large sample would be required in order to provide sufficient statistical power for the analysis. And this, finally, raises the problem of cost. Subsidizing college education is extremely expensive, so a substantial investment would be required in order to obtain a sufficiently large sample.

For all these reasons, an experimental approach to the question of college impact would be difficult – though certainly not impossible – to implement. We recommend it to institutions with the necessary resources to undertake it.

A GLOBAL ANALYSIS

Given the challenges of implementing natural experiments and survey experiments outside Romania, we adopt what might be regarded as a least-bad alternative for generalizing from the RNE: observational data drawn from cross-national surveys.

The most extensive global survey is the WVS. The seventh wave, completed between 2017 and 2020, was carried out in partnership with the EVS, generating a combined dataset with seventy-nine countries (Haerpfer et al. 2020). The characteristics of these surveys, as well as the joint dataset, are summarized in Table 3.3.[16]

Four countries – Germany, Romania, Russia, and Serbia – are included in both the WVS and EVS. Thus, the number of polities in the joint dataset is not exactly the sum of the number of countries in the EVS and WVS. Note also that while most country samples in the WVS and EVS range from 1,000 to a little

[16] We might have chosen to enlist previous waves of the WVS in our analysis. However, those surveys do not include measures of the respondent's social class, a potential confounder in our regression analysis. Additionally, since we want to compare WVS and RNE results, it makes sense to focus on the same time period.

TABLE 3.3 *World Values Survey and European Values Survey samples*

	European Values Survey (EVS)	World Values Survey (WVS)	EVS/ WVS
Wave	5th	7th	Joint
Questions (N)	49	60	49
Respondents (N)	56,491	70,867	127,358
Polities (N)	34	49	79
Polities	Albania, Azerbaijan, Austria, Armenia, Belarus, Bosnia/ Herzegovina, Bulgaria, Croatia, Czechia, Denmark, Estonia, Finland, France, Georgia, *Germany*, Great Britain, Hungary, Iceland, Italy, Lithuania, Montenegro, Netherlands, North Macedonia, Norway, Poland, Portugal, *Romania*, *Russia, Serbia*, Slovakia, Slovenia, Spain, Sweden, Switzerland	Andorra, Argentina, Australia, Bangladesh, Bolivia, Brazil, Myanmar, Chile, China, Taiwan, Colombia, Cyprus, Ecuador, Egypt, Ethiopia, *Germany*, Greece, Guatemala, Hong Kong, Indonesia, Iran, Iraq, Japan, Jordan, Kazakhstan, Kyrgyzstan, Lebanon, Macau, Malaysia, Mexico, New Zealand, Nicaragua, Nigeria, Pakistan, Peru, Philippines, Puerto Rico, *Romania, Russia, Serbia*, South Korea, Tajikistan, Thailand, Tunisia, Turkey, Ukraine, United States, Vietnam, Zimbabwe	

Period of data collection: 2017–2020. Countries in italics are included in both the EVS and the WVS. Source: www.worldvaluessurvey.org/WVSEVSjoint2017.jsp.

over 3,000, in these four countries the combined samples are somewhat larger because of the combination of the two surveys.[17]

Fortuitously, the WVS/EVS includes a large battery of questions pertaining to social and political attitudes. By design, many of the questions chosen for the RNE were drawn directly from the WVS, meaning that they are exact replications (though of course RNE does not replicate the question *ordering*

---

[17] In this situation, one might weight observations so that each country carries equal influence in the regression analysis. However, because we include country fixed effects in all analyses, we do not anticipate that differences in sample sizes across countries have much impact on the aggregate results.

of the WVS/EVS). Regrettably, some questions on the WVS are not included in the EVS, as reflected in the second row of Table 3.3. Consequently, most of our analyses include the joint WVS/EVS dataset while a few are restricted to the WVS sample.

Coverage for the chosen variables across the WVS and EVS datasets is strong. However, we want to ensure that all samples are identical so that results are fully comparable. To solve this problem, and to mitigate any sample biases that might arise from missingness, we impute missing values for (a) the combined WVS/EVS dataset and (b) the WVS dataset (consisting of several variables not included in the combined WVS/EVS dataset). For each dataset, ten imputed datasets are generated using the Amelia algorithm (Honaker et al. 2011).

To impute the individual variables in both datasets, we use the joint multivariate normal (MVN) approach in which the data is modeled as a sample from a joint MVN distribution. Three control variables (father's education, mother's education, father's job) are nominal, and are imputed following the procedure in Enders (2010). Once the individual variables are imputed, the individual indexes introduced in Chapter 4 are computed based on the imputed values (one index per dataset).

The imputed datasets contain 6.3 percent and 6.9 percent more data than the original EVS/WVS and WVS datasets (counting only the imputed variables). Since this is a small portion of the total, there is no reason to imagine that our results would be any different if imputed observations were excluded. All statistics reported in this book are drawn from analyses on these imputed datasets, whose variability embodies the underlying uncertainty of imputed observations – an uncertainty reflected in standard errors and confidence intervals.

Causal Inference

To reach causal inferences about the impact of university education on attitudes and behavior with observational data, we fall back on the traditional strategy of conditioning on background factors that might serve as confounders. Accordingly, all regression analyses include country fixed effects (to control for all manner of country-specific characteristics) and covariates measuring pretreatment characteristics of subjects including age, sex, father's educational attainment, mother's educational attainment, and father's job when the respondent was a child. Insofar as these factors affect selection into treatment (attendance at university) and outcomes of interest (social and political attitudes), we should be able to account for these relationships.

Our hope is that this conditioning strategy eliminates, or at least reduces, selection biases that might affect our estimates. However, we do not want to oversell results from these regression-based analyses. For one thing, some of the background covariates depend upon self-report and may be subject to recall bias or other factors that themselves could be driven by university attendance.

We do not know in which direction that bias might run. University-educated respondents may *over*estimate their social class in order to feel that they fit in. Or, they may *under*estimate their family background, which appears diminished by reference to their more affluent peer group. Reassuringly, robustness tests that exclude these covariates – while maintaining country fixed effects – show estimates of university effects on social and political attitudes that are similar to those in our benchmark models.

A more serious problem is that we cannot measure other possible confounders such as personality, motivation, and intelligence. Regression-based corrections are loaded with assumptions – about which factors are properly measured (without measurement bias), which factors are pre- and post-treatment, and which factors influence the decision to attend college – as discussed in Chapter 2. In the RNE analyses, we assume that those narrowly above and below the passage threshold for the *bac* are similar on average in these relevant confounders, whether observable or unobservable. But in the WVS/EVS analyses we must rely on stronger assumptions pertaining to our choice of background covariates, their measurement, and their functional forms.

Although we have (much) less faith in the point estimates, it seems reasonable to use the WVS/EVS analyses to compare the size of coefficients for university attendance across different outcomes. This presumes that the unmeasured confounders, whatever they happen to be, do not operate differently on different outcomes – a reasonable assumption for most comparisons, but perhaps not for all.[18]

All things considered, we believe that our regression models are better identified than most survey-based analyses of this topic, as reviewed in Chapter 2. The WVS/EVS include questions about age, sex, father's educational attainment, mother's educational attainment, and father's job when the respondent was a child – all of which are pretreatment (with the caveat that answers about the latter depend upon subject recall). Most regression-based analyses cannot draw on such a broad set of pretreatment covariates, and are therefore forced to rely on a more parsimonious model or on covariates that are likely to be post-treatment.

In any case, our regression analyses serve as a useful adjunct to our natural experiment, offering clues into causality on a much larger scale than can be managed with the narrowly focused RNE. If the same relationship between college education and an outcome is found across these two very different designs – RNE and WVS/EVS – we are inclined to believe that it is truly causal and general in purview.

---

[18] Let us say that ambition and motivation are the missing confounders. It may be reasonable to assume that these factors do not have differential effects on views of abortion and democracy. But it may be unreasonable to suppose the same for political participation: someone who is ambitious is a *do*-er, and therefore more likely to be engaged in politics.

SOCIAL DESIRABILITY BIAS

Many of the questions on the RNE and WVS/EVS surveys tap into widely shared norms. For example, questions about political participation tap into a norm of civic engagement. Questions about crime and corruption tap into norms of law-abidingness. And so forth.

Accordingly, one must be concerned that responses reflect what the respondent believes is the correct answer rather than the answer that accurately reflects their views. Respondents may say that they are intolerant of corruption when in fact they do not object. Or they may express general opinions that do not conform to actual behavior. For example, they might indicate their support for free speech as an ideal but not in specific situations where a person with unpopular views is prohibited from expressing them. Or they may simply misreport behavior, saying that they vote regularly when they actually vote rarely or not at all.

We can expect that many responses on our surveys are marred by some sort of social desirability bias, a genre of error that is virtually impossible to avoid in survey-based research. Helpfully, if *all* subjects are susceptible to social desirability bias, the latter poses a minor nuisance. The most likely repercussion is a truncated distribution on the response variable, the product of responses that are bunched up around what is perceived to be the "correct" answer.

Social desirability bias becomes a serious threat to inference only if correlated with the treatment of theoretical interest. Thus, we must consider whether college-educated respondents are more susceptible to social desirability bias than non-college-educated respondents, or vice versa.

There is some evidence, for example, that more educated survey respondents in the US are more likely to overreport turnout; that is, to say they voted when they did not.[19] This increased overreporting could produce overestimates of the effect of university attendance on turnout (and perhaps, similarly, on other political activities).[20]

In the same vein, it is sometimes alleged that what students learn in college is not greater tolerance per se but rather the ability to mask their intolerance in socially acceptable ways (Jackman 1978; Jackman and Mulha 1984). For example, college-educated respondents may articulate greater confidence in an abstractly framed question about the importance of free speech because they have been socialized to accept this abstract ideal – but be no more willing than less-educated respondents to permit speech by people they fundamentally disagree with.

---

[19] See Ansolabehere and Hersh (2012), Bernstein and colleagues (2001), and Enamorado and Imai (2019).
[20] Unfortunately, turnout is not public record in most countries (including Romania) as it is in the US, so we are limited in our ability to address this threat to inference directly.

One clue to this problem can be found in comparing questions that are framed in an abstract fashion with those (on the same general topic) that are framed in a specific fashion. If we find a larger treatment effect (in the liberal direction) for the former, then we might worry that social desirability bias is greater for educated respondents than for less educated respondents.

Happily, there is little evidence of this in the results presented in Chapter 4. For example, two questions in the RNE address the respondent's propensity to vote. The first asks the question in a general fashion: "Here are some forms of political action that people can take. For each one, indicate your involvement." Response options include: (a) I would never under any circumstances do this, (b) I might do this, and (c) I definitely would do this or have done this. "Voting" is the first of several actions listed. The second question on the RNE survey having to do with voting is much more specific. "In the 2019 European Union elections, did you vote?" Response options include: (a) Yes, (b) No, (c) Don't remember, and (d) Not old enough to qualify. Figure 4.1 shows that the estimated effect of a college education is greater for the latter than the former (though the differences are not statistically significant). In other words, the more generally framed question – where one might expect social desirability bias to be stronger – does not generate a larger causal effect.

It should also be noted that most of the questions on the RNE survey and WVS/EVS are fairly specific. For example, in ascertaining views of corruption, the surveys ask about specific acts that some might call corrupt; they do not ask about corruption in general. As such, they may be less susceptible to social desirability bias.

There is still a nagging worry that a college education might teach students the correct way to answer questions rather than altering their actual opinions and behavior. Perhaps they are more likely to treat the survey as an exam, with correct and incorrect answers, while less educated respondents do not think of it that way or do not care so much about their score.

If this is the case, it suggests an interpretation of (some of) the results reported in Chapter 4. Specifically, it suggests that college education enhances people's sensitivity to social cues. College students, and former students, may have a stronger desire to conform to widely held values than non-college-educated respondents.

It is difficult to believe that this urge to conform is all for show and has no echo in actual behavior. Perhaps (in this interpretation) the real differences between college and non-college respondents are not as great as the effects registered in Chapter 4. Nonetheless, they should be in the same direction. People who *say* they support equal rights for homosexuals are probably more likely to *actually* support equal rights for homosexuals than those who say they do not.

Additionally, we would point out that social and political change often begins with changing ideas about social desirability. Consider the history of racism in the US. At a certain point in time, openly racist sentiments (e.g., use of the "N-word") were proscribed. One may surmise that many people still had (and have) racist thoughts. But the fact that they do not express them publicly is important, and may serve as the first step toward overcoming deeply ingrained prejudices. Accordingly, even if the immediate impact of a college education centers on social desirability, we should not dismiss this as trivial.

In any case, many of our survey questions do not feature an obviously "correct" (socially acceptable) answer. This includes questions about membership in various organizations, political activities other than voting, and party ideology. On these questions – a substantial portion of the total – we also find that university attendance has a causal effect. Moreover, the direction of the effect is usually in the same liberal direction as those questions that have a generally accepted "correct" response. Here, social desirability bias cannot be at work, or its impact is very minimal. The fact that college matters here suggests that social desirability bias is not driving all of our results.

CONCLUSIONS

In this chapter, we introduced our methods of analysis. We began by clarifying the treatment of theoretical interest – university education – explaining why we chose to focus on tertiary rather than primary or secondary education. Next, we introduced the RNE. This was followed by a discussion of its generalizability and the potential for future replications in other settings. In the fourth section, we introduced the WVS/EVS data that forms the basis of our global analyses. The final section discussed potential problems emanating from social desirability bias, which, for a variety of reasons, we do not view as a serious threat to inference.

While this groundwork is somewhat technical, and very detailed, it is essential for understanding the evidence that will be presented in the chapters that follow.

4

Findings

In the previous chapter, we introduced two complementary approaches to the question of how higher education impacts social and political attitudes.

The first relies on a natural experiment conducted in Romania focused on high school graduates whose scores fall just above and below a threshold score on a national baccalaureate test (the *bac*) that determines entrance to university. Students on either side of the threshold are assumed to be similar on background characteristics, establishing the basis for a regression discontinuity (RD) design. We refer to this as the Romanian Natural Experiment (RNE).

The second relies on survey data from the latest round of the World Values Survey (WVS), administered between 2017 and 2020 in tandem with the European Values Survey (EVS). Regression analyses include country dummies along with covariates measuring age, sex, father's educational attainment, mother's educational attainment, and father's job when the respondent was a child.

Where questions are identical, we present results from the RNE and WVS/ EVS side by side. (For details, see Appendices A and B, which reproduce the RNE and WVS/EVS questionnaires.) Several caveats apply when comparing results from these very different research designs.

First, the two sets of analyses are not directly comparable since they draw from different demographic groups. RNE includes only students aged eighteen to twenty-five whose scores fall in a narrow bandwidth around the exam passage threshold, while WVS/EVS includes respondents of all ages and all levels of academic ability. Second, the RNE estimates are more likely to be correctly identified, estimating the causal impact of university education while avoiding selection bias due to unmeasured (or imperfectly measured) variables such as parental resources, persistence, or responsibility, all of which might relate to university attendance and also affect our dependent variables of interest. By contrast, the WVS/EVS analyses are more likely to be generalizable (if true) and are also more precise, owing to the much larger sample.

Outcomes are measured with multiple indicators as well as composite indices. Bear in mind that measurement error is likely to be larger for the former than for the latter. This is evident in the size of the confidence intervals, which are greater for individual variables than for composite indices. One source of error stems from the distribution of responses. For a few questions, responses are clustered at one end of the scale, leading to a highly skewed distribution in which estimates depend on a small number of unusual values. Because the disaggregated results are more susceptible to stochastic variability and truncated distributions, we have greater confidence in results for the composite indices. This applies to both datasets but especially to the RNE, where the sample is modest in size and therefore more vulnerable to outliers.

Outcomes of theoretical concern are divided into seven main topics, each of which forms a section of this chapter: *social capital* (political participation, membership in civil society organizations, trust), *democracy* (popular rule, civil liberty), *law-abidingness* (crime and corruption), *culture* (the family, sexuality and deviance, gender, race, ethnicity, religion, science), *cosmopolitanism* (regions and regional associations such as the European Union, global associations such as the United Nations), *economics* (taxes, redistribution, the welfare state), and *overall ideology* (left–right self-placement, environmentalism versus growth).

Recall (from Chapter 1) that each of these topics is regarded as an element of *liberalism*, understood in what is variously referred to as its original, classic, nineteenth-century, or European sense. Liberalism entails a commitment to freedom, the rule of law (also known as constitutionalism), law-abidingness (e.g., opposition to corruption), democracy, citizenship, progress, education, individualism, tolerance, openness to new ideas, rationalism, secularism, cosmopolitanism, and equality with respect to rights, duties, and dignity – but not redistribution or the welfare state. To be a liberal in the twentieth century usually also entails support for political parties classified as left wing or progressive; but partisanship is just one aspect of this wide-ranging worldview.

Survey responses classified as liberal are indicated in Tables 4.1 to 4.7 that follow. For now, it is sufficient to note that liberalism is a capacious label, one we adopt partly out of convenience and partly out of an intuition that there might be connecting threads across these topics.

SOCIAL CAPITAL

Social capital refers here to civic and political engagement along with social and political trust. We disaggregate this topic into four components: (a) voting, (b) other modes of political participation, (c) membership in voluntary associations, and (d) trust. Each is measured by a number of questions, as shown in Table 4.1. For each question, we indicate the response that we consider to be "liberal," defined as higher social capital. The final columns indicate the variable tags for the survey(s) in which that question appears (reproduced in Appendices A and B). A blank cell indicates that a variable is not included in a survey.

TABLE 4.1 *Indicators of social capital*

	"*Liberal*"	RNE	WVS	EVS
VOTING				
Voting: have done or would do	Yes	q7_1	Q222	E264
Voted in the 2019 European Union elections	Yes	q4		
OTHER MODES OF POLITICAL PARTICIPATION				
Interested in politics	Yes	q5	Q199	E023
Political party: active member	Yes	q6_5	Q98	A068
Signing a petition: have done or would do	Yes	q7_2	Q209	E025
Joining in boycotts: have done or would do	Yes	q7_3	Q210	E026
Attending peaceful demonstrations: have done or would do	Yes	q7_4	Q211	E027
Joining strikes: have done or would do	Yes	q7_5	Q212	E028
Any other act of protest: have done or would do	Yes	q7_6		
MEMBERSHIP				
Sport or recreational organization: active member	Yes	q6_2	Q95	A074
Art, music, or educational organization: active member	Yes	q6_3	Q96	A066
Labor union: active member	Yes	q6_4	Q97	A067
Environmental organization: active member	Yes	q6_6	Q99	A071
Professional association: active member	Yes	q6_7	Q100	A072
Humanitarian or charitable organization: active member	Yes	q6_8	Q101	A080_01
Consumer organization: active member	Yes	q6_9	Q102	A078
Self-help group, mutual aid group: active member	Yes	q6_10	Q103	A080_02
Other organization: active member	Yes	q6_11	Q105	A079
TRUST				
Most people can be trusted	Yes	q2_1	Q57	A165
Political leaders can be trusted	Yes	q2_2		

Measures of social capital. "Liberal": coded as a liberal response. RNE: Romanian Natural Experiment; WVS: World Values Survey; EVS: European Values Survey. Variable tags correspond to those in the original surveys, reproduced in Appendices A (RNE) and B (WVS/EVS).

Response options for these questions differ. A few are interval scales while most are ordinal. To aid interpretation, they are rescaled so that 0 is the lowest level of social capital and 1 indicates the highest level of social capital. Therefore, treatment effect estimates can be interpreted as a fraction of the response-scale range that attending university would be expected to move a person (e.g., an estimate of 0.2 implies that university attendance causes, on average, an increase of 20 percent of the response-scale range on that item).

Figure 4.1 examines the impact of higher education on each of the individual measures of social capital listed in Table 4.1. RNE analyses show considerable variability, though most of the estimates are positive. WVS/EVS analyses are consistently positive. These RNE effects are especially strong for social and political trust. Both trust in people and trust in politician items show effect estimates near 0.2. Given that both of these variables can range only from 0 to 1, this is a very large effect. Perhaps this reflects a sense on the part of those who have the good fortune of gaining access to university that the system is working, the world is a benevolent place, and therefore people can be trusted. Or, perhaps the experience of being drawn out of a parochial world where their ambit is limited into a wider world with connections to people from far away and a broader set of ideas instills confidence in that wider world.

One RNE result is rather surprising. University attendance appears to have a large negative effect on political interest. This is all the more surprising given the clear positive effects estimated for other indicators related to voting and party membership. Although we are unable to pinpoint the specific mechanism driving this surprising result, we suspect that those exposed to university might interpret the response scale of this question differently. For example, university attenders might be exposed to an environment where those around them appear to be highly politically engaged; by this standard, they might view their own engagement as minimal, and answer the question accordingly. For example, someone who votes some of the time and reads political news once a week on average might consider themselves "Somewhat interested" in politics if they were in a non-university environment. But that same person, if they were to attend university and be around others who voted and read about politics even more often than they do, might answer that they are "Not very interested." Unfortunately, the RNE lacks a set of anchoring vignettes or other ways to test the impact of peer comparisons so this explanation is necessarily speculative. Furthermore, the fact that the WVS/EVS estimate a positive effect for university attendance on political interest may call this explanation into question.

Overall, though, the estimated effects of university attendance on these social capital indicators paint a picture of higher education having a positive impact on a broad range of traits related to social capital. Those who attend university are on average more trusting and more involved with their communities, and participate more in politics than those who do not attend university. This general finding holds for both the RNE and the cross-country WVS/EVS data.

To measure the overall effect of university education on social capital, we combine the foregoing indicators into an overall measure of social capital – one for the RNE sample and another for the WVS/EVS sample. We do so in several steps (following our pre-analysis plan).

First, we generate four component indices – Voting, Other modes of political participation, Membership, and Trust – as indicated in Table 4.1. To do so, we take a simple average of all items within the component, each first standardized by subtracting off the mean and dividing by the standard deviation so that each

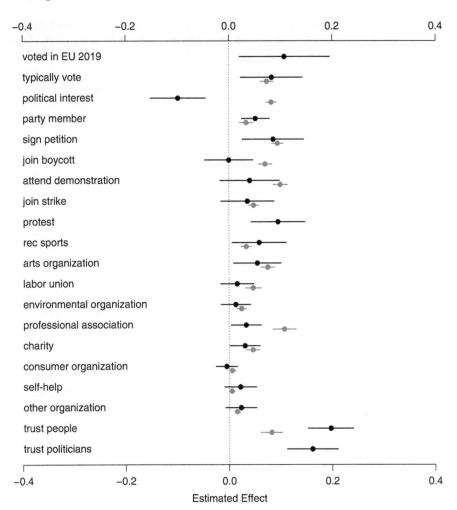

FIGURE 4.1 University impact on social capital indicators

Indicators are scaled so that higher scores indicate higher social capital. RNE estimates (in black) are fuzzy RD effect estimates (two-stage least squares). $N=1,210$ (542 below the threshold, 668 above), with slightly smaller sample sizes for some individual items due to missingness. WVS/EVS estimates (in gray) employ ordinary least-squares regression with country fixed effects and covariates measuring pretreatment characteristics of subjects including age, sex, father's educational attainment, mother's educational attainment, and father's occupation when the respondent was a child. Analyses are conducted on imputed samples. $N=123,163$ for "typically vote" (where we must discard respondents who are under the legal voting age); 126,690 for all others.

component contributes similarly to the overall index. Next, we generate an overall index of social capital. To do so, we take a simple average of the four component indices, then subtract off the sample mean and divide by the sample standard deviation to produce an easily interpretable measure of social capital that has a mean of 0 and a standard deviation of 1. This index, then, can be interpreted as a measure of social capital for a given person as compared to the typical values of this variable (or, equivalently, as a z-score for social capital relative to its overall distribution in our sample). Values of this index near 0 indicate that someone has a typical (roughly average) social capital level. Values near 1 (−1) indicate that someone has fairly high (fairly low) social capital. Values near 2 (−2) or further away from 0 would represent an exceptionally high (low) level of social capital.

This same procedure is followed for the RNE sample and the WVS/EVS sample. The only difference is that in the latter case we rely on the slightly smaller number questions on these surveys, meaning that two of the components (voting and trust) are formed by a single variable, as noted in Table 4.1.

Figure 4.2 shows the estimated effect of university attendance on each of these aggregated social capital indices. The RNE point estimate for the social capital index is 0.66 with a standard error of 0.09. Recall that this index has a mean of 0 and a standard deviation of 1, meaning that the causal effect is around two-thirds of a sample standard deviation – a substantial effect. The 95 percent confidence interval ranges from 0.49 to 0.84, which includes only effect sizes that are positive and quite large in magnitude. Furthermore, the p-value from a null hypothesis test of zero effect is below 0.001, meaning we can strongly reject the null hypothesis of zero effect.

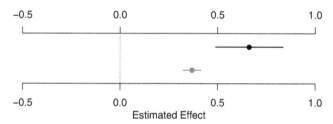

FIGURE 4.2 University impact on social capital index
Social capital index is scaled to have a sample mean of 0 and sample standard deviation of 1 within each sample. A higher score indicates more social capital. RNE estimate (in black) is a fuzzy RD effect estimate (two-stage least squares). N=1,210 (542 observations below threshold, 668 observations above threshold) for social capital index, with slightly smaller sample sizes for individual items due to missingness. WVS/EVS estimate (in gray) employs ordinary least squares with country fixed effects and covariates measuring pretreatment characteristics of subjects including age, sex, father's educational attainment, mother's educational attainment, and father's occupation when the respondent was a child. Analyses are conducted on imputed samples. N=123,163.

The WVS/EVS estimate is more modest but also more precisely estimated (signaled by narrower confidence bounds). Readers should bear in mind that precision is not the same thing as unbiasedness, and the WVS/EVS estimates, which are based on observational data analyzed using regression models rather than the natural experimental design used in the RNE, are much more likely to be systematically biased, for reasons discussed at length in this chapter and the next.

Because some of the questions related to social capital that were included in the RNE were not included in the WVS/EVS, this might complicate the comparisons of the social capital indices estimated separately for each of these datasets. To address this concern, we have also estimated the same effect for the RNE while forming our social capital indices using only items that were included on both the RNE and the WVS/EVS. The correlation between these two social capital indices in the RNE sample is quite high ($\rho=0.92$), which is unsurprising since only three of the twenty RNE social capital questions are not also in the WVS/EVS. Furthermore, the estimated effect of university attendance on the social capital index using only the WVS/EVS items is similar to that for the index using all twenty of the RNE social capital questions (0.59 versus 0.66, both with p-values less than 0.001). Therefore, our overall conclusion does not seem driven by small differences in the items used to compose these indices.

When looking at both the RNE and the broader WVS/EVS samples, the effect of university attendance is substantial. University education enhances social capital. This is consistent with prior studies, as reported in Chapter 2.

DEMOCRACY

Next, we look at the relationship between university education and attitudes toward democracy. Unfortunately, the RNE survey does not include questions tapping into such attitudes. Therefore, analyses reported here rely entirely on the WVS/EVS. For each question listed in Table 4.2, we indicate the response that we interpret as "liberal," in this case greater support for democratic values.

Figure 4.3 shows the analyses of these fourteen outcomes. In nearly all cases, those with university education hold positions that we regard as more supportive of democracy than those who have not been exposed to higher education. Only two effects are indistinguishable from 0.

As previously, we create an index from all of these questions pertaining to democracy. Our index is derived from the first dimension of a principal component analysis across the fourteen questions. To ease interpretation, the scores on this first dimension are standardized to have a mean of 0 and a standard deviation of 1.

Estimates for this index are shown in Figure 4.4. It is very strong. Again, we conclude that a university education enhances support for democracy. This is consistent with prior studies, as reported in Chapter 2.

TABLE 4.2 *Indicators of democracy*

	"Liberal"	WVS	EVS
Importance of giving people more say in government decisions	Yes	Q154	E003, E004
Importance of protecting freedom of speech	Yes	Q154	E003
People choose leaders in free elections – important	Yes	Q243	E226
The army takes over when government is incompetent – essential	No	Q245	E228
Civil rights protect people's liberty against oppression – essential	Yes	Q246	E229
People obey their rulers – essential	No	Q248	E233B
Living in a country that is governed democratically – important	Yes	Q250	E235
Having a strong leader – good	No	Q235	E114
Having experts, not government, make decisions – good	No	Q236	E115
Having the army rule the country – good	No	Q237	E116
Having a democratic political system – good	Yes	Q238	E117
Government has right of video surveillance	No	Q196	H009
Government has right to monitor emails and other information exchanged on internet	No	Q197	H010
Government has right to collect information about anyone living in country	No	Q198	H011

Measures of support for democracy. "Liberal": coded as a liberal response. WVS: World Values Survey; EVS: European Values Survey. (None of these questions appear in the RNE.) Variable tags correspond to those in the original surveys, reproduced in Appendix B (WVS/EVS).

LAW-ABIDINGNESS

In this section, we explore attitudes and behavior associated with crime and corruption, which we call *law-abidingness*. Unfortunately, one cannot reasonably ask whether respondents have engaged in these unsavory activities. This might be unethical and in any case is likely to be unavailing.[1] Accordingly, most of our questions tap into the respondent's *tolerance* for crime and corruption. This is an important topic unto itself insofar as it presumably has political ramifications; for example, a willingness to support anti-crime and anti-corruption policies and political parties and candidates that have comparatively clean records.

It is also widely viewed as a proxy for how likely people are to engage in criminal or corrupt activities. Reassuringly, tolerance of corruption is strongly

[1] We do not have a sample that is large enough to allow for a list experiment in Romania, which would obscure the identity of those who might be engaging in corrupt or illegal activities and hence improve the accuracy of their reports.

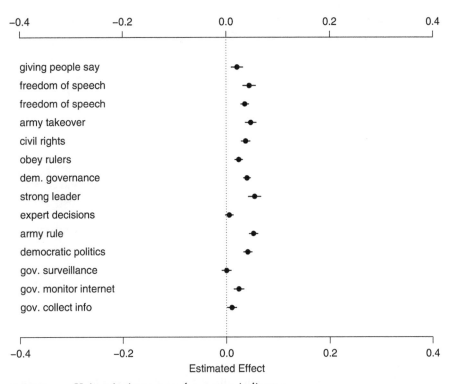

FIGURE 4.3 University impact on democracy indicators
Indicators are scored so that higher values indicate greater support for democracy. WVS/EVS analysis using ordinary least-squares regression model with country fixed effects and covariates measuring pretreatment characteristics of subjects including age, sex, father's educational attainment, mother's educational attainment, and father's occupation when the respondent was a child. Analyses are conducted on imputed samples. N=70,530 (WVS/EVS sample).

correlated with perceptions of corruption when measured at national levels (Erlingsson and Kristinsson 2019: 155). Countries with low tolerance of corruption have little of it (by self-report). Of course, this does not mean that the individuals who say they are intolerant of corruption are doing something about it. However, there are good reasons to suppose that answers to questions about corruption tolerance are not merely rhetorical. After all, it would generate considerable cognitive dissonance if a person who committed corrupt acts on a regular basis professed to be disgusted by the practice. This is the stuff of literature and film but we doubt it is common among survey respondents. Indeed, analyses reported in Chang and Kerr (2017: 79) show that intolerance for corruption is correlated with opposition to the incumbent in eighteen countries in sub-Saharan Africa where corruption (by all reports) is quite high. People who (say they) do not like corruption are not inclined to

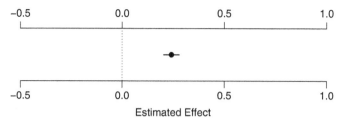

FIGURE 4.4 University impact on democracy index
Democracy index is scaled to have a sample mean of 0 and sample standard deviation of
1 within each sample. Higher values indicate more support for democracy. The WVS/
EVS estimate employs ordinary least squares with country fixed effects and covariates
measuring pretreatment characteristics of subjects including age, sex, father's
educational attainment, mother's educational attainment, and father's occupation
when the respondent was a child. Analyses are conducted on imputed samples.
N=126,690 (WVS/EVS).

support ruling parties in countries where corruption is rife. This is not
a smoking gun, but it supports the view of researchers who regard questions
about corruption tolerance as indicative of behavior.

Questions pertaining to law-abidingness drawn from the RNE, WVS, and
EVS questionnaires are listed in Table 4.3. It will be noted that we have a much
wider array of questions on this topic for the RNE than for the WVS and EVS.

Figure 4.5 shows estimates of the impact of higher education on all of these
indicators. In every case, university attendance is associated with greater
probity. Estimates are weaker for WVS/EVS than for the RNE. However,
because of the greater precision of the former, they can be distinguished from
results that might be obtainable by chance.

To summarize the impact of university education on law-abidingness, we
combine the indicators shown in Table 4.3 into two indices, one from the
RNE sample and the other from the WVS/EVS sample. To do so we follow our
pre-analysis plan, employing the first component of a principal component
analysis using all variables for which data is available. This means that the
RNE index is weighted toward corruption and the WVS/EVS index is
weighted toward crime, and includes many fewer items. Even so, these
variables are all highly correlated so the mismatch across indices is unlikely
to be very consequential.

These items appear to be strongly structured by a first underlying
dimension. In the RNE sample, the first principal component explains
nearly half (46.6 percent) of the overall variance, which is quite high for
these sorts of survey items. All of the factor loadings carry the expected
signs. Note that although we standardize and sign each item so that higher
values indicate higher levels of law-abidingness, we do not impose the
restriction that all items relate to the estimated scale in the same way;

TABLE 4.3 *Indicators of law-abidingness*

	"Liberal"	RNE	WVS	EVS
CRIME				
Claiming government benefits to which you are not entitled is justifiable	No	q1_1	Q177	F114A
Avoiding a fare on public transport is justifiable	No	q1_2	Q178	F115
Stealing property is justifiable	No	q1_3	Q179	
Cheating on taxes if you have a chance is justifiable	No	q1_4	Q180	F116
CORRUPTION				
Someone accepting a bribe in the course of their duties is justifiable	No	q1_5	Q181	F117
A magistrate or police officer accepting a bribe to close a case is justifiable	No	q1_13		
Providing information obtained from your job to interested parties is justifiable	No	q1_14		
A police officer who receives money in exchange for not fining someone is justifiable	No	q1_15		
To help a friend's firm to obtain funds/contracts from public institutions is justifiable	No	q1_16		
For a bureaucrat to accept a present to hasten the issuing of a document is justifiable	No	q1_17		
Helping relatives or friends avoid sanctions or gain advantage is justifiable	No	q1_18		
To hire a relative in a public institution is justifiable	No	q1_19		
For a public employee to receive a present *after* favorably pursuing a request is justifiable	No	q1_20		
To offer money or presents to a doctor to treat you is justifiable	No	q1_21		
To give money or presents to a doctor because you are happy with your treatment is justifiable	No	q1_22		
To give presents to a teacher who educated your children is justifiable	No	q1_23		
Punishment for corruption is too mild	Yes	q2_3		
Corruption is inevitable, and has always been around	No	q2_4		
Corruption is forgivable if no alternative is available in order to get something done	No	q2_5		
If I witnessed an act of corruption, I would report it	Yes	q2_6		
Giving or receiving bribes is common practice among people you know	No	q3		

Measures of law-abidingness. "Liberal": coded as a liberal response. RNE: Romanian Natural Experiment; WVS: World Values Survey; EVS: European Values Survey. Variable tags correspond to those in the original surveys, reproduced in Appendices A (RNE) and B (WVS/EVS).

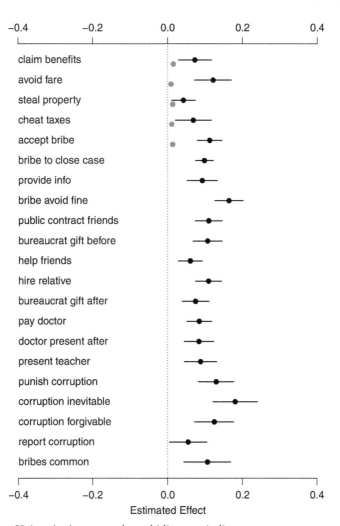

FIGURE 4.5 University impact on law-abidingness indicators
Indicators are scored so that higher values indicate greater law-abidingness. RNE estimates (in black) are fuzzy RD effect estimates (two-stage least squares). N=1,216 (546 observations below threshold, 670 observations above threshold) with slightly smaller sample sizes for some individual items due to missingness. WVS/EVS analysis using ordinary least-squares regression model with country fixed effects and covariates measuring pretreatment characteristics of subjects including age, sex, father's educational attainment, mother's educational attainment, and father's occupation when the respondent was a child. Analyses are conducted on imputed samples. N=70,530 for "steal property" (WVS sample); 126,690 for all others (WVS/EVS sample).

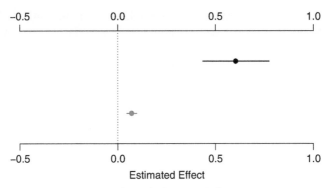

FIGURE 4.6 University impact on law-abidingness index
Law-abidingness index is scaled to have a sample mean of 0 and sample standard deviation of 1 within each sample. Higher values indicate less tolerance of, or lower propensity to, crime and corruption. RNE estimate (in black) is a fuzzy RD effect estimate (two-stage least squares). N=1,216 (546 observations below threshold, 670 observations above threshold). The WVS/EVS estimate (in gray) employs ordinary least squares with country fixed effects and covariates measuring pretreatment characteristics of subjects including age, sex, father's educational attainment, mother's educational attainment, and father's occupation when the respondent was a child. Analyses are conducted on imputed samples. N=126,690.

nonetheless, the principal component estimates suggest that this is the case for each item.[2]

Figure 4.6 shows estimates for these composite indices of law-abidingness. The RNE analysis suggests that attending university causes an increase of 0.61 in law-abidingness, well over half a sample standard deviation. This substantively large estimated effect is also highly significant (p=<.001). The WVS/EVS estimate is similar, though smaller, in magnitude, and with a much tighter confidence band. University education appears to lower people's overall tolerance for crime and corruption (i.e., increase their law-abidingness).

Because only four of the twenty-one variables used in the RNE were also included in the WVS/EVS data, one might worry about comparing the estimated effect of university attendance on law-abidingness with the indices estimated based on each of these two datasets. To address this, we also estimated a law-abidingness index using the RNE data while including only the four items that were also in the

---

[2] Although we believe the principal component analysis is a sensible way of measuring the underlying construct, the specific approach we use does not seem to make a large difference. For example, in the RNE, the first principal component is correlated at 0.98 with a simple average of the (appropriately signed and standardized) indicators. Therefore, readers who prefer can loosely think of our measure as a simple average of the questions related to our conception of law-abidingness.

WVS/EVS. Although the correlation between these two indices in the RNE data is moderate (ρ=.30), the estimated effect of university attendance using our fuzzy RD is similar when using the subset of variables to form our index (0.52) to when using all of the relevant variables from the RNE (0.61).

Across all our tests, we find a relationship between university attendance and law-abidingness – understood, in most cases, as intolerance for crime and corruption. This is consistent with a handful of previous studies, as reported in Chapter 2, though it must be added that the topic has not received much attention from scholars.

CULTURE

In this section, we examine a range of topics commonly associated with the concept of *culture*, which we understand in a wide-ranging fashion. What social roles, norms, and values are people expected to subscribe to and abide by?

Topics falling into this broadly defined domain include the family; sexuality and deviance; gender; race, ethnicity, and religion; religiosity; and science. The final item shown in Table 4.4 refers to party conflict, understood across a cultural dimension.

Tests estimating the impact of university education on each outcome in Table 4.4 (except party affiliation) are shown in Figure 4.7. As previously, each variable is scaled so that a higher score indicates a more liberal position – that is, greater tolerance, secularism, rationalism, and equality – and so that each individual item's values range from 0 to 1.

We find that university education is estimated to have a liberalizing effect on twenty-two of the twenty-nine indicators from the RNE, with most of those estimates being statistically significant. The WVS/EVS data shows a similar overall pattern, albeit with more precise estimates and generally smaller magnitudes.

Questions in the family subtopic generally show insignificant estimates that are small in magnitude for the RNE but moderately sized and statistically significant for the WVS/EVS. It should be noted that for the questions on beating one's wife or children, most RNE respondents gave the response "Never justifiable" (the lowest value on the ten-point response scale), meaning that these items did not have much meaningful variation in the sample.

The strongest pattern of support appears to be for items related to gender equality. Eight out of nine RNE questions – and all of the WVS/EVS questions – on this subject register a positive effect and most of these effects are sizeable.

The one exception may be attributable to confusion on the part of respondents. In one section of the survey, we ask, "How do you feel about the following statements?" Response options include: "Strongly agree," "Agree," "Neither agree nor disagree," "Disagree," and "Strongly disagree." Here are the questions that follow:

When jobs are scarce, men should have more right to a job than women.

TABLE 4.4 *Indicators of culture*

	"*Liberal*"	RNE	WVS	EVS
FAMILY				
Parents beating children justifiable	No	q1_12	Q190	
One of my main goals in life has been to make my parents proud	No	q13_1	Q27	D054
Abortion justifiable	Yes	q1_8	Q184	F120
Divorce justifiable	Yes	q1_9	Q185	F121
SEXUALITY, DEVIANCE				
Sex before marriage justifiable	Yes	q1_10	Q186	
Unmarried couples living together as neighbors acceptable	Yes	q12_7	Q25	
Homosexuality justifiable	Yes	q1_6	Q182	F118
Homosexuals as neighbors acceptable	Yes	q12_5	Q22	A124_09
Prostitution justifiable	Yes	q1_7	Q183	F119
Drug addicts as neighbors acceptable	Yes	q12_1	Q18	A124_08
People who have AIDS as neighbors acceptable	Yes	q12_3	Q20	
GENDER				
When jobs are scarce, men have more right to a job than women	No	q8_1	Q33	C001_01
If a woman earns more money than her husband, it's almost certain to cause problems	No	q8_3	Q35	
Having a job is the best way for a woman to be an independent person	Yes	q8_4		
A man beating his wife justifiable	No	q1_11	Q189	
When a mother works for pay, the children suffer	No	q13_2	Q28	D061
On the whole, men make better political leaders than women do	No	q13_3	Q29	D059
A university education is more important for a boy than for a girl	No	q13_4	Q30	D060
On the whole, men make better business executives than women do	No	q13_5	Q31	D078
Being a housewife is just as fulfilling as working for pay	No	q13_6	Q32	
RACE, ETHNICITY, RELIGION				
When jobs are scarce, employers should prioritize people of this country over immigrants	No	q8_2	Q34	C002_01
People of a different race as neighbors acceptable	Yes	q12_2	Q19	A124_02

(continued)

TABLE 4.4 *(continued)*

	"Liberal"	RNE	WVS	EVS
Immigrants/foreign workers as neighbors acceptable	Yes	q12_4	Q21	A124_06
People who speak a different language as neighbors acceptable	Yes	q12_8	Q26	
People of a different religion as neighbors acceptable	Yes	q12_6	Q23	
RELIGIOSITY				
Involvement in church or religious organization	No	q6_1	Q94	A065
Attend religious services	No	q9	Q171	F028
Importance of God in your life	No	q10	Q164	F063
SCIENCE				
The world better off because of science and technology	Yes	q11	Q163	
PARTY AFFILIATION				
Support for parties with liberal policies on cultural issues (not part of the cultural values index)	Yes	q14	Q233	

Measures of cultural values. "Liberal": coded as a liberal response. RNE: Romanian Natural Experiment; WVS: World Values Survey; EVS: European Values Survey. Variable tags correspond to those in the original surveys, reproduced in Appendices A (RNE) and B (WVS/EVS). Note that q8_3 was asked in WVS6 but dropped from later waves of WVS, and thus appears only in the RNE.

When jobs are scarce, employers should give priority to people of this country over immigrants.

If a woman earns more money than her husband, it's almost certain to cause problems.

Having a job is the best way for a woman to be an independent person.

Note that the implications of the response options are flipped on the final question, which is the only question for which university appears to have a conservative effect on attitudes toward gender equality. We suspect that many respondents, perhaps in a hurry, did not take notice of this and simply checked the same or a similar response as they had for previous questions. As a result, the more supportive one is of gender equality, the less supportive one appears to be of women entering the workforce. (This question is not included in the WVS/EVS so we cannot compare responses outside Romania.) Although we cannot be certain this is the case, this would imply that the non-liberal effect of university estimated for this question is simply an artifact of survey design and response.

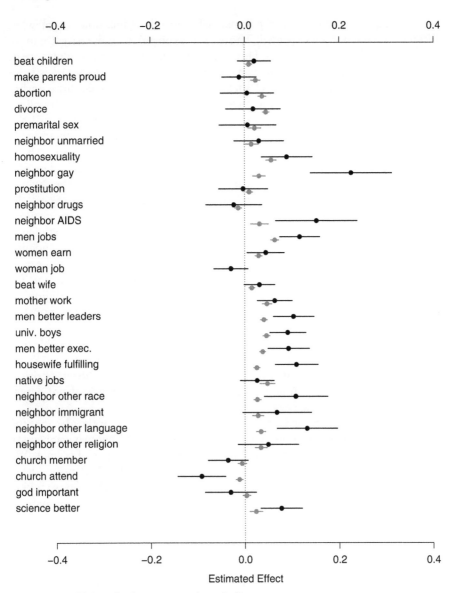

FIGURE 4.7 University impact on culture indicators
Indicators are scaled so that higher values indicate more liberal responses (see Table 4.4).
RNE estimates (in black) are fuzzy RD effect estimates (two-stage least squares).
N=1,216 (546 observations below threshold, 670 observations above threshold), with
slightly smaller sample sizes for some individual items due to missingness. WVS/EVS
estimates (in gray) employ ordinary least squares with country fixed effects and
covariates measuring pretreatment characteristics of subjects including age, sex,
father's educational attainment, mother's educational attainment, and father's
occupation when the respondent was a child. Analyses are conducted on imputed
samples. N=126,690 for regressions using the combined WVS/EVS survey; N=70,530
for regressions using the WVS survey (see Table 4.4).

With respect to religiosity, the impact of university education is somewhat different from what we expected. Those with exposure to university are more likely to attend religious services. However, other questions – the importance of God in one's life and membership in a religious organization – do not register an effect that is differentiable from chance. This divergent pattern confirms earlier work on the subject (Glaeser and Sacerdote 2008; Schwadel 2011). If college enhances other forms of participation, as shown in the first section of the chapter, it is not surprising that it might also enhance participation in religious activity. In addition, we should note that many universities have denominational affiliations, and some are governed by church bodies and impose mandatory religious education as part of the curriculum. Even where universities are formally secular, religious organizations seem to regard the campus as a convenient – and strategically important – recruiting ground. One can expect to find a Newman center catering to Catholic students, a temple catering to Jewish students, a mosque catering to Islamic students, and at least one Protestant association. These clerical organizations serve as community centers, a focus for student activity, and a mechanism for maintaining connections to one's ancestral – or recently adopted – religion. In this light, as well, it is not surprising if college attendance prompts a boost in religious involvement.

Our data, of course, is limited to a particular point in time. It is possible that higher education had a secularizing effect in earlier periods. In the 1920s, Paula Fass (1977: 139) asserts that American college life "tended to foster a critical attitude toward the church and made for religious indifference, if not actual hostility" (see also Leuba 1921).

Finally, higher education is estimated to increase support for the idea that the world is better off because of science and technology. Obviously, university coursework might emphasize the contributions and importance of science. We also separately estimated the effect of university attendance for RNE respondents who pursued a science track (as opposed to the humanities track) prior to taking the *bac*. Unfortunately, the effects are not estimated precisely enough to confidently say which of these groups has the larger effect for this question.

For the most part, the indicators shown in Table 4.4 are highly correlated in the expected direction. However, the correlations are not very high, suggesting that there may be multiple dimensions to the far-flung concept of cultural values.

To generate an overall estimate of the impact of university education on cultural values, we combine these indicators into two indices – one for RNE and the other for WVS/EVS – using the first component of principal component analyses. This first component is then standardized, subtracting the mean and dividing by the standard deviation, to aid interpretation.

This first principal component explains just over 15 percent of the variation in these cultural values indicators, but the principal component index is highly correlated with a simple average of the twenty-nine signed and standardized indicator variables ($r=0.94$), and all but three of the twenty-nine factor loadings for these items are of the expected sign (the three loadings that are estimated to be negative are quite close to 0, suggesting that these items do not meaningfully load onto this first dimension of cultural values). Although we believe our approach to measuring cultural values is more principled, the main results are similar when using the simple average measure of cultural liberalism as the dependent variable.

Figure 4.8 shows the impact of university education on these cultural values indices. In the RNE, the estimated effect of university attendance on cultural values from the RNE analysis is 0.61, which is more than half a sample standard deviation. The p-value on the null hypothesis of no effect is less than .001, indicating that we have a very high degree of confidence that the true effect is positive. The WVS/EVS results are similar, though slightly smaller in magnitude (and of course more precise). These results provide strong evidence that university attendance fosters a more liberal attitude toward most cultural topics.

As with previous indices for the RNE and the WVS/EVS, the two datasets include slightly different sets of questions related to the concept of cultural liberalism. Here, eighteen out of the thirty variables in the RNE are also found in the WVS/EVS. When constructing an index of cultural liberalism for RNE respondents using only the eighteen items in common across all surveys, we obtain a measure that is correlated with the full index at 0.93. The estimated effect of university attendance across this index is also quite similar.

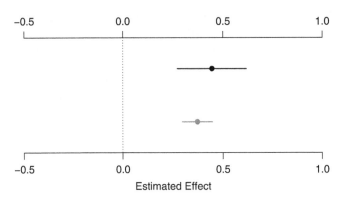

FIGURE 4.8 University impact on culture index
The cultural values index is scaled to have a sample mean of 0 and sample standard deviation of 1 within each sample. Higher values indicate greater cultural liberalism. RNE estimate (in black) is a fuzzy RD effect estimate (two-stage least squares). N=1,216 (546 observations below threshold, 670 observations above threshold). The WVS/EVS estimate (in gray) employs ordinary least squares with country fixed effects and covariates measuring pretreatment characteristics of subjects including age, sex, father's educational attainment, mother's educational attainment, and father's occupation when the respondent was a child. Analyses are conducted on imputed samples. N=70,530.

As a final test of the impact of higher education on cultural values, we examine party affiliation to see whether attendance at university leads respondents to support parties that take a more liberal view of cultural issues. To determine this, we incorporate information from several sources.

Questions on the RNE survey and WVS/EVS ask about the respondent's party affiliation. To locate each party on a scale of cultural values for our RNE analysis, we employ the well-known GALTAN index from the Chapel Hill survey (Bakker et al. 2015). For the analyses with WVS/EVS data, we draw on the V-Party dataset (Lührmann et al. 2020), as the Chapel Hill survey only covers European countries. In the V-Party project, experts assign each party a score that represents its position on a variety of cultural issues including minority rights (v2paminor), immigration (v2paimmig), LGBT social equality (v2palgbt), national cultural superiority (v2paculsup), use of religious principles (v2parelig), and equal participation of women in the workforce (v2pawomlab). Since V-Party offers no overall measure of cultural liberalism, we employ the GALTAN index from the Chapel Hill survey (Bakker et al. 2015) as our benchmark. GALTAN scores are available for a sample of parties (N=283) and countries (N=23) that are also covered by WVS/EVS. With this sample, we regress the GALTAN score on the six variables listed above from V-Party. Regression coefficients from this analysis provide a prediction of GALTAN scores for all parties in the V-Party survey that have been coded along the foregoing six variables, extending the range of our analysis to 178 parties from 41 countries.[3] Finally, we rescale and reorient the original scale so that a score of "0" signifies a party that is culturally conservative and a score of "1" signifies a party that is culturally liberal.

Figure 4.9 shows the impact of university education on the cultural dimension of party conflict using these scales as the outcome. It will be seen that those with university experience are more likely to support culturally liberal parties. The effects are fairly similar for the RNE and WVS/EVS. Note that because the dependent variable is scaled to range theoretically from 0 (the least liberal possible) to 1 (the most liberal possible), the effects are reasonably large. For example, the 0.05 estimated effect of university attendance on party affiliation along the cultural dimension is more than a quarter of a sample standard deviation, a substantively significant impact.

Overall, our findings offer confirmation of previous work on issues related to family, gender, sexuality, ethnicity, xenophobia, and other social issues, as reported in Chapter 2, where, with the notable exception of religiosity, university education is associated with a more liberal outlook.

---

[3] The EVS sample is not included as this survey does not ask about vote choice. However, separate analyses based on the European Social Survey replicate those for the WVS.

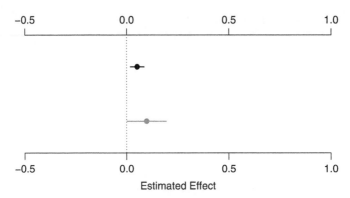

FIGURE 4.9 University impact on party affiliation along the cultural dimension
Party affiliation on cultural values index is measured using GALTAN index, rescaled so
its theoretical range goes from 0 (least culturally liberal) to 1 (most culturally liberal).
Note that Romanian parties in the RNE sample range from 0.175 to 0.7375 on this
measure. Higher values indicate greater cultural liberalism of the party. RNE estimate (in
black) is a fuzzy RD effect estimate (two-stage least squares). N=1,121 (503 observations
below threshold, 618 observations above threshold). The WVS/EVS estimate (in gray)
employs ordinary least squares with country fixed effects and covariates measuring
pretreatment characteristics of subjects including age, sex, father's educational
attainment, mother's educational attainment, and father's occupation when the
respondent was a child. Analyses are conducted on imputed samples. N=70,530.

COSMOPOLITANISM

Cosmopolitanism refers to the idea that we are all citizens of the world, and that
our identity as members of the human species is in certain respects more
fundamental than other identities; for example, as members of a nation,
a social group, or a locality. The idea may be traced back in Western thought
to ancient Greeks such as the Cynic Diogenes, though it has only recently
become prominent in works of political theory and philosophy (Appiah 2006;
Heater 1996).

Although questions about cosmopolitanism were not included in the
RNE, several relevant questions speak to the idea in the WVS and EVS, as
shown in Table 4.5. These hinge on trust in regional and international
organizations or on feelings of closeness to the continent one inhabits and
to the world at large.

Analyses of these variables are displayed in Figure 4.10. There, we can see
that university education is associated with more cosmopolitan views across all
four outcomes and that these effects are differentiable from 0, though not
enormous.

To summarize the impact of university education on cosmopolitanism, we
combine the four indicators into a single index using the first component of

TABLE 4.5 *Indicators of cosmopolitanism*

	"Liberal"	*WVS*	*EVS*
Trust in major regional organization (e.g., European Union)	Yes	Q82	E069_18A
Trust in the United Nations	Yes	Q83	E069_20
Close to your continent	Yes	Q258	G062
Close to the world	Yes	Q259	G063

Measures of cosmopolitan attitudes. "Liberal": coded as a liberal response. WVS: World Values Survey; EVS: European Values Survey. (None of these questions appear in the RNE.) Variable tags correspond to those in the original surveys, reproduced in Appendix B (WVS/EVS).

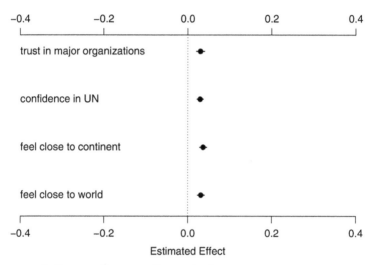

FIGURE 4.10 Indicators of cosmopolitan attitudes
Indicators are scored so that higher values indicate more cosmopolitan attitudes. WVS/EVS analysis using ordinary least-squares regression model with country fixed effects and covariates measuring pretreatment characteristics of subjects including age, sex, father's educational attainment, mother's educational attainment, and father's occupation when the respondent was a child. Analyses are conducted on imputed samples. $N=126,690$ (WVS/EVS sample).

a principal component analysis. This analysis, shown in Figure 4.11, confirms that university attendance is associated with a more cosmopolitan worldview. Of course, we must bear in mind that there is no corresponding evidence from the RNE, so our conclusion rests solely on observational evidence.

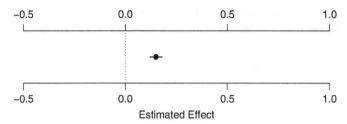

FIGURE 4.11 University impact on cosmopolitanism index
Cosmopolitanism index is scaled to have a sample mean of 0 and sample standard deviation of 1 within each sample. Higher values indicate more cosmopolitan attitudes. The WVS/EVS estimate employs ordinary least squares with country fixed effects and covariates measuring pretreatment characteristics of subjects including age, sex, father's educational attainment, mother's educational attainment, and father's occupation when the respondent was a child. Analyses are conducted on imputed samples. N=126,690 (WVS/EVS).

ECONOMICS

Our fifth category of social and political attitudes focuses on issues of an economic nature. This includes redistribution, market regulation, social provision, and other aspects of the welfare state. Questions about these topics, listed in Table 4.6, are asked only on the WVS/EVS survey. Because these questions were not included in the RNE survey, the only way we can infer the effect of university attendance on economic views from the RNE is by examining party affiliation along the economic dimension, as we do at the end of this section.

To aid interpretation, each indicator listed in Table 4.6 is scaled so that a higher value indicates a more liberal position, which in this case means more support for the market and less support for government intervention and redistribution. (Note that this is the opposite of the common meaning of the term "liberal" in the American political context.)

Figure 4.12 shows estimates of the impact of university attendance on these outcomes. Along five of these outcomes, one can discern a slight liberal effect, though two tests reveal an estimate that is indistinguishable from null.

To generate an index of economic values, we utilize the first component of a principal component analysis including all variables shown in Table 4.6 (except the last, indicating party affiliation). This first component is then standardized, subtracting the mean and dividing by the standard deviation, to aid interpretation. The resulting test, shown in Figure 4.13, substantiates results for component indicators in Figure 4.12. University attendance appears to foster a more free-market ("laissez-faire") view of economic issues, though the effect is not huge.

TABLE 4.6 *Indicators of economic attitudes and behavior*

	"Liberal"	*RNE*	*WVS*	*EVS*
Private ownership of business should be increased	Yes		Q107	E036
Individuals should take more responsibility for personal welfare	Yes		Q108	E037
Competition is good	Yes		Q109	E039
Government should tax the rich and subsidize the poor	No		Q241	E224
People should receive state aid for unemployment	No		Q244	E227
Incomes should be made more equal	No		Q106	E035
The state should make incomes more equal	No		Q247	E233A
Support for parties with liberal (pro-market, anti-state) policies on economic issues (not part of economic index)	Yes	q14	Q233	E179_WVS7

Measures of economic attitudes and behavior. "Liberal": coded as a liberal response. RNE: Romanian Natural Experiment; WVS: World Values Survey; EVS: European Values Survey. Variable tags correspond to those in the original surveys, reproduced in Appendices A (RNE) and B (WVS/EVS).

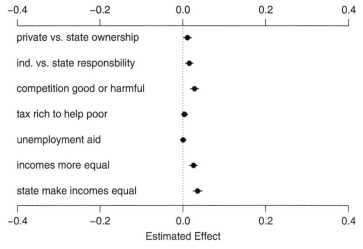

FIGURE 4.12 University impact on economic indicators
Indicators are scored so that higher values indicate more liberal economic views, with 0 and 1 being the lowest and highest values for each one. WVS/EVS analysis using ordinary least-squares regression model with country fixed effects and covariates measuring pretreatment characteristics of subjects including age, sex, father's educational attainment, mother's educational attainment, and father's occupation when the respondent was a child. Analyses are conducted on imputed samples. $N=70,530$ (WVS/EVS sample).

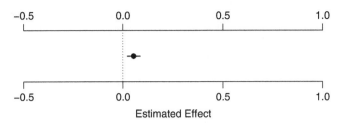

FIGURE 4.13 University impact on economics index
Indicators are scored so that higher values indicate more liberal economic views, with o and 1 being the lowest and highest values for each one. WVS/EVS analysis using ordinary least-squares regression model with country fixed effects and covariates measuring pretreatment characteristics of subjects including age, sex, father's educational attainment, mother's educational attainment, and father's occupation when the respondent was a child. Analyses are conducted on imputed samples. N=126,690 (WVS/EVS sample).

As a final test, we examine the impact of university attendance on party affiliation, this time understood along an economic dimension. To do so, each party is given a score based on expert coding from the V-Party project that represents that party's position on economic issues. The original coding of this variable (v2pariglef_mean) extends from o ("far-left") to 6 ("far-right"). We rescale this outcome from o to 1. The results of these tests are shown in Figure 4.14. There, we show a positive effect for the RNE and a null effect (indistinguishable from o) for the WVS/EVS.

Considered together, the evidence presented in this section suggests that university attendance exerts a small liberalizing effect on the economic dimension of attitudes and party affiliations.

This is more or less consistent with previous studies of public sentiment for redistribution, the welfare state, and social policies, which yield mixed findings, as shown in Chapter 2. It must be added that that these topics have not been widely studied (our extensive survey uncovered only four published studies). Clearly, more work is needed on this important topic.

OVERALL IDEOLOGY

Summary measures of ideology can be misleading, particularly when party- or issue-conflict is multidimensional. Nonetheless, many party systems feature a dimension of party conflict that citizens recognize as left–right (Hooghe et al. 2002) – a conceptualization that harks back to the French Revolution and was reinforced in subsequent centuries by the growth of socialist and communist movements on the left and fascist movements on the right.

We adopt a question from the WVS/EVS that asks respondents to situate themselves on such a scale: "In political matters, people talk of 'the left' and 'the right.' How would you place your views on this scale, generally speaking?"

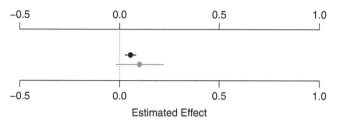

FIGURE 4.14 University impact on party affiliation along the economic dimension
Party affiliation along an economic dimension in the RNE is determined by LRECON
variable from Chapel Hill Expert Survey, rescaled to (theoretically) range from 0 (least
economically liberal) to 1 (most economically liberal). This variable ranges from 0.3375
to 0.7357 and has a standard deviation of 0.15 in the RNE sample. Party affiliation along
an economic dimension in the WVS/EVS determined by arraying parties using the
V-Party measure of economic ideology. A higher score indicates a more liberal
position; that is, more support for the market and less support for government
intervention and redistribution. The RNE estimate (in black) is a fuzzy RD effect
estimate (two-stage least squares). N=1,121 (503 observations below threshold, 618
observations above threshold). The WVS/EVS estimate (in gray) employs ordinary least
squares with country fixed effects and covariates measuring pretreatment characteristics
of subjects including age, sex, father's educational attainment, mother's educational
attainment, and father's occupation when the respondent was a child. The social
dimension and the economic dimension are constructed based on the V-Party dataset,
as described earlier. Analyses are conducted on imputed samples. N=31,448.

Closely related is the apparent conflict between environmentalism and
economic growth, which may tap into an overarching political identity. We
adopt a question on the WVS/EVS that asks respondents to choose one of the
following statements: "Protecting the environment should be given priority,
even if it causes slower economic growth and some loss of jobs" or "Economic
growth and creating jobs should be the top priority, even if the environment
suffers to some extent." We code the first as liberal and the second as
conservative. This question might also be interpreted as a way of gauging the
relative importance of the cultural and economic dimensions of ideology.

Both of these questions are shown in Table 4.7. Regrettably, they were not
included in the RNE, so these analyses are limited to observational data from
the WVS/EVS.

The estimated impact of university attendance on these outcomes is shown in
Figure 4.15. Both register a positive effect, though the overall left–right outcome
is very close to 0. We infer that this is because the cultural and economic
dimensions of ideology, displayed in previous sections of this chapter, exert
countervailing influences. University education pushes subjects toward the left
along the cultural dimension and to the right along the economic dimension of
party conflict.

TABLE 4.7 *Indicators of overall ideology*

	"Liberal"	*WVS*	*EVS*
Protecting environment more important than economic growth	Yes	Q111	B008
Political views on a right–left scale	Left	Q240	E033

Measures of overall ideology. "Liberal": coded as a liberal response. WVS: World Values Survey; EVS: European Values Survey. Variable tags correspond to those in the original surveys, reproduced in Appendix B (WVS/EVS).

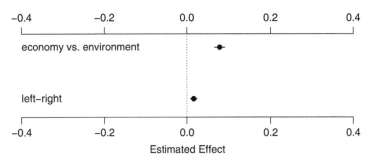

FIGURE 4.15 University impact on indicators of overall ideology
Indicators are scored so that higher values indicate more liberal economic views, with 0 and 1 being the lowest and highest values for each one. WVS/EVS analysis using ordinary least-squares regression model with country fixed effects and covariates measuring pretreatment characteristics of subjects including age, sex, father's educational attainment, mother's educational attainment, and father's occupation when the respondent was a child. Analyses are conducted on imputed samples. $N=126{,}690$ (WVS/EVS sample).

In this respect, our findings diverge somewhat from previous work, where eight out of nine studies report a strongly liberal effect, as shown in Chapter 2. By the same token, the preference for environmentalism over growth shown in Figure 4.15 is consistent with previous studies of environmentalism, which is strongly associated with university attendance in all four published studies.

CONCLUSIONS

In this chapter, we have shown the possible impact of university education on seven outcomes: *social capital* (political participation, membership in civil society organizations, trust), *democracy* (popular rule, civil liberty), *law-abidingness* (crime and corruption), *culture* (the family, sexuality and deviance, gender, race, ethnicity, religion, science), *cosmopolitanism* (regions and regional associations such as the European Union, global associations such as the United Nations), *economics* (taxes, redistribution, the welfare state), and *overall ideology* (left–right self-placement, environmentalism versus growth). Each is measured by multiple variables, and all but the last include a composite index.

This is a lot of empirical ground, setting our study apart from other studies of the university, which tend to be more narrowly focused (see Chapter 2). Yet, these questions are closely interconnected. One's views of sexuality, religion, and politics are probably not independent, for example. Likewise, insofar as university attendance affects these outcomes, the mechanisms at work are likely to be similar. And, where the impact of university *varies* across these outcomes, we ought to be able to learn from this variation. If we see a positive relationship for one outcome and a null or negative relationship for another, that is potentially informative. It shows where university education matters and where it does not, or matters differently, and offers hints into the mechanisms that may be at work. Thus, for theoretical and empirical reasons it seems helpful to consider a wide range of outcomes.

Across most of the outcomes surveyed in this chapter, and across *all* of the composite indices, university education appears to exert a liberalizing influence on social and political attitudes. Those who attend college are more likely to have higher levels of political participation and trust, greater support for democracy, less tolerance for crime and corruption, more tolerant views of non-traditional behavior, more egalitarian views toward outgroups such as women and minorities, greater support for science, greater support for parties with liberal perspectives on cultural issues, greater support for global institutions and cosmopolitan ideals, lower support for taxes, redistribution, and the welfare state, and a slightly more left-wing position on the left–right scale.

All in all, the results fit our thesis – that college attendance boosts liberalism. In the next part of the book we explore various extensions of these findings.

PART III

EXTENSIONS

5

Nuances

In Part II of the book we focused on the impact of university attendance on social and political attitudes. Our analyses, based partly on a natural experiment situated in Romania (the Romanian Natural Experiment [RNE]) and partly on survey data from around the world (the World Values Survey [WVS] and European Values Survey [EVS]), show that university attendance is associated with more liberal attitudes and behavior across a wide variety of outcomes, summarized at the conclusion of Chapter 4.

In this chapter, we explore some of the nuances associated with these results. First, we discuss the question of effect sizes. (How large are the causal effects?) Second, we test the robustness of effects. (How much do estimates change when potential confounders are included or excluded?) Third, we explore variation across different samples and research designs. (How much consistency is there across the RNE and WVS/EVS analyses?) Fourth, we interrogate variation across countries. (Where does a university education appear to have the greatest impact?) Fifth, we examine the liberalizing effect through the life-cycle of respondents in the WVS/EVS survey. (How long does the effect endure and does it change over time?) Sixth, we test various individual-level moderators that might enhance or mitigate the impact of university on social and political attitudes. (Does the sex, urban/rural location, social-class background, and discipline of students moderate the impact of university on social and political attitudes?) Seventh, we explore the impact of university education on the stability of party identification. (Does attending college affect the probability that a student will adopt a party affiliation that is different from their parents'?) Finally, we examine the aggregation problem. (Do the individual-level effects of college scale up to societal levels?) In a chapter appendix, we explore the dimensionality of social and political attitudes, as captured in our many outcome variables.

(How many empirical dimensions are contained in these indicators and how closely do these dimensions map onto our a priori categories?)

These are a lot of topics and they are rather disparate. Readers should feel free to browse selectively. Unlike other chapters, this one does not build in a cumulative fashion.

EFFECT SIZES

Assuming that university education really does carry a liberalizing effect, how large are these effects? How much does a university education matter? Is the effect trivial, as suggested by a number of skeptics (e.g., Caplan 2018)?

This is not an easy question to answer since most of the questions on our surveys deal with attitudes rather than behavior. As such, they do not have a natural interpretation. Adding to the confusion, we have leaned heavily on aggregate indices of these concepts, which are less susceptible to measurement error but also less straightforward to interpret.

Under the circumstances, one approach to judging effect sizes is to compare the influence of university to other factors often regarded as important influences on social and political attitudes such as income, father's occupation (blue collar or white collar), sex (male or female), and age. The WVS allows us to compare these factors side by side as predictors of the six aggregate outcomes examined in Chapter 4 – social capital, democracy, law-abidingness, culture, cosmopolitanism, and economics.

Of course, we must be cognizant of the usual threats to causal inference, as discussed in Chapters 2 and 3. In particular, current education and income may be endogenous to father's occupation, sex, and age. Thus, we conduct two analyses. The first is a bivariate regression with only one right-side variable of theoretical interest, accompanied by a vector of country dummies. The second includes all variables in a "kitchen-sink" specification. The results are shown in Table 5.1.

Because our interest is in the size of the effects (rather than their statistical significance), and because we want to compare effects to each other across different predictors and outcomes, estimates are normalized to indicate the impact of a one-standard deviation change in the independent variable on a one-standard deviation change in the outcome – a standardized ("beta") regression coefficient.

Table 5.1 shows that age is the strongest predictor of cultural values (older people are more conservative) and law-abidingness (older people are less tolerant of crime and corruption). Income is the strongest predictor of economic values (wealthier people view matters of taxing, redistribution, and the welfare state more negatively) and cosmopolitanism (wealthier people have more favorable attitudes toward international institutions and are more likely to identify as citizens of the world). Income also has the strongest

TABLE 5.1 *Predictors compared*

Outcome	Social capital index						Democracy index					
Model	1	2	3	4	5	6	7	8	9	10	11	12
University education	.158					.143	.097					.091
Income of respondent		.092				.063		.021				-.000
Father's occupation			.066			.032			.051			.034
Female				-.101		-.094				-.008		-.005
Age					.021	.052					-.007	.009
R^2	.19	.17	.17	.18	.17	.21	.32	.31	.32	.32	.32	.33

Outcome	Law-abidingness index						Culture index					
Model	13	14	15	16	17	18	19	20	21	22	23	24
University education	.021					.039	.110					.080
Income of respondent		-.030				-.027		.063				.029
Father's occupation			-.005			.002			.072			.039
Female				.020		.023				.043		.045
Age					.087	.089					-.136	-.114
R^2	.13	.13	.13	.13	.13	.14	.53	.53	.53	.53	.54	.55

(continued)

TABLE 5.1 (*continued*)

Outcome	Cosmopolitanism index						Economics index					
Model	25	26	27	28	29	30	31	32	33	34	35	36
University education	.055					.038	.042					.025
Income of respondent		.067				.055		.063				.054
Father's occupation			.043			.026			.031			.016
Female				-.014		-.003				-.020		-.018
Age					-.018	-.003					-.026	-.014
R^2	.10	.10	.10	.10	.10	.11	.15	.14	.14	.14	.14	.15

Ordinary least squares (OLS) estimates, calculated as standardized coefficients (betas), of the impact of several factors on five indices of liberalism. The construction of indices is explained in Chapter 4. All models include country dummies. Countries: forty-nine. Observations: 70,867. Data: WVS. Father's occupation: records his job when respondent was age fourteen. Coded as blue collar (=0) if skilled worker (e.g., foreman, motor mechanic, printer, tool and die maker, electrician), semi-skilled worker (e.g., bricklayer, bus driver, cannery worker, carpenter, sheet metal worker, baker), unskilled worker (e.g., laborer, porter, unskilled factory worker, cleaner), farm worker (e.g., farm laborer, tractor driver), or farm proprietor/manager. Coded as white collar (=1) if professional or technical (e.g., doctor, teacher, engineer, artist, accountant, nurse), higher administrative (e.g., banker, executive in big business, high government official, union official), clerical (e.g., secretary, clerk, office manager, civil servant, bookkeeper), sales (e.g., sales manager, shop owner, shop assistant, insurance agent, buyer), or service (e.g., restaurant owner, police officer, barber, caretaker).

relationship to law-abidingness; however, wealthier people are apparently *more* tolerant of crime and corruption – not what one might expect.

University education has the strongest and most consistently liberal effect on social and political attitudes overall. Looking at bivariate relationships, higher education is the strongest predictor of social capital and democracy, the second strongest predictor of cultural values, cosmopolitanism, and economic values, and the third strongest predictor of law-abidingness. Relative to other predictors, the impact of higher education is generally stronger in the full specifications.

Taken in tandem with the one hundred or so individual outcomes explored in Chapter 4, this validates our claim that higher education is a wide-ranging influencer. Its impact is broad but also deep. Indeed, it is difficult to identify a social or political outcome that is *not* affected in some way by the experience of a university education.

SPECIFICATIONS

The results presented in Chapter 4 suggest that university education exerts a liberalizing effect on a wide range of social and political variables, and the previous section suggests that they are non-trivial. In this section, we test the robustness of these findings.

Recall (from Chapter 3) that the RNE leverages a regression discontinuity (RD) research design to estimate causal effects by focusing on the exogenous variation in university attendance that occurs between those scoring narrowly below versus narrowly above the passage threshold on the baccalaureate exam (*bac*). This is not a true randomized experiment and hence it merits investigating whether the assumption of as-if random variation in the treatment variable is valid. We show in Chapter 3 that the differences between narrow passers and failers of the *bac* are generally small in magnitude. However, they are statistically significant for some variables that could themselves plausibly affect our dependent variables (see Figure 3.5 and Table 3.2).

In order to assess robustness, we re-run the benchmark RNE analyses for each of the main indices, this time adding a set of background covariates assumed to be pretreatment. This includes childhood socioeconomic status (SES), father's education, humanities/social science track (assigned at age fourteen), age, gender, and the location (coded as urban/rural) of the respondent's high school.

Figure 5.1 compares the estimated effect of university attendance from the original analyses without controls (plotted with black circles) with supplementary analyses that include these six potential confounders (plotted with black squares). For all six outcomes, estimated effects are very close, corroborating the assumption that assignment to treatment is as-if random.

Of course, it is possible that (unmeasured) confounders persist. Even so, it seems doubtful that their inclusion in the model would dramatically alter our findings. Sensitivity analyses (presented in Apfeld et al. 2022a, 2022b, 2023) suggest that our results would remain statistically significant even in the presence of an omitted confounder that predicts over ten times as much variation in *bac* passage, university attendance, and the dependent variable as any of the included control variables.

Turning to the WVS/EVS, readers will recall that this regression-based format includes several pretreatment controls – age, sex, father's educational attainment, mother's educational attainment, and father's occupation when the respondent was a child. In Figure 5.1, we compare the results from this benchmark specification (plotted with gray squares) with a second specification (plotted with gray circles) that includes only the predictor of interest – a dummy variable marking whether the respondent has a university degree. (Both analyses include country fixed effects.)

Normally, we expect background covariates to serve a confounding role when subjects self-select into treatment. However, these two specifications yield very similar results, as shown in Figure 5.1. The only outcome where choices in specification appear to matter is with respect to cultural values. Even here, the two estimates are both positive and highly significant. The robustness of these tests in the face of dramatic changes in model specification gives us confidence that the observational data analysis provided by the WVS/EVS is not subject to arbitrary modeling choices.

Readers will note that estimates provided by the RNE and the WVS/EVS are generally fairly close – with the exception of law-abidingness. In this case the apparent difference is actually a product of varying outcomes, as we have many more questions pertaining to law-abidingness on the RNE survey ($N=21$) than on the WVS/EVS ($N=5$), as shown in Table 4.3. Comparisons across these two research designs can only be assessed by examining questions that are shared across surveys, a topic to which we now turn.

SAMPLES AND RESEARCH DESIGNS

In Chapter 4, we looked for general causal effects, estimated separately across the RNE and WVS/EVS datasets. Here, we investigate how the estimated effects of university attendance vary across research designs and samples. To do so, we examine all items that are shared across the RNE and WVS/EVS, a total of fifty questions. As previously, each outcome is rescaled from 0 (the least liberal response) to 1 (the most liberal response).

Four sets of estimates are considered for each outcome variable, as shown in Table 5.2. The first is the benchmark RNE, which uses an RD estimator (described in detail in Chapter 3) to estimate the effect of university attendance among young Romanian adults who scored close to the passage threshold on the *bac*. The second is the WVS/EVS regression analysis including adults of all ages but restricted to surveys from Romania. The third is the WVS/EVS analysis restricted to the Organisation for Economic Co-operation and Development

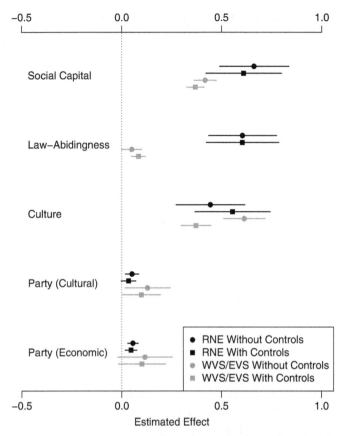

FIGURE 5.1 University impact on main dependent variables with and without control variables

RNE estimates for each dependent variable (with 95 percent confidence intervals) from a fuzzy RD effect estimate (two-stage least squares) using (a) the usual design (black circles) and (b) with covariates measuring childhood SES, father's education, humanities/ social science track, age, gender, and urban high school (black squares). N=1,121 (503 observations below threshold, 618 observations above) (slightly fewer observations in models with control variables due to some missing values). WVS/EVS estimates (with 95 percent confidence intervals) based on regression models (a) without covariates (gray circles) and (b) with the usual set of covariates – age, sex, father's educational attainment, mother's educational attainment, and father's occupation when respondent was a child (gray squares). Country fixed effects are included in both WVS/ EVS models.

(OECD). The fourth is the WVS/EVS analysis with the full sample. All WVS/ EVS samples include a wide range of adult respondents, roughly representative of the populations of the countries analyzed.

TABLE 5.2 *Results across varying samples and research designs*

Set	Mean	Correlation 1.	2.	3.	4.
1. RNE (Romania)	.034	1			
2. WVS/EVS, Romania only	.026	.40	1		
3. WVS/EVS, OECD only	.042	.38	.32	1	
4. WVS/EVS, entire sample (benchmark)	.035	.39	.39	.96	1

Analyses of university impact on fifty common outcomes are compared using different research designs, specifications, and samples. The first column shows the mean estimate across all outcomes. Subsequent columns show the Pearson's *r* correlation between estimates derived from different analyses of the same outcome.

For each set of fifty analyses, Table 5.2 displays the mean estimate for university attendance in the first column. A higher value indicates that university attendance is more strongly associated with liberal outcomes. In the second section of the table, we note correlations across the fifty estimates.

Intercorrelations across the various sets of analyses in Table 5.2 are generally modest, showing considerable variability in estimated university effects when disaggregated by question. The exception is among sets 3–4, where a strong correlation appears – which is not surprising given that these datasets are largely overlapping.

Of greater interest are the mean estimates across all outcomes, displayed in the first column. Here, one can see that the RNE estimates (set 1) are comparable to the other sets – slightly stronger than the WVS/EVS focused on Romania (set 2), slightly weaker than the WVS/EVS for the OECD (set 3), and almost identical to the WVS/EVS benchmark analysis for the entire sample (set 4).

The comparison between sets 1 and 2 is of special interest as it displays results for two quite different research designs conducted on respondents from the same country. We have much greater faith in estimates drawn from the RNE than estimates from the WVS/EVS, for reasons discussed at length in Chapter 3. A particular worry is that self-selection into treatment (intrinsic to the observational design of the WVS/EVS) might bias results in favor of the "liberalizing" university effect. Plausibly, youth with liberal leanings are more likely to attend university. In this light, it is somewhat surprising to discover that the RNE yields slightly higher estimates of the university effect than the WVS/EVS.

We do not want to read too much into this small difference, which could be stochastic. Alternatively, it could be the product of contrasting survey design features. Specifically, the RNE is a much shorter survey instrument than the WVS/EVS, which contains nearly 300 questions. If respondents are fatigued or distracted, this would presumably introduce noise, attenuating the true effect of university education on social and political attitudes.

In any case, the important point is that quasi-experimental and observational results are very close. Insofar as there is a difference, the observational analysis yields weaker estimates.

Interestingly, studies of human capital also find a rough correspondence between quasi-experimental and observational designs. A recent review of the literature concludes that "naïve cross-sectional comparisons and studies with strong quasi-experimental research designs yield very similar estimates of the economic return to education" (Deming 2022: 77). Perhaps, in this arena, biases introduced by self-selection into treatment are amenable to measurement (and thus can be conditioned in a statistical model) or are not so serious to begin with.

Other comparisons contained in Table 5.2 pertain to the various samples of the WVS/EVS. Of particular note is set 4, which includes the entire global sample – the evidentiary basis for the results presented in Chapter 4. This estimate (0.035) is nearly indistinguishable from the RNE (0.034).

It is comforting to discover that analyses based on the natural experiment and on observational data reveal similar results. Of course, it does not obviate all concerns about the external validity of the former or the internal validity of the latter. But it is at least consistent with our assumption that they are measuring the same quantity.

COUNTRIES

Up to now, global analyses have focused on aggregate results across the entire WVS/EVS sample, composed of seventy-nine countries. In this section, we explore variation across countries (minus the US dependency of Puerto Rico).

To do so, we employ seven indices that measure the central concepts of our inquiry: social capital, democracy, law-abidingness, culture, cosmopolitanism, economics, and overall ideology. For each composite outcome, we estimate regression models with the usual background covariates – age, sex, father's educational attainment, mother's educational attainment, and father's job when respondent was fourteen – replicating the benchmark model in Chapter 4.

Table 5.2 shows the estimated coefficients on university attendance for each country on each outcome. Mean values across all countries are displayed across the bottom row. There, it will be seen that all values are positive, meaning that university attendance is associated with more liberal attitudes across all seven dimensions. However, some coefficients are stronger than others. The effect on social capital is especially strong, while the effect on economics is weakest, as noted in Chapter 4.

We also calculate the mean for each country across all seven dimensions, displayed in the penultimate column of Table 5.2. This value is positive in all cases except Lebanon and Cyprus, where it is very slightly negative. It appears that the liberalizing effect of college education is nearly ubiquitous.

As a final summary statistic, we conduct a principal component analysis of the seven dimensions. A country's score on the first component of this analysis is presented in the last column of Table 5.2, and countries are ordered by their score along this component. By this metric, university education has the greatest liberalizing effect in France, the US, Poland, Slovenia, the UK, Switzerland, Colombia, Tunisia, the Netherlands, and Denmark. It has the weakest liberalizing impact in Egypt, Turkey, Azerbaijan, Iraq, Armenia, Vietnam, Chile, and Bangladesh. In Lebanon and Cyprus the university effect on liberalism is slightly negative, as noted.

How can we account for these patterns? Why might tertiary education have a stronger liberalizing effect in some countries than in others?

To examine this question, we regress the outcomes in Table 5.3 against a large number of country characteristics. This battery of tests includes per capita GDP; urbanization; population; ethnic, linguistic, and religious diversity; educational attainment; number and proximity of universities; university enrollment; state history; colonial history; regional dummies; and many additional factors.

Readers should bear in mind all the caveats usual to cross-country analyses limited to a single cross-section, along with the caveats already issued pertaining to our use of observational data. Skepticism is warranted. Even so, something may be learned from this exercise.

After testing dozens of potential causal factors, we find only two that strongly predict country-level coefficients. The first measures the share of a country's population whose ancestors hail from Europe (Gerring et al. 2022). This is positively correlated with university effects on social capital, culture, cosmopolitanism, and on the two overall indices (the grand mean and the principal components). Apparently, the university's liberalizing effect is greatest in countries that share a European demographic heritage. This is not too surprising given that both the modern university and the ideology of liberalism found their first expressions in Europe and its offshoots.

The second factor that appears to predict the university effect is democracy. Our measure, known as the Polyarchy index (Teorell et al. 2019), is drawn from the Varieties of Democracy project (Coppedge et al. 2020). To account for a country's democratic experience over the entirety of its history (since 1789), we calculate a stock measure with a 1 percent annual depreciation rate.[1]

For seven of the nine outcomes tested in Table 5.4, this index of democracy appears to serve as a moderator. It is easy to see why this might be so. In a free society, students and teachers are free – or, at any rate, relatively free – to develop a liberal curriculum and to openly display liberal perspectives on matters pertaining to politics and society. All of the causal mechanisms

---

[1] For further discussion of the construction and utility of the stock conception of democracy, see Gerring and colleagues (2005). The untransformed "level" measure of Polyarchy also predicts university effects, though not quite as robustly.

TABLE 5.3 *Countries compared*

	Social capital	Democracy	Law-abiding	Culture	Cosmopolitan	Economics	Ideology	Mean	pci
France	0.55	0.51	0.13	0.32	0.25	0.01	0.29	0.29	3.21
US	0.67	0.53	0.19	0.18	0.17	0.18	0.25	0.31	2.72
UK	0.62	0.44	0.00	0.24	0.37	-0.05	0.25	0.27	2.65
Poland	0.54	0.34	0.07	0.37	0.16	0.32	0.26	0.29	2.60
Slovenia	0.51	0.41	0.16	0.35	0.16	0.03	0.24	0.26	2.55
Switzerland	0.49	0.35	0.03	0.35	0.27	0.05	0.24	0.25	2.38
Austria	0.67	0.25	0.01	0.22	0.41	-0.08	0.31	0.26	2.29
Netherlands	0.55	0.30	0.04	0.23	0.35	0.08	0.31	0.27	2.21
Australia	0.52	0.39	-0.06	0.21	0.20	-0.05	0.30	0.22	1.89
Denmark	0.46	0.35	0.08	0.25	0.20	-0.11	0.30	0.22	1.88
Colombia	0.52	0.33	0.42	0.23	0.02	0.00	0.28	0.26	1.78
Iceland	0.59	0.30	0.02	0.28	0.19	-0.10	0.20	0.21	1.73
Finland	0.43	0.36	0.00	0.32	0.19	-0.04	0.16	0.20	1.62
Taiwan	0.37	0.33	-0.01	0.34	0.14	0.14	0.17	0.21	1.46
Spain	0.47	0.26	0.06	0.26	0.06	0.09	0.31	0.21	1.45
Estonia	0.54	0.26	0.07	0.27	0.18	0.33	0.16	0.26	1.42
Tunisia	0.20	0.47	0.14	0.23	-0.10	-0.01	0.37	0.19	1.36
Sweden	0.52	0.41	0.13	0.19	0.18	0.09	0.12	0.23	1.33
Albania	0.28	0.26	0.04	0.25	0.28	0.32	0.29	0.25	1.32
Portugal	0.48	0.30	0.14	0.29	0.33	0.11	0.04	0.24	1.29
Georgia	0.26	0.34	0.14	0.20	0.25	0.05	0.28	0.22	1.24

(continued)

TABLE 5.3 (continued)

	Social capital	Democracy	Law-abiding	Culture	Cosmopolitan	Economics	Ideology	Mean	PCI
Brazil	0.50	0.25	0.29	0.27	0.23	0.14	0.09	0.25	1.22
Norway	0.41	0.30	0.10	0.18	0.09	-0.05	0.32	0.19	1.12
Bolivia	0.29	0.43	0.19	0.14	0.21	0.05	0.23	0.22	1.07
Macedonia	0.41	0.34	0.19	0.21	0.26	0.25	0.07	0.25	0.95
Germany	0.54	0.23	-0.02	0.16	0.27	0.06	0.19	0.21	0.90
Hungary	0.39	0.29	0.08	0.23	0.21	0.18	0.14	0.22	0.87
Greece	0.40	0.13	0.02	0.24	0.26	0.10	0.26	0.20	0.86
Ecuador	0.17	0.38	0.25	0.24	-0.04	0.17	0.26	0.20	0.82
Czechia	0.53	0.39	0.05	0.17	0.22	0.33	-0.04	0.24	0.72
Nicaragua	0.37	0.17	0.18	0.19	-0.01	0.13	0.35	0.20	0.65
New Zealand	0.44	0.29	-0.04	0.19	0.16	-0.06	0.18	0.16	0.65
Ethiopia	0.39	0.33	0.11	0.17	0.27	0.37	0.07	0.24	0.65
Iran	0.20	0.39	0.23	0.17	0.02	0.27	0.21	0.21	0.56
Croatia	0.35	0.28	0.06	0.20	0.10	0.14	0.16	0.18	0.41
Slovakia	0.27	0.35	0.29	0.10	0.23	0.29	0.12	0.24	0.33
Andorra	0.59	0.21	0.02	0.09	0.09	0.01	0.21	0.17	0.31
Italy	0.34	0.23	0.12	0.14	0.23	0.22	0.17	0.21	0.28
China	0.43	0.14	-0.09	0.30	-0.02	0.14	0.15	0.15	0.27
Hong Kong	0.46	0.24	-0.03	0.19	0.09	0.17	0.09	0.17	0.22
Myanmar	0.01	0.11	0.22	0.40	0.12	0.43	0.15	0.20	0.13
Bosnia/Herz.	0.33	0.14	0.16	0.22	0.15	0.15	0.13	0.18	0.00

(continued)

Nigeria	0.48	0.20	-0.02	0.21	0.15	0.14	-0.02	0.16	-0.12
Mexico	0.32	0.18	0.14	0.14	0.15	0.20	0.12	0.18	-0.29
Argentina	0.45	0.13	0.03	0.18	0.01	0.17	0.11	0.15	-0.29
Romania	0.15	0.28	0.16	0.18	0.05	0.27	0.09	0.17	-0.38
Philippines	0.32	0.25	0.52	0.10	0.14	0.06	0.01	0.20	-0.40
Macao	0.21	0.29	0.24	0.12	0.09	0.01	0.11	0.15	-0.46
Japan	0.35	0.30	-0.03	0.06	0.15	0.06	0.10	0.14	-0.47
Ukraine	0.31	0.15	0.13	0.10	0.32	0.14	0.06	0.17	-0.56
Zimbabwe	0.63	0.29	-0.03	0.19	-0.45	0.61	-0.12	0.16	-0.76
Bulgaria	0.33	0.12	0.03	0.11	0.22	0.11	0.07	0.14	-0.88
Serbia	0.26	0.16	-0.15	0.11	0.09	0.17	0.16	0.11	-0.89
Guatemala	0.19	0.23	0.14	0.12	0.08	-0.16	0.10	0.10	-0.92
Kyrgyzstan	0.24	0.17	0.12	0.15	-0.09	0.14	0.11	0.12	-1.03
Tajikistan	0.40	0.10	0.10	0.14	0.26	0.10	-0.11	0.14	-1.12
Peru	0.39	0.09	0.18	0.05	0.16	0.14	0.04	0.15	-1.17
Indonesia	0.19	0.30	0.31	0.05	0.04	0.21	-0.02	0.16	-1.17
Montenegro	0.22	0.19	0.04	0.19	-0.05	-0.30	0.04	0.05	-1.18
Kazakhstan	0.25	0.08	0.07	0.05	0.19	0.01	0.14	0.11	-1.31
Malaysia	0.17	0.19	0.34	0.10	-0.06	-0.01	0.07	0.11	-1.33
Pakistan	0.19	0.20	0.13	0.03	-0.01	0.25	0.13	0.13	-1.40
Belarus	0.21	0.02	0.08	0.12	0.10	0.14	0.12	0.11	-1.45
Russia	0.15	0.09	0.01	0.06	0.23	0.07	0.09	0.10	-1.59
Jordan	0.24	0.15	-0.03	0.08	-0.19	-0.05	0.14	0.05	-1.70

(continued)

TABLE 5.3 (continued)

	Social capital	Democracy	Law-abiding	Culture	Cosmopolitan	Economics	Ideology	Mean	pc1
South Korea	0.27	0.05	0.10	0.04	0.12	-0.10	0.07	0.08	-1.83
Thailand	0.05	0.03	-0.01	0.09	0.04	0.18	0.19	0.08	-1.91
Lithuania	0.30	0.06	-0.03	0.06	0.15	0.19	-0.03	0.10	-1.93
Egypt	0.30	0.09	0.11	0.00	-0.08	0.25	0.00	0.10	-2.23
Turkey	0.14	0.03	-0.03	0.06	0.04	-0.02	0.05	0.04	-2.43
Azerbaijan	0.26	0.10	-0.11	-0.01	0.08	0.15	-0.04	0.06	-2.46
Iraq	0.09	0.15	0.34	0.02	-0.14	-0.16	0.02	0.04	-2.50
Armenia	0.13	0.00	0.06	0.07	0.15	0.03	-0.02	0.06	-2.51
Vietnam	0.22	0.06	0.02	0.12	-0.20	0.11	-0.06	0.04	-2.57
Chile	0.46	-0.17	-0.18	-0.05	0.27	0.12	0.03	0.07	-2.61
Bangladesh	0.27	0.07	0.01	-0.06	0.38	-0.03	-0.18	0.06	-2.77
Cyprus	0.33	-0.07	-0.18	0.06	-0.16	-0.04	-0.02	-0.01	-3.03
Lebanon	-0.03	0.05	0.03	0.04	0.01	-0.23	-0.15	-0.04	-3.69
Mean	*0.35*	*0.23*	*0.09*	*0.16*	*0.12*	*0.10*	*0.13*	*0.17*	*0.00*

Outcomes include indices for social capital, democracy, law-abidingness, culture, cosmopolitanism, economics, and overall ideology – all of which are standardized. For each country, the chosen outcome is regressed against university attainment (a dummy measuring whether a respondent has a bachelor's degree or higher) along with covariates measuring the pretreatment characteristics of subjects including age, sex, father's educational attainment, mother's educational attainment, and father's occupation when the respondent was a child. We report the coefficient on university attainment in each cell. The final columns show the mean across these six dimensions and the first component from a principal component analysis of the six dimensions. Mean values for each column are displayed across the last row. Countries are ordered by their score in the final analysis (pc1), highest to lowest.

discussed in the next chapter should develop to their full potential, unhindered (or less hindered) by the state. By contrast, in an authoritarian context, there are constraints – often very strong constraints. Faculty are often compelled to toe the government line while students are not able to express themselves openly. Accordingly, universities operating in an authoritarian context are less likely to serve as avatars of liberalism.

We find, more specifically, that democracy is associated with a stronger liberalizing effect for social capital, democracy, cosmopolitanism, ideology, and the two overall measures (the grand mean and the principal components index). This is consistent with previous studies showing enhanced university effects for democracies on outcomes such as tolerance of homosexuality (Zhang and Brym 2019) and tolerance of Jews (Weil 1985), though it is inconsistent with studies showing an enhanced effect on religiosity (Scheepers et al. 2002).

The democracy index also predicts an *anti*-liberal effect for economic outcomes. That is, conditional on living in a democracy, attending a university may make one more inclined to support the welfare state and redistributive policies. We are not sure how to interpret this countervailing effect.

In summary, both of the moderators tested in Table 5.4 seem highly plausible. At the same time, it is important to bear in mind the weaknesses of this research design, as discussed. One should also be acutely aware that these two factors explain a modest portion of the variance (a fifth to a third, judging by the model-fit statistics in Models 8–9). This may be a product of measurement error, error stemming from our underlying causal models, or error from missing factors that we have not been able to identify. We leave these matters for future research.

DURATION

With virtually any causal effect one must be concerned about duration. Perhaps the liberal effect of attending college attenuates quickly. Former students, having assumed the roles and responsibilities of middle age and lost touch with their alma mater, may not be as liberal as they once were.

Alternatively, the impact of a college education may cumulate over time. In this scenario, college is a critical juncture setting students off on a very different path than they would have otherwise pursued. As the paths of those with and without college diverge, so might their social and political attitudes.

Jennings and Stoker (2008) find little attenuation with age, and enhancement on a few outcomes. Likewise, the Bennington panel study shows that attitudes of graduates remained remarkably stable five decades after graduation (Alwin et al. 1991). Both studies are focused on the US, raising questions about generalizability.

TABLE 5.4 *Regression analysis of country coefficients*

Outcome	Social capital	Democracy	Law-abiding	Culture	Cosmopolitanism	Economics	Ideology	Mean	pci
	1	2	3	4	5	6	7	8	9
Europeans (%)	0.001***	0.001	-0.000	0.001***	0.001***	0.001	0.001	0.001***	0.015***
	(2.800)	(1.530)	(-0.268)	(3.489)	(3.324)	(1.378)	(1.590)	(3.155)	(3.466)
Democracy stock	0.004***	0.002***	-0.001	0.000	0.001*	-0.003***	0.002***	0.001*	0.032***
	(5.391)	(2.839)	(-0.979)	(0.883)	(1.672)	(-2.835)	(3.899)	(1.842)	(3.755)
R-squared	0.429	0.206	0.0212	0.222	0.247	0.108	0.234	0.322	0.421

Indices displayed in Table 5.3 regressed against country-level covariates. Ordinary least squares, t-statistics in parentheses. $N=76$ (countries) *** $p<.01$, ** $p<.05$, * $p<.1$.

Descriptive statistics

Variable	Mean	Std. dev.	Min	Max
Social capital	0.35	0.16	-0.03	0.67
Democracy	0.23	0.14	-0.17	0.53
Law-abidingness	0.09	0.13	-0.18	0.52
Culture	0.17	0.10	-0.06	0.40
Cosmopolitanism	0.12	0.15	-0.45	0.41
Economics	0.10	0.15	-0.30	0.61
Ideology	0.13	0.12	-0.18	0.37
Mean	0.17	0.08	-0.04	0.31
pci	0.00	1.64	-3.69	3.21
Europeans (%)	43.74	42.74	0.00	100.00
Democracy stock	27.93	17.97	5.46	66.75

We cannot employ the RNE sample to investigate this question as all respondents fall within a narrow age range. Accordingly, our analyses enlist the WVS/EVS sample, which includes adults of all ages. We shall assume that most respondents attended college as young adults, which means that age is a proxy for years since university. Respondent age is classified into five subsets: 18–29, 30–39, 40–49, 50–59, and 60 or older. We then estimate regression models (including the standard set of covariates and country dummies) separately for each of the six core indices.

The results, displayed in Figure 5.2, offer some evidence for the proposition that effects increase with time, particularly for social capital and democratic values. For other outcomes, there is no apparent pattern, or a much subtler one.

It is true that this analysis cannot effectively disambiguate between *duration* effects and *age* or *cohort* effects. That is the nature of the data-generating process. Most people attend college (if they do so at all) as young adults, so age, cohort, and time since college are confounded.

To deal with this issue, we employ a much larger sample drawn from the US and including multiple waves of National Election Surveys conducted from the 1950s to the present. This analysis (not shown) is able to disambiguate cohort and age effects. Consistent with previous studies (Alwin et al. 1991; Jennings and Stoker 2008), we find little attenuation in college effects on social and political attitudes even when examining cohorts from different decades.

In summary, there is little evidence that the effects of university attendance attenuate as people grow older and become more removed from their university experience. It may even grow stronger, at least for some outcomes. In any case, it seems likely that the liberalizing effects of university persist for most people throughout their lives.

INDIVIDUAL-LEVEL MODERATORS

Having looked at macro-level factors that might generate heterogeneous effects, as well as the duration of the university effect, we turn to individual-level moderators; that is, factors that distinguish individuals in our sample that might enhance or diminish the impact of going to college on social and political attitudes. This includes sex, urbanization, social class, and discipline. For each topic, we employ data from the RNE and WVS/EVS wherever possible.

To our surprise, we have little to report. Along a few outcomes, women may be more affected by the experience of college than men according to regression analyses of the WVS/EVS. However, the difference is not great and is not replicated in the RNE. With respect to various measures of social-class background (e.g., father's education, childhood SES), urbanization (e.g., urban/rural high school in the RNE), and disciplinary tracks, there is little evidence of moderating effects. (For a detailed example focused on disciplinary tracks, see Figure 6.1.)

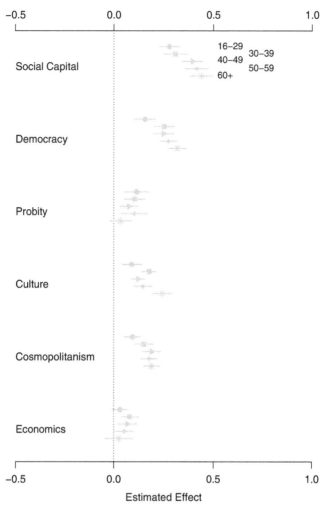

FIGURE 5.2 University effect by age
Indices are scaled to have a sample mean of 0 and sample standard deviation of 1. Higher values indicate greater liberalism. The WVS/EVS estimates are based on separate age-specific subsets of the data and employ ordinary least squares with country fixed effects and covariates measuring pretreatment characteristics of subjects including age, sex, father's educational attainment, mother's educational attainment, and father's occupation when the respondent was a child. Analyses are conducted on imputed samples. Sample sizes vary by subgroups and range from 11,281 to 31,294.

This does not mean that college affects everyone equally. But it does suggest that, at least with respect to the tested factors, moderating effects are likely to be rather small.

PARTISANSHIP

Most of the measures employed as outcomes in the foregoing analyses have a partisan dimension. This is explicit in our analysis of vote choice and implicit in other analyses. This raises an important question: does university attendance prompt students to deviate from their parents' party affiliation?

We are familiar with the truism that most people obtain their political orientation from their parents (Campbell et al. 1960). And yet, not everyone follows in their parents' ideological footsteps. (If they did, party systems would be completely frozen.)

To find out whether attending a university affects this critical aspect of politics, we ask student-age respondents of our RNE survey about their own partisan preference and the preference of their father (or mother if their father is deceased or out of contact). The outcome in this analysis is coded 1 for those who identify with a different party than their father (or mother) and 0 for those who identify with the same party as their father (or mother).

Figure 5.3 shows an effect of 0.14 for university attendance on the binary dependent variable. This implies an increase of 14 percent in the probability of deviating from the parent's partisanship – a substantial effect that is also highly significant (p=.001).

There is no analogous question on the WVS/EVS so we cannot say how generalizable this result might be. Insofar as party change is responsive to party system size – citizens, one imagines, are more likely to change parties if there are more choices available – it is relevant to note that the Romanian party system features seven major parties (see Table 4.7). Across the world's democracies this may be regarded as about average (Bértoa 2013). It is much larger than the two- and three-party systems found in the US and the UK but much smaller than the fragmented party systems found in countries with proportional electoral rules, large districts, and no (or very low) statutory thresholds such as the Netherlands and Israel, or first-past-the-post rules combined with extreme ethnic heterogeneity, as in India.

In any case, the result displayed in Figure 5.3 suggests that university education may be one of those rare experiences that wrests individuals from their inherited identification with a particular party. If so, this is important for understanding party politics in an increasingly partisan age.

SCALING UP

All of the empirical tests from the RNE and the WVS/EVS, as well as previous studies reviewed in Chapter 2, focus on individuals as units of analysis. This was a strategic choice. If causality cannot be established at this level, it is doubtful that it will ever be sorted out in larger units.

However, one cannot assume that micro-level results always aggregate up at macro-levels. If higher education nurtures a more liberal outlook among

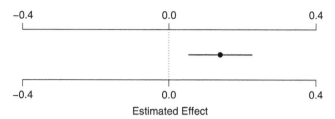

FIGURE 5.3 Deviation from parental partisanship
RNE estimate (in black) is a fuzzy RD effect estimate (two-stage least squares). $N=1,016$ (538 observations below threshold, 578 observations above threshold). Dependent variable equals 1 if respondent supports different party from father (or mother), 0 for those who identify with the same party as their father (or mother).

individuals who attend college, does an increase in higher educational attainment across a *population* lead to a more liberal outlook?

The aggregation problem (Humphreys and Scacco 2020) is best explained by looking at a particular situation where it is alleged to exist. Consider the example of education and political participation. If education fosters turnout and other acts of political engagement at individual levels, one would expect that higher levels of education in a society would generate higher participation at a societal level. And yet, this expected pattern does not appear in longitudinal data on educational attainment and turnout for most countries. In the US, for example, educational levels have risen continuously over the postwar period while participation rates have fallen or held steady, depending upon the period under review (Brody 1978).

One possible explanation for this paradox is that education is a "rival" or "positional" good. An individual's enjoyment of higher education is contingent upon how many other people possess higher education. The explanation is intuitive when applied to jobs. If there are a fixed number of jobs in the economy and the best jobs are allocated on the basis of educational qualifications, then one's employment prospects are determined by one's own education relative to everyone else's. In this situation, one would not expect educational investments to scale up (Caplan 2018). Of course, many economists view the jobs available in an economy as endogenous to human capital. Here, greater human capital generates more good jobs; the pie is not fixed. However, this is presumably a long-term effect.

In any case, let us consider how this debate pertains to outcomes such as participation. Nie, Junn, and Stehlik-Barry (1996: 6) argue:

Formal education influences political engagement by allocating scarce social and political ranks that place citizens either closer to or further from the center of critical social and political networks that, in turn, affect levels of political engagement. The rank to which individuals are assigned is the result of the impact of education on a long train of life circumstances, including occupational prominence, voluntary associational membership, and family wealth. For political engagement, formal education works as a sorting mechanism, assigning ranks on the basis of the citizen's *relative* educational attainment. Relative education is not the absolute number of years attained but the amount of education attained compared to those against whom the citizen competes. As the aggregate amount of absolute education in the population changes over time, the relative significance of a given number of actual years of education will vary.

From this perspective, the critical mechanisms are social networks operative across a society. Nie and colleagues view these networks as fixed in size, with education levels determining who is "in" and who is "out." Space is limited.

In our view, this argument is not very plausible. A static view of social networks would make sense if those networks were governed entirely by organizations of fixed size; for example, country clubs, parent–teacher associations, and so forth. However, many networks are informal and loosely governed, and thus not limited in size. Consider networks based on friends, neighbors, or internet platforms like Facebook. There is no limit, in principle, to how many people may participate in these loosely defined networks. So, insofar as education enhances network engagement, and engagement in networks drives higher rates of voting and other acts of political participation, there is no barrier to scaling up. Education is not a rival good.

Moreover, a static view of social networks runs against a sizeable literature that views the construction of networks as endogenous. A central research question is to understand why some societies have dense networks, generating high social capital, while others have weak networks. Education plays a role in many of these causal models (Huang et al. 2009). If one believes that education empowers citizens, opening up avenues of communication that would not otherwise be present, then one must conclude that networks are endogenous to education.

This seems self-evident in an illiterate society, as primary education offers basic skills necessary for social and political inclusion. We grant that the social capital payoff of education probably increases in a sublinear fashion: increases at the top of the scale will matter less than those at the bottom. So, increasing the number of university graduates in a society where everyone has a high school diploma may have less impact on the density of social networks operative in that society than increasing the number of citizens with primary or secondary diplomas. Still, we imagine that the impact is likely to be positive. A society with more college graduates is likely to have denser social networks and more social capital, and this should translate into greater participation at societal levels.

Empirically, the argument is hard to parse because it is difficult to distinguish "absolute" and "relative" effects of education on political participation. However, one recent evaluation confirms that increases in education do not, in fact, attenuate participation (Helliwell and Putnam 2007).

Data from the WVS offers further purchase on the problem. If there were ceiling effects, one would expect to find a stronger relationship between university education and participation in countries with low educational attainment, where presumably there is greater space for additional members in existing social networks – and hence less crowding out. We should find that higher education is more strongly related to voting in Kenya than in the US, for example. As it happens, there is little evidence of an inverse relationship between overall educational attainment and the strength of the education–turnout relationship. (Although not reported in Table 5.4, we found no overall measure of educational attainment that successfully mediates the impact of college education on social and political attitudes.)

Importantly, even skeptics like Nie and colleagues view education as having some relative and some absolute effects on participation. It is not an entirely zero-sum game. Moreover, the other outcomes investigated in our study do not seem to be susceptible to the aggregation problem suggested for participation. Corruption, ideology, and attitudes toward social groups and social practices are not positional goods subject to sorting effects. Accordingly, we are fairly confident that the findings reported in Chapter 4 are scalable.

Possibly, the aggregated effect of higher education is even *greater* than the sum of individual effects. Note that many societal outcomes involve threshold effects in which individual effects are magnified by their interaction. We can expect this sort of positive reinforcement for most of the social and political attitudes under investigation. The more people vote, the more peer pressure there is for others to vote. The more people are intolerant of corruption, the more pressure there is on others to rethink old attitudes of acceptance and resignation. The more people regard gays and lesbians as full and equal citizens of society, the more the stigma of sexual deviance is lifted. In these respects, the impact of higher education is probably self-reinforcing.

This does not mean that our micro-level evidence provides precise point estimates for how higher education affects social and political attitudes at societal levels. For this, we must consult studies focused on macro-level outcomes. Instead of individuals, one may examine subnational regions or countries as units of analysis. Although this sort of study is open to many confounders, it is not subject to the scaling problem precisely because the scale is already huge. If we find that higher levels of educational attainment, or the existence of universities, are correlated with liberal outcomes when using regions or countries as units of analysis, we have greater assurance that our micro-level findings are scalable.

The most straightforward approach would be to aggregate survey results from the WVS/EVS for each country in our dataset. This variable could then be regressed against a country-level measure of university education or overall educational attainment along with relevant covariates. Unfortunately, the WVS/EVS offers an incomplete sample of countries ($N=79$) and only a few observations through time (even if we enlist all available waves of the WVS).

Better data can be obtained from other sources. An additional advantage is that these other sources are often more objective in nature. Rather than relying on respondents' self-report – which, as we observed, is subject to error (Chapter 3) – these measures are constructed by expert coders (e.g., corruption) or are directly observable and countable (e.g., turnout). This does not mean they are free from measurement error. It means that they are subject to a different sort of measurement error, and thus serve as a cross-check on findings presented in Chapter 4 that rely on self-report. Topics for which a global measure – or at least a global analog – can be found include (a) participation, (b) crime and corruption, and (c) democracy.

PARTICIPATION

The most common way to operationalize the concept of participation is through voter turnout, the share of eligible voters who cast a ballot in national elections. This statistic is widely reported and meaningful in countries with contested elections.

In a cross-national study, Gallego (2010) finds that educational attainment is generally correlated with higher turnout, corroborating our finding. However, the relationship is mediated by the difficulty of voting. Where voting is easy, for example because of compulsory voting, education has little impact on the propensity to vote. Where voting is hard, requiring sacrifices on the part of the voter without sanctions for non-voting, as in the US, the relationship between educational attainment and voting is quite strong.

Another measure of participation focuses on voluntary associations. Relying on Gale's *Encyclopedia of Associations*, Schofer and Longhofer (2011) construct an index measuring the number of associations in each country over time. This outcome is regressed against a number of predictors including educational attainment. The latter turns out to be a robust predictor: more education translates into more associational activity.

CRIME AND CORRUPTION

The relationship of education to crime is another topic of considerable interest. The usual approach is to measure crime cross-nationally with the homicide rate, as this is the most widely reported – and by all accounts the least biased – cross-national measure, as well as being the outcome of greatest concern. As elsewhere, education is usually operationalized as educational attainment. Since crime rates do not offer a long time-series, most analyses are cross-sectionally dominated. Some studies show the expected negative relationship (Furqan and Mahmood 2020; Pridemore 2008). One study finds divergent effects between male (–) and female (+) schooling (Cole and Gramajo 2009). Other studies show no relationship (Fajnzylber, Lederman, and Loayza 2002).

Closely related to crime is the concept of corruption. The usual approach to the latter adopts a contemporary measure of corruption such as the World Bank's Worldwide Governance Indicators or the Transparency International

Corruption Perceptions Index. This measure is regressed against an index of overall educational attainment, or tertiary educational attainment, along with relevant covariates. The results generally show a statistically significant relationship: more education is correlated with lower corruption (Cheung and Chan 2008). A variant of this approach measures education in the nineteenth century so as to estimate the long-term effect (Uslaner and Rothstein 2016).

Another approach measures the prevalence of universities (arguably more exogenous than educational attainment and in any case much easier to measure) on the right side and employs longitudinal data on corruption from the Varieties of Democracy dataset. This allows for a sample that includes all country-years from 1789 to the present, facilitating a fixed-effect estimator. The results show that universities are associated with lower corruption (Apfeld et al. 2022c).

Still another approach focuses on US states, employing federal corruption convictions of state officials as an indicator of corruption. Glaeser and Saks (2006) find that convictions are greater in states with lower education.

DEMOCRACY

Of all the topics relevant to the present question, that which is most commonly studied at aggregate levels is the relationship between education and democracy. This line of research begins with Lipset (1959) and includes a great many studies, only a few of which we shall mention here.[2]

Focusing on the period prior to World War I, Kurzman and Leahey (2004: 994) examine six democratizing episodes: Russia in 1905, Iran in 1906, the Ottoman Empire in 1908, Portugal in 1910, Mexico in 1911, and China in 1912. They note that these countries "ousted dictators or forced them to accept significant limits on their power . . . promulgated or reinstituted constitutions . . . held elections and convened parliaments in an atmosphere of relative freedom [and] . . . witnessed the almost overnight emergence of a boisterous press." Most important for our purposes, each of these democratizing movements was led by intellectuals with substantial support from the university sector (Kurzman 2008: 13). Kurzman and Leahey (2004) argue that the success of these and other democratization movements is contingent on the size of the intellectual class. That this class was diminutive in these countries may be a key to the failure of these movements. For our purposes, however, what is significant is that universities were on the vanguard of democracy movements in the early twentieth century.

In more recent times, when the intellectual class has grown, student movements have played key roles in democratization movements in South Korea (Mi 2005), Burma/Myanmar, Indonesia (Budiman 1978), Hong Kong (Ortmann 2015), mainland China (discussed in Chapter 7), Hungary (Paloczi-Horvath 1971), Czechoslovakia, Poland (Bernhard 1993; Junes 2015),

---

[2] For further discussion, see McGinn and Epstein (1999, 2000).

Albania (Rama 2019), Greece, Turkey, Iran, and many Latin American countries. Exactly what causal weight to assign to student activists is an open question, and not all of these transitions to democracy were successful. Nonetheless, it shows that sentiment at many universities has trended in a democratic direction, lending credence to the argument for universities as a democratizing influence.

Another approach to this issue focuses on the location of political protest. Dahlum and Wig (2021) show that universities are often chosen as sites of protest in Africa, Central America, and the Caribbean, and that many of these protests are oriented toward achieving democratic rights. Related studies show that higher levels of education induced higher levels of protest during the Arab Spring (Campante and Chor 2012; Dahlum and Wig 2019). Thus, from various perspectives, one may conclude that the existence of a university constitutes a threat to dictatorship (Brancati 2016; Connelly and Grüttner 2010).

To grapple with this question on a global scale, researchers have employed a cross-national regression framework. Here, a measure of democracy is placed on the left side (most commonly the Polity2 variable from the Polity IV dataset) and a measure of educational attainment on the right side. Some studies take a cross-sectional approach, leveraging variation across countries (Glaeser et al. 2004; Kurzman and Leahey 2004; Sanborn and Thyne 2014). Others adopt a panel format, leveraging variation through time, perhaps with instruments for educational attainment (Benavot 1996; Bobba and Coviello 2007; Murtin and Wacziarg 2014). Unfortunately, data on educational attainment is scarce prior to 1960 so a longer time-series must focus on a smaller panel of countries. Most of these studies (including those cited in this paragraph) find a positive association between education and democracy. A few question the consensus, arguing that there is no relationship once an appropriate estimator is adopted (e.g., Acemoglu et al. 2005).

CONCLUSIONS

In this chapter, we explored various extensions of the main results, presented in Chapter 4. The results from these analyses may now be briefly reviewed.

First, causal effects registered by higher education on social and political attitudes are comparable to, or greater than, those associated with sex, age, and social class. Second, effects from the RNE and WVS/EVS models are robust when potential confounders are included, or excluded, from a benchmark model. Third, estimates are stable across the RNE and WVS/EVS, and across various subsamples of the WVS/EVS. Fourth, the impact of education is enhanced in countries with a large share of citizens of European ancestry and in countries with democratic regimes. Fifth, the impact of education does not attenuate through time, and may actually become more pronounced with respect to some political and social attitudes. Sixth, no moderating effects can be detected with respect to individual-level characteristics such as sex, age, urbanization, social class, and discipline. Seventh, university attendance appears to nudge students away from the party identification of their parents. Finally, the available evidence suggests that individual-level treatment effects scale up to societal levels.

These ancillary analyses reinforce our confidence in the results posted in Chapter 4 and also flesh out the meaning and import of those results. In the next chapter, we delve into potential causal mechanisms. Why does a college education carry such wide-ranging effects?

APPENDIX: DIMENSIONALITY

Chapter 4 divides up the vast subject of "social and political attitudes" into six topics: social capital, democracy, law-abidingness, culture, cosmopolitanism, and economics based on our predefined expectations about what concepts these items relate to. To what extent are these dimensions recognizable in the data? Do answers to questions across the RNE survey and WVS/EVS group together as anticipated?

To assess this issue, we conduct exploratory factor analyses of respondents' answers to all of the questions examined in Chapter 4. The goal of this analysis is to understand the empirical structure of responses to these items, including how strongly associated they are with each other and whether the pattern of association is consistent with our preconceptions.

Figure 5a.1 shows the eigenvalues from the components produced by these factor analyses (with varimax rotation). RNE and WVS/EVS surveys are analyzed separately, as they involve different samples and somewhat different sets of questions. However, the results are fairly similar. Scree plots show that most of the variability is explained by the first four components.

Table 5a.1 shows the factor loadings for the first four or five factors obtained from the factor analyses. Because the variables contained in these two datasets are not identical, the results are not mirror images of each other. However, both datasets show evidence of a few prominent dimensions, with subsequent dimensions tapering off in explanatory power. Moreover, the dimensions estimated in each analysis correspond in a rough fashion to the concepts we defined ex ante in our preregistered studies.

The ordering and structure of these dimensions, however, show notable differences between the RNE and WVS/EVS data. This should not be surprising given the different mix of questions in the two datasets. In particular, the RNE includes many more questions related to law-abidingness than does the WVS/EVS, while the WVS/EVS includes many items related to economics that are not in the RNE. Questions about democracy and cosmopolitanism are asked only in the WVS/EVS.

Table 5a.1 provides our own interpretation of each identified dimension, based on the reported factor loadings. For the RNE, we discern four dimensions: (1) law-abidingness, (2) social capital, (3) culture I, and (4) culture II. Since the latter refer to different aspects of culture, we infer that there are two empirical dimensions to this concept. For the WVS/EVS, we discern five dimensions: (1) culture I, (2) social capital I, (3) social capital II, (4) culture II, and (5) economics. Here, we infer that both culture and social capital contain two empirical dimensions.

Note again that the results of any factor analysis are a product of the variables chosen. Since there are many more measures of economic ideology in the WVS/EVS than the RNE, it is not surprising that this dimension is a recognizable component of the former but not the latter.

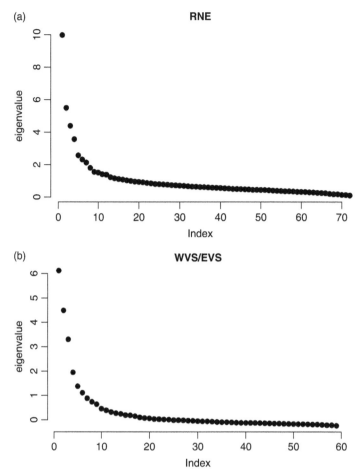

FIGURE 5A.1 Scree plots for Romanian Natural Experiment and World Values Survey/
European Values Survey
Scree plots from factor analyses with varimax rotation using the factanal function in
R. RNE: 72 questions, 1,235 observations. WVS/EVS: 61 questions, 189,488 observations.

In any case, the empirical patterns discovered in the data for the RNE and WVS/
EVS conform fairly closely to our a priori categories, which were defined before
analyzing the data, both in total number and in substance. This suggests that if we
restructured the indices employed in Chapter 4 to conform to the empirical patterns
in the data, we would end up with a very similar set of results. However, we believe
that it makes more sense to construct indices that conform to recognizable concepts
than those that happen to conform to a particular set of responses, especially as the
latter is contingent upon potentially idiosyncratic (and therefore non-generalizable)
samples and sets of questions.

TABLE 5A.1 *Factor loadings*

Survey	RNE				WVS				
Factors	1	2	3	4	1	2	3	4	5
Labels	Law-abidingness	Social capital	Culture I	Culture II	Culture I	Social capital I	Social capital II	Culture II	Economics
Voted in EU 2019	–				–	–	–	–	–
Typically vote									
Political interest								0.201	
Party member		0.448							
Sign petition		0.414							
Join boycott		0.351						0.229	
Attend demonstration		0.409	0.206	−0.273				0.204	
Join strike		0.444		−0.239				0.240	
Protest		0.455		−0.216					
Recreational sports		0.522			0.212				
Arts organization		0.581					0.264		
Labor union		0.317							
Environmental org.		0.640			0.209		0.295		
Professional association		0.567					0.226		
Charity		0.598			0.227		0.233		
Consumer organization		0.569			0.204		0.259		
Self help		0.657					0.261		
Other organization		0.599							
Trust people									
Trust politicians									

(continued)

TABLE 5A.1 (continued)

Survey	RNE				WVS				
Factors	1	2	3	4	1	2	3	4	5
Labels	Law-abidingness	Social capital	Culture I	Culture II	Culture I	Social capital I	Social capital II	Culture II	Economics
Homosexuality			0.518	0.330			-0.228		
Prostitution			0.413	0.517	0.203		-0.223		
Abortion			0.432	0.504					
Divorce			0.468	0.409					
Premarital sex			0.463	0.317					
Beat wife				-0.446					
Beat children				-0.354					
Church member		-0.381							
Men jobs			0.571						
Men native			0.309						
Women earn			0.374						
Woman job									
Church attend				0.280					
God important				0.317					
Science better									0.204
Neighbor drugs									
Neighbor other race			0.297						-0.305
Neighbor AIDS			0.374						0.253
Neighbor immigrant			0.231					0.223	-0.256
Neighbor gay			0.383						
Neighbor other religion			0.278					-0.263	
Neighbor unmarried			0.237					-0.242	

Neighbor other language						−0.240
Make parents proud		0.260	0.200			
Mother work		0.270				
Men better leaders		0.403				
University boys		0.500			0.257	
Men better executives		0.544				
Housewife fulfilling	0.212	0.551	−0.214			0.292
Claim benefits			0.441		0.213	
Avoid fare			0.511	−0.205	0.233	
Steal property			0.480	−0.202	0.240	
Cheat taxes			0.455		0.204	
Accept bribe	0.325		0.534		0.248	
Bribe to close case	0.468		0.253			
Provide info	0.772		0.154			
Bribe avoid fine	0.701		0.224			
Public contract friends	0.832					
Bureaucrat gift before	0.852					
Help friends	0.848					
Hire relative	0.871					
Bureaucrat gift after	0.883					
Pay doctor	0.896					
Doctor present after	0.887					
Present teacher	0.874					
Punish corruption	0.669					
Corruption inevitable	0.672					
Corruption forgivable	0.575					
Report corruption	0.577					

(continued)

TABLE 5A.1 (continued)

Survey	RNE				WVS				
Factors	1	2	3	4	1	2	3	4	5
Labels	Law-abidingness	Social capital	Culture I	Culture II	Culture I	Social capital I	Social capital II	Culture II	Economics
Witness corruption	0.466				–	–	–	–	–
Cultural ideology									
Economic ideology									
Left–right position	–	–	–	–					
Incomes more equal	–	–	–	–					
Private vs. state ownership	–	–	–	–					
Individual responsibility	–	–	–	–					
Competition good	–	–	–	–					
Economy vs. environment	–	–	–	–					
Tax the rich	–	–	–	–					
Aid for unemployment	–	–	–	–					
State makes incomes equal	–	–	–	–					
Private ownership	–	–	–	–					
Trust in regional org.								0.327	
Trust in the UN								0.322	
Close to your continent								0.205	0.282
Close to the world								0.204	0.291

Factor loadings from factor analyses with varimax rotation using the factanal function in R. Values small in magnitude (between –0.2 and 0.2) are omitted. RNE: 72 questions, 1,235 observations. WVS: 67 questions, 30,821 observations. Dash indicates that the question was not asked on a survey. EU = European Union; UN = United Nations.

6

Mechanisms

How can one account for the pattern of main effects reported in Chapter 4? What about the university experience nudges students in a liberal direction?

Attending university is a complex treatment. There is a formal curriculum as well as many informal activities including study and recreation. In the course of their education, students encounter professors, administrators, and peers. For many, college involves leaving home and taking up residence in a different part of the country or the world, often in an urban environment. This may involve mastering a language other than the one they grew up speaking. Completion of a college education is accompanied by a degree, which may change an individual's social status and their self-conception, and often opens the way to occupations with enhanced earning power (relative to what they would have been able to achieve otherwise). After college, there are often enduring ties to friends, perhaps to a spouse whom one met while at college, and to the alma mater itself. All of this is part of the university experience and hence must be considered part of the treatment.

The control condition, a residual category, is even more disparate. Those who do not enter university (or who attrit) may do any number of things with their lives. That said, there are some statistical regularities that, we expect, hold constant across most settings. The non-college set is likely to get married and have children at an earlier age, less likely to migrate outside their natal region, and less likely to hold a white-collar job. Presumably, their pattern of life is more traditional in the sense of adhering to local norms and customs (whatever they happen to be).

The set of *outcomes* of theoretical interest is also diverse. In Chapter 4, we explored a range of social and political attitudes and behaviors spanning the concepts of social capital, democracy, law-abidingness, culture, cosmopolitanism, economics, and overall ideology.

In the face of all this diversity, it might seem reasonable to suppose that different aspects of the college experience have divergent effects. That is, different mechanisms are responsible for different outcomes. This is the narrowly targeted approach adopted (implicitly) by most journal articles.

Even so, the various components of the university treatment are difficult to unbundle, and there seems to be some consistency across its various effects – which we characterized as *liberal* (Chapter 1). Accordingly, it is plausible to suppose that there might be common factors at work. Indeed, the literature reviewed in Chapter 2 invokes several explanatory frameworks with great frequency.

In this chapter, we review three mechanisms that seem to promise broad applicability: *empowerment, allocation,* and *socialization.* We argue that the latter offers the most compelling overall explanation. At the same time, we acknowledge that this is a difficult claim to establish empirically. In the concluding section, we discuss the difficulties of causal inference at greater length. In this instance, as in many others, it is easier to estimate a causal effect than to identify the mechanisms at work in that effect.

EMPOWERMENT

University education is a powerful tool. For the same reasons that literacy empowers,[1] higher education presumably empowers.

There is, first of all, knowledge about the world that a university education imparts. There is, secondly, a generalized competency. This includes communicative skills, a feeling of confidence with respect to a variety of social roles, ease of travel across urban and rural boundaries and across countries, an ability to navigate the internet, and so forth – all of which should contribute to an individual's capacity to respond to life's myriad challenges.

Together, the impact of education on knowledge and overall competency is sometimes referred to as a *cognitive* model.[2] With these competencies, university students and graduates are likely to cultivate a larger network of personal acquaintances, generating a positive effect on social capital.[3]

All things considered, university-educated citizens are more likely to feel at home in the world than those with less education. Accordingly, the highly educated may be less susceptible to feelings of anxiety and threat. This, in turn, should foster a more tolerant, cosmopolitan, and inclusive worldview – a mechanism sometimes referred to as *psychodynamic.*[4]

---

[1] See Freire (1970), Giroux (1988), and Goody (1975).

[2] See Hyman and Wright (1979), Nie, Junn, and Stehlik-Barry (1996: 6), Stephens and Long (1970), and Weil (1985).

[3] See Buerkle and Guseva (2002), Nie, Junn, and Stehlik-Barry (1996), and Sondheimer and Green (2010).

[4] See Jenssen and Engesbak (1994), Lottes and Kuriloff (1994: 51), and McClosky and Brill (1983).

Empowerment may also broaden perspectives. Knowledge of others' lives and viewpoints may lead to an enlargement of one's own views (van de Werfhorst and Kraaykamp 2001: 313). Rather than seeing oneself as a member of a particularistic unit – a family, clan, ethnicity, or region – one may be encouraged to think of oneself as a citizen of a country and perhaps also of the world, a cosmopolitan perspective. This intellectual background, or *Bildung*, should foster changes in attitudes and behavior. Specifically, the ethic of helping oneself and one's people may be displaced by a more universalistic ethic that calls into question inherited or particularistic obligations and justifications.

Unfortunately, direct measures of empowerment are scarce, as the concept is so difficult to distinguish from outcomes of interest. How, for example, can one distinguish a feeling of political efficacy from actions such as voting?

One feature that is measurable is knowledge and sophistication. However, these features do not appear to play a strong mediating role with respect to political behavior (Luskin 1987, 1990).

The World Values Survey (WVS) asks one question (Q48) that bears directly on feelings of empowerment. "Some people feel they have completely free choice and control over their lives, while other people feel that what they do has no real effect on what happens to them." Responses range from 1 ("no choice at all") to 10 ("a great deal of choice").

We employ this variable in a series of mediation analyses centered on the six indices of liberalism introduced in Chapter 4 – social capital, democracy, law-abidingness, culture, cosmopolitanism, and economics. The results, displayed in Table 6.1, offer very little support for the empowerment thesis. Insofar as we can tell, the liberalizing effect of a university education is not (or only very slightly) mediated by feelings of empowerment. This is true even for social capital, where one might imagine the connection would be strongest.

Of course, we do not suppose that this minimal evidence has disposed of the thesis. All we can really say with any assurance is that we cannot find evidence for the thesis with the data available to us.

ALLOCATION

A good deal of research suggests that college education boosts the employment and marriage prospects of those who attend.[5] This has been characterized as an *allocative* effect since it advances material prospects (Kerckhoff 1976).

Insofar as income affects social and political attitudes, it is reasonable to suppose that income, and the broader implications of social class, might serve as an important mediator. Specifically, it ought to incline those with higher education against economic policies such as redistributive taxation that would impinge on their earnings – especially as they presumably have less need of

---

[5] See Barrow and Malamud (2015), Deming (2022), and Zimmerman (2014).

TABLE 6.1 *The mediating effect of efficacy*

Outcome	Social capital	Democracy	Law-abiding	Culture	Cosmopolitanism	Economics
Average mediating effect (ACME)	.006***	.006***	.007***	.002***	.011***	-.001**
Average direct effect (ADE)	.350***	.236***	.058***	.170***	.141***	.044***
Total effect (ATE)	.356***	.241***	.065***	.172***	.152***	.045***
Proportion mediated (ACME/ATE)	1%	2%	10%	1%	7%	0%
Countries	78	78	76	78	78	78
Observations	102,471	102,471	97,209	102,471	102,471	102,471

Efficacy is measured with the question: "Some people feel they have completely free choice and control over their lives, and other people feel that what they do has no real effect on what happens to them. Please use the scale to indicate how much freedom of choice and control you feel you have over the way your life turns out." Responses are arrayed on a ten-point scale from "Not at all" to "A great deal." The index construction for each of the outcomes is explained in Chapter 4. Analyses were conducted with the paramed package in Stata (Emsley and Liu 2013) using unimputed data from the WVS and EVS. *** p>.01; ** p>.05; * p>.1.

public services than their less fortunate brethren without higher education. This effect can be found in our own analyses, displayed in Figures 4.12 to 4.14.[6]

Along other outcomes, however, it is not obvious how the allocative effect would or should matter. It is not clear, for example, that tolerance for sexual deviance has any economic costs or benefits (for those who are non-deviant). With respect to political participation, a sacrifice of time is required, and if a college education enhances the value of one's time, then the opportunity cost of participation is increased. This would suggest that college should have a negative impact on participation – quite the opposite of what we find. To be sure, forms of participation that require financial sacrifice such as contributing to a campaign may be enhanced by the income effect of a college degree.

To test the allocative effect of education, we undertake a series of mediation analyses with data from the WVS. (The European Values Survey [EVS] uses a somewhat different measure of income, which means it would be difficult to compare results.) As previously (in Figure 6.2), six indices of liberalism compose the outcomes, while the income of respondents (self-assessed) is treated as the potential mediator.

The results in Table 6.2 indicate that income is a negligible mediator for social capital, democracy, law-abidingness, and cultural values. The proportion mediated ranges from 0 percent to 12 percent and in the latter case bears the wrong sign. There is a bit of evidence for income as a mediator with respect to cosmopolitanism, and a good deal of support for the idea that income mediates attitudes toward economic issues, where it explains 61 percent of the total effect.

We conclude that the allocative effect of a college education is important, but primarily for pocketbook outcomes. Here, one's class position matters because the policy under consideration directly affects one's material self-interest. For other issues, we do not see much of an allocative effect.

This finding is bolstered by studies of lottery winners, where the allocation effect is randomized through a natural experiment. One such study finds that affluence "increases hostility toward estate taxes, marginally increases hostility towards government redistribution, but has little effect on broader attitudes concerning economic stratification or the role of government as a provider of social insurance." Doherty and colleagues (2006: 441) conclude, "the findings suggest the limited influence that material concerns have on one's broad political outlook."

Moreover, although income is an important mediator for university's effect on economic values, we should bear in mind that the total impact of a university education on economic values is modest relative to education's impact on other outcomes. This is evident in Table 6.2 (see ATE [total effect]), in the various analyses shown in Chapter 4, and in Table 5.1, where we compare standardized

---

[6] This is consistent with Bullock's (2021) study of the impact of secondary education on attitudes toward redistribution.

TABLE 6.2 *The mediating effect of income*

Outcome	Social capital	Democracy	Law-abiding	Culture	Cosmopolitanism	Economics
Average mediating effect (ACME)	.022***	-.000	-.009***	.007***	.017***	.023***
Average direct effect (ADE)	.288***	.217***	.087***	.159***	.081***	.015
Total effect (ATE)	.310***	.217***	.078***	.167***	.097***	.038***
Proportion mediated (ACME/ATE)	.07%	0%	12%	4%	18%	61%
Countries	47	47	48	48	47	48
Observations	42,859	42,390	51,758	41,949	38,812	49,991

Analyses conducted with the paramed package in Stata (Emsley and Liu 2013). Sample limited to the WVS (unimputed data only). The index construction is explained in Chapter 4. Mediator: income, measured by respondents' self-location on a ten-point scale. All specifications include covariates measuring father's occupation when respondent was a child, father's education, mother's education, sex, age, and dummies for each country. ***$p<.01$; **$p<.05$; *$p<.1$.

coefficients. In summary, the allocative effect of higher education is a strong mediator of a modest causal effect, and it has few implications for other (non-economic) dimensions of the university's influence.

SOCIALIZATION

A final explanatory framework centers on the university as an agent of socialization. According to Niemi and Klingler (2012: 33), "mid- to late-adolescence through early adulthood is ... when individuals establish many of the habits, orientations, and feelings that guide them throughout their lives."[7] For those who attend college, this institution lies at the center of the tradition to adulthood. It is here that students adapt to their new role as educated persons and whatever entailments seem appropriate for that role.[8]

The socializing effects of college may be a relatively new development in the long sweep of history. Recall that prior to the twentieth century college education was a rarity. Few families could afford higher education or saw fit to invest in it. College was a marginal experience of little notice and little sociological import.

In the twentieth century, opportunities for higher education – as well as rewards – skyrocketed. Accordingly, college became an integral part of the transition from youth to adulthood for a significant portion of the population. No longer a diversion from regular life, it is now a rite of passage for members of the middle classes throughout the world. The college student has also become a recognized social identity, one with its own set of norms and expectations.

Both of these developments should enhance the socializing effects of a college education, for it is through this institution that one learns how to become an adult. The influences of peers, professors, the curriculum, and other aspects of college life are thereby magnified, as are cohort effects. Whoever attended university during the 1960s shares a common set of experiences; likewise for other generations, though perhaps not to the same extent.[9]

The stress associated with getting accepted to college, gaining the acceptance of one's college peers, and pursuing a successful college career signals its centrality to modern life. Because college matters, we can expect it has a greater influence on social and political attitudes than it did in previous historical eras.

---

[7] See also Jennings and Markus (1984) and Jennings and Niemi (1981). For work on young adulthood from an anthropological, psychological, and sociological perspective, see Arnett (2014) and Clydesdale (2008).

[8] For general treatments of political socialization, see Hyman (1959) and Wasburn and Covert (2017). For socialization as a mediator for educational effects, see Dey (1997), LeVine (1966), Meyer (1977), Stubager (2008), Surridge (2016), and Weidman (1989).

[9] This may have been true as early as the 1920s in rich countries like the US (Fass 1977).

Those who commend the liberal social and political attitudes and values instilled by higher education may be inclined to describe the socialization process as one of *enlightenment*, casting students as active agents of their own intellectual and moral awakening.[10] Those who are critical of this effect may describe it as *indoctrination*, implying that students are passive receptacles of an ideology propounded by professors or college activists. Nowadays, this critique is more likely to be voiced from a conservative angle.[11] However, we observed in Chapter 2 that leftists often charge the university with melding young minds to suit a capitalist, militarist, or quietist agenda.[12] Operationally, "enlightenment" and "indoctrination" are difficult to distinguish, which is why we collapse them into the more neutral concept of socialization.

What does it mean to socialize someone into a liberal worldview? Reviewing her own field of social psychology, Deborah Prentice (2012: 516–517) identifies the following phenomena:

> felt pressures to conform to liberal views; a reluctance to express nonliberal views; an assumption that liberal views are even more prevalent and extreme than they are; a tendency to explain the field's liberal bias in terms of the properties of conservatives, not liberals, that produce it; and ... an inclination to derogate and punish [faculty and students] who express conservative views.

Arguably, the socialization process in a university context carries extra freight insofar as substantive conclusions are associated with objective, scientific truths. During the postwar era, Andrew Jewett (2014: 192–193) notes:

> liberal professors knit their own political views into the very fabric of reality and dismissed their political opponents as hopelessly out of touch with the world – perhaps even clinically insane. This realist stance, along with Keynesian economics and, in some circles, an emphasis on individual rights, set the tone of postwar academic liberalism. Postwar liberals portrayed natural and social scientists as the spokespersons for reality in the political process. They littered their writings with phrases like "history reveals," "experience tells us," "responsible observers agree," "the truth of the matter is," and "deeply ingrained in the structure of." Silently turning "oughts" into "ises," these veiled normatives filled the academic discourses of the 1950s with a welter of "to be" verbs and passive, agentless phrasings. According to this necessitarian outlook, professionals with the proper training and technical skills could easily discern the meanings of social phenomena.

Although this sort of "naturalizing" may have been especially characteristic of the American academy during the postwar decades, it presumably extends to other times and other places. Note that the work of the university – or at least of

---

[10] See Davis and Robinson (1991), Hyman and Wright (1979), Nie, Junn, and Stehlik-Barry (1996), and Nunn, Crockett, and Williams (1978).

[11] See Greer (2017), Horowitz (2009), and Lott (1990).

[12] See Aufderheide (1992), Feldman (1989), Giroux (2015), Leslie (1993), Schrecker (1986), Scott (2019), Sinclair (1923), and Wallerstein and Starr (1971).

the social and natural sciences – is to explore the world in a scientific fashion; in this light, it is no surprise that conclusions would be presented as natural or objective truths.

We are not trying to tear down the edifice of science. Our point is simply that, whether justified or not, this is one of the rhetorical features that distinguishes socialization on a university campus from socialization in other venues. Because it masks the process of persuasion under the guise of objective truth, or "sound methodology," a university education may enhance the effectiveness and durability of whatever norms it purveys.

Some writers view the socialization process as reproducing the dominant (or core) values of a society.[13] We shall assume that this refers to the values held by most people. It follows that the experience of a college education should pull students closer to the mean across a population. While this interpretation might make sense of some of the outcomes of concern (e.g., law-abidingness), many of the outcomes addressed in this study are not consistent with a dominant-ideology explanation. Those who have attended university are more liberal than those who have not attended university, even along dimensions that lie far from the mainstream in many countries such as support for immigrants, minorities, women's rights, homosexuality, and civil liberty. Since the effect registered in our WVS/EVS sample is fairly consistent across countries, it cannot represent a reversion to the mean. We shall assume, therefore, that socialization effects do not simply reinforce currently dominant social values.

Many questions remain. In particular, there are multiple agents of socialization. This includes (a) professors, (b) disciplines, (c) peers, (d) civic education, and (e) overall gestalt.

Professors

Many studies conclude that college faculty are more liberal than the general public, an issue reviewed in Chapter 7. It is not far-fetched, therefore, to suppose that professors might construct lectures and course material that reflect their social and political views, and that students exposed to those views would be influenced by them.[14]

However, one study does not find a strong connection between professors' ideology and their students' ideological shifts during the course of a semester (Woessner and Kelly-Woessner 2009a). Likewise, a comparison of student ideological self-placement through time in thirty-eight universities does not find an association between professorial liberalism and greater shifts in a liberal direction (Mariani and Hewitt 2008).

---

[13] See Baer and Lambert (1982), Dunn (2011), Phelan and colleagues (1995), Schnabel (2018), Weakliem (2002), and Weil (1985).
[14] See Phelan and colleagues (1995).

It could be that professors do not care to parade their personal views in front of the classroom, or that their curriculum does not allow space for this sort of proselytizing. Or it could be that professors prognosticate but students are not receptive to these messages, either out of disinterest or skepticism (Caplan 2018; Gross 2013).

Disciplines

Some disciplines, generally located in the humanities and social sciences, are especially liberal (see Chapter 7). It follows that the liberalizing effect of college might be more marked for students concentrating in these disciplines (Hastie 2007). It also follows that there might be some spillover in attitudes toward society and politics from the humanities and social sciences to students concentrating in other disciplines. Those studying sociology are likely to have more impact on general views about race, gender, and sexuality than those studying engineering, for example. Altbach (2007: 339) notes, "Student activists come largely from the social sciences and to some extent from the humanities." Accordingly, what these students think, and what they learn during the course of their studies, is likely to have a broader impact.

Many studies claim to find a disciplinary effect on social and political attitudes.[15] Some show that the impact of studying humanities and social sciences is more liberalizing than studying science, technology, engineering, and mathematics (STEM) disciplines (Haley and Sidanius 2005; Hanson et al. 2012; Sidanius et al. 1991). Fischer and colleagues (2017) find a robust effect on economics students – toward a neoliberal view of economic issues – but little effect for students in other disciplines (see also Kirchgässner 2005). At least one study reports that scientific disciplines induce a more liberal effect than non-scientific disciplines (Ma-Kellams et al. 2014), running contrary to the general expectation. Many studies find only weak or inconsistent disciplinary effects (Elchardus and Spruyt 2009; Jacobsen 2001; Weisenfeld and Ott 2011). Adding to the confusion, all studies that we are aware of are marred by problems of self-selection, as students are likely to select disciplines that accord with their worldviews.[16]

Longitudinal research designs, where student attitudes are measured over time, offer some correction for this bias. However, it seems likely that those who select more liberal disciplines are not only more liberal at the time of selection but also predisposed to adopt more liberal views in the future. They are hankering to move left, and await the occasion to abandon views held by their parents or their local community. By contrast, those who select more conservative disciplines may be predisposed to adopt conservative views

---

[15] See Astin (1993), Benenson and Bergom (2019), Guimond and Palmer (1990, 1996), Hillygus (2005), Rich (1977), and Woessner and Kelly-Woessner (2020).

[16] See Astin (1978), Feldman and Newcomb (1969), and Elchardus and Spruyt (2010).

during and after college. They are hankering to move right. In this respect, trend-lines can be deceiving.

The Romanian Natural Experiment (RNE) offers a somewhat stronger research design in this respect, as students in Romania are compelled to choose an educational track at age fourteen. This track, either natural science or humanities/social science, is generally maintained through college (for those who matriculate). Indeed, it is quite difficult to change. Accordingly, we can regard it as relatively fixed.

It is true of course that this choice could also be forward-looking. However, at such an early age, students are less likely to be aware of the ideological proclivities of different disciplines; they may not even understand very much about ideology. In any case, they are likely to be heavily influenced by teachers and parents. In this sense, we might regard the choice as exogenous (though certainly not random).

Figure 6.1 shows estimates of the effect of university attendance on each of the major indices, calculated in the same way as our main estimates in Chapter 4 but this time analyzed separately for respondents in the two major tracks recognized at university levels: humanities/social science and natural science/ engineering.

In each paired analysis, the effect estimate is larger for humanities/social science students than for natural science/engineering students.[17] Granted, none of these differences are statistically significant; they are probably a product of small samples and resulting imprecision. Nonetheless, the results are suggestive and in line with expectations that less scientific fields of study may more directly emphasize the themes of a liberal education and thus have a greater impact on social and political attitudes. Bear in mind that all of the subjects in the RNE fall very close to the baccalaureate exam (*bac*) threshold and thus possess, at least by this measure, similar intelligence, skill, and motivation.

The greatest differences in effect size are on cultural values and law-abidingness, while the estimated effect of university attendance on social capital is fairly similar for the students in the two tracks. One might surmise that social habits and connection with one's community, key features of social capital, are less a product of the curriculum than of the general university environment, affecting all students equally regardless of their disciplinary track.

The estimated impact of university on party support, both on the cultural and economic dimension, is larger for humanities than for natural sciences. It bears

---

[17] One subtle point that merits mentioning is that, as a regression discontinuity design, the RNE estimates the average effect of university attendance for those scoring at the passage threshold on the baccalaureate exam (*bac*). When separately analyzing humanities and science test takers, we must recognize that the exams taken by these two groups are somewhat different, meaning that the type of respondent who would score at (or very close to) the passage threshold might be somewhat different.

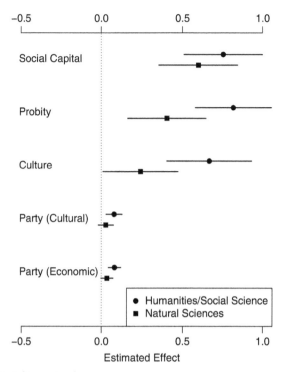

FIGURE 6.1 Disciplinary tracks
Estimates for each dependent variable (with 95 percent confidence intervals) based on
RNE subsetted by academic concentration. Estimates are from fuzzy regression
discontinuity (two-stage least squares) using the same basic design as in Figures 4.2,
4.6, 4.8, 4.9, and 4.11. For humanities/social science, N=644 (313 observations below
threshold, 331 observations above). For natural sciences, N=572 (233 observations
below threshold, 339 observations above).

mentioning that the scale of the social capital, law-abidingness, and cultural values
indices (standardized to have a mean of 0 and standard deviation of 1) is different
than for the two party-support measures, which are scaled to have a theoretical
range of 0 to 1. Therefore, the estimated effect sizes (and differences between the
two groups) are larger than they might at first appear. But for neither party-support
measure is the difference between the two disciplinary tracks statistically
significant.

Overall, these results provide some support for the idea that a humanities or
social science education has a greater liberalizing impact than a technical or
natural science education. But readers should bear in mind that these findings
are suggestive rather than conclusive, given the imprecise estimates available
from subsets of the RNE data.

Peers

Peer effects are thought to be particularly strong for young adults, and there is plenty of work attesting to this in the literature on education and human capital (Sacerdote 2011). Decades ago, Feldman and Newcomb (1969: 240) remarked: "Students have mutual and reciprocal influence on each other. In the interaction they develop consensual and shared sets of expectations regarding each other's behavior and regarding important aspects of their common environment. These consensual and shared expectations – known as norms and standards – form the basis of the student peer group's power over individual members." It follows that students exposed to liberal friends and acquaintances may be likely to move in a liberal direction, and vice versa.[18]

Since peer groups formed in college often last through life, these networks may have enduring significance long after the chords of *Pomp and Circumstance* have faded away. More broadly, we can imagine that one's social circle in later life might be strongly affected by one's educational background. University graduates are more likely to seek out the company of other university graduates; likewise, those without higher education may feel they have more in common with others of similar backgrounds. In this respect, peer effects may be far-reaching and enduring.

However, it is not clear whether peer effects can explain the aggregate university effects we have observed. This depends upon how the effect is conceptualized and modeled.[19]

Commonly, a peer effect is understood as a movement within a group of peers toward the mean of that group along whatever outcome is under consideration. If so, peer effects should lead to tighter clustering around the mean but not a change in the mean value, as movements in a liberal direction are countered by movements in the opposite direction. This is exactly what a systematic panel study of peer effects finds. "Students attending liberal colleges become more liberal over time, whereas those attending conservative colleges become more conservative," reports Dey (1997: 408; see also Dey 1996).

For peer effects to explain aggregate university effects, additional assumptions are needed. For example, it is possible that liberal students are more vocal about their political and social views than their conservative peers. Although most students in Latin America expressed conservative or centrist views in opinion polls taken in the 1960s, leftists were considerably more prominent in student politics and managed to win most university elections (Liebman, Walker, and Glazer 1972: 130). Likewise, although many American college students supported the Vietnam war, many campuses – especially elite

---

[18] See Bryant (2003), Dey (1997), Hanson and colleagues (2012), Klofstad (2007), Milem (1998), Newcomb (1943), Newcomb and Wilson (1966), Rauf (2021), and Strother and colleagues (2020).

[19] The perils of modeling peer effects are discussed in Angrist (2014).

campuses – were dominated by antiwar protests during the late 1960s and early 1970s.

These observations are consistent with the conservative charge of "PC-ism." While it is cool to speak out against racism, sexism, imperialism, and other hated -isms, it is not so cool to defend religion, the military, and the status quo. While it is okay to be communist or anarchist, it is not okay to be fascist. Extremism on the left is more acceptable than extremism on the right in a college setting, one might argue.

Perhaps leftists are more politically motivated; they work harder and with greater urgency, petitioning their friends and acquaintances, organizing events, sponsoring speakers and debates, and engaging the questions of the day. If their hard work makes them more effective representatives of student interests, this might explain their dominance of student elections in Latin America (Liebman, Walker, and Glazer 1972: 131).

Perhaps the motivation of liberals and leftists derives in some degree from what they perceive as a favorable setting. Years ago, Newcomb (1943: 59) observed that students with ambitions to become student leaders at Bennington College, Vermont, felt obliged to "fit in to what they believe to be the college pattern." If this pattern is perceived to be liberal, then it follows that student leaders will echo that liberal ethos, reinforcing it among the rank and file.

This may help to explain why student activism often has a liberal or left-wing cast. Philip Altbach (2007: 330) notes:

The university is a particularly favorable environment for the development of organization and movements among students. There is an active intellectual environment that stresses independent thought and analysis. Universities are institutions that stress intellectual values and ideals – theories and values that may call into question established social and political norms. Professors, through their teaching and research, may also provide – albeit sometimes indirectly – an atmosphere that legitimates dissent.

If universities establish a liberal ethos, then those who share that ethos, or are willing to adopt that ethos, may be more prominent in the public life of the university and in private spaces where contentious social and political issues are often hashed out. This would explain a peer effect that seems (insofar as our analyses are correct) to tilt in a liberal direction. However, we do not have systematic evidence of this pattern.

Civic Education

Another potential mechanism consists of training students for civic activity, which may have ramifications for political participation, social trust, and law-abidingness – and possibly for other outcomes that we have characterized as liberal.

Good citizens are not formed naturally. There must be some sort of preparation. Educational systems have striven to provide that preparation since time immemorial (Heater 2003). Although civic education is often focused on at primary and secondary levels, university may also contribute to that preparation, either with courses or lectures focused on this topic and/or activities on- and off-campus that provide experience working in the community (McIlrath and Lyons 2012; Saltmarsh and Zlotkowski 2011).

Many studies suggest that civic education of the scholastic or practicum variety makes a difference to civic engagement in later years.[20] Other studies are skeptical (Langton and Jennings 1968).[21] In any case, it is doubtful whether civic courses affect the attitudes and behavior of most students, as these programs tend to be small and are attended on a voluntary basis in most colleges. Outside the Anglo-American world, our impression is that they are rare, as the topic of civics is normally taught in high school rather than college. And where they exist in authoritarian contexts such as China, they are unlikely to register liberal effects (Cantoni et al. 2017).

Even if students are not exposed to a course or practicum on civic education, they may nonetheless learn a good deal about democratic citizenship as part of their college experience. Students play an important role in governance in many Southern European universities (following the Bologna model) and in most Latin American countries, where students composed a share of the governing bodies from the very beginning (Liebman, Walker, and Glazer 1972: 2), a role that was enhanced by the wave of Córdoba reforms in the early twentieth century. In Latin America, it is common for one-third of a university's governing body to be composed of students (Lipset 1967: 23).

Elsewhere, presidents, trustees, administrators, and professors are usually appointed, and are not directly responsible to the student body. However, nearly all universities feature elective positions among the faculty (e.g., department chairs, faculty councils) and among the students (e.g., club members and leaders, student councils and presidents). In this capacity, universities serve as training grounds for democracy, encouraging students to uphold democratic virtues and practice responsible citizenship.[22] We do not know to what extent this experience impacts general attitudes toward society and politics.

Gestalt

A final approach to the socialization question treats universities in a holistic fashion, with the idea that each university has a different gestalt and should therefore register a different impact on its students. This approach is less

---

[20] See Astin, Sax, and Avalos (1999), Checkoway (2001), Galston (2001), and Johnson (2004).
[21] For a general survey, see Arthur, Davies, and Hahn (2008).
[22] Arguments along these lines have been made many times before, as noted in Chapter 7.

revealing with respect to causal mechanisms as university effects may stem from faculty, disciplines, peers, or some combination of the foregoing. All are merged into a single omnibus treatment.

Yet, there are some observable – and hence testable – features stemming from this thesis. Insofar as a university education changes attitudes and behavior through a socialization process, one might conjecture that certain types of schools would experience stronger effects. Specifically, socialization should be enhanced in colleges that are small, selective in recruitment, homogeneous, isolated (e.g., in a rural area), with a distinct ideological profile, and where students live predominantly on-campus. Here, school identity and esprit de corps are likely to be strongest.[23]

One of the earliest studies of socialization focused on Bennington College, Vermont, which seems to incorporate all of these features (Newcomb 1943). Of course, to test the idea that college types matter, one must compare socialization effects across different universities that vary along the foregoing dimensions. In this vein, Hanson and colleagues (2012) find that small liberal arts colleges have a greater liberalizing effect on student attitudes than other university environments. Other studies find small or inconsistent between-college effects.[24] None are free from the threats posed by self-selection. Once again, we are faced with inconclusive evidence.

CONCLUSIONS

Universities are complex organisms, so it would not be surprising if their impact on social and political attitudes operated through multiple pathways. Our discussion has highlighted three mechanisms – empowerment, allocation, and socialization – that seem to have the most general purview.

We cast doubt on the overall importance of empowerment and allocation. These factors might play an important role for a few outcomes. For example, the more conservative views of those with college education on economic policies are probably a result of their improved class status. However, college has only a modest impact on economic values and there is no evidence to suggest that allocative effects apply to other outcomes.

We are more optimistic with respect to socialization, which seems to have an expansive range of application. However, socialization is a large concept – really, a bundle of mechanisms. Since these are difficult to test, our conclusions must be regarded as preliminary.

In the end, we are left with a speculative view of the mechanisms at work in the relationship between university education and liberalism. These are summarized in Figure 6.2. The arrows going to and from each mechanism

---

[23] In this vein, Clark and Trow (1966: 61) remark, "the most potent instrument of value change is the quasi-total institution, where members sleep, play, and work in the same place."

[24] See Feldman and Newcomb (1969), Pascarella and Terenzini (1991, 2005).

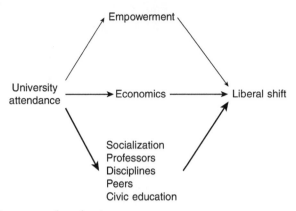

FIGURE 6.2 Summary of mechanisms

offer a rough indication of how important we think they might be in explaining the overall liberal shift in social and political attitudes that results from a college education.

Why are these pathways so slippery? Why are our conclusions to this chapter so speculative?

As it turns out, this is a common state of affairs. Social scientists generally know more about X's impact on Y than the pathways through which the effect flows. This is especially the case for treatments like university education that involve (a) multiple potential mechanisms that are (b) difficult to measure, (c) entangled with each other, (d) non-manipulable (or at least difficult to manipulate), and (e) subject to self-selection.[25]

We do not mean to say that the task is hopeless. And certainly, it bears further research. Our point is simply that any uncertainties associated with the causal effect of education on social and political attitudes are magnified when it comes to ascertaining the mechanisms at work. That is unlikely to change because it is inherent in the problem of causality.

---

[25] For general discussion, see Gerring (2010) and Imai and colleagues (2011).

PART IV

HISTORY

7

The Rise of a Liberal University

Having shown considerable evidence of the liberalizing effect of college education in the twenty-first century, we are faced with a question about origins. When did this effect arise? How long have universities been exerting a liberal influence on societies?

Unfortunately, in previous historical eras we have no satisfactory way of ascertaining whether universities affected the social and political attitudes of those who attended – and, if so, in what direction. All of the methodological obstacles discussed in Chapter 2 are magnified as we move further back in time.

What we *can* reasonably address is a set of descriptive questions. When did universities become more liberal than the societies they were situated within and how much more liberal are they today? To answer these questions, we need to compare the views and values of the university – variously defined by its faculty, students, activities, and graduates – with the societies in which they were/are embedded.

To be clear, showing that universities were/are more liberal than the societies they inhabit does not mean that they have a liberalizing effect. But it is probably a necessary condition. Insofar as the university ethos was liberal – relative to society at large – it is plausible to suppose that attendance at such an institution might have exerted a liberal influence. If not, the proposition is difficult to sustain.

We begin this chapter with a capsule history of the growth of higher education around the world, demonstrating that although the university has been around for a long time, its current position of social prestige is comparatively recent. Prior to the modern era, the university could not have had much impact on society because universities were small and of peripheral importance.

The rest of the chapter focuses on the modern era. In each section, we examine a different component of our topic: intellectuals, university faculty, student activism, university constituencies, and university graduates. In the final section, we compare the social and political attitudes of faculty, university students, former students, and the general public to each other in Romania, the US, and globally at the present time.

A few caveats about the evidence are in order before we begin. First, the paucity of sources in earlier historical eras obliges us to focus primarily on the Western world, where university histories are long and data sources plentiful (relatively speaking). Second, many of our sources are of questionable representativeness, especially those that reach back prior to the development of random-sample survey technology.

Finally, historical data is generally limited to the partisan/ideological components of liberalism; for example, party affiliation, placement on a left–right spectrum, or the existence of radical protests and intellectual movements. Consequently, we are simply unable to systematically evaluate other aspects of liberalism prior to the late twentieth century. In this part of the book, therefore, our empirical treatment of liberalism is narrower – though our theoretical understanding still encompasses the wide range of subjects defined as liberal in Chapter 1.

Despite these limitations, this chapter addresses essential questions and does so with the best evidence available. Further thoughts on the informativeness – and limitations – of the data are offered in the conclusion of this chapter, where we also provide a concise summary of the long-term ideological trajectory of the modern university. We reserve speculation on the causes of these developments for Chapter 9. This chapter is primarily descriptive.

UNIVERSITIES

As long as there have been complex civilizations, there have been centers of learning. At first, these tended to be informal gatherings of scholars and students such as Plato's Academy and Aristotle's Lyceum. Many of these early intellectual centers were focused on training of a spiritual nature. In the latter category, Al-Azhar University (in present-day Cairo), whose roots extend back to the tenth century, is sometimes regarded as the world's oldest continuously operating center of higher learning.

In Chapter 3, we adopt a narrower definition of the university, one consistent with contemporary understandings. So defined, the history of our topic may be traced back to institutions founded in the eleventh and twelfth centuries in Bologna, Paris, and Oxford. By 1215, these institutions embodied the ideal of *studia generalia*, whose

> guild-like organizations of masters and students exercised a high degree of legal auton-
> omy, elected their own officers, controlled their own finances, attracted students from
> a wide area (*generale*), offered instruction in one or more of the higher faculties of law,
> medicine, or theology as well as the seven foundational liberal arts, and conferred
> degrees and teaching licenses that were, in theory at least, honored by other universities.
> (Axtell 2016: 4)

Universities of this sort also have a long history in some European colonies. Universidad Santo Tomás de Aquino was founded in 1538 in what is now the Dominican Republic. The Universidad Michoacana de San Nicolás de Hidalgo, in central Mexico, was founded in 1540. The Universidad Nacional Mayor de San Marcos, in Lima, Peru, was founded in 1551. The University of Santo Tomas, in the Philippines, was founded around 1611. Harvard University was founded in the colony of Massachusetts in 1636.[1]

These early cases notwithstanding, universities were still quite rare prior to the modern era. The takeoff for universities in the Americas occurred in the nineteenth century, in Asia at the turn of the twentieth century, and in Africa in the late twentieth century. Regional trajectories, along with the global trajectory, are plotted in Figure 7.1 over the course of a millennium.[2]

We are not able to measure university enrollment in a comprehensive fashion prior to the modern era, but we know that these institutions were quite small (Stone 1964). After all, few jobs required a diploma.

In the modern era, the university's position in society underwent a dramatic shift.[3] Figure 7.1 shows the dramatic increase in the number of universities across the world in the twentieth century. Figure 7.2 shows the share of young adults who attended an institution of higher learning from the mid-twentieth century to the present. A steep upward slope is notable, especially in Europe and the Americas, where higher education transitioned from an elite to a mass activity.

In rich countries, a majority of young adults now attend an institution of higher learning. Roughly three-quarters now do so in the US, though overall tertiary education is less impressive because of the inclusion of older cohorts with less education. In poor countries the share is much lower, as shown in Figure 7.3. But even in the poorest parts of the world tertiary education is on the rise. Lant Pritchett (2013: 25) notes "the average developing-country adult in 2010 had more years of schooling than the average adult in an advanced country in 1960."

Within countries, there is considerable variation in the regional accessibility of higher education. To provide a more finely grained picture, Figure 7.4 shows a map of the world with dots indicating the location of nearly 12,000 universities that meet our definitional criteria. This provides a bird's-eye view of the geographic penetration of universities across the globe in the present era.

Institutions of higher education have increased in number and also in standing over the modern era. This is especially notable when compared with

---

[1] Connections between the British empire and the spread of universities are discussed by Newton (1924) and Pietsch (2015). The development of Latin American universities is discussed in Lanning (1940) and Maier and Weatherhead (1979).

[2] Histories of the university have been written for Europe (e.g., Ridder-Symoens 2003a, 2003b; Rüegg 2004, 2011), the Middle East (Makdisi 1981), and the US (e.g., Geiger 2014). Other regions are not well studied.

[3] See Barro and Lee (2013) and Schofer and Meyer (2005).

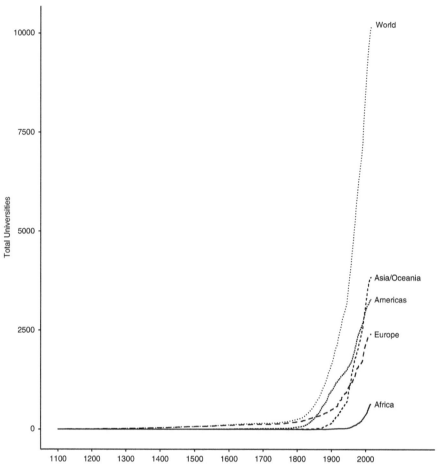

FIGURE 7.1 The global proliferation of universities
Number of universities globally and by region. N=11,915 (Apfeld 2019).

what one might consider to be their main competitor in the ideational realm, namely religion. Figure 7.5 displays the frequency of "university" and "church" in the English language over the past four centuries as represented by the Google Books database. As one can see, the trajectory of these two terms is negatively correlated. From the mid-nineteenth century onward, declines in "church" are matched by increases in "university," offering a neat visualization of the long-term process by which secular authorities gradually displaced spiritual authorities.[4]

---

[4] See Bruce (2011), Norris and Inglehart (2011), and Voas and Chavez (2016).

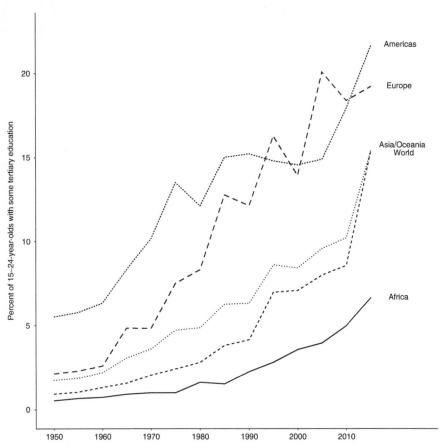

FIGURE 7.2 Tertiary educational attainment, 1950–2015
Tertiary educational attainment among youth (aged fifteen to twenty-four) from 1950 to
2015. All countries weighted equally (Barro and Lee 2013).

Of course, a repository of published words is not a perfect reflection of the
values of the general populace. The Bible is perhaps still the most commonly
read book in Christian societies, and those who do not consume books are
unrepresented in this exercise. Google Books is, however, a reasonably good
indication of the ideas and interests of those who write and read on a regular
basis.

While the intellectual class was dominated by clergy up until the twentieth
century, in more recent times intellectuals have deserted the church and flocked
to universities. We suppose that similar transformations have occurred in many
non-Anglophone societies. Frank and Mayer (2020: 18) conclude that in the
contemporary world, "the university plays a role analogous to that of the high
church in the medieval world . . . . It offers authoritative answers to all of life's

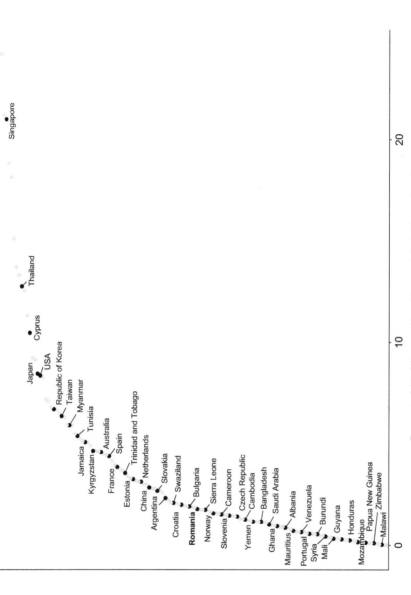

FIGURE 7.3 Tertiary educational attainment in 2015

Partial or complete tertiary educational attainment among fifteen- to twenty-four-year-olds in 2015. Every third country is labeled. *N*=146 (Barro and Lee 2013).

FIGURE 7.4 University penetration across the world
Dots represent the location of universities in 2019. N=11,915 (Apfeld 2019).

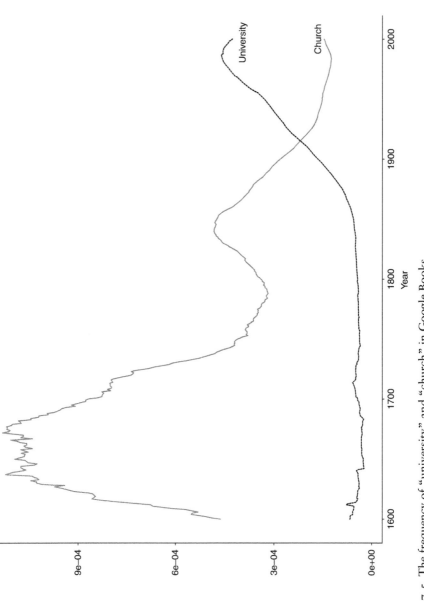

FIGURE 7.5 The frequency of "university" and "church" in Google Books

The relative frequency of each 1-gram (word) as a fraction of all 1-grams published (in English) within a given year, averaged across a six-year moving window. Terms are case-insensitive and aggregate results for both singular and plural forms of each noun. Data provided by Google Ngram (Michel et al. 2011).

ultimate questions .... Professors, not priests ... unlock the secrets of the universe."

So far as we can tell, the demand for academic credentials is growing virtually everywhere. One may suppose that this trend will continue into the foreseeable future as technologies advance and jobs shift from brawn to brain, increasing the need for high-level training and diplomas attesting to proficiency in specialized areas of expertise.

To be sure, there are challenges ahead. The cost of a university education has spiraled and students worry about economic returns on their investment. Families, like governments, struggle with the issue of how much to invest in tertiary education.[5] But even if enrollments stabilize over the next few decades, it seems clear that the university will remain a central institution in modern society for the foreseeable future. (Further thoughts on this question are offered at the end of Chapter 10.)

INTELLECTUALS

Having sketched the history of the university, we now set our gaze on intellectuals, broadly construed as individuals whose influence arises from the force of their ideas (though they may also have taken part in important events or held important nonacademic offices).

In premodern times, intellectuals did not enjoy great autonomy unless they happened to be independently wealthy. Learned men (few women were literate and even fewer held positions of prominence) tended to serve well-established institutions such as the church or the state, or a wealthy patron. Universities, as noted, were scarce, small, and underfunded. Teaching was a service occupation.

During the European Enlightenment, intellectuals rose to prominence in public affairs for the first time and were no longer so tightly constrained. To be a writer in the age of the printing press meant that one had a platform for new and provocative ideas, ideas that might challenge conventional norms and established institutions. From this vantage point, it is no surprise that an association between radical ideas and men (occasionally women) of letters arose in the early modern era.

Many of the revolutions and reform movements of the modern era – including the American Revolution, the French Revolution, the Chartist movement, the revolutions of 1848, the Paris Commune, the Russian Revolution, and virtually every nationalist and independence movement – were led by

---

[5] In light of these challenges, some anticipate a major shake-up in which students and policymakers pursue cheaper alternatives for advanced training such as massive open online courses (MOOCs) (Carey 2016; Collins and Halverson 2018; Kamenetz 2010). Thus far, MOOCs have served as a supplement to rather than a replacement of traditional college education. But we cannot predict what the future might hold.

writers and thinkers. These movements were *intellectual*, not just social or political.[6]

Yet, radical ideas emanating from the eighteenth and nineteenth centuries were not, as a rule, propounded by university professors. Many leading intellectuals including Ben Franklin and Thomas Paine were not even university educated. Others, though university educated, did not have academic positions. This describes people like Charles Fourier, Karl Marx, and Pierre-Joseph Proudhon, who were denizens of the library but not of the university. Indeed, it is difficult to imagine the radical ideologies of the day – anarchism, socialism, communism, and other "-isms" – arising from a university context. Nor did these ideas have much of a following among university faculty or students.

In the twentieth century, all this would change. Several turning points in this history deserve mention (Jennings and Kemp-Welch 1997). The first is the Dreyfus affair in France (1894–1906), which galvanized the intellectual class and was instrumental in establishing the concept of the intellectual throughout the Anglo-European world (Charle 2015; Drake 2005). The second is composed of the intertwined events of World War I and the Russian Revolution, after which many intellectuals turned away from nationalist ideals and toward a more cosmopolitan and/or socialist vision of society (Stern 2006). The third is the Great Depression, which seemed to augur the dying days of capitalism and offered another spur for radical organizing (Cohen 1993). The fourth is the expansion of universities during the postwar era, leading to a mass constituency of students and a more differentiated organizational structure (Schofer and Meyer 2005). The fifth is the 1960s, which highlighted the Vietnam War and the more general problem of US imperialism amidst a general cultural and political awakening (De Groot 1998; Fink, Gasset, and Junker 1998; Horn 2007; Jian et al. 2018). The sixth is the advent of multiculturalism, LGBQTY rights, and other forms of what is sometimes known as "identity politics" (Fukuyama 2018) or the "cultural left" (Rorty 1998).

Throughout the twentieth century, intellectuals appeared at the forefront of movements for independence, self-determination, liberty, democracy, and equality (in the sense of equal rights). But what was their role overall? Evidently, not all intellectuals were situated on the liberal left.

As a first pass at measurement, we employ the Google Books database to examine the citation trajectory of two intellectuals who embody what are perhaps the most influential traditions on the left. Karl Marx (1818–83) is the generally acknowledged point of departure for modern socialist and communist movements, as well as for intellectual work focused on social class, revolution,

---

[6] On intellectuals and popular politics, see Baud and Rutten (2004), Beecher (2021), Lipset (1967: 10–12), and Pipes (1961).

and capitalism.[7] Michel Foucault (1926–1984) is probably the most widely cited intellectual figure on the cultural or post-structuralist left.

Figure 7.6 shows the prominence of these two progenitors in published work over the past century and a half. Marx, it seems, had little resonance for writers in the nineteenth century. But his fortunes picked up in the twentieth century, reaching a peak around 1980, after which a marked decline is visible. Foucault gained traction in his own lifetime and his popularity has increased in a fairly steady fashion in subsequent decades. Today, he is cited almost half as often as Marx, which is remarkable given that there are no political parties, governments, or social movements bearing his philosophy.

By way of contrast, influential intellectuals with a less radical profile such as Adam Smith, Émile Durkheim, and Max Weber have not attracted increased support in the course of the past century. Their trend lines, had we bothered to show them in Figure 7.6, would be flat.

To obtain a more comprehensive view of intellectual currents, we assemble a database of prominent Western intellectuals who lived from the mid-seventeenth century to the present. "Western" is understood loosely to refer to the world of letters articulated in European languages. This does not mean that intellectuals are only counted if they emanated from the West; it means that their fame must have reverberated in the West (as in the cases of Mao or Gandhi).

We consider an individual to be prominent if they appear in a historical biography or encyclopedia with a broad purview (not one limited to a single country). We consider that their fame is at least partly intellectual if they are known for their ideas or their publications, though they may also hold a formal position of power. Thomas Jefferson was a prominent intellectual in addition to serving as the third president of the US. George Washington, although more famous, was not famous for his words or ideas and hence is not included in our sample.

Four hundred and thirty-one individuals meet these loose criteria. We cannot pretend that this is an authoritative list. Additional names could surely be added and some might be subtracted, depending upon how strictly one interprets the foregoing criteria. It is in any case the only such database that we are aware of, and good enough for present purposes.[8]

Our goal is to ascertain the academic position and general political leanings of these individuals. If an intellectual held a university appointment for most of their career, they are coded as faculty. Political leanings

---

[7] Victor Brombert (1961: 139) remarks, "no single ideology or spiritual force in the twentieth century has come close to rivalling the prestige of Marxism among European intellectuals." Similar statements could be made for other regions of the world.

[8] Collins (1998) compiles a similar list of intellectuals from earlier historical eras.

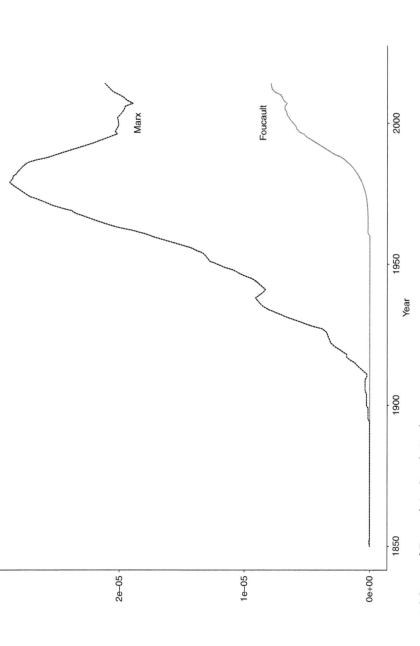

FIGURE 7.6 Marx and Foucault in Google Books
The relative frequency of "Marx" (and variants) and "Foucault" as a fraction of all phrases published (in English) within a given year, averaged across a three-year moving window. Data provided by Google Ngram (Michel et al. 2011).

are coded on a three-point scale: (1) conservative or right wing, (2) centrist or non-political, or (3) liberal, left, or radical. These matters are understood relative to the tenor of politics in their part of the world during their lifetime. For this, we consider the issue(s) for which each individual was most well known, leaving aside their views on other subjects. (Mao's intellectual contribution was to communism; his views on the family are less well known and therefore less relevant for present purposes.)

Importantly, our coding conflates liberal, left, and radical. Some of the individuals coded in this generic category were not liberals in the sense in which we defined the term (in Chapter 1). For example, they may have compromised liberty and democracy for other goals. Some gave priority to economic equality, which falls outside our understanding of liberalism. And yet, most of these intellectual movements could be characterized as *more liberal than the status quo*. In this sense they qualify as avatars of liberalism.

Results from these codings are plotted through time from 1700 to the present in Figure 7.7. (Centrists and those without a clear ideological affiliation are omitted.) This assessment suggests that intellectuals have been liberal/left of center throughout the modern era, an ideological leaning that becomes more marked through time, though it seems to have stabilized over the past half-century.

An even more dramatic change is noticeable in the occupation of intellectuals. Prior to the twentieth century, most did not hold university positions. Beginning in the mid-nineteenth century, however, they begin to migrate into faculty jobs. At present, 80–90 percent of all those identified as intellectuals work in a university setting or have done so for a significant portion of their lives. Intellectual activity has been professionalized. The age of the gentleman intellectual (e.g., Thomas Jefferson) or activist intellectual (e.g., Karl Marx) is seemingly waning. To be sure, intellectuals still engage in politics; but those who do so often hold a day-job as a professor.

This trend speaks to the long-term politicization of the university. While the nineteenth-century university may have qualified as an ivory tower, our data suggests that this is no longer the case. Prominent public intellectuals, most of whom are left-liberal in orientation, address the world from lecture podiums.

FACULTY

Having surveyed the movement of intellectuals into college faculty, we now zoom in to take a closer look at the social and political attitudes of this professional class.

Over the years, a number of surveys have been conducted of professors (faculty) or academics (including scholarly researchers who may or may not be employed at teaching universities). However, many are limited to a single

FIGURE 7.7 Ideologies and pedigrees of Western intellectuals
Western intellectuals (N=431). In each year, percentages are calculated based on all intellectuals over the age of nineteen. Liberal embraces those whose politics are liberal, left, or radical. Conservative embraces those whose politics are right wing. Centrists and those without a clear ideological orientation are omitted (Benewick and Green 1998; Claeys 2004; Sheldon 2001; https://en.wikipedia.org/wiki/List_of_intellectuals_of_the_Enlightenment).

university or a single discipline. Others do not include a clear comparison between the views of academics and the views of the general public, making it difficult to reach firm conclusions.[9] These surveys seem to indicate that

---

[9] Where the same question is asked in surveys of the general population, or where the outcome is voting behavior, it is easy enough to compare faculty to the general population. But where the question is more specific, or there is no comparable general population survey, one must speculate.

professors are fairly liberal, but since there is no explicit comparison group, it is difficult to say for sure.[10]

Our review is limited to published studies (no working papers) whose scope extends beyond a single university or discipline and where there is an explicit contrast with some non-university reference group. We are able to locate only fifteen studies that meet all of these criteria, as shown in Table 7.1. There, we list the study, the year(s) in which the survey or surveys were administered, the target of the survey (faculty or academics), and the comparison group (e.g., the general public), as well as the general topic or topics (e.g., income inequality or party affiliation). Where a single study undertakes multiple topics that yield different findings, they are listed on separate rows. The final column indicates the finding; that is, whether faculty or academics are more (↑) or less (↓) liberal than the comparison group. If the findings are mixed or the differences are trivial, this is registered as a null effect. ("Liberal" is defined as it is elsewhere in this book, which means that liberals are critical of redistribution and the welfare state.)

Most of these studies focus on the US or the UK. Other countries are neglected, though a wide range of European countries are included in van de Worfhorst (2020). The International Social Survey (Brooks 2014) covers nineteen countries, most of which are in Europe and none of which are in the developing world.[11] Although it seems likely that systematic surveys exist in other countries, all the studies we have been able to unearth are centered on the Organisation for Economic Co-operation and Development (OECD).

Most studies were conducted over the past several decades. Only a few stretch back prior to 1970 and only one prior to 1940. All of these early studies are located in the US. The earliest, conducted in 1936 (Kornhauser 1938), was limited to a single city and is of dubious quality since techniques of random sampling were not well developed at the time.

Most studies center on overall ideology (judged on a left–right spectrum) or party affiliation, with academics shown to be generally to the left. The exception is a study of social scientists in Sweden, which show them leaning to the right (Berggren et al. 2007). Since this conflicts with most other studies, we need to understand why.

---

[10] See Cardiff and Klein (2005), Eitzen and Maranell (1968), Faia (1974, a meta-analysis), Gross and Simmons (2009), Hamilton and Hargens (1993), Kim (1978), Klein and Stern (2005a, 2005b), Klein and Western (2004–2005), Kuvvet (2021), La Falce and Gomez (2007), Langbert (2018), Langbert, Quain, and Klein (2016), Larregue (2018), Larson and Witham (1998), Lehman (1975), Lipset (1982), Lazarsfeld and Thielens (1958), Maranell and Eitzen (1970), Mariani and Hewitt (2008), Nakhaie and Brym (1999, 2011), Pritchard, Fen, and Buxton (1971), Schonberg (1974), Spaulding and Turner (1968), Smith, Mayer, and Fritschler (2008), Stolzenberg and colleagues (2019), Turner and Spaulding (1969), and Zipp and Fenwick (2006).

[11] International Social Survey Program (ISSP) covers Australia, Britain, Czechia, Denmark, France, Germany, Ireland, New Zealand, Norway, Poland, Portugal, Russia, Slovenia, Spain, Sweden, Switzerland, and the United States.

Berggren and colleagues' (2007) study is based on a coding based on party coalitions. From 2006 to 2014, Sweden was governed by a coalition of center-right parties that called themselves "the Alliance for Sweden." Most academics seem to have supported the Liberal Party ("fp"), probably the most left-leaning party inside the Alliance. As such, Swedish academics could be said to support the most left-leaning party inside a right-leaning coalition. With this important caveat, it is correct to say that the Liberal Party – the party that attracts the vote of many Swedish academics – has been in opposition to Social Democratic governments, the dominant party of the left.[12] In this respect, Sweden is different from most other countries represented in Table 7.1, where academics generally adhere to the left-wing party or coalition.

On issues of income inequality and redistribution (including support for the welfare state), two studies find academics to the right of the general public (which is to say, adopting a more "liberal" policy) and one study (Brooks 2014) finds the reverse. On other issues – religiosity/secularism, foreign policy, civil liberties, and cultural issues – academics are almost uniformly more liberal. However, relatively few studies address these issues, so one must tread carefully in search of a conclusion.

Time-Series Data

The studies reviewed in Table 7.1 are focused on different populations and different outcomes. Accordingly, it is difficult to construct a vision of how patterns have changed – or not – over time.

In the sections that follow, we attempt to construct time-series data that allows us a peek into this crucial question. Have faculty always been to the left of center? Have they moved further in this direction in recent years?

Four national surveys shed light on the political affiliations of British academics in the contemporary era, beginning in 1964 (Carl 2017: 5). To summarize the data in a useful fashion, we calculate their support for the Conservative Party, the main party on the right, which is compared with support for the party in the general electorate (as revealed in national elections occurring near the time of the survey).

Figure 7.8 shows that, relative to the general electorate, academics were already somewhat less inclined to support the Tories in the 1960s. Later, during the Thatcher years, they moved much further away, embracing a variety of alternatives on the liberal left including Labour, Liberal/Liberal Democrat/Social Democratic Party, Greens, and other smaller (mostly regional) parties. Today, support among British academics for the Tories falls roughly twenty-five points below Tory support in the general electorate.

Another angle on the changing party affiliations of academics is provided by financial contributions to political campaigns. The US offers a finely grained picture

---

[12] We are indebted to Jan Teorell for this explication.

TABLE 7.1 *Surveys of university faculty*

Study	Year(s)	Target and reference group	Topic	Finding
UNITED STATES				
Kornhauser (1938)	1936	600 citizens of Chicago, including academics and nonacademics	Income inequality, New Deal	↓
Howard (1958)	1956	Faculty at 47 colleges compared to surveys of the general public	Party affiliation	↑
Bayer (1970); Ladd and Lipset (2001)	1969	Faculty at 2,433 colleges compared to surveys of the general public	Party affiliation, left–right placement, foreign policy, culture	↑
Gross and Fosse (2012)	1974–2008	326 professors culled from multiple waves of a national survey (General Social Survey, GSS) with a total of 44,029 respondents	Left–right ideology; secularism	↑
Gross and Fosse (2012)	2006	1,471 professors compared to surveys of the general public	Ideology et al.	↑
Rothman et al. (2005)	1999	1,643 faculty at 183 universities compared to surveys of the general public	Left–right placement	↑
FRANCE				
Francois et al. (2016)	2011	2,000 academics compared to surveys of the general public	Left–right ideology, secularism	↑

(*continued*)

TABLE 7.1 (continued)

Study	Year(s)	Target and reference group	Topic	Finding
UNITED KINGDOM				
Halsey (1992: ch. 11)	1976, 1989	4,737 faculty and non-faculty staff in universities and polytechnics	Left–right placement, party support	Ø
Halsey and Trow (1971)		1,397 faculty compared to surveys of the general public	Interest in politics	↑
			Religiosity	Ø
Carl (2017)	2015	General survey including some academics	Party affiliation	↑
Carl (2018)	2015	22,444 citizens including some academics	Left–right scale derived from multiple measures	↑
SWEDEN				
Berggren et al. (2007)	2006	1,512 social scientists compared with surveys of the general public	Party identity/sympathies, left–right placement, public opinion	→
AUSTRALIA				
Etzioni-Halevy (1986)		Academics compared with surveys of the general public	Left–right placement	↑
EUROPE				
van de Werfhorst (2020)	2012	Academics compared with other professionals as part of survey of 234,306 professionals	Left–right ideology; immigration; European integration	↑
			Income equality	→
OECD				
Brooks (2014)	1993–2008	International Social Survey Program (ISSP) includes faculty and the general public	Civil liberties, gender equality, homosexuality tolerance, church/state separation, welfare state	↑

Finding: relative to the comparison group, the surveyed faculty or academics are more liberal (↑), less liberal (↓), or indistinguishable (Ø).

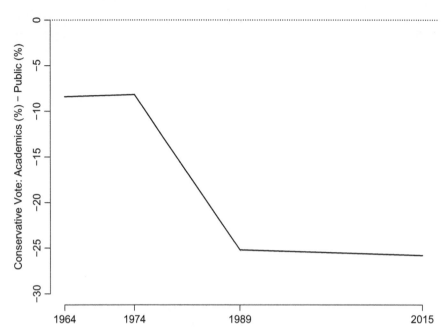

FIGURE 7.8 Party affiliations of British academics
Party affiliations of British academics, judged by their support of the Conservative Party (from Carl 2017: 5) relative to that party's support in the general electorate (from national election results).

of donations since the 1970s, when the Federal Elections Commission began collecting data (per statutory directive). Although the time-series is relatively short, Figure 7.9 shows a sharp increase in leftward preferences over the past several decades. It is worth noting that while all professional groups have trended left, academics are among the most left-leaning at the present time (Bonica 2016).

Of course, one should bear in mind that making a financial contribution to a political campaign is not an activity that everyone engages in. One can suppose that only those professionals who are deeply engaged in politics are likely to do so on a regular basis. Even so, there is apt to be a correlation between changes at the extreme and changes at the center. Moreover, those who are most engaged are likely to set the political tone on college campuses across the country, so their views are of special relevance to our quest to understand the impact of university attendance on social and political attitudes.

STUDENT ACTIVISTS

Having looked at intellectuals and academics, we turn our attention to students.

In the premodern era, the experience of attending a university was scarcely conducive to moral or political awakening. For most students, their period of

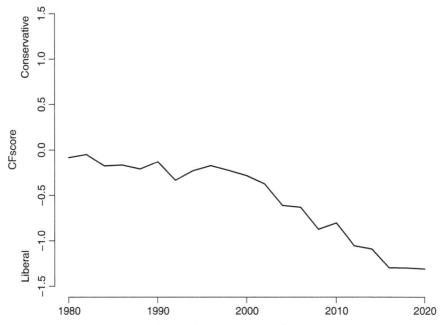

FIGURE 7.9 Campaign contributions by American academics
Average CFscore of candidate positions among contributions by contributors employed by universities (Bonica 2016).

study was akin to an apprenticeship; they had a narrowly vocational view of their training and what it could do for them. For others who came from aristocratic backgrounds and cared less about learning or degrees, there was plenty of time for entertainment – drinking, brawling, sports, and amorous exploits. Neither type of student was especially motivated to question the status quo.

We do not mean to imply that students were passive receptacles. Indeed, they were often in conflict with their nominal masters (professors), with townspeople (the perennial town versus gown strife), and with each other (Boren 2001; Dhondt and Boran 2017). However, these conflicts were highly localized. They concerned issues of lodging, rules of decorum, parietal rules, the curriculum, the assignment of grades and diplomas, and the defense of university rights and privileges. These sorts of localized conflicts persist in the twentieth century. Indeed, an instigating factor in the reform movement at the University of Córdoba in 1918 was the closing of a student dormitory (Liebman, Walker, and Glazer 1972: 9). An instigating factor in *les événements* at the Nanterre campus of the University of Paris in 1967–8 was the regulation of night-time visits between male and female students. Yet, in the twentieth century local conflicts spiraled into national – sometimes international – conflicts. There is little sign of this in the premodern era.

Cobban (1975: 164–5) offers this summation of the political engagements of a student in a European university in the Middle Ages.

Doubtless the medieval student would speculate on the structure of society; he would debate the main theological and political issues of his day and he would have the opportunity to attend the magisterial disputations on matters of public concern; he would criticize the established order of things; but, while at university, he would have little interest in changing the world in which he lived. The overriding student consideration was to become part of the established social pattern. In his later career, the graduate's skills might be employed, for example, in the propagandist warfare of ideological conflict in the papal, imperial or royal service. To this extent, the university student might eventually be involved in movements which promoted adjustments within the social order. But, at the university phase, the student's world was geared to conservative modes of thought.

This apolitical experience began to change in the nineteenth century, prompted by the rise of student associations. Beginning in Germany (as noted earlier), the organizational craze spread.

Sweden had its Verdandi (begun in 1882), a student society dedicated to radical liberalism, as well as its Heimdal (founded in 1891), an association seeking to preserve Swedish student conservatism and tradition. In France the first apolitical secular organization, the Association Generale des Etudiants, formed in 1877, and by 1900 every university town in France boasted at least one chapter. And Great Britain saw the birth of the Students' Representative Council, organized in 1884 at Edinburgh. All over Europe, students joined organizations – some political in nature, others expressly apolitical, and many of these organizations joined forces to form associations of organizations, so that by the twentieth century European universities were the sites of complex networks of interrelated student groups. (Boren 2001: 42–43)

According to Gevers and Vox (2004: 272), "Poland in 1793, after the second Polish partition, provided the first example of students as a group putting themselves at the service of the national community, and whose calling was adopted by following generations."

In Latin America, student participation in the affairs of the university and in national affairs has an especially long history, stretching back to the early nineteenth century. Richard Walter (1968: viii) summarizes:

The graduates of ... institutions of higher learning provided much of the intellectual, military, and political leadership during the Latin American Wars for Independence against Spain (1810–1825). A dozen years later, a group of young Argentine intellectuals, the "Generation of 1837," led the liberal movement which eventually overthrew the dictator Juan Manuel de Rosas in 1852. Although Brazil did not have a full-fledged university until the twentieth century, students from the law school in Sao Paulo composed much of the leadership for the campaigns which abolished slavery (1888) and replaced the empire with a republic (1889). Venezuela's university youth formed one of the principal groups opposing and, finally, bringing to an end the dictatorship of Antonio Guzman Blanco (1888).

Around the turn of the twentieth century, university life and various currents of radicalism came together in a concerted fashion for the first time. This is shown by general studies of student movements and intellectuals[13] and by regional studies focused on Europe (Klemenčič, Bergan, and Primočič 2015), Latin America (Levy 1991), Asia (Weiss and Aspinall 2012), Africa (Zeilig 2007), and North America (Altbach 1989; Lipset and Altbach 1969).

By the end of the twentieth century the campus radical was an established trope. The hopes and dreams invested in this mythical figure are reflected in the words of the Córdoba Manifesto, often regarded as the opening knell of student activism in Latin America: "Youth is always surrounded by heroism. It is disinterested: it is pure. It has not yet had time to contaminate itself" (quoted in Liebman, Walker, and Glazer 1972: 34). The potential force of this social grouping is brought out by Samuel Huntington (1968: 290), who writes, "The city is the source of opposition within the country; the middle class is the focus of opposition within the city; the intelligentsia is the most active oppositional group within the middle class; and the students are the most coherent and effective revolutionaries within the intelligentsia." Whether students will ever fulfill their revolutionary potential remains to be seen. But it is clear that they have played a substantial role in politics in the twentieth century.

During this century, student organizations became international, though these bodies were intermittent and never played a major role in student movements (Altbach and Uphoff 1973). In the twenty-first century, students find each other online. It is worth recalling that Facebook, the world's largest social network, was born as a medium for Harvard University students to interact with each other. Now, online sites are international, and since most students around the world are conversant in English, there are few barriers to communication. Adegbuyi (2021) reports on a new phenomenon he calls the "study web."

The Study Web is a constellation of digital spaces and online communities – across YouTube, TikTok, Reddit, Discord, and Twitter – largely built by students for students. Videos under the #StudyTok hashtag have been viewed over half a billion times. One Discord server, *Study Together*, has over 120 thousand members. Study Web extends far past study groups composed of classmates, institution specific associations, or poorly designed retro forums discussing entrance requirements for professional programs. It includes but transcends Studyblrs on Tumblr that emerged in 2014 and eclipses various Reddit and Facebook study groups or inspirational images shared across Pinterest and Instagram. Populated mostly by Gen Z and the youngest of millennials, Study Web is the

---

[13] See Altbach (1997, 2007), Bessant, Mesinas, and Pickard (2021a, 2021b), Boren (2001), Brooks (2016), DeConde (1971), Emmerson (1968), Habermas (1971), and Klemenčič (2014).

internet most of us don't see, and it's become a lifeline for students from junior high to college.

So far, the use of this new tool seems mostly geared toward professional and personal goals. However, it is easy to imagine that it might also become a tool for political discussion and organization. After all, students are one of the largest international communities with a shared identity and (arguably) common interests.

Student Protest in the US

To gain a more comprehensive view of student activism in the US, we draw on a study conducted by Nella van Dyke (2003). Van Dyke focuses on protests occurring on nine college campuses in the US, which are recorded from student newspaper archives for each college from 1900 to 1990. The results are displayed in Figure 7.10.

By this account, student movements/protests experienced a small peak in the 1930s and a much higher peak in the 1960s and 1970s, declining thereafter but remaining far above previous levels. Of 2,700 protest events in her database,

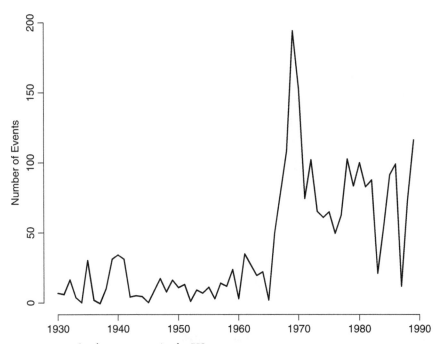

FIGURE 7.10 Student protests in the US
Number of university protests (coalition or non-coalition) on nine US college campuses (van Dyke 2003: 235, figure 1).

van Dyke (1999) reports that only 56 were initiated by right-wing activists. This confirms our sense that left-wing activists are generally more active than right-wing activists. (Exceptions must be made for countries with strong fascist movements such as Italy and Germany during the interwar period.)

In earlier work, van Dyke (1999) breaks down the action by decade. In the 1930s, colleges in her database were absorbed with antiwar activities. In the 1940s, opposition to war continued along with agitation for civil rights. In the 1950s, protests centered on the McCarthy proceedings and the anti-communist witch hunt. In the 1960s, students turned to disarmament, opposition to war, and civil rights. In the 1970s, peace activities were accompanied by movements for women's rights, against nuclear power, and against the Apartheid regime in South Africa. In the 1980s, these causes were joined by protests against US involvement in Central America and for (and occasionally against) abortion rights. Through it all, students were motivated by issues associated with university organization and campus life.

Student Movements in Latin America

Patterns are apt to be different outside the Anglo-European world. Latin America, in particular, has a long and boisterous history of student protest. This is captured in Imanol Ordorika's (2021) coding of student movements across the continent in the twentieth century, reproduced in Figure 7.11.

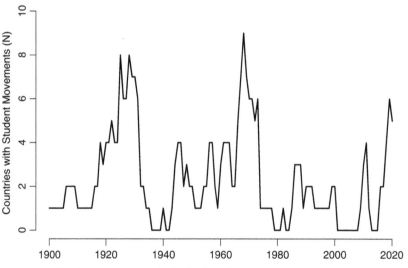

FIGURE 7.11 Student movements in Latin America
Number of countries in Latin America with student movements (Ordorika 2021); see also Ordorika, Rodríguez-Gómez, and Antón (2019).

Ordorika describes the late nineteenth and early twentieth centuries as fairly quiet. From 1918 to 1935 he marks the first wave of university reform movements, beginning with the landmark Córdoba Reform. This is coupled with protests against US imperialism. From 1940 to 1963, students engaged in further protests centered on university reform as well as protests aimed at challenging authoritarian governments and defending democracy. From 1960 to 1978, protests centered on the ideals of democracy and/or radical (often socialist) transformations of society. From 1985 to the present, protests have been mounted against structural adjustment policies ("neoliberalism") and tuition increases, as well as in defense of democratic institutions. Of course, these are just the major trends; many protests are focused on issues specific to a particular country or time-period.

Discussion

None of our historical sources tell us *how many* students (and faculty) participated in student movements and protests. A few belligerents can make the headlines of a newspaper and become an entry in a book; this does not mean that their less adventurous colleagues shared their views. Typically, those who are intensely engaged in politics constitute a small minority; this is true in universities (Soares 1967a) as well as in society at large (Verba, Schlozman, and Brady 1995). What we can reasonably infer is that *some* students participated in these movements. So long as sampling biases are constant over time, the trends manifested in the foregoing figures should be interpretable.

In any case, extremists (we use this term in a non-judgmental fashion) were an important part of the campus experience for many students. Being a student at a college campus in the 1930s meant coming into contact with communist classmates and Marxist ideas, for example. This is bound to have had some impact on the average student and possibly also on the faculty. It may have prompted discussions about social equality, democracy, and capitalism. Perhaps it shifted some opinions to the left. If so, the tails of the distribution are indicative of the center of the distribution. In this sense, it is informative to track the history of campus activism.

Acknowledged, the left-wing movements that received support from some faculty and students through the twentieth century were *illiberal* in many respects. The Bolshevik Revolution, the Chinese Revolution, the Cuban Revolution, the Sandinista Revolution, and other less successful attempts to revolutionize society along Marxist lines did not inaugurate liberal democracies. However, the vision of these movements that was popular in university circles tended to emphasize their popular and democratic nature. Once these movements gained power, clamping down on opposition forces and establishing one-party states, they usually lost support in university circles.

As an example, one might consider the college craze for the Nicaraguan Sandinista movement. Their popularity was evident everywhere in the Americas during the 1970s and 1980s, a point when they seemed to represent change in a democratic direction – at the very least, a shift from the autocracy of the Somoza regime. In later years, as the Sandinista National Liberation Front (FSLN) clamped down on opposition parties and rigged elections, they lost their status as a cause célèbre. Sandino t-shirts no longer adorn students lounging in cafes. Here, as for many other causes – the Spanish Civil War, the Cuban Revolution, the Vietnam War – it seems reasonable to regard campus support for radical leftist causes as embodying a liberal impulse.

UNIVERSITY CONSTITUENCIES

In this section, we focus attention on university constituencies. This might refer to a constituency reserved for graduates of a particular university, a constituency containing a university (and hence including many students, faculty, and former students), or students currently attending a university. As elsewhere in this chapter, we have been opportunistic in our selection of data and sources, drawing sustenance wherever we can.

University Constituencies in the UK

In 1603, two constituencies, focused respectively on the universities of Oxford and Cambridge, were introduced in England. Much later, similar constituencies were added for other universities across the British Isles, as shown in Table 7.2.

TABLE 7.2 *University constituencies in the UK*

University	Number of MPs	Years
Cambridge	2	1603–1950
Oxford	2	1603–1950
Dublin	1 (1801–1832), 2 (1832–1922)	1801–1922
Edinburgh and St. Andrews	1	1868–1918
Glasgow and Aberdeen	1	1868–1918
London	1	1868–1950
Combined English universities	2	1918–1950
Combined Scottish universities	3	1918–1950
National University of Ireland	1	1918–1922
Queen's University of Belfast	1	1918–1950
University of Wales	1	1918–1950

Source: Humberstone (1951).

All such constituencies were abolished by the middle of the twentieth century. (They persisted in the Irish upper house but most members of parliament (MPs) were elected as independents, offering little grist for our mill.)

A university constituency was unique because it was not geographically defined. Its constituents included all those who graduated from a particular university, regardless of where they happened to live. Graduates of these universities thus possessed two votes: one in their university constituency and another in their residential constituency. In some respects, this makes the university constituency even more suited to our purposes; it is the closest thing to an actual survey of university graduates in periods prior to the existence of such surveys.

Thanks to the labors of Lloyd Humberstone (1951), we know the identities of the individuals who were selected to represent these constituencies and a bit about them, including their factional or party identity (if any). Our dataset covers the years 1603–1951, marking the creation and abolition of university constituencies. Within this timespan, 194 individuals were elected to serve university constituencies in the British House of Commons, several of whom served non-consecutive terms.

For simplicity, these university MPs are classified into three groups: (a) Independent (including those explicitly identified as Independent as well as those without a clear factional or party identification), Tory/Conservative (including Unionists of all stripes and National Labour), and Whig/Liberal. This reflects their faction/party identity at the point of their election, as best as can be determined. The share of university MPs falling into each of these categories over time is displayed in Figure 7.12. Trends are smoothed, so readers should not imagine that historical transitions are precisely marked in this figure. Now, let us try to make sense of these trends.

Originally, campaigns for parliament were mostly local in character and scarcely coordinated. Accordingly, candidates campaigned on their own, running as "independents" (as we would now say). In the early years, university MPs would be difficult to distinguish from other MPs as none had a very clear or consistent factional identity. Nearly all MPs were nonpartisan at the outset, as shown in Figure 7.12.

Beginning in the eighteenth century, factions known as Tories and Whigs arose, which meant somewhat different things in different eras. The Tory faction was originally sympathetic to the Catholic cause, and in particular to those who supported the right of James I to the throne ("Jacobites"). Later, Tories identified as Anglicans and with the squirearchy, and were generally regarded as royalists; that is, supporters of the government appointed by the king or queen. Whigs, by contrast, were more supportive of non-conformists (including Scottish Presbyterians), originally opposed to James. By the end of the eighteenth century, one might say that the Tory Party, under William Pitt the Younger, represented the gentry and other groups closely allied with the crown. The Whig Party, under Charles James Fox, represented dissenters,

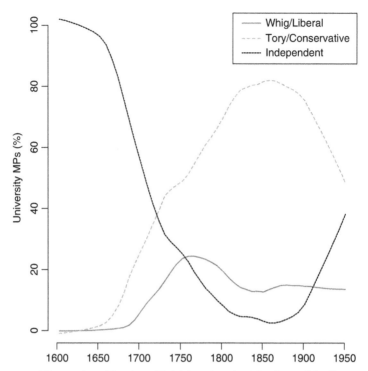

FIGURE 7.12 The partisan identity of British university Members of Parliament
Partisanship of MPs from university constituencies in Britain, smoothed lines
(Humberstone 1951, supplemented by Wikipedia entries). Percentages are smoothed
over time using loess.

industrialists, and reformers of various stripes. Figure 7.12 reflects how the
share of university MPs changed as British politics transitioned from an era of
independents to an era of factional conflict.

By the end of the nineteenth century, Whig and Tory factions were replaced
by Liberal and Conservative parties, with national party programs, national
campaigning, and strong party discipline. And around the turn of the century,
the Labour Party became a challenger, eventually supplanting the Liberals as
the second major party. This history is doubtless familiar to most readers so it
need not be rehearsed. In coding Tories with Conservatives and Whigs with
Liberals, we do not mean to suggest that these distinctions are meaningless. This
is merely an acknowledgment that the terms were used synonymously for
a number of years in the late nineteenth century.

Throughout the age of factional and party conflict, Tory/Conservatives
outnumbered Whig/Liberals among the university delegations in the House of
Commons. This is clearly illustrated in Figure 7.12. That said, university MPs
were not exactly party hacks. Indeed, by the mid-twentieth century university

MPs established a reputation as independents who resisted the growing power of political parties (Rex 1946). This can be seen in the upswing among university independents during the last years of our period.

Some university MPs were quite radical in their own (nonpartisan) ways. Eleanor Rathbone, one of the representatives for the combined English universities from 1929 to 1946, campaigned for a family allowance and for women's rights. George Maitland Lloyd won office in 1923 from the University of Wales constituency as an Independent Christian Pacifist, after which he caucused with the Labour Party. Ramsay MacDonald, one of the founders of the Labour Party and the first Labour MP, won election from the combined English universities district in the by-election of 1937. However, by this point he had been expelled from the Labour Party by virtue of his participation in the Conservative-dominated governments of the interwar period. Consequently, he campaigned as a member of the National Labour Party, a splinter group that struggled to distinguish itself from the Tories and dissolved after World War II.

Strikingly, no Labour Party candidates were selected from any university constituency, even though the Labour Party was improving its standing in the national polls through the early twentieth century and gained a national majority in 1945. One must bear in mind that the Labour Party's constituency was almost entirely working class at a time when very few members of the working class could gain entrance to university (or would even contemplate applying). Although some university MPs were on the left, they were not on the Labour left. Regrettably (for our purposes), university constituencies were abolished in 1948 so we cannot use this source to track the evolution of opinion among university graduates after mid-century.

British Constituencies with a University

Another approach to discerning university attitudes extends closer to the present and thus allows a peek into the evolution of opinions in the late twentieth century. Here, we compare geographically based constituencies that possess a university with those that do not. (University constituencies, which have no geographic boundaries, are excluded.)

This is possible because of painstaking work conducted by Danny Dorling (2012), who has reconstructed voting behavior in UK constituencies back to the first Reform bill. This involves matching constituencies as they existed in 1997 with constituencies as they existed in the past, taking into account myriad redistrictings. To do so, votes are reallocated from neighboring constituencies to get a sense of how those who lived in the territory of a 1997 constituency voted in each previous election. Although some assumptions are involved in this process, it is the only way in which we can approach British constituencies as consistent units through time.

Our question of interest concerns those constituencies that happen to contain a university. We draw this list from Apfeld (2019), which marks

FIGURE 7.13 Ideology of British constituencies with a university, 1900–1997
Conservative vote share (%) in British constituencies (excluding Northern Ireland) with
at least one university *minus* Conservative vote share in other constituencies within the
same NUTS region, averaged across all NUTS regions in each election from 1900 to 1997
(Dorling 2012).

the year in which each university was founded and its location. To
compare these constituencies with others (that do not contain a university),
we examine votes for the Conservative Party, the dominant party in modern
British politics and the party that has largely defined ideological conservativism
for the British electorate. Comparisons are drawn within a NUTS
(Nomenclature of Territorial Units for Statistics) region, and then averaged
across all NUTS regions, to provide a single point for each general election
from 1900 to 1997.[14]

A clear trend is visible across the twentieth century in Figure 7.13. Over time,
university constituencies have become markedly less inclined to support
Conservative candidates. The trend-line since 1960 is especially strong.

Cornell University

Universities have never enjoyed special reserved constituencies in the US.
However, there are constituencies where a single university dominates the

---

[14] Prior to that, the nature of party competition, and the scarcity of universities, make interpretation difficult.

electorate. Here, the electorate is assumed to include faculty, students and former students, university staff, family members of the former groups, and industries closely associated with university life and dependent on university patronage. We shall assume that there are shared political perspectives across these closely linked constituencies.

One such community is Ithaca, New York, home of Cornell University. To ascertain the voting behavior of Cornell-affiliated voters, Delphia Shanks, Isabelle Mireille Aboaf, and Richard Bensel gathered data from archives maintained by the Tompkins County Board of Elections. In a few instances where those archives were incomplete, election returns were taken from the archive of the *Ithaca Journal* and, in one instance where neither source could provide information, they used publicly available county returns. The Cornell community is defined as those who voted in precincts immediately adjoining the Cornell campus. In most cases, precinct boundaries were readily available. In a few cases, ward data (ordinarily containing more than one precinct) was substituted. Shanks, Aboaf, and Bensel note that their definition of the "Cornell community" does not take into account historical changes in the city of Ithaca and Cornell University. They suspect, for example, that the proportion of all Cornell-affiliated voters residing in chosen precincts was somewhat higher in earlier periods because housing for students, faculty, and staff has spread out to areas more distant from campus, hence outside the chosen precincts. With these caveats, we are able to compare the voting behavior of the Cornell University community with that of the general public in presidential elections from 1868 to the present, as shown in Figure 7.14.

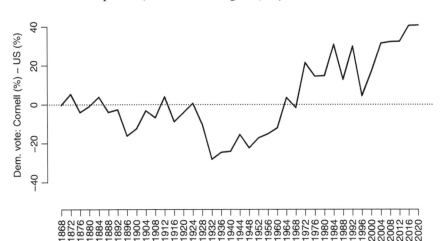

FIGURE 7.14 Cornell University community voting preferences
Share of Cornell University community that cast ballots for the Democratic presidential candidate minus the share of the US electorate that cast ballots for the Democratic presidential candidate. Data gathered and analyzed by Delphia Shanks, Isabelle Mireille Aboaf, and Richard Bensel, and generously provided to the authors.

Through the nineteenth and early twentieth centuries, it will be seen that this community's voting behavior mimicked the general public fairly closely, though it was slightly more Republican in most years as one might expect for a northern region of the US. During the Great Depression and the early postwar decades, Cornell moves solidly into the Republican camp, registering resounding tallies against Franklin Roosevelt, Truman, Stevenson, and Kennedy. During the 1970s, Cornell is on the fence between the two parties. But in 1972 it registers a dramatic shift toward the Democratic Party. This jump in support surely owes something to the fact that this was the first year in which voters aged eighteen to twenty-one qualified for suffrage. It was also a peak year of campus activism surrounding the Vietnam War, and George McGovern (the Democratic candidate in that year) was known as the antiwar candidate. All of this may have boosted the performance of the Democratic Party in the Cornell community (relative to the national electorate, where the youth vote comprised a much smaller share of the total). However, it cannot explain the entire shift from the 1950s to the 1970s. Nor can it explain the subsequent increase in Democratic support registered over the past two elections, both of which featured Donald Trump at the top of the Republican ticket.

Harvard University

A different sort of evidence is provided by straw polls. Beginning in 1860, Harvard University conducted occasional informal surveys of its students during quadrennial presidential elections. Samples average about 2,700 per poll, though they are smaller in earlier years (as was the Harvard student body). Some elections were missed or the data was not preserved. Even so, enough of a time-series is available to suggest broader trends in the student body.

Granted, there is no pretense of sampling in these polls; respondents are self-selected. One may speculate as to the sort of bias this might introduce. One assumption is that majority opinion is overrepresented, as students with minority views may be shy about expressing them (we are not clear about the extent to which these polls respect the anonymity of participants). Another assumption is that self-selection overrepresents the opinions of those with stronger political commitments and (often) more extreme views.

Whatever sort of self-selection bias exists, we propose that this bias is likely to be constant through time. As such, long-term trends may be interpretable – with the caveat that we do not know exactly what sort of Harvard student is represented in the trend.

Figure 7.15 shows that respondents to the Harvard straw poll were less supportive of the Democratic Party in the landmark election of 1860, bespeaking Harvard's regional position as a northern ("Yankee") university. However, once the slavery issue receded from the public agenda, little difference

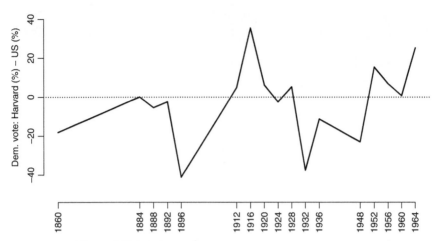

FIGURE 7.15 Harvard University students
Straw polls of Harvard undergraduates reported in back-issues of the *Harvard Crimson*. Results are calculated as the share of respondents who supported the Democratic candidate *minus* the share of voters across the US in that general election who supported the Democratic candidate.

can be found between the preferences of Harvard men and the general public in the closely fought elections of 1884–1892. During the realigning election of 1896, when William Jennings Bryan – the noted populist – captured the Democratic ticket, Harvard men abandoned the party to support the Republicans, understood as the party of order. Another switch is discernible during the Progressive era, when Harvard men plumped for Wilson's version of progressivism. However, during the 1930s and 1940s, when the Democratic Party was defined by the New Deal, Harvardians felt obliged to defend tradition against the perceived depredations of the state. It is not until the 1950s and 1960s that these straw polls show a shift toward the Democratic Party (relative to the general populace). If we had data from more recent straw polls, we suppose that this trend would be even more marked.

We conclude that Harvard students sat on the conservative side of the political spectrum until the late twentieth century, when everything shifted. This is mirrored in data from other American universities (see earlier) and in standard histories of Harvard University (Keller and Keller 2001).

Flagship University Counties in the US

To obtain a broader picture of our subject, we now shift our attention to college communities across the US. We do so by comparing the aggregate vote in counties where large "flagship" state universities are located with other counties in the same state. The outcome of interest is the difference between

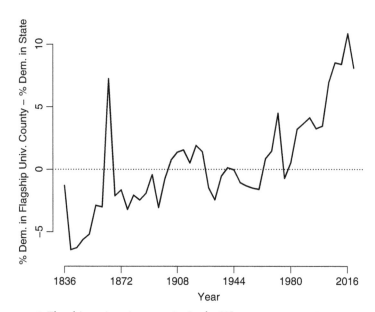

FIGURE 7.16 Flagship university counties in the US
Difference between county with flagship university and state-wide Democratic presidential vote, averaging all states. Data from Peter Nardulli and MIT Election Lab.

(a) the Democratic vote in the county containing a flagship university and (b) the Democratic vote in the state as a whole. These statistics are then averaged across all states to produce a country-level mean from 1836 to the present, as shown in Figure 7.16.[15]

One should bear in mind that the votes tabulated in counties with flagship universities are not primarily from students, most of whom could not vote prior to the passage of the 26th Amendment. However, we anticipate that a sizeable number of those casting ballots in these counties are students, former students, faculty, university staff, and persons directly tied to the university. We interpret this as the political environment that students encounter as they pursue their degree – a potentially important instrument of socialization.

Figure 7.16 demonstrates that through most of American history flagship university counties were less Democratic than the states they were situated in. Exceptions arose in 1864 and in the Progressive era. Beginning in the 1960s, this long-term pattern reversed. Now, flagship university counties are much more likely to support the Democratic candidate for president. In recent elections, the

---

[15] This is not an entirely balanced sample. States enter the sample when they are admitted to the union and when a flagship university is established. However, the trends exhibited in Figure 7.16 do not seem to be driven by the changing composition of the sample – whose composition is, in any case, fairly constant across the past century and a half.

Democratic vote in "flagship" counties is about 10 percent higher on average than in the rest of the state. This confirms the adage that college towns are liberal towns. Sometimes they are liberal oases, as in the case of Austin, Texas; Gainesville, Florida; Chapel Hill, North Carolina; Athens, Georgia; and Bloomington, Indiana.

UNIVERSITY GRADUATES

Leaving aside university constituencies, we may compare university graduates with those who did not obtain a university degree. This is consistent with the main causal question of the book, which asks whether university education affects social and political attitudes – though the data presented here is regarded as descriptive rather than causal (for reasons that will shortly become clear).

To do so, we draw on recent work by Thomas Piketty and collaborators (Gethin et al. 2022), who put together a unique dataset encompassing roughly 300 national elections in 21 Western democracies during the postwar era. Primary data sources are national election studies, supplemented (where necessary) by ad hoc surveys. For each election, the authors distinguish votes for parties on the left, understood as including socialist, social democratic, communist, and green parties. Using this dataset, we are able to compare the voting behavior of university graduates to those without university degrees.

Figure 7.17 demonstrates that over the past six decades a remarkable trend has been in motion. While highly educated voters once voted overwhelmingly for right and center parties, they are now more likely (by a small margin) to support left-wing parties. If one controls for background characteristics such as income, sex, and age, this trend-line shifts upward. Controlling for background factors, university graduates are *much* more likely to support parties on the left. The trends – both the raw descriptive trend shown in Figure 7.17 and the adjusted trend – are monotonic and virtually linear. For six decades, citizens with university degrees have been moving away from center and conservative parties and toward the left (broadly defined).

It is tempting to interpret this trend-line in a causal fashion. Previous sections of this chapter have established that universities have moved in a liberal-left direction over the course of the twentieth century; perhaps they have inculcated these values in their students.

However, it is important to bear in mind that party systems have also changed. New parties have formed and old parties have evolved. Generalizing broadly, one might say that the parties grouped together on the left end of the spectrum are more attentive to noneconomic, non-redistributive issues than they were a half-century ago. Likewise, the parties grouped together on the right end of the spectrum are less focused on economic issues and more on issues like immigration and nationalism, while many sport a populist ethos. In this light, it is no surprise that there is now a positive association between university education and support for left parties.

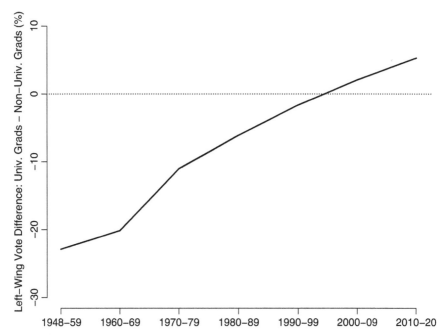

FIGURE 7.17 Partisanship and university education in the Organisation for Economic Co-operation and Development
The difference between the share of university graduates and non-university graduates voting for left-wing (socialist, social democratic, communist, and green) parties over time. Mean values across all countries in the (unbalanced) sample: Australia, Austria, Belgium, Britain, Canada, Denmark, Finland, France, Germany, Iceland, Ireland, Italy, Luxembourg, Netherlands, New Zealand, Norway, Portugal, Spain, Sweden, Switzerland, United States (Gethin, Martínez-Toledano, and Piketty 2022: appendix figure A7).

PROFESSORS, STUDENTS, FORMER STUDENTS,
AND THE GENERAL PUBLIC

In this section, we compare the views of key groups discussed throughout the chapter – university professors, university students, former students (the college-educated), and the general public.

The best way to do so is evidently with systematic surveys, many of which have been conducted over the years. Frustratingly, most do not include relevant comparisons across groups. They are focused on one group to the exclusion of others, leaving comparisons implicit.

A tantalizing example is Gillespie and Allport's (1955) survey of college students in ten countries – the US, New Zealand, South Africa, Egypt, Mexico, France, Italy, Germany, Japan, and Israel. This cross-national survey, undertaken in 1949–1951, inquires into attitudes about gender equality, racial equality, the family, nationalism, democracy, and other issues of direct concern to our own study. However, it is difficult to know what to make of the answers as they are not accompanied by surveys of the general public incorporating the same set of questions.[16]

Our review of extant surveys, limited to those that include explicit comparisons, is contained in Table 7.3. It will be seen that they are mixed in their findings. Three show university communities to be more liberal than the general public and four find no significant differences between the two groups.

The earliest of these studies reports on a poll taken during the 1924 presidential election. Here, the preferences of American college students mirrored those of the general electorate, as registered in the nationwide vote. Lipset (1972: 166) notes that since most college students in the 1920s came from well-to-do families, who generally voted Republican, this may have represented a shift to the left relative to their upbringing.

One of the first systematic surveys of college opinion in the US, conducted in the 1950s, focused on eleven campuses chosen to represent a range of college types: Cornell University, Dartmouth College, Fisk College, Harvard University, University of Michigan, University of North Carolina, University of Texas at Austin, University of California–Los Angeles, Wayne State, Wesleyan University, and Yale University (Goldsen et al. 1960). The authors found that partisanship correlated strongly with selectivity. Elite institutions such as Dartmouth, Yale, Wesleyan, and Cornell tilted toward the Republican Party while the less elite institutions tilted toward the Democrats. Across these campuses, the authors find "a remarkable absence of any intense or consuming political beliefs, interests or convictions on the part of the college students . . . [as well as] extreme political and economic conservatism" (Goldsen et al. 1960: 97). This conclusion, the authors note, is "in marked contrast to the radicalism usually attributed to American college students in the thirties, and said to be a traditional aspect of student culture in other countries."

One recent study, focused on the US, the UK, and Canada, finds a clear liberal tilt among students relative to the general publics in these countries (Kaufmann 2021). However, this study focuses on doctoral students, whose views are probably much more liberal than the average undergraduate (and whose numbers, as a share of the general population, are extremely small).

---

[16] There are a great many additional surveys of university communities – mostly in the US – that do not include explicit comparisons with the views of the general public. See the Allport (1929), Blau (1953), Boldt and Stroud (1934), Breemes and colleagues (1941), Bugelski and Lester (1940), Fay and Middleton (1940), Garrison and Mann (1931), Gilliland (1940, 1953), Goldsen and colleagues (1960), Harris and colleagues (1932), Hoge and Bender (1974), Jones (1926, 1938), Knode (1943), La Falce and Gomez (2007), Leuba (1921), Moore and Garrison (1932), Nogee and Levin (1958), Pace (1939, 1949), Pressey (1946), Riffer (1972), Rosenberg (1956), Stember (1953), Symonds (1925), and Woessner and Kelly-Woessner (2020).

TABLE 7.3 *Extant surveys of university communities*

Study	Year(s)	Target and comparison group	Topic	Finding
UNITED STATES				
Lipset (1972: 166)	1924	National survey, comparing college students and other voters	Party affiliation	Ø
Havemann and West (1952)	1937	951 young adults in Minnesota and several other states, comparing college graduates and non-graduates	Liberalism (30 statements)	↑
Goldsen et al. (1960)	1950s	Survey of students at 11 colleges, whose views are compared with the general public	Party affiliation, disparate opinions	Ø
Middleton and Putney (1963)	1961	1,440 students in 16 colleges relative to their parents	Left–right ideology	↑
Wright (1975)	1970	938 citizens, comparing college- and non-college-educated	War, race	Ø
ISRAEL				
Shapira et al. (1986)	1977, 1980	835 citizens, comparing students and the general public	Left–right ideology	Ø
OECD				
Kaufmann (2021)	2012, 2017, 2020	1,100 PhD students in US, UK, and Canada compared with general publics in those countries	Left–right ideology, discrimination, Trump support	↑

Finding: relative to the comparison group, college students or college communities (at large) are more liberal (↑), less liberal (↓), or indistinguishable (Ø).

Romania and the World

To address these questions, we focus on Romania, the site of the natural experiment that forms a major part of the empirical analyses in Parts II and III of the book. Surveys include (a) our Romanian natural experiment (RNE) survey, (b) a survey we conducted with faculty at Bucharest University (the largest and by all accounts the most influential university in Romania), (c) a survey we commissioned of college-age youth in Romania conducted by Mercury Research (a Romanian survey firm), and (d) general population surveys conducted by the World Values Survey (WVS) and European Values Survey (EVS) focused on Romania. (Since the WVS and EVS of Romania employed nearly identical questionnaires and sampling procedures, results are combined.) As a basis of comparison, we also include (e) global results for the seventh wave of the WVS/EVS.

All surveys were conducted between 2018 and 2021. To assure comparability, questions of theoretical interest are identical across all surveys. Coverage is not universal, as a few questions were omitted from the RNE. Responses are coded as indicated in parentheses so that higher values indicate greater liberalism (as defined in Chapter 1). The bottom row tallies the grand mean across all available questions for each group.

From these surveys, we are able to identify seven groups within Romania of relevance to the present project: (1) college faculty at Bucharest University, (2) college students aged nineteen to twenty-three, (3) non-college students aged nineteen to twenty-three, (4) students whose baccalaureate (*bac*) scores fall near (usually just above) the threshold required for admittance to college, (5) non-students whose *bac* scores fall near (usually just below) the threshold required for admittance to college, (6) adults of any age with university degrees, and (7) adults of any age without university education. The final columns in Table 7.4 identify respondents throughout the world (8) with university education and (9) without university education.

At present, we focus on four patterns contained in Table 7.4. First, college faculty are considerably more liberal overall than every other group. This appears to be true for virtually every question except redistribution and overall political views on a left–right scale. Second, students are generally more liberal than non-students, though the differences are not great and on one question – the importance of God – non-students are more liberal (secular). Third, respondents with a university education are marginally more liberal than those without. This pattern is evident in Romania as well as across the world.

Finally, differences across these nine groups seem to be driven primarily by questions about political interest, voting, trust, democracy, law-abidingness, corruption, divorce, homosexuality, gender, race, religion, and science/technology. There is less variability with respect to party affiliation, left–right placement, and questions about economic policy. This suggests that the cleavage between university communities and those outside the ivory tower

TABLE 7.4 Social and political attitudes of Romanians, circa 2020

	Romania							World	
Source:	Authors	Mercury		RNE		WVS/EVS		WVS/EVS	
Year:	2021	2021		2019–2020		2017–2020		2017–2020	
Group:	Bucharest	Age 19–23		Near *bac* threshold		Adult		Adult	
Sub-group:	Faculty University	Students	Non-students	Students	Non-students	University degree	No university degree	University degree	No university degree
N:	(369)	(1,080)	(773)	(853)	(645)	(402)	(2,376)	(30,922)	(95,390)
	1	2	3	4	5	6	7	8	9
Interested in politics (+)	.68	.56	.46	.62	.66	.37	.33	.52	.42
Voting: have done or would do (+)	.93	.85	.66	.75	.68	.78	.75	.81	.74
Most people can be trusted (+)	.61	.52	.55	.21	.37	.15	.12	.40	.24
Living in country that is democratic – important (+)	.97	.77	.65			.87	.81	.87	.83
Cheating on taxes if you have a chance is justifiable (-)	.88	.49	.41	.75	.70	.86	.84	.88	.87
Accepting a bribe in the course of one's duties is justifiable (-)	.98	.82	.73	.87	.80	.95	.93	.92	.91

(continued)

Divorce justifiable (+)	.66	.57	.49	.52	.51	.49	.38	.59	.46
Homosexuals as neighbors acceptable (+)	.93	.74	.58	.48	.35	.55	.44	.67	.57
Men make better business executives than women do (-)	.73	.57	.46	.42	.35	.71	.62	.68	.60
People of a different race as neighbors acceptable (+)	.99	.96	.94	.83	.77	.83	.81	.87	.82
Importance of God in your life (-)	.39	.27	.21	.28	.35	.16	.14	.42	.32
World better off because of science and technology (+)	.83	.70	.60	.75	.71	.68	.64	.70	.66
Affiliation with culturally liberal parties (+)	.53	.53	.43	.43	.38	.40	.40	.48	.47
Government should tax the rich and subsidize the poor (-)	.43	.56	.57			.48	.37	.40	.39

(*continued*)

TABLE 7.4 (continued)

	Romania							World	
	Authors	Mercury		RNE		WVS/EVS		WVS/EVS	
Source:	2021	2021		2019–2020		2017–2020		2017–2020	
Year:	Faculty	Age 19–23		Near bac threshold		Adult		Adult	
Group:	Bucharest University								
Sub-group:	University	Students	Non-students	Students	Non-students	University degree	No university degree	University degree	No university degree
N:	(369)	(1,080)	(773)	(853)	(645)	(402)	(2,376)	(30,922)	(95,390)
	1	2	3	4	5	6	7	8	9
Affiliation with economically liberal (pro-market) parties (+)	.64	.60	.58	.61	.57	.53	.49	.44	.46
Political views on a left–right scale (left)	.47	.53	.55			.46	.48	.52	.48
Mean	.73	.63	.53	.58	.55	.59	.54	.64	.58

Scales range from 0 to 1, with higher scores indicating more liberal views. Coding for each question indicated in parentheses.

may have more to do with culture and political culture than with overall political ideology (as the latter is usually understood).

The US

To supplement analyses of Romania we turn to the US, a country that has featured prominently in our discussion and in broader debates on these matters. To do so, we draw on the Politics of the American Professoriate (PAP) survey conducted by Gross and Simmons (2014b) in 2006. As a basis of comparison, we enlist the General Social Survey (GSS), a biannual survey conducted by the National Opinion Research Center (NORC) at the University of Chicago (with principal funding from the National Science Foundation). Because some of the categories of interest are quite small (e.g., college students aged nineteen to twenty-three), we pool GSS surveys from 1996 to 2016 in order to obtain a sufficient sample to make meaningful comparisons. Since this range of years brackets 2006, the year in which PAP was administered, we anticipate that any opinion trends across those years are balanced on either side of the middle year (2006). All questions that bear on our subject matter and are asked in identical form across PAP and GSS are included in Table 7.5. As previously, a grand mean, calculated across all survey questions, is listed on the bottom row.

Differential responses exhibited across demographic categories in the US are quite similar to patterns found in Romania. University faculty hold the most liberal opinions and exhibit the most liberal behavioral patterns. College students are more liberal than non-college students. Those with a university education are more liberal than those without. These differences are quite marked, judging from the grand means.

One difference between the two countries is apparent. In Romania, the views of college faculty on economic issues (addressed in a question about whether government should tax the rich and subsidize the poor) are indistinguishable from the general public. In the US, the views of college faculty on reducing differences between rich and poor are more left wing (less liberal) than the general public. In the US, therefore, one might conclude that professors ought to be labeled "leftists" rather than "liberals." We do not know which label would be more appropriate in other countries around the world.

CONCLUSIONS

The liberal nature of the university is the theme of many recent studies, as noted in various sections of this chapter. Likewise, the intertwined history of the university and liberalism is a well-established theme. The institution and the worldview developed in tandem and undoubtedly influenced each other. In these respects, our chapter confirms a broad consensus among scholars.[17]

---

[17] See Halstead (1996), Rothblatt (1976), and Shils (1989).

TABLE 7.5 *Social and political attitudes of Americans, 1996–2016*

	PAP	GSS		GSS	
	2006	1996–2016		1996–2016	
	Adults	19–23		Adults	
Source: Year(s): Age: Group:	Professors	College students	Never college	University degree	No university degree
N:	(1,115–1,400)	(553–1,008)	(533–1,017)	(4,921–12,077)	(9,863–15,531)
	1	2	3	4	5
Liberalism (partisan) on a 7-point scale	.60	.54	.51	.49	.46
Party identity: non-Republican	.82	.70	.74	.62	.70
Oppose death penalty for persons convicted of murder	.59	.39	.35	.34	.29
Govt not obliged to reduce differences b/w rich and poor	.40	.42	.36	.49	.42
Abortion legal for any reason	.68	.50	.34	.51	.33
Same-sex sexual relations are not wrong	.69	.61	.50	.52	.30
Preschool children do not suffer if the mother works	.65	.62	.58	.58	.52
Women need not stay home to care for family	.79	.70	.61	.64	.51
African-Americans suffer discrimination in jobs	.44	.45	.44	.37	.37

(continued)

African-Americans have less educational opportunities	.76	.53	.37	.51	.40
African-Americans are not unmotivated	.79	.60	.46	.60	.41
Do not believe in God	.34	.31	.24	.22	.13
Do not attend religious services	.55	.61	.66	.54	.56
Voted in past presidential elections	.99	.55	.27	.80	.59
Mean	.65	.54	.46	.52	.43

Scales range from 0 to 1, with higher scores indicating a more liberal outcome. *N*: the sample range for each survey across all questions listed in the table. PAP: Politics of the American Professoriate survey (Gross and Simmons 2014b); GSS: General Social Survey (NORC 2019).

Yet, the attachment of the university to liberal ideas has not been traced in a systematic fashion over time. Extant studies do not offer strong conclusions about *when* the university moved into the liberal camp. That is what we have grappled with in this chapter, and that is our intended contribution to this extensive literature.

To address the question, we took several cuts at the material. After demonstrating the dramatic rise of the university in the modern era, we focused on particular components of our topic – intellectuals, university faculty, student activism, university constituencies, and university graduates. In each section, we assembled data that sheds light on long-term historical trends. The previous section of the chapter employs survey data to compare attitudes among college students, former students, college faculty, and general publics in Romania and the US at the present time.

This collection of evidence is limited in various ways, as acknowledged in the following subsection. Nonetheless, it is probably the largest and most wide-ranging of its kind. This is not by accident, as we build on the labors of many scholars whose work is reflected in the tables and figures of the chapter. Our hope is that by drawing information from diverse sources, we might be able to compensate for the deficiencies of each data source considered on its own. Now, we shall do our best to weave together these multifarious strands into a concise account.

Let us begin with the premodern era, when universities did not stray very far from the norms of the societies they inhabited. By and large, they played a peripheral role in these societies, training youths in fields like theology, classics (i.e., the study of ancient languages and texts), medicine, and law that were well established. Academic monographs, textbooks, and university courses were expected to gather together accumulated knowledge on a subject, not to break new ground. The emphasis was on learning the tradition, not novelty.

Of the medieval university, Alan Cobban (1975: 167) writes,

Study took the form of the critical evaluation and discussion of a prescribed corpus of writings by means of the commentary, the disputation and the question. As ultimate truth lay beyond the reach of human understanding, study and dialectical inquiry could serve only to elucidate within an a priori thought system. The mastery of a difficult discipline, the sharpening of the critical faculties, the ability to expound logically, the careful digestion of approved knowledge, these were the features of the average university education. Teaching and learning were innately conservative processes and, at the ordinary student stage, questioning was conducted as a form of training within an accepted intellectual framework .... For the most part, the universities provided an undergraduate training designed rather to perpetuate a body of doctrine than to promote independent lines of thought. Students went to university to absorb the material set before them and, to a large extent, this was based on memory work and rote learning.

One could hardly argue that university students in the medieval or early modern eras were inducted into a distinctive way of viewing the world.

Works devoted to the history of universities suggest that prior to the twentieth century, these institutions could be viewed as apostles of certain very general liberal ideals such as freedom, the rule of law, tolerance, rationalism, cosmopolitanism, and humanism. However, defenses of these principles were often couched in a parochial manner. Universities defended academic and religious freedom because it was essential to their business model (Hofstadter 1955). When they advocated for liberty, it was sometimes presented as a privilege reserved for universities, not a right of citizenship – much less a human right.

In the nineteenth century, this limited, parochial vision of liberalism began to broaden, and in the twentieth century, university life adopted a more forthright liberal hue and a more politically engaged perspective. By the end of the twentieth century, liberal ideals were heartily embraced.

It is always perilous to mark a single point of inflection in a long-running trend. That said, if one had to identify the moment when universities moved decisively into the liberal camp, it would be the decades following World War II. During the second half of the twentieth century many of the trend lines tracked in this chapter experienced their steepest ascent.

This is corroborated by public perceptions captured in the Google Books database. Our simple query includes two search terms: "liberal university" and "conservative university." The results are shown in Figure 7.18. It will be seen that occurrences of the former were scarce to nonexistent prior to the nineteenth century. This is not because "liberal" was uncommon; indeed, this term reaches peak usage in Google Books at the end of the eighteenth century. However, it was not until the mid-nineteenth century that the concept of liberalism was joined to the university, and it was not until the late twentieth century that liberal references consistently outnumbered conservative references. This confirms our conclusion that the university became a haven for liberal ideas sometime in the past century.

Caveats and Clarifications

Before concluding, it is important to acknowledge the limitations of our historical evidence.

Highly salient aspects of university history such as student movements and protests are much easier to study than the subtler aspects of that history; for example, what people thought about outgroups like minorities, homosexuals, or immigrants. Consequently, our analyses privilege the big, the dramatic, the eventful aspects of university life. We know more about student movements than about students, for example. And political attitudes are privileged over social attitudes.

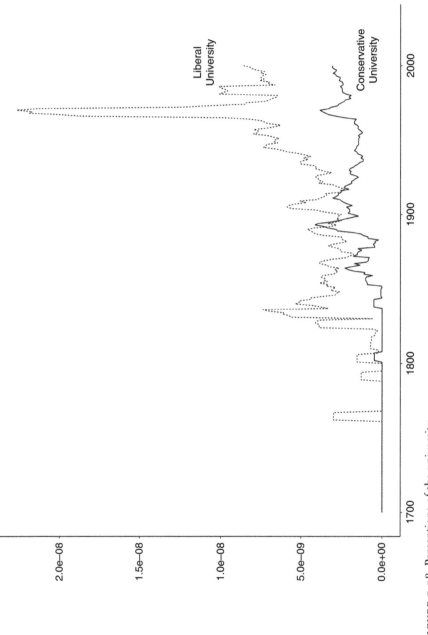

FIGURE 7.18 Perceptions of the university

The relative frequency of "liberal university" and "conservative university" as a fraction of all phrases published (in English) within a given year, averaged across a three-year moving window. Data provided by Google Ngram (Michel et al. 2011).

Among political attitudes, ideology is often reduced to "-isms," to a unidimensional left–right scale, or to support for specific parties. We know this is an oversimplification, obscuring much of the action. Additionally, the meaning of "left" and "right" – as well as the agendas of specific parties – has changed a good deal over the past two centuries (Gerring 1998). So, when we say that the university is more left-leaning today than in the past, this statement must be understood as a product of changes within the university as well as changes in the way that parties have defined their mission.

In particular, we note that the association between universities and parties on the left is accentuated wherever the right assumes a populist or authoritarian complexion and wherever the left champions democracy and the rights of minorities – in other words, wherever party cleavages place liberalism (defined in Chapter 1) solidly on one side of the spectrum. In situations where liberals are cross-pressured, as, for example, in elections that turn on economic and class issues of a redistributive nature, we expect their allegiances to be divided.

Our discussion in this chapter focuses primarily on overall ideology. Other elements of our capacious vision of liberalism such as social connectedness, law-abidingness, and support for democracy are neglected. Unfortunately, it is difficult to find historical measures of views on these subtle features, so we cannot address the extent to which university communities may have been distinctive along these dimensions.

Another shortcoming is the limited length of many of our time-series. Although we have searched diligently, most historical sources do not extend into the nineteenth century, and many are limited to the postwar era. Large surveys, the most useful source for tracking opinions over time, are scarce.

Our data also raises serious questions about sample bias. Early polls did not rely on random sampling. The MPs selected from British university districts presumably represented their constituents in some respects, but we do not know much more than their factional or party affiliation. Straw polls of Harvard students may reflect response biases. Voting behavior within the Cornell University community is somewhat more informative, but we do not know for sure whether the situation was similar among other academic communities. Student protests that show up in van Dyke's coding reflect the views of *some* students; but the greater number may have been oblivious to the tumult, or turned off by the militants.

It is important to appreciate that our sources lean heavily toward the West and especially the US. In some respects, this focus may be justified as Europe was the historic home of the university and the most influential universities, journals, libraries, research institutes, and funding bodies are still located in Europe and the US. This means that scholars and administrators at top universities across the world are often trained in the West and the model of the contemporary internationalized university is to a considerable extent a Western model. However, we cannot say with assurance that the ideational trajectories observed for the US and Europe are mimicked in other countries.

One can appreciate that the character of university politics is to some degree a response to the character of national politics. In autocratic settings, this means support for democracy. In countries where core liberal rights are assured (at least for some citizens), this means the embrace of a more expansive agenda, which often involves the extension of core rights and recognition to outgroups; for example, women, minorities, immigrants, and those whose sexual identity differs from the mainstream. In this respect, the university histories of Russia and China (on the autocratic end of the spectrum) and the US and Europe (on the democratic end) are linked. They are all liberal, but they emphasize different elements of that diffuse worldview (sketched briefly in Chapter 1 and in the conclusion to that chapter).

To be sure, university actors whom we call liberal did not necessarily embrace that moniker. In the twentieth century, radicals of all persuasions were likely to view "liberalism" as a mainstream ideology associated with a defense of the status quo. However, liberal ideals often undergirded movements of a radical flavor. For example, movements for civil rights, multiculturalism, feminism, and LGBTQ rights, as well as movements against imperialism, are liberal insofar as they seek to extend rights and privileges enjoyed by dominant social groups to outgroups. Even socialist movements are liberal in many respects, albeit not in their drive to strengthen the state and redistribute wealth. Communist movements often take little notice of democracy and civil liberty; here, a leftist position seems patently illiberal.

Significantly, ideological transformations on university campuses over the course of the twentieth century generally reinforced the trend toward a liberal worldview. Fascism, to the extent that it had a foothold in university environments in Europe, quickly lost appeal. Communism's demise came later, with key turning points occurring after the Hitler–Stalin pact (1939), the Moscow trials (1936–1938), and the suppression of the Hungarian Revolution (1956). While the appeal of socialism endured longer in Latin America, the brutality of left-wing movements such as the Shining Path, and the turn toward autocracy in Cuba, Nicaragua, and Venezuela, signaled its fading luster on university campuses.

Disillusioned with the Old Left, student movements embraced the New Left, a vaguely libertarian and radically democratic philosophy that informed many of the movements of the 1960s and thereafter; for example, "identity" movements based on gender, sexuality, race, or ethnicity. All emphasized (at least implicitly) ideals of equal rights and tolerance for the individual, who exercises free range in defining him/her/their self. Finally, environmental movements arose, extending the ethic of care to natural phenomena.

These developments reinforce our sense that the university climate is considerably more liberal in its overall gestalt at the turn of the twenty-first century than it had been a century earlier. At the same time, we must acknowledge that the advocacy of liberal ideals is sometimes pursued in rather illiberal ways; for example, by casting aspersions on opponents or refusing to hear opposing views. This has led to charges of "PC-ism" and "cancel culture," generating the impression of an illiberal academy more committed to being "woke" than to rational inquiry (D'Souza 1991). It is too soon to project how these issues will play out, though we suspect that in the long run liberal commitments to free speech, civility, tolerance, and reason will outweigh the urge to proselytize.

8

Disciplinary Differences

When speaking of universities, one is evidently lumping together a great many disciplines, each with a distinctive complexion and unique history. In this chapter, we interrogate these differences and attempt to make sense of them. As in Chapter 7, our focus is primarily on ideology, understood through left–right self-placement and party affiliation. Other aspects of liberalism, laid out in Chapter 1, are left aside simply because it is difficult to explore them historically in a rigorous empirical fashion.

To access the partisan component of liberalism, we begin with an original coding of intellectual leaders in selected fields, observed across a century and a half. Next, we enlist survey research, whose retrospective coding extends back to the early twentieth century. Finally, we examine recent data drawn from the early twenty-first century. In the conclusions, we explore possible explanations for the ideological differences manifested across academic disciplines.

LEADING INTELLECTUALS WITHIN THREE DISCIPLINES

We begin with intellectual leaders, understood as those whose work is influential in a discipline during their lifetime. By this criterion, Karl Marx does not qualify because he was not widely influential in any organized academic discipline until after his demise. (This exercise is therefore rather different from that which was introduced in the previous chapter.) For each chosen figure, we attempt to determine their political leanings based on standard biographical accounts, as we did for intellectuals at large (see previous chapter). In this fashion, we are able to trace the evolving politics of various disciplines.

Of course, this approach involves some strong assumptions. We must assume that the political views of these leaders are in some respects exemplary of the disciplines they worked within. We believe this is a reasonable assumption in the humanities and social sciences, where politics intermingles with the subject of theoretical interest and the influence of an intellectual leader is often connected to their professed ideology. It is difficult to imagine that Foucault would have been as influential if his politics had been to the right, for example. (The same approach would be less viable in the natural sciences, where politics and subject matter are more clearly divorced. That is why this effort is limited to the social sciences and humanities.)

Within this ambit, we focus on three fields with strong political orientations and disciplinary histories that extend back to the late nineteenth century: *sociology*, *philosophy*, and *literary criticism* (Baldick 1996; Furner 1975; Ross 1992). The latter is defined broadly so as to include the intertwined fields of English, American studies, cultural studies, foreign languages, comparative literature, and classics.

Within each of these disciplines, we attempt to identify those whose work has been most influential. As with the database of intellectuals that informs Figure 7.7, our judgments might be questioned. No two canons are identical. Nonetheless, there is likely to be a great deal of overlap among lists of leading academics focused on the same discipline. Small differences are unlikely to affect the outcomes of interest, which are focused on political identities.

The most challenging task is arriving at a summary coding of each figure's political leanings, which we categorize as (1) conservative, right wing, (2) centrist or without a clear ideological orientation, or (3) liberal, left, or radical. As in our previous coding exercise in Chapter 7 (which relies on the same categories), these judgments are made against the background of the time and place in which individuals lived.

Even so, some may regard this adventure in coding as crudely reductionist, especially given the intellectual richness and sophistication of our subjects and, in some instances, their long and varied history of political engagement. So it is. Yet, in order to analyze trends, we must be able to mark progress through time, and this requires some simplification.

To visualize historical trends, our codings are graphed through time, from 1880 to 2020, in Figure 8.1. A point on this graph represents the share of (living, adult-age) academics in a discipline who espouse a left/liberal/radical ideology in a particular year.

Over this period of nearly a century and a half, each discipline moved decisively to the liberal left – though at different times and with different trajectories. Leading sociologists have progressed in a fairly monotonic fashion toward the left end of the spectrum. Leading figures in literary criticism were moderate in outlook until the 1960s, at which point they moved left such that they now occupy the most left-wing position. The field of philosophy, by this reckoning, has the most jagged history. Influential philosophers initially leaned to the right, swung back to the center-left during the middle of the century, tacked back to the right at the end of the twentieth century, and then moved sharply to the left in the twenty-first century. Another point to note is the declining variability across fields in the twenty-first century, with all three disciplines ending up in the liberal camp.

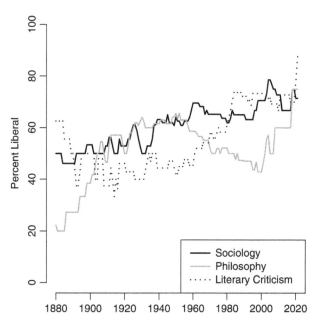

FIGURE 8.1 Liberalism among leading figures in three disciplines
The share of leading figures in sociology, philosophy, and literary criticism (N=137) that
embrace a liberal, left, or radical ideology. For each year, percentages are calculated
based on all intellectuals alive over the age of nineteen.

DISCIPLINES THROUGH TIME

In this section, we narrow our gaze from intellectuals (at large) to college faculty
in the US, the one country where historical surveys prior to 1960 are available.
We must also narrow our historical scope, which extends back to the 1920s.
The benefit is that we shall obtain a more comprehensive view of academic
disciplines – extending across the humanities, social sciences, and natural
sciences – and one that accesses the political views of rank-and-file academics,
not just intellectual leaders.

    We are aware of only one survey of American academics that includes the
early years of each discipline. Between 1959 and 1964 Turner and Spaulding
(1969) administered retrospective questionnaires to US academics in
philosophy, sociology, political science, history, psychology, botany, geology,
mathematics, and engineering. Respondents were asked to state their previous
voting choices in presidential elections beginning in 1924 or the first year in
which they were eligible to exercise the franchise. This generates a time-series
that we construct as the Republican vote share (%) minus the Republican vote
share of the general electorate in each election.

We focus on Republican vote share rather than Democratic vote share because there is a good deal of third-party voting among respondents and most of these presidential candidates (e.g., Robert Lafollette, Norman Thomas, and Henry Wallace) were on the left end of the political spectrum. Deviations from the Democratic vote would therefore understate the liberal sentiment of respondents. For the same reason, calculating ideology as a ratio of support for Democrats and Republicans (Duarte et al. [2015] do for the field of psychology) exaggerates the conservativism of the profession's early years.

Several potential biases of this methodology should be noted. First, respondents may misremember their voting choices, and this pattern of error may be tilted in the direction of their current party affiliation. Accordingly, variation through time may be underestimated. Second, the size of the sample declines as one moves back through time, so earlier estimates are more subject to stochastic error. Third, there may be cohort effects. Specifically, estimates from earlier years rest on older respondents. If we assume that these older respondents are more conservative (both because people grow more conservative because they age and because changing patterns of recruitment mean that younger scholars have more liberal views), this may exaggerate changes in a liberal direction through time. Unfortunately, we do not have access to the raw data so it is not possible to attempt to correct for these biases through model adjustments. We must accept the data for what it is, appreciating the rarity of historical data on this subject.

To get a sense of how these disciplines evolved in the contemporary period, we integrate data from Turner and Spaulding (1969) with later surveys. This includes the Carnegie Commission Survey of Student and Faculty Opinion carried out in 1969 (Bayer 1970; Ladd and Lipset 2001), the 1999 North American Academic Study Survey (Rothman, Nevitte, and Lichter 2005), the Politics of the American Professoriate survey (PAP), carried out in 2006 by Gross and Simmons (2014a), and a survey conducted in 2017 by Langbert (2018).

The first three panels in Figure 8.2 focus on disciplines within the humanities, the social sciences, and the sciences, respectively. The final panel integrates all three divisions in a single graph. In each instance, we compare party affiliations of academics with those of the general electorate. Party affiliations are judged by reported vote choice or (where the latter is unavailable) by party identification.

Panel (a) in Figure 8.2 suggests that faculty in the discipline of history echoed the partisan affiliations of the general electorate in 1924, the first year in our time-series. Subsequently, historians moved left (relative to the general electorate) in a fairly monotonic fashion. (We do not know what to make of an apparent move back toward the center in 2017.)

Other humanities disciplines were already to the left of the American electorate in the 1920s, a position they retained throughout the subsequent century. Although a few data points purport to show members of fine arts or philosophers to the right of their colleagues in history and languages (English, foreign language), we do not read too much into these possibly errant data points. (Samples for individual disciplines are not very large.)

Faculty in the social sciences, depicted in Panel (b) of Figure 8.2, appear to have moved away from the Republican Party somewhat later, during the era of the Great Depression and the New Deal.

Even sociology, the most left-wing discipline among our group of social science fields, was fairly close to the general electorate in the 1928 and 1932 elections. By 1936, however, it had moved far from the center, rejecting Republican candidates by large margins in every succeeding election. Although sociologists may have always been somewhat more liberal than the general electorate, historical survey data suggests that those differences were not large – judged in partisan terms – until the New Deal was well underway.[1]

The trajectory of political science is similar to sociology, if not quite so far left. In the 1928 election political scientists were reportedly more Republican than the general electorate. But by 1936 they had moved solidly into the Democratic column, where they have remained ever since.[2]

Of all the social science disciplines, psychology appears to have moved most dramatically to the left over the course of the past century. In the 1920s, their voting behavior was indistinguishable from the general electorate. By the mid-twentieth century, psychologists were far to the left.[3]

Economics faculty are somewhat less Republican than the general public, but not dramatically so – until the Trump era. By contrast, the partisan affiliation of business professors tracks the affiliations of the general public fairly closely. It would appear that the most conservative faculty in the American university today are centrists, whose support was roughly equally divided across the two parties – at least until the Trump era.[4]

Partisan predilections among natural science faculty (including math and engineering) are depicted in Panel (c) of Figure 8.2. Here, a clear trend-line is also noticeable. Faculty in these allied fields moved from the Republican column into the Democratic column over the course of the past century. Differences among disciplines are not easy to spot, though faculty in the life sciences seem to be somewhat more liberal than others.

The final panel in Figure 8.2 aggregates all disciplines into three camps – humanities, social sciences, and natural sciences. Here, a striking pattern emerges. The humanities and social sciences are located to the left of the general electorate from the beginning of our time-series (with one possible

[1] For further discussion of the field of sociology, see Calhoun (2008), Lipset and Ladd (1972), McFalls and colleagues (1999), Smith (2014), and Turner (2014).
[2] For further discussion of the field of political science, see Adcock (2014), Adcock, Bevir, and Stimson (2009), Ladd and Lipset (1971), and Turner and colleagues (1963).
[3] For further discussion of the field of psychology, see Duarte and colleagues (2015), McClintock and colleagues (1965), and Prentice (2012).
[4] For further discussion of the field of economics, see Bernstein (2014), Klein and Stern (2007), and Landreth and Colander (2001).

exception, in 1928). There is only a modest trend in a leftward direction over the century-long period of observation. By contrast, the natural sciences begin solidly on the right, as strong Republicans, and proceed in a fairly linear fashion to the left as the decades unfold – converging with their fellows in the humanities and social sciences at the end of the series. Whether this convergence is permanent or a temporary response to the populist character of the Republican Party under Trump (as we suspect) remains to be seen. Although this movement in the natural sciences has received little attention from scholars, it is by far the most important trend observable in the data. Movements in a leftward direction among American academics in the twentieth century are mostly a product of changes within the allied fields of the life sciences, the physical sciences, math, engineering, and health.

Before concluding, we should remind readers of potential errors in the data used to compile Figure 8.2. We have already discussed potential problems with Turner and Spaulding (1969), which relies on recall and where sample attrition occurs as one moves backward in time – meaning that trends prior to 1960 cannot be clearly differentiated from cohort effects. Our time-series also depends upon cobbling together surveys taken at different times by different researchers with different response rates, different sample sizes, and different sampling procedures. This is not a normal procedure but it is the best that can be managed under the circumstances. In most cases, we do not have access to the original datasets and therefore cannot make adjustments so as to harmonize these diverse samples.

For all these reasons, we want to guard against looking too closely at variability across elections or across individual disciplines. The broader trends, and especially those aggregated by area (natural sciences, social sciences, humanities), are probably more reliable – though these are subject to aggregation effects (since somewhat different baskets of disciplines are surveyed in each year).

CONTEMPORARY COMPARISONS

To gain a clearer picture of variability across disciplines in the US, it is important to avoid the – possibly transitory – effects of the Trump era, an era when academics feel under attack by a leader, and a party, with openly populist tendencies. (Note the remarkable convergence of disciplines in the final survey of Figure 8.2.) If the Republican Party reverts to form, ending its rhetorical battle against intellectuals, universities, and science, we suspect that academics will return to patterns registered in previous surveys.

Accordingly, we choose a survey from an earlier period. For our purposes, it is essential to locate a sample containing enough respondents within each discipline to make meaningful comparisons. In this respect, a fairly recent survey conducted by Cardiff and Klein (2005) is ideal. The authors rely on voter registration lists (which are public), which are then compared with faculty

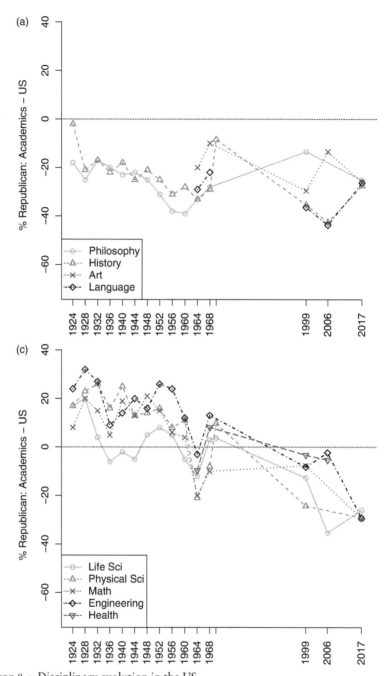

FIGURE 8.2 Disciplinary evolution in the US

Republican vote share (1924–1970) or party ID (1999, 2004, 2017) of US college faculty *minus* Republican vote share of the general electorate in the nearest presidential election. Party ID calculated as Republican share of two-party vote; independents are therefore excluded. Data for 1924–1960 (N=2,389) drawn from Turner and Spaulding (1969). Data for 1964 (N=48,750) and 1968 (N=50,161) drawn from the 1969 Carnegie Commission Survey of Student and Faculty Opinion (Ladd and Lipset 2001). Data for 1970 (N=1,204) drawn from Political Attitudes and

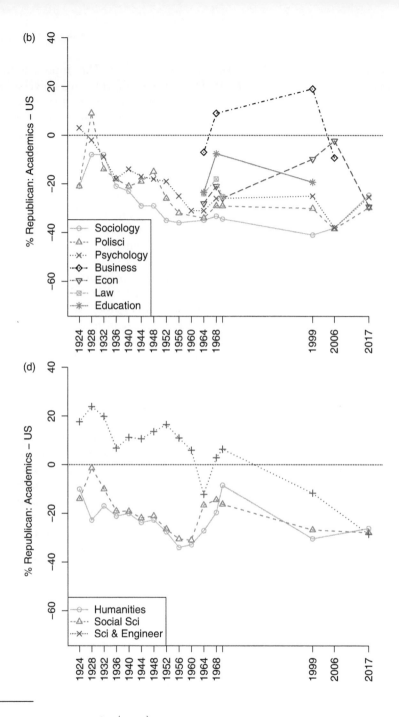

CAPTION FOR FIGURE 8.2 (cont.)
Participation of American Academics, 1970 (Turner and Hetrick 1970). Data for 1999 (N=1,622) drawn from the 1999 North American Academic Study Survey (Rothman, Nevitte, and Lichter 2005). Data for 2004 (N=1,274) drawn from the Politics of the American Professoriate survey (PAP) described in Gross and Simmons (2014a). Data for 2017 (N=8,688) drawn from Langbert (2018).

rosters to determine the political leanings of academics. This approach yields a sample of over 6,000 subjects located in eleven California-area universities.

In addition to yielding a large sample, this approach obviates the differential non-response problem. To be sure, not all voters are found on the voter registry list, perhaps because they do not vote or are not eligible to vote, because they vote in another county, or because of confusion among names. But it seems reasonable to suppose that this sort of missingness is random and therefore unlikely to affect comparisons across disciplines.

One might also wonder about a sample drawn entirely from a single state, especially one as liberal as California. However, the authors are careful to include a range of universities (listed in the note to Table 8.1), some of which are undoubtedly on the liberal end and others of which are more conservative. In any case, our goal is not to compare faculty to the general public (as we do later in this chapter) but rather to compare faculty across different disciplines. So long as the political complexions of disciplines are fairly stable across states and regions, one can safely extrapolate these results to the rest of the country.

In defining disciplines, we stick as closely as we can to those identified in Figure 8.2. In some cases, this means combining categories originally reported separately in Cardiff and Klein (2005). This is also advisable insofar as it generates larger sub-samples that are less prone to stochastic variability.

To distinguish the party affiliations of academics in various fields, one may focus on support for the Democratic Party or the Republican Party, or the ratio of Democratic to Republican support. These measures are highly correlated, as one can see. However, they are not identical and for the purposes of comparison it is important to identify that which we have greatest confidence in. The problem with any indicator focused on Republicans is the paucity of Republican support in our sample. Although the sample is large, Republicans are rare. This means that any statistic grounded in Republican support is susceptible to stochastic error. Accordingly, our discussion focuses on the Democratic partisans as a share of the entire discipline, the criterion we used to order the disciplines in Table 8.1.

Readers should bear in mind that independents are excluded from this analysis. Since there are many more registered Democrats than registered Republicans in most disciplines, one can safely assume that many of those who do not register as Democratic would nonetheless end up voting for Democratic candidates, especially in an era without a strong third-party challenger. (A very small number are registered as members of the Green Party.) In any case, our goal is to compare disciplinary party affiliations with each other. Readers should focus on the relative placement of these disciplines in Table 8.1 – with the most left-wing disciplines at the bottom – not on absolute numbers.

TABLE 8.1 *US disciplines compared in 2004–2005*

Discipline	Division	Faculty (N)	Dem (N)	Dem/ total (%)	Rep (N)	Rep/ total (%)	Dem/ Rep (ratio)
Business/management	Social science	330	100	30	71	22	1.41
Engineering/CS/IT/ aerospace	Natural science	745	224	30	99	13	2.26
Economics	Social science	262	85	32	30	11	2.83
Mathematics	Natural science	342	136	40	24	7	5.67
Health/medicine	Natural science	359	162	45	43	12	3.77
Physical sciences	Natural science	681	309	45	72	11	4.29
Law	Social science	254	119	47	30	12	3.97
Fine arts/performing arts/ music	Humanities	313	151	48	20	6	7.55
Philosophy/religious studies	Humanities	195	95	49	16	8	5.94
Education/social welfare	Social science	310	152	49	30	10	5.07
Languages and literature	Humanities	511	262	51	22	4	11.91
Political science	Social science	225	124	55	19	8	6.53
Life sciences	Natural science	626	351	56	31	5	11.32
Psychology/psychiatry	Social science	425	240	56	27	6	8.89
History	Humanities	290	164	57	15	5	10.93
Sociology/ethnic studies/ anthropology	Social science	347	200	58	11	3	18.18
Total (mean)		6215	2874	(46)	560	(9)	(6.91)

Party affiliation (Democrat/Republican) of faculty across disciplines in 2004–2005 according to voter registration records. Includes faculty from eleven California universities: University of California–Berkeley, Stanford University, Santa Clara University, University of San Diego, Point Loma Nazarene University, Pepperdine University, Claremont McKenna College, California Institute of Technology, San Diego State University, University of California–San Diego, and University of California–Los Angeles. Source: Cardiff and Klein (2005).

CONCLUSIONS

Table 8.1 confirms the truism that "harder" disciplines are located to the right of "softer" disciplines.[5] But this does not go very far toward an explanation, and there are a number of glaring exceptions such as psychology and the life sciences (on the left). We speculate that three factors may be at work, operating independently upon the ideological proclivities of academic disciplines.

First, let us assume that those who enter the academy with strong political views are primarily interested in reforming society in a liberal direction. (This issue is explored in depth in Chapter 9.) Accordingly, those with the strongest political views should be drawn to disciplines most closely connected to aspects of society in need of reform. Mary Furner (1975: xii; see also Turner 2014) explains how sociology (the most left-wing discipline in the Cardiff and Klein sample and in many other surveys) grew out of a general interest in social reform after the Civil War.

Social scientists were concerned citizens from various walks of life, brought together by a common interest in helping people who became casualties of industrial society. In 1865 they formed the American Social Science Association (ASSA) to gather information and develop techniques for ameliorating bad social conditions. As long as these amateur social scientists devoted most of their energy to humanitarian causes, they added little to basic social science knowledge. When some ASSA leaders gradually shifted their attention from the unfortunate victims of social change to processes affecting society as a whole and then embarked upon empirical studies to discover how society worked, they took the first tentative steps toward professionalization as social scientists.

Many years later, Christian Smith (2014: 7–8) describes the field of sociology as a sacred engagement, "committed to the visionary project of realizing the emancipation, equality, and moral affirmation of all human beings as autonomous, self-directing, individual agents (who should be) out to live their lives as they personally so desire, by constructing their own favored identities, entering and exiting relationships as they choose, and equally enjoying the gratification of experiential, material, and bodily pleasures."

The point is strongly stated; surely this does not describe everyone currently engaged in the field of sociology. Even so, one can recognize a wide-ranging set of commitments that are likely to be appealing to a certain sort of young person as they decide what sort of career they wish to pursue. If this pattern of recruitment holds across the academic fields, one may surmise that those with a reforming bent would be motivated to study the things they want to change. The most "political" disciplines should draw the most politicized practitioners.

---

[5] See Cardiff and Klein (2005), Hamilton and Hargens (1993), Howard (1958), Klein and Western (2004–2005), Ladd and Lipset (1975), Langbert (2018), Langbert, Quain, and Klein (2016), and Rothman and colleagues (2005). Eitzen and Maranell's (1968) survey of 979 US faculty in 1962 finds that social scientists (sociologists and psychologists) are predominantly identified with the Democratic Party while both physical scientists and humanities faculty (from the fine arts) are predominantly Republican – a partial vindication of the usual pattern.

This may help to account for why the natural sciences are, on the whole, less leftist than the other disciplines. There is not much one can do to reform society as a physicist. To be sure, one can use the platform provided by one's academic position to address political questions, as Albert Einstein did. But one cannot use one's training as a physicist to do so, and one can hardly incorporate such matters into the curriculum or into published work of an academic nature.

However, there are limits to this explanation. If the most political subjects draw the most politicized academics, one would expect the social sciences to occupy the leftmost position in the academy, as their subject matter – politics, economics, society – is most closely associated with social reform. This may have been true initially; that is, in the late nineteenth and early twentieth centuries (see Figure 7.10). However, it no longer appears to be the case. Since the 1960s, the humanities have caught up to the social sciences on the left-wing vanguard (see Figure 8.2), suggesting that our first explanatory factor is insufficient, on its own, to account for variability across the disciplines.

A second factor to consider is the methodology employed by various disciplines. Scientific disciplines, we suppose, employ a "positivist" epistemology centered on generalizable theories and falsifiable tests. This provides a good deal of structure to any empirical venture. Where there is no empirical referent – for example, in pure math and some abstract areas of physics – structure is provided by the postulates of mathematics. Anyone undertaking to conduct research in these fields must be willing to accept these constraints. They are also encouraged to adopt a dispassionate view of research, in which findings are separable from priors and in which one is occasionally (perhaps regularly) proven wrong. In these fields, the commitment to science may override the commitment to social reform.

These strictures apply unevenly to the social sciences. It depends upon the specific subject under investigation, norms specific to that subfield, and the norms of the individual researcher. There is a lot of wiggle room. But not nearly as much as one finds in the humanities. The humanities are not tightly bound to a single methodology. There are many methodologies, one might say, and none are especially confining. Similarly, the subject matter of the humanities is fairly unbounded. The study of English is limited only by what is written in English, the study of art to what is called art (itself an endless subject of debate), the study of film to what is filmed, and so forth. From this perspective, it is not surprising that the political agenda of the humanities has swung dramatically over the course of the twentieth century. In the nineteenth century, the fields now classified as humanities were oriented around study of the classical age. Greek and Roman were the preferred languages, and scholars sought to recapture the magic of that era and the meanings contained in ancient texts. By the end of the twentieth century, these fields were enmeshed in theory – Marxist, feminist, deconstructionist, post-structuralist, and so forth – and engaged in strident critiques of bourgeois culture and mainstream politics, as discussed. Radical imaginations found a welcoming home in the study of culture.

The extent to which scientific methodology structures the work of academics affects how much opinionizing they can introduce into their work and into their teaching. It also presumably affects recruitment. Those with strong political views may prefer a field that allows some scope for their expression over a field that imposes scientific blinkers, restricting investigations to phenomena that can be measured and tested in a scientific fashion. One must bear in mind that a good deal of importance to humankind is not amenable to research conducted in a "scientific" mode. This is where one would expect scholars with strong convictions to congregate.

One final influence deserves consideration. At the present time, disciplines focusing on human beings and human action seem to be more liberal than those focused on inanimate objects or abstract structures.

The study of the humanities is humanistic, which is to say it focuses on human action, in all its specificity and individuality. The emphasis of history, literary criticism, and the fine arts is on differences and particularity. In this respect, philosophy departs from the norm among other humanities disciplines. Here, the goal is generality, abstraction. In sync with our argument, it is on the conservative end of the humanities disciplines.

The social sciences also study humans but they generally do so in a mechanistic or structural fashion – as the product of incentives and constraints, things that individuals have little control over. The goal is to abstract from these contexts a more general theory about what is going on. Within the social sciences, psychology and anthropology, two very different disciplines that are nonetheless focused on individual actions and perceptions, are more liberal than economics, which is generally focused on larger structures.

The natural sciences, for their part, have no truck whatsoever with "agency." Yet, even within the natural sciences the life sciences are much more liberal than the physical sciences, confirming the general pattern. (Medicine and health appear to buck this trend, though in other surveys they are generally on the left end of the spectrum.)

Note that these are not methodological differences; they stem instead from the nature of the subject matter. Work that focuses on individual people, living or dead, is more liberal in political outlook than disciplines where human action is understood in the aggregate, through abstract structures or systems, or inanimate objects.

In summary, if we want to explain ideological differences across contemporary disciplines, no single explanatory framework will suffice. It is not a simple matter of "hard" versus "soft." Our sense is that at least three factors – political relevance, methodology, and human-ism – operate independently.

Other factors may also be in play. For example, one might surmise that salary plays a part in conditioning political attitudes across disciplines. Those in business and law schools and economics departments generally command the highest earnings, followed by faculty in the natural sciences. Humanities faculty are generally the least well remunerated. This fits with a materialist understanding of ideology, since the softer disciplines are also the most left-liberal.

On the other hand, if one considers the *opportunity costs* of an academic career, it is the natural scientists who take the greatest hit. They could earn much larger salaries in the private sector. Accordingly, one might imagine they would be envious of their brethren in the private sector, which should translate into greater support for the left.

On the third hand, if one considers social class as an *inheritance*, humanities faculty probably surpass their colleagues in other disciplines. Few humanities professors come from working-class backgrounds and most are native-born, while it is not uncommon to find scientists and engineers who rose from humble beginnings and many immigrate from abroad. However, the relatively privileged upbringing enjoyed by humanities professors does not endear them to capitalism.

In summary, we find materialist logic to be rather ambiguous in its predictions. In our view, the nature of each discipline and self-selection into that profession plays a more important role in determining the ideological proclivities of various disciplines.

Having obsessed in this chapter about differences across disciplines, we must not lose sight of the fact that these ideological differences are fairly small and have seemingly become even smaller over time. *All* academic fields congregate on the liberal left at the present time. Even the "right wing" of the academy, which according to most surveys is located in business and engineering schools, is to the left of the general public. Accordingly, we have little to say in the remainder of this book about interdisciplinary differences except when they pertain to understanding and explaining broader movements across the university, a task to which we now turn.

9

Explanations for the Liberal Shift

In Chapter 7 we explored the association between liberalism and the university, taking a long view of the matter. As we pointed out, there are many limitations to the historical evidence. First, the paucity of sources in earlier historical eras obliges us to focus primarily on the Western world. Second, many of our sources are of questionable representativeness, especially those that reach back prior to the development of random-sample survey technology. Finally, because historical data is generally limited to the partisan/ideological components of liberalism, our treatment of liberalism is narrower than elsewhere in the book. With these important caveats, we offered some tentative conclusions.

Although some very general tenets of liberalism such as the value of free inquiry may stretch back to the origins of the university in the Middle Ages, the differentiation of the university from the rest of society along partisan-ideological lines seems to be a much more recent development. There are no signs of this anywhere in the nineteenth century. In countries for which we possess longitudinal evidence of voting behavior, partisan affiliations, or left–right ideology, it seems that the university was at least as conservative as society at large until the twentieth century. After this point, a dramatic divergence begins in which university faculty – and, to a lesser extent, students and former students – move into the liberal-left camp.

In this chapter, we assess some of the possible causes of this liberal shift. Why did the ideology of the university diverge from society, and why did it move in a liberal direction?

We begin by reviewing several common explanations. Next, we introduce a functionalist approach focused on the long-term consequences of an institution with a high degree of organizational autonomy whose goal is to seek general truths about nature and society.

COMMON EXPLANATIONS

Drawing on the literature reviewed in Chapter 2, we are able to identify seven common explanations for the liberal shift: (a) the university as weathervane, (b) class interests, (c) public sector employment, (d) genetics, (e) intellectual activity, (f) the expansion of higher education, and (g) self-selection.

Some of these factors apply selectively to faculty or to students, while others apply to both components of the academy. We shall argue that although each may play some role in explaining the liberal shift in universities observed over the course of the twentieth century, the last factor is probably the most significant.

University As Weathervane

Universities are places where young adults congregate in large numbers in cohort-specific cadres. There, they share their lives for a period of years, often regarded as formative. In this crucible, often separated from their families and their natal communities, students may be uniquely open to the winds of change.

According to one view, whatever direction the cultural and political winds are blowing, youthful enthusiasm will fill their sails. Since the winds have been blowing in a liberal direction through most of the modern era, it is not surprising that universities have adopted a liberal hue. However, if the current of history should someday move in a conservative direction, universities would be first adopters.[1]

This is a difficult theory to test, as the wind of history is not a treatment that can be easily identified and measured, much less manipulated. However, some evidence may be adduced from the example of countries where politics has moved in an *anti*-liberal direction. A short list includes the communist revolutions in Russia and China, the Islamic revolution in Iran, the Sandinista revolution in Nicaragua, the Bolivarian revolution in Venezuela, and populist governments led by Victor Orbán in Hungary, Jair Bolsonaro in Brazil, Rodrigo Duterte in the Philippines, and Donald Trump in the US. Each of these movements enjoyed widespread popular support. It is difficult to say exactly how many citizens embraced these but there is no question that they embodied the general tenor of public opinion for a period of time in these countries.

However, these were not student movements, by any stretch of the imagination. To be sure, initial support could be found among some college students and faculty. However, initial enthusiasm soured as these movements turned repressive. From that point, universities became places of resistance, or (in the most repressive regimes) sullen compliance.

Accordingly, the historical record does not provide much support for the weathervane theory of university ideology. For the most part, universities have

---

[1] We are indebted to Kurt Weyland (personal communication) for this idea.

occupied a liberal position relative to society over the past century, even when the local political and cultural climate has moved in an illiberal direction.

Class Interests

What scholars think about society may rest on where they stand in society. According to one long-standing view, intellectuals adopt a critical attitude toward society in situations where they experience downward mobility or blocked upward mobility.[2]

By a similar logic, wherever there are more people with advanced degrees than there are suitable (white-collar) jobs to accommodate them, this provokes a radical response (Kotschnig 1937). With little hope of obtaining a job commensurate with their training, students and former students may despair, and this in turn may incline them to radical (generally left-wing) politics. Corresponding to this view, those with the fewest occupational opportunities – in the humanities and social sciences – are generally the most radical. The chronic over-supply of humanities PhDs relative to the academic (and nonacademic) jobs available may also be viewed as a cause of discontent, and of leftist ideology in particular.

Running contrary to these claims, we find similar patterns of university liberalization in countries with the lowest unemployment rates such as South Korea and Japan. Moreover, we see no sign of a direct relationship between levels of white-collar employment – and hence economic opportunity – and radicalism. Indeed, the 1960s were a period of prosperity, expansion, and low unemployment in most Western nations – a condition that extends to those with university degrees and in particular to those pursuing careers in higher education. And yet, student and faculty protest movements were strongest and, arguably, most radical at the pinnacle of postwar prosperity, a time when academic posts were relatively easy to obtain.

A more specific rendition of the class-interest thesis locates radicalism in a mismatch between cultural capital and economic capital. Bourdieu (1984: 397–465; 1988) points out that academics have a great deal of the first but less of the second – at least relative to those who might be regarded as their reference-group. This, he argues, is a recipe for discontent, which manifests in all manner of leftish dissent.

Although plausible, Bourdieu's influential explanation runs into a number of empirical snags. First, one must measure the ambiguous concept of cultural capital. If it is (roughly) equivalent to the social status of intellectuals, one might speculate that it is quite high in France (with its mandarin culture) and in East Asian societies (the original mandarin societies, who share a Confucian heritage). By contrast, intellectuals occupy a lower position on the totem pole in the US, often described as an anti-intellectual political culture (Hofstadter

[2] See Mandel (1969), Mannheim (1936: 155), and Michels (1915).

1966). Accordingly, one should see more academic dissent and leftism – relative to society at large – in mandarin societies than in the egalitarian (and, arguably, anti-intellectual) society of the US. Such patterns are not obvious.

Second, one would expect that better-paid intellectuals would be less discontent, and therefore less radical, as there is less of a disjuncture between their cultural and economic capital. This is consistent with patterns across disciplines, where those with lower salaries (e.g., in the humanities) often have more radical and more left-wing views than disciplines with higher salaries (e.g., in economics, business schools, and the natural sciences), as shown in Chapter 8.

However, there is no evidence to suggest that the pattern holds *within* departments, as Bourdieu's theory would seem to suggest. We have no reason to believe that highly remunerated members of an English department are more conservative than their less well-paid colleagues, for example. Indeed, the intellectual stars – whose salaries doubtless reflect their status – often seem to be more radical than those whose careers have less luster. Likewise, prestigious universities, offering generous compensation, are not more conservative than lesser universities, with lower salaries. In the US, radicalism seems to be positively correlated with salary and prestige (Ladd and Lipset 1975). Harvard University is more radical than the University of Worcester.

Finally, Bourdieu's theory predicts that academics have strong views on economic issues, where they will adopt an egalitarian (redistributionist) position. Yet, surveys of academics are ambiguous on this point. We find that the views on economic issues are not so different from the general public, as shown in Tables 7.4 and 7.5. The main point of differentiation is on *non*-economic issues, where their views are much more liberal.

In these respects, one may question whether the dislocation between cultural and economic capital causes academics to adopt more left-wing views. The counter-argument, discussed later, is that academics already held those views when they entered the academy.

Public Sector Employment

Many academics work for public universities, and even those who work for private universities are in some sense reliant on state support; for example, for student loans that pay for tuition or government grants that pay for research. College students are also often reliant on government support for stipends, loans, or tuition. As such, the self-interest of college faculty and students may lead them to support left-leaning political parties and ideologies that promote increased public sector spending. That is how their bread is buttered (Lamont 1987). In this respect, the university may follow trends found among public sector employees, who are known to be left of center (Svallfors 2004).

However, this channel of influence – like the previous – would seem to operate primarily upon *economic* issues, and has no obvious bearing on cultural issues. With respect to economic issues, we have observed that support for the redistributive aspects of the welfare state among academics is not so different from that of the general public. By contrast, support for cultural issues is extremely strong. This is the reverse of the typical pattern found among public sector workers who are not highly educated such as those who work for public utilities or transportation departments.

Likewise, if self-interest were the driving feature of academic attitudes, one would expect that academics working for public universities would be more left wing than those working for private institutions. This may be true in some parts of the world but we see little sign of it in the US. Again, the evidence seems weak, or at best limited in purview.

Genetics

A growing body of research suggests that genetic endowments affect the development of social and political attitudes and behavior, including many of the features that we have characterized as liberal.[3]

Now consider the implications of a meritocratic recruitment process to universities. Although once reserved for people of a certain race, class, and gender, universities are now open – or at least fairly open – to talent (leaving aside a few blatant meritocratic violations such as legacy slots in American universities). Gaining entrance to the academy as a student or a faculty member is an extremely arduous process, one that probably hinges on intelligence to a greater degree than it did a century ago. As a consequence, one might imagine that the intelligence differential between those inside and outside the academy is considerably greater at the turn of the twenty-first century than it was at the turn of the twentieth century.

Putting these two pieces of information together, one might imagine that genetics is the underlying cause affecting both liberalism and the growing attitudinal differentiation between those with and without university degrees. More intelligent people, goes the story, are more likely to regard the world in an open-ended fashion, are more tolerant of differences, are less anxious about maintaining order, are less respectful of authority, and are less inclined toward a hierarchical social order. All of these features should lead one in a liberal direction. If these are the same sorts of people who tend to enter the academy,

---

[3] For early studies examining the connection between intelligence and political attitudes, see Allport (1929), Harper (1927), and Symonds (1925). For more recent work, see Bell, Schermer, and Vernon (2009), Carl (2015), Carney and colleagues (2008), Deary and colleagues (2008), Dodson (2014), Fowler and Dawes (2008, 2013), Fowler, Baker, and Dawes (2008), Ganzach (2020), Hodson and colleagues (2012), Jost (2009), Jost and Hunyady (2005), Kanazawa (2010), Kleppestø and colleagues (2019), Lockyer and colleagues (2018), Makowsky and Miller (2014), Peterson and Somit (2017), Pratto and colleagues (1994), Rindermann and colleagues (2012), Schoon and colleagues (2010), and Smith and colleagues (2012).

then genetics could be the hidden factor that explains growing liberalization in the academy and among its graduates.

There is something to be said for this view. But, even if true, there are also reasons to doubt that it can explain much of the variation that we observe across populations today. For one thing, genetic influences as revealed by twin studies tend to be fairly small in magnitude. As such, they are unlikely to account for the very large differences in beliefs and values that separate college professors, and many students, from the general public (as revealed in Chapter 7).

More important, if native intelligence were the critical feature leading to a liberal academy, one would expect that faculty in more intellectually demanding fields such as pure math or physics would be more liberal than faculty in disciplines with lower thresholds such as the humanities and social sciences. The actual pattern is the reverse of what intelligence would lead us to predict. The "softer" the discipline, the more liberal its social and political attitudes, as shown in Chapter 8.

Another objection is that intellectually gifted students often pursue jobs in the private sector that are better remunerated than university jobs. If intelligence exerts a strong influence on social and political attitudes, one would expect that those at the top of private sector professions – as engineers, lawyers, bankers, businesspeople, and so forth – would have more liberal views than those at lower ranks (assuming these career ladders are relatively meritocratic). There is no evidence of this. Lawyers are more liberal than engineers, but not necessarily smarter; nor are top lawyers more liberal than lawyers at the middle and lower tiers of their profession.

Finally, if intelligence was the hidden driver of university liberalism, then estimates of the university's impact on social and political attitudes derived from our natural experiment would diverge sharply from estimates based on observational data. This is not what we find, as shown in comparisons of estimates drawn from the Romanian Natural Experiment (RNE) and World Values Survey (WVS)/European Values Survey (EVS) in Chapter 4, which are generally quite close and – on average – extremely close (Table 5.2).

For all of these reasons, we conclude that native intelligence does not offer a compelling explanation of the modern university's liberal trajectory.

Intellectual Activity

Rather than native intelligence, it could be that intellectual *activity* leads one to adopt more liberal views. The more one finds out about the world, the more liberal one becomes. This could be because cognitive faculties become more developed, because knowledge is obtained that leads one in a liberal direction, and/or that intellectual activity leads one to question established beliefs, resulting in views of a more liberal nature (Ladd and Lipset 1975; Lazarsfeld and Thielens 1958).

The hypothetical experiment suggested by this hypothesis might look something like this. Recruit a sample of volunteers and assign them (randomly) to one of the following tasks. The control group performs manual labor or repetitive office tasks. One treatment group would attend a course in math (an abstract intellectual task). A second treatment group would investigate a topic in the real world (a social science endeavor). The difficulty with the latter, evidently, is that one must engage the literature on the topic, which is bound to have some sort of ideological slant (probably liberal). In any case, we do not know what the results of such an experiment would be, and so far as we know, nothing like it has ever been tried.

However, there have been longitudinal studies that follow students as they proceed through their educational journey. These studies find that academics do not continue growing more liberal as their intellectual experiences accrue and their knowledge and expertise about a subject grows. The "advanced" part of one's education, that which qualifies professors to hold faculty positions, does not seem to make them more liberal than they were when they initially signed up. Those completing their PhDs are not more liberal than those just beginning their doctorate (Fosse, Freese, and Gross 2014; Gross 2013: 75). Nor is there any evidence to suggest that older academics, who have been investigating their respective topics for decades, are more liberal than younger academics, fresh out of graduate school.

Finally, it is implausible to suppose that intellectual activity, by itself, makes one more liberal. If this were the case, a similar cognitive dynamic should have been operative from the founding of the first universities. And yet, as we have seen, there is little evidence of a liberal shift in the academy prior to the twentieth century.

The Expansion of Higher Education

In Chapter 7, we noted the vast expansion of higher education that occurred in the twentieth century. This expansion involved lifting barriers to entry for students and faculty from disadvantaged socioeconomic backgrounds and previously excluded groups such as minorities and women. As a consequence, the constituency of a typical college campus is considerably more representative of society at large than it was a century ago. This, in turn, may be an important factor in the liberalization of the academy. In particular, one might expect less privileged constituencies to assume a more inclusive view of many issues.

Survey research offers some support for this thesis. New entrants to the university often hold more liberal views than older denizens. In the US, for example, college-educated Jews, Blacks, Hispanics, Asians, and women are more liberal on a range of issues and more likely to affiliate with the Democratic Party than their White, male, Protestant classmates (Ladd and Lipset 1975; Smith, Mayer, and Fritschler 2008). In Latin America, Africa, and China, surveys suggest that students from lower-class backgrounds often assume more radical positions (Lipset 1967: 29). Several studies situated in Latin America find that students from working-class backgrounds are more likely to engage in student protests (Disi Pavlic 2017; Liebman, Walker, and Glazer 1972: 101).

Since women and minority groups are often situated to the left of men and majority groups in the general population, it is no surprise that the same patterns would arise within the academy. Yet, demographic diversification, by itself, cannot account for the liberalization of the university. Insofar as the university becomes more demographically representative of society, it should become *more* ideologically representative, not less. This is not what we see.

It could be that those members of outgroups who end up in higher education (as students or faculty) are not typical members of their social group. Perhaps they are more liberal. And perhaps the ideological differences between those who do and do not attend university, or pursue a university career, are even greater among women and minority groups than among males of the majority group. This would make sense insofar as outsiders must strive harder, and must be especially motivated, to gain entrance to an institution they were historically excluded from. For them, the university is not a default option. If so, the selection effects that we discuss in the next section apply with special force.

It could be that the educational experience of outgroups, once they arrive at university, is different from the educational experience of ingroups (Reyes 2018). Perhaps it has a radicalizing effect on the former that is not experienced by the latter. One can imagine that a class in African-American studies has a different impact on Black and White students, for example.

One must also consider spillover effects. The admission of outgroups on university campuses diversifies everyone's life experiences, which may lead students (of all backgrounds) to hold more liberal positions than they otherwise would – at least on issues of race and gender (Sidanius et al. 2008). This is especially likely if the entrance of previously excluded groups fosters new disciplines and subdisciplines that appeal to particular social groups; for example, Black studies (Rojas 2007), ethnic studies (Rojas 2014), multicultural studies (Fass 1991), migration studies (Gold and Nawyn 2019), women's studies (Boxer 2001), and queer studies (Dynes 1995).

Even so, we doubt that the opening up of the university to outgroups is the critical factor behind the liberal shift in universities around the world. Note that liberalization seems to have occurred everywhere, even in societies with few ethnic, religious, or racial differences such as South Korea, Japan, Chile, and Finland. And in more diverse societies, the fact that universities are beginning to resemble society demographically should lead to greater ideological convergence between universities and the societies they are situated within, as we pointed out.

Self-Selection

The simplest explanation for why the university has become more liberal is that it recruits liberal people to join its ranks. University professors do not become more liberal as they accumulate more years in the archives, in the laboratory, or in front of the computer. (Arguably, they move to the center as they age, a common life-cycle pattern.) They were more liberal to begin with.[4]

Initial recruitment patterns into the academy are likely to be self-reinforcing. If current denizens of the academy lean left, this presumably influences the choice of occupation for the next generation. After all, making a career as an academic means spending one's professional life in the midst of other academics. This can be uncomfortable if your colleagues hold different views.

It is especially uncomfortable to hold views that are considered retrograde and subject to epithets (racist, sexist, homophobic, xenophobic, logocentric, Western-centric, et al.). This experience is probably more common in the social sciences, where one's research is closely connected to topics about which liberals and conservatives disagree. Engineers may avoid awkward conversations about politics, but it is hardly possible for sociologists and political scientists to do so.

Many studies suggest that conservatives feel unwelcome in university settings, and especially in humanities and social science departments. Conservatives who choose to brave this hostile territory may also face subtle, or not so subtle, discrimination from their liberal colleagues.[5] This, at least, is the perception of many conservatives (Smith, Mayer, and Fritschler 2008: 85), some of whom fear that they cannot reveal their political identity without risking their career.

The thesis of ideological discrimination is supported by regression analyses showing that conservative ideology is associated with diminished professional advancement.[6] Of course, other (unmeasured) factors could also account for this correlation, and many studies find no direct evidence of ideologically based discrimination in hiring and promotion.[7] Even so, all conservatives presumably feel the weight of norms, in-jokes, assumptions, and friendship networks that are based on an ingroup assumption of fealty to liberal ideology.

---

[4] In this context, it is important to distinguish overall ideology from partisanship. Our claim is that overall ideology stabilizes by the time someone enters graduate school – and certainly by the time an individual completes their academic degree. By contrast, partisan affiliation may change, especially if the major parties realign on key issues of concern to academics. For example, the embrace of civil rights by the Democratic Party in the 1960s may have encouraged many liberal academics to switch their party affiliation from Republican to Democratic. This is consistent with findings of a partisan shift in the postwar era (Wright, Motz, and Nixon 2019).

[5] See Klein and Stern (2005a, 2005b), Klein and Western (2004–2005), and Shields and Dunn (2016).

[6] See Rothman and colleagues (2005) and Rothman and Lichter (2009).

[7] See Fosse, Gross, and Ma (2014), Gross (2013), La Falce and Gomez (2007), Prentice (2012), and Smith, Mayer, and Fritschler (2008).

Moreover, in the humanities and social sciences the nature of the job itself is shaped by liberal ideology. The subjects we study – for example, racism, sexism, homophobia, exclusion, discrimination, inequality, imperialism – are often a response to liberal critiques of society. The theorists we cite and whose work shapes our thinking about the world are, likewise, critical of the status quo, usually from a left or liberal perspective.

Values like freedom, equality, and democracy loom large in the humanities and the social sciences. Most topics relate in some fashion to these liberal ideals. One may surmise that academics who choose to study other topics, or whose work does not seem to support these values, have a more difficult time getting published or getting noticed.

Our purpose in dwelling on these features of everyday life in the academy is to make a simple point. A liberal environment is likely to be more inviting to those with liberal inclinations than to those with conservative inclinations. Neil Gross (2013: 105) observes, "for historical reasons the professoriate has developed such a strong reputation for liberalism that smart young liberals today are apt to think of academic work as something that might be appropriate and suitable for them to pursue, whereas smart young conservatives see academe as foreign territory and embark on other career paths." Many studies echo this line of reasoning.[8]

From this perspective, liberalism is a self-reinforcing cycle. The liberalism of the university reinforces a pattern of recruitment, which in turn generates greater liberalism in the university. We find the explanation convincing, but also incomplete.

A FUNCTIONALIST EXPLANATION

Following our discussion in the previous section, we shall assume that self-selection is the most important proximal explanation for why the university faculties liberalized over the course of the twentieth century. Liberals are much more likely than conservatives to pursue a career in the academy. A similar selection effect may operate among students, though we assume that ideology is a minor factor in the decision to go to college.

However, self-selection cannot address the prior question. Why did universities move in a liberal direction in the first place?

In answering this question, it is tempting to identify a specific turning point after which universities began to tack in a liberal direction. In Chapter 7, we noted several events – the Dreyfus affair, World War I and the Russian Revolution, the Great Depression, and the 1960s. Each was probably associated with a shift in a liberal direction, at least in some countries.

---

[8] See also Ladd and Lipset (1975), Lazarsfeld and Thielens (1958: 150), and Woessner and Kelly-Woessner (2009b, 2020).

However, it is questionable whether any of these can be regarded as a cause in the counterfactual sense. That is, it is difficult to imagine the ideological proclivities of the modern university playing out differently in the absence of these events. Undoubtedly, these events hastened the evolution of universities in a liberal direction so they qualify as token causes. However, without them it seems nearly certain that the liberalization of the modern university would still have occurred, even if more slowly.

Note also that these events did not bear equally on every region of the world. The Dreyfus affair occurred in France. The impact of World War I and the Russian Revolution was felt most directly in Europe. The Great Depression was probably harshest in the US. The events summarized as "the Sixties" had the greatest impact on the US and several countries in Western Europe. If these events were determinative, one would expect to see local effects: universities in the affected areas should have experienced the greatest shifts in a liberal direction and these differential shifts would have stuck. However, the liberalness of the contemporary university appears to be a global phenomenon. It is not limited to certain countries or even to the West.

A second point to bear in mind is a product of our efforts to track the process of liberalization in Chapter 7, which reveal no sharp temporal discontinuities. As near as we can tell, the liberalization of universities is a continuous process with traces that extend back to the nineteenth century or at least the early twentieth century.

All of this suggests that some fairly general cause(s) is at work. It is not plausible to suppose that a critical juncture reverberated throughout the world, affecting career choices, faculty hiring and promotions, and the creation and transformation of disciplines everywhere and forever.

The Necessity of Universities

A core mission of the modern university is rational inquiry; that is, the aim to develop general explanations that are empirically verifiable and that fit within an overarching body of knowledge in a logical and coherent fashion. A case can be made that this function is essential to the workings of a modern society. We need science, and the best way to produce and disseminate science is through an institution that looks very much like a modern university.[9]

Consider the alternatives.

Corporations have the financial wherewithal to support scientific research, and to a limited extent they do so. Yet, their goals are generally limited to research that promises to generate marketable products in the near future. Longer-term research projects are likely to be neglected. Moreover, private labs devoted to company interests are unlikely to share results that impair the long-run development of science. In recent years, private labs such as those

---

[9] For a very general statement of the modernization argument, see Kerr and colleagues (1960).

funded by General Electric and Bell Telephone have lost stature, a signal that their functions are residual – of interest to their funders but not to the larger scientific community. It is difficult to imagine a scenario in which the private sector carries the burden of providing a public good such as basic research.

Another scenario for providing scientific research would be a government agency, where research is directly supervised by career bureaucrats or political appointees. Every national agency employs scientists and some of these people do research, so there are exemplars for this organizational model. However, those exemplars also demonstrate the limits of what might be accomplished by a purely bureaucratic approach to science. The principal danger is that rational inquiry would become politicized, with appointments being made on the basis of partisan or personal loyalties and scientific agendas responding to constituency demands. Alternatively, directives from the top might insist that all research be "applied," with immediate policy objectives in mind. Both of these outcomes would impede the long-term progress of science.

Arguably, if the pursuit of truth is to be productive, the process of inquiry must be untrammeled (Braben 2008). This claim has been made on many occasions. Johann Fichte, in his inaugural address as rector of the University of Berlin (1811), declared: "If ... a university is to achieve its purpose and be what it really pretends to be, it must be left to itself thenceforward; it needs, and rightly demands, complete external freedom" (quoted in Brubacher 1967: 237).

Much later, Vannevar Bush (1945) described the work of science as "the free play of free intellects, working on subjects of their own choice, in the manner dictated by their curiosity for exploration of the unknown." This is why universities, and the semi-autonomous fields of scholarly endeavor they nurture, are necessary.

From this perspective, the *republic of scholars* is not just a rhetorical flourish. William Kirby (2022: 12) concludes, "The most basic requirement for plentiful, high-quality research output from faculty is academic autonomy." A submissive university is unlikely to perform effectively as a creator and purveyor of knowledge. Ambitious and creative faculty and students will avoid such an institution if other alternatives are available. And even if capable people are found, their industry will not be very fruitful, as avenues of inquiry will be blocked and the free exchange of ideas prevented. Free inquiry demands a zone of free speech. The development of expertise requires a "marketplace of ideas" (Post 2012).

It is for this reason, one may surmise, that universities – and especially top universities – have often enjoyed a greater degree of autonomy than is afforded other institutions. Universities in Europe generally received charters from the pope, from a monarch, or from a legislature. The charter established the autonomy of that body vis-à-vis local rulers, granting privileges that could not be (except in cases of overriding need) infringed upon. This allowed for greater freedom of expression within the university than without, despite concerns about apostasy (Courtenay 1989; Hofstadter 1955).

So it was in most European colonies. Even Spain's highly centralized empire recognized the importance of autonomy for the university, "one of the few corporate bodies in the Spanish colonial world to be given this status" (Liebman, Walker, and Glazer 1972: 2). Although not scrupulously observed, the grant of autonomy is an implicit recognition of the functional need for independence in scholarly affairs. Much later, in 1918, this desideratum was guaranteed by a set of university reforms instituted in Argentina and subsequently adopted by other nations in Latin America.

In the US, the importance of university autonomy was recognized by the landmark Supreme Court case *Dartmouth College* v. *Woodward* (1819), which preserved the college from New Hampshire's attempt to control the appointment of trustees (and coincidentally laid the basis for contract law [Brubacher 1967]). In the mid-twentieth century, the institution of academic tenure was widely adopted by colleges and universities with the express purpose of protecting faculty from arbitrary dismissal and thereby protecting academic freedom (Hertzog 2017).

Even in authoritarian settings, universities have often enjoyed a limited zone of autonomy. This was true, for example, in Latin America during periods of dictatorship (Liebman, Walker, and Glazer 1972), in imperial Japan (Marshall 1992), and in imperial Russia (Brower 1970, 1975). It is true today in places like Hong Kong, Singapore, and the United Arab Emirates, where most universities enjoy a good deal of independence to pursue scholarly research.

From a broader perspective, one might view the open-ended quest for truth, the willingness to consider novel explanations, and a culture of progress as key elements of long-term economic development. This feature, which arguably distinguished Europe from other parts of the world, is often viewed as key to the advance of the West in the medieval and early modern eras, paving the way for the industrial revolution in the modern era (Landes 2006; Mokyr 2016). Some regard science as critical (Jacob 1997); others see science as incidental, noting that the most important inventions occurred in an ad hoc fashion in response to particular needs, demands, and accidents, and without institutional support (Landes 1975).

In any case, over time the need for a systematic body of knowledge, and a cadre of properly trained experts to deploy and advance that science, became more and more evident. In the early modern era, universities may have supported the growth of scientific knowledge (Mokyr 2016: 172–173), but the most important institutions fostering scientific research such as the Royal Society of London for Improving Natural Knowledge (founded in 1660) and the French Academy of Science (1666) were not universities in the modern sense insofar as they had no formal system of providing education, no students, and no real control over their membership. This was the age of the gentleman-scholar, who financed his own research or sought out a wealthy patron to provide support. Over time, these relatively uncoordinated activities were appropriated by universities, who became the principal bodies supporting the quest for scientific advance as well as scientific education.

The key era of transition from the medieval model of the university to the modern model was probably the nineteenth century. At the outset of that illustrious century, universities were devoted primarily to preserving knowledge, recovering the wisdom of the ancients. A good deal of university energy and resources centered on training clergy, an activity that was in no respect scientific. Legal training consisted then, as it does today, of learning the law of the land, certain general principles of law, and various applications. No scientific method was needed, as there were no fundamental discoveries to make; it was not an empirical exercise in the usual sense of the term. Medical training, the third professional arm of the medieval and early modern academy, was the closest in spirit and practice to what one might call science. However, it had not advanced very far and – quite rightly – held little public esteem. (Prior to the nineteenth century, one's chances of survival were probably worsened, rather than improved, by the application of Western medicine.)

With respect to funding and internal organization, most universities had little to recommend them. Poorly funded and with little autonomy, faculty positions were not a desirable station and did not attract the best and the brightest. Since neither entrance to university nor entrance to academic ranks was subject to meritocratic criteria, one can be sure that even among those who applied, the best were not chosen. Students were poorly motivated, prone to disorder and unrest, and not keen to absorb knowledge – except the minimal amount needed to achieve their professional aspirations. Universities were not places of prestige and accomplishment.

Over the course of the nineteenth century, and continuing into the twentieth century, these features underwent a slow but fairly steady revolution. The beginning of this transformation might be dated to reforms instituted by Wilhelm von Humboldt at the University of Berlin in the early nineteenth century, which asserted the university's right to autonomy and academic freedom, and set forth a vision of higher education devoted to general knowledge and universal citizenship, thus moving beyond the more parochial and vocational orientation of the early universities. Later in the nineteenth century, many universities came to see themselves as institutions that fostered original research and discovery, not just the preservation of the past. Research and subsequent publication – signifying one's contribution to a body of knowledge – became an essential element of the job. This was accompanied by the growth of doctoral programs, culminating in a thesis or dissertation, and by the founding of professional organizations and academic journals representing each discipline. Universities gained support from governments, increased tuition, or attracted private donations, providing funding for improved faculty salaries and research. Entrance to the university, and to the faculty, became more meritocratic.[10] All of these developments enhanced the status and autonomy of the university, which began to attract the brightest and most ambitious intellects.

One might argue that all of these later developments were preordained once universities were founded in the Middle Ages. Or one might take a contingent view of the matter. After all, some bodies of higher education did not make the transition to a fully professionalized organization and to open-ended, rational, and scientific investigation. Their devotion to the classics (e.g., in China) or to theology (e.g., madrasas in the Middle East) did not allow for such a transition. This is immaterial to our argument.

What matters is that a university system developed along modern lines over the course of the past two centuries. From a functionalist perspective, one could argue that it had to happen – maybe not exactly in the way that it did but in some analogous manner. No one has discovered a better mechanism for developing and purveying scientific knowledge. And scientific knowledge is essential for the operation of modern economies and governments. Testament to this is the diffusion of this university model from Europe to the rest of the world such that it is, today, virtually universal.

Synergies

Now, we can return to our main question. If modern universities are places one goes to think rationally about the world, and if these institutions must be granted a degree of autonomy in order to carry out their mission, what sort of person is likely to end up in this sort of institution?

It seems likely that the career path of a university professor will appeal to those with liberal inclinations. By contrast, those with a taste for money, adventure, spiritual transcendence, or dissipation are likely to choose different paths.

Likewise, the setting of a university is likely to provide a comfortable platform for those with liberal views, validating their perspectives on politics and society. By contrast, those of a more traditional or conservative cast may feel that their values and virtues are out of place and perhaps illegitimate. This may lead to a peer effect. Liberal students may speak louder and more self-confidently than conservatives or traditionists, as we speculate in Chapter 6.

In some sense, the ideal of liberalism might be regarded as a reflection of the university's core mission. To pursue truth effectively, scholarly bodies require freedom from outside interference, tolerance of diverse viewpoints and backgrounds, trust (so that scholars can cooperate), and cosmopolitanism (because there are no boundaries to truth). These are features of liberalism, in our capacious definition. One follows from the other. Accordingly, the

[10] On European universities generally, see Rüegg (2004) and Torstendahl (1993). On Germany, see Turner (1974). On France, see Weisz (1983). On the US, see Geiger (1986, 2014).

university must defend these principles – especially free speech – if its mission is to be successful. The institutional mission of a university places it ineluctably in the liberal camp.

Moreover, since the independence of the university is never safe from political interference outside the framework of a democratic constitution, university leaders are incentivized to advance and defend democracy. Their freedom and that of society at large are linked.

The synergy between universities and freedom is best illustrated in situations where they come into conflict. Reflecting on Russian history (both the imperial and Soviet periods), Marshall Shatz (1980: 10) writes,

Th[e] modern educated elite has presented its creator with one of its most intractable dilemmas. The dilemma arose when the state discovered that it could not keep the educated elite within the narrow intellectual boundaries it had set for it. First of all, even strictly technical training requires a certain amount of broad intellectual preparation and intellectual curiosity. Inevitably, some of the more thoughtful and sensitive educated individuals, newly equipped with the tools of inquiry, began delving into matters of public concern that the government insisted on reserving for its own judgment. Second, even professional and technical specialists require a certain amount of creative autonomy and self-expression in their work in order to carry it out properly. This in itself can bring them into conflict with a government which, through censorship, attempts to supervise and control intellectual activity along with all other aspects of national life. Third, and perhaps most important, the educated elite has to be given a certain degree of social and economic privilege. If their skills are in short supply, yet are essential for the country's development, educated individuals must be given both material incentives and social prestige in order to induce them to apply their talents. These very privileges, however, breed a sense of pride and self-esteem that leads them to resent the restrictions and arbitrary treatment they must sooner or later encounter at the hands of a paternalistic government.

From this perspective, there is something intrinsic to the academic enterprise that breeds dissent from arbitrary authority. Having built universities, the tsars created the conditions for a rebellious intelligentsia. More generally, it is difficult to conceive of an institution unencumbered by government restrictions that is designed to explore the world rationally – and, where possible, empirically – that does not endorse values such as democracy, engagement, law-abidingness, rationalism, science, tolerance, and cosmopolitanism.

In this light, it is not surprising that fascism, communism, and other totalitarian utopias have not had enduring appeal to the college set. They were briefly fashionable on some college campuses in the early to mid-twentieth century. But their appeal was greater for students than for faculty. And that appeal proved to be transitory, as noted.

Populist movements have never had much appeal to university communities or to the highly educated. It is not hard to see why, as they are generally hostile to universities, to intellectuals, and to higher learning more generally.

Intellectuals are viewed as an integral part of the elite that conspires against the interests of the common people.[11] Conversely, it is lack of education that qualifies someone as a man (or woman) of the people. That is why populist leaders trumpet their common origins and express themselves in a colloquial fashion. The opposition of universities to populism is preordained, and the more prominent the role of populism in popular politics, the greater the rift between gown and town is likely to become. Leaders like Bolsonaro, Chavez, Duterte, Orbán, and Trump are calculated to drive universities, and the university-educated, into the opposition camp.

Finally, for those interested in changing the status quo, education is an obvious tool. To John Dewey (1897: 16), "Education is the fundamental method of social progress and reform." Not surprisingly, reformers are often drawn to careers in education. Stand-patters will find other occupations. Thorstein Veblen, Friedrich Hayek, and many others have speculated that those characteristics of mind and personality that "lead people to reject the established order are closely tied to those that foster scholarly or artistic activity" (Lipset 1982: 148).

It is conceivable that reform might involve a return to the past, restoring the wisdom of the ancients or of God and thereby reversing the corruption of the modern era. A classical, "Great books" approach to education, or one centered on religious texts, is seemingly well suited to this vision of reform as restoration. We have observed that this vision was quite common through the nineteenth century.

However, if the modern university is defined by a quest for rational explanation, for empirically verifiable truths, and for scientific progress, a backward-looking vision of reform is not in keeping with university ideals. Instead, reforms that resonate on university campuses usually involve some species of change that is progressive in the sense of embracing the future and the ideal of improvement through time, whether incremental or revolutionary. A progressive notion of time is of course in keeping with the liberal project as it has been understood since the Enlightenment.

CONCLUSIONS

We began this chapter by reviewing a number of explanations for why universities have trended in a liberal direction over the course of the past century. This includes (a) the university as weathervane, (b) dislocation between cultural and economic capital, (c) public sector employment, (d) genetics, (e) intellectual activity, (f) the expansion of higher education, and (g)

---

[11] Since many prominent intellectuals, radicals, and college professors are of Jewish heritage, the anti-Semitic strain of many populist movements also comes into play. For populist leaders like Viktor Orbán, who is now attempting to banish the European university from Budapest, these features dovetail.

self-selection. Self-selection, we argued, is probably the most important proximal cause.

Next, we inquired into distal causes. If self-selection is the proximal cause, why is it that liberals, rather than conservatives, seem inclined to pursue careers as academics? Our explanation followed a functionalist logic.

Universities, we argued, are necessary to modern economies, governments, and societies. In order to fulfill their mission – which (among other things) involves the pursuit of general truths through rational inquiry – they must enjoy a degree of autonomy from outside pressures. Since rational inquiry is an important component of the liberal worldview, the curriculum's liberal tilt derives from its core mission. Since this orientation is likely to appeal to those with liberal sympathies, their influx shapes the development of the institution, creating new disciplines and reshaping old ones in a more liberal mold. This, in turn, reinforces a process of recruitment in which those with liberal inclinations are more likely to enter the academy. Briefly, universities are liberal today because their mission is attractive to people with a liberal worldview. This is recognized in the concepts of *liberal education* and *liberal arts*.

Granted, none of these assertions are measured and tested, and it is not entirely clear how they might be. Our arguments must therefore be regarded as speculative. Even so, we find the functionalist framework plausible as an explanation of the long-term intellectual trajectory of universities across the modern world.

PART V

CONCLUSIONS

10

Synthesis

Higher education is a perennial topic of debate. Some advocate expansion, making higher education available and affordable for all. Others advocate retrenchment, on the grounds that scarce public resources are better spent elsewhere (Caplan 2018) or that the functions of traditional universities can be achieved more efficiently by massive open online courses (MOOCs) (Haber 2014). The same debate is engaged among individuals and families, who must decide how much of their time and money a university degree is worth.

In this book, we leave aside economic questions to focus on the university's role as an influencer. What impact does a university education have on the social and political attitudes – and, by extension, the behavior – of those who attend? Are university graduates different? Do they view the world, and themselves, differently than they would have if they had not attended an institution of higher learning?

Having inundated the reader with a barrage of methods, arguments, and findings, it is time to pause so that we may arrive at a more synthetic view of our subject. We begin by examining evidence pertaining to the university's effect on student social and political attitudes, introduced in Part II of the book. Next, we address some of the nuances connected to those findings as well as the mechanisms at work, presented in Part III of the book. In the third section, we delve into the history of the university, the topic of Part IV of the book. The penultimate section adopts a long view of our subject, stretching from the origin of universities to the present-day effects of higher education. The final section speculates on the overall impact of universities on societies in the modern era, which we conceptualize as "soft power."

THE UNIVERSITY EFFECT

In Chapter 1, we introduced an overarching thesis – that universities have a liberalizing effect on their students. We employ the keyword *liberalism* in its original (also known as classic, nineteenth-century, or European) incarnation. This includes the ideals of freedom and liberty as well as commitments to the rule of law, law-abidingness, democracy, citizenship, progress, education, individualism, tolerance, openness to new ideas, rationalism, secularism, cosmopolitanism, and equality with respect to rights, duties, and dignity – but not redistribution or the welfare state. This worldview is associated with liberal or left political parties so it also has an explicitly political expression. But liberalism as we use the term is much broader than partisanship and many of its characteristics are not partisan at all.

In Chapter 2 we reviewed a long history of work dealing with the influence of education on the youth. At the end of the chapter we provided a systematic review of recent studies that offer an estimate of the causal effect of university attendance on social and political attitudes. An overwhelming majority of these studies indicate that universities exert a liberalizing effect (see Table 2.2).

Even so, we do not regard these studies as entirely conclusive. First, there are mixed findings for some outcomes such as religiosity and economics. Second, extant studies are generally focused on the US or Western Europe; the rest of the world is scarcely touched. Third, most studies rest on strong assumptions about the data-generating process, raising questions about potential bias. A smaller number of quasi-experimental studies report mixed, or much weaker, results.

For these reasons, the existing literature on university effects is inconclusive. This does not mean it should be jettisoned. Granted, if we could conduct experimental or quasi-experimental studies in countries throughout the world, we might propose to wipe the slate clean and start all over again with stronger evidence. But this is not possible at present and is unlikely to be possible in the foreseeable future, for reasons discussed in Chapter 3. Accordingly, as we reach for general conclusions about the relationship of higher education to social and political attitudes, we draw on the extant literature as well as our own analyses.

The first of these enlists a natural experiment in Romania, where a national exam (the baccalaureate, *bac*) regulates access to higher education, offering an opportunity for a regression discontinuity design centered on those whose scores fall just above and below the cutoff. We refer to this set of analyses as the Romanian Natural Experiment (RNE).

The second set of analyses rests on data from the World Values Survey (WVS), implemented in the most recent wave in conjunction with the European Values Survey (EVS). These surveys integrate data from over 120,000 respondents located in 79 countries around the world (Table 3.3). Our regression analyses of this data include country fixed effects along with covariates measuring age, sex, father's educational attainment, mother's educational attainment, and father's occupation when the respondent was a child.

These two research designs exhibit complementary strengths and weaknesses with respect to internal and external validity, as discussed in Chapter 3. Neither is fully conclusive on its own. But viewed together, we should be in a good position to evaluate the impact of university education on social and political attitudes.

The results from tests of the university effect on social and political attitudes across nearly 100 outcomes conducted with the RNE and WVS/EVS research designs are presented in Chapter 4 and summarized in Table 10.1. An upward arrow indicates a liberal effect, a downward arrow an anti-liberal effect, and a null symbol an effect that is so close to zero it cannot be distinguished from chance. Effects that surpass the conventional 95 percent confidence threshold are printed in bold. (Empty cells indicate that data is not available for that analysis.)

Table 10.1 suggests that the liberal thesis is mostly true. University education seems to enhance most outcomes classified as liberal. As in extant studies, the results are not quite as consistent for religiosity and economics as they are for other outcomes.

We suggested (in Chapter 4) that mixed findings for various aspects of religiosity may be due to the countervailing effects of higher education on participation (↑) and belief (↓). Highly educated people, it seems, are more likely to attend church (a participation effect) but no more likely to believe in a deity or in the existence of supernatural powers – presumably because of their commitment to rational, naturalistic ways of understanding the world.

EXTENSIONS

Having characterized the main findings, we turn to various extensions, presented in Part III of the book. We begin with nuances associated with the university effect and proceed to discuss possible mechanisms at work in this causal relationship.

Nuances

A great many issues were explored in Chapter 5, which we shall now attempt to summarize briefly.

First, we discussed the question of effect sizes, which are difficult to judge since they pertain mostly to attitudes rather than behavior. (How much is a shift from 3 to 4 on a five-point scale measuring support for women working outside the home?) One basis of evaluation is provided by other factors that are commonly regarded as important influences on social and political attitudes such as income, father's occupation (blue collar or white collar), sex (male or female), and age. When evaluated side by side with university education, we find that the latter is the strongest predictor overall. Thus, although we cannot answer the half-empty/half-full question, we can say that university education appears to have a greater impact on social and political attitudes than other demographic factors.

TABLE 10.1 *Results summarized*

	RNE	WVS	Fig.
Social capital index	⬆	⬆	4.2
Voting: have done or would do (+)	↑	⬆	4.1
Voted in the 2019 European Union elections (+)	↑		4.1
Interested in politics (+)	⬇	⬆	4.1
Political party: active member (+)	⬆	⬆	4.1
Signing a petition: have done or would do (+)	↑	⬆	4.1
Joining in boycotts: have done or would do (+)	↓	⬆	4.1
Attending peaceful demonstrations: have done or would do (+)	↑	⬆	4.1
Joining strikes: have done or would do (+)	↑	⬆	4.1
Any other act of protest: have done or would do (+)	↑		4.1
Sport or recreational organization: active member (+)	↑	⬆	4.1
Art, music or educational organization: active member (+)	↑	⬆	4.1
Labor union: active member (+)	↑	⬆	4.1
Environmental organization: active member (+)	↑	⬆	4.1
Professional association: active member (+)	↑	⬆	4.1
Humanitarian or charitable organization: active member (+)	↑	⬆	4.1
Consumer organization: active member (+)	↓	↑	4.1
Self-help group, mutual aid group: active member (+)	↑	⬆	4.1
Other organization: active member (+)	↑	⬆	4.1
Most people can be trusted (+)	⬆	⬆	4.1
Political leaders can be trusted (+)	⬆		4.1
Democracy index (+)		⬆	4.4
Importance of giving people more say in government decisions (+)		⬆	4.3
Importance of protecting freedom of speech (+)		⬆	4.3
People choose leaders in free elections (+)		⬆	4.3
The army takes over when government is incompetent (−)		⬆	4.3
Civil rights protect peoples' liberty against oppression (+)		⬆	4.3
People obey their rulers (−)		⬆	4.3
Living in a country that is governed democratically (+)		⬆	4.3
Having a strong leader (−)		⬆	4.3
Having experts, not government, make decisions (−)		Ø	4.3
Having the army rule the country (−)		⬆	4.3
Having a democratic political system (+)		⬆	4.3
Government has right of video surveillance (−)		Ø	4.3

(*continued*)

TABLE 10.1 (*continued*)

	RNE	WVS	Fig.
Government has right to monitor emails and other information exchanged on internet (–)		↑	4.3
Government has right to collect information about anyone living in country (–)		↑	4.3
Law-abidingness index (+)	↑	↑	4.6
Claiming government benefits to which you are not entitled is justifiable (–)	↑	↑	4.5
Avoiding a fare on public transport is justifiable (–)	↑	↑	4.5
Stealing property is justifiable (–)	↑	↑	4.5
Cheating on taxes if you have a chance is justifiable (–)	↑	↑	4.5
Someone accepting a bribe in the course of their duties is justifiable (–)	↑	↑	4.5
A magistrate or policeman accepting a bribe to close a case is justifiable (–)	↑		4.5
Providing information obtained as part of your job to people to whom it is of interest is justifiable (–)	↑		4.5
A policeman who receives money in exchange for not fining someone while in traffic is justifiable (–)	↑		4.5
To favor the firm of a friend to obtain funds/contracts from/with public institutions is justifiable (–)	↑		4.5
For a bureaucrat to accept a present to hasten the issuing of a document is justifiable (–)	↑		4.5
To help relatives or friends avoid sanctions or be advantaged in solving some problems is justifiable (–)	↑		4.5
To hire a relative in a public institution is justifiable (–)	↑		4.5
For a public employee to receive a present AFTER favorably pursuing your request is justifiable (–)	↑		4.5
To offer money or presents to a doctor to treat you is justifiable (–)	↑		4.5
To give money to a doctor because you are happy with the way they treated you is justifiable (–)	↑		4.5
To give presents to a teacher because you are pleased with their performance is justifiable (–)	↑		4.5
Punishment for corruption is too mild (+)	↑		4.5
Corruption is inevitable, and has always been around (–)	↑		4.5
Corruption is forgivable if no alternative is available in order to get something done (–)	↑		4.5
If I witnessed an act of corruption, I would report it (+)	↑		4.5

(*continued*)

TABLE 10.1 (*continued*)

	RNE	WVS	Fig.
Giving or receiving bribes for favors or work conducted is common among people you know (−)	↑		4.5
Cultural values index (+)	⬆	⬆	4.8
Parents beating children justifiable (−)	↑	⬆	4.7
One of my main goals in life has been to make my parents proud (−)	∅	⬆	4.7
Abortion justifiable (−)	∅	⬆	4.7
Divorce justifiable (+)	∅	⬆	4.7
Sex before marriage justifiable (+)	∅	⬆	4.7
Unmarried couples living together as neighbors acceptable (+)	↑	↑	4.7
Homosexuality justifiable (+)	↑	⬆	4.7
Homosexuals as neighbors acceptable (+)	↑	⬆	4.7
Prostitution justifiable (+)	∅	⬆	4.7
Drug addicts as neighbors acceptable (+)	↓	↓	4.7
People who have AIDS as neighbors acceptable (+)	↑	⬆	4.7
When jobs are scarce, men have more right to a job than women (−)	↑	⬆	4.7
If a woman earns more money than her husband, it's almost certain to cause problems (−)	⬆	⬆	4.7
Having a job is the best way for a woman to be an independent person (−)	↓		4.7
A man beating his wife justifiable (−)	↑	⬆	4.7
When a mother works for pay, the children suffer (−)	⬆	⬆	4.7
On the whole, men make better political leaders than women do (−)	↑	⬆	4.7
A university education is more important for a boy than for a girl (−)	⬆	⬆	4.7
On the whole, men make better business executives than women do (−)	⬆	⬆	4.7
Being a housewife is just as fulfilling as working for pay (−)	↑	⬆	4.7
When jobs are scarce, employers should prioritize people of this country over immigrants (−)	↑	⬆	4.7
People of a different race as neighbors acceptable (+)	⬆	⬆	4.7
Immigrants/foreign workers as neighbors acceptable (+)	↑	⬆	4.7
People who speak a different language as neighbors acceptable (+)	↑	⬆	4.7
People of a different religion as neighbors acceptable (+)	↑	⬆	4.7
Involvement in church or religious organization (−)	↓	↓	4.7

(continued)

Synthesis   259

TABLE 10.1 *(continued)*

	RNE	WVS	Fig.
Attend religious services (–)	↑	↓	4.7
Importance of God in your life (–)	↓	Ø	4.7
The world better off because of science and technology (+)	**↑**	**↑**	4.7
Support for parties with liberal positions on cultural issues (+)	**↑**	**↑**	4.9
Cosmopolitanism index (+)		↑	4.11
Feeling close to one's continent (+)		↑	4.10
Feeling close to the world (+)		↑	4.10
Trust in the UN (+)		↑	4.10
Trust in regional organization (+)		↑	4.10
Economic index (+)		↑	4.13
Private ownership of business should be increased (+)		↑	4.12
Individuals should take more responsibility for personal welfare (+)		↑	4.12
Competition is good (+)		↑	4.12
Government should tax the rich and subsidize the poor (–)		Ø	4.12
People should receive state aid for unemployment (–)		Ø	4.12
Incomes should be made more equal (–)		↑	4.12
The state should make incomes more equal (–)		↑	4.12
Support for parties with liberal (pro-market, anti-state) positions on economic issues (+)	**↑**	Ø	4.14
Environmental preservation preferred to economic growth (+)		↑	4.15
Your political views on a right–left scale (+)		↑	4.15

Summary of results presented in Chapter 4. Indices printed in italics; components of each index shown in indented entries following each index. RNE: Romanian Natural Experiment. WVS: World Values Survey, conducted in tandem with the European Values Survey (EVS). University influence: ↑ (liberal), Ø (null), ↓ (anti-liberal), bold (p<.05). Empty cells indicate that a question was not included in the RNE or WVS/EVS surveys.

Second, we tested the robustness of effects estimated from the RNE and WVS with and without controls for potential confounders. We find that the inclusion or exclusion of these factors has very little impact on the main results.

Third, we explored variations across different samples and research designs. To do so, we examined all outcomes that are shared across the RNE, WVS, and EVS, a total of fifty questions. The most important comparison is between samples drawn from Romania. Here, we find that estimates from the RNE and the WVS/EVS, when averaged together (to obtain an overall university effect), are remarkably close. In other words, results from the quasi-experimental analysis parallel those from the observational analysis. Insofar as differences can be detected, the liberalizing effect of university education appears slightly stronger in the RNE than the WVS/EVS, suggesting that any biases contained in the WVS/EVS lean against our main hypothesis. This lends credence to our multimethod methodology. (Recall that we have greater faith in the RNE than in the observational data drawn from the WVS/EVS.)

Fourth, we interrogated variations in effect sizes across all seventy-nine countries in the WVS/EVS sample. To do so, we employed the indices that we have used throughout this study to measure the central concepts of our inquiry: social capital, democracy, law-abidingness, culture, cosmopolitanism, economics, and overall ideology. For each outcome, we estimated regression models with the usual background covariates in our benchmark model (age, sex, father's educational attainment, mother's educational attainment, and father's job when respondent was a child). Here, these models are estimated separately for each country. We find that all values are positive, meaning that university attendance is associated with more liberal attitudes. However, some coefficients are stronger than others. The social capital effect is especially strong while the economic effect is weakest, as noted in Chapter 4.

We also calculated the mean causal effect for each country across all seven dimensions (social capital, democracy, and so on). This value is positive in all cases except Lebanon, where it is very slightly negative. One may conclude that the liberalizing effect of college education is nearly ubiquitous. However, it is stronger in some countries (e.g., France, the US, Poland, Slovenia, the UK, Switzerland, Colombia, Tunisia, Netherlands, and Denmark) than in others (e.g., Iraq, Vietnam, Lithuania, Turkey, Azerbaijan, Armenia, Cyprus, Chile, Bangladesh, and Lebanon).

To explain cross-country variability in the university effect, we regressed each outcome against a large number of country-level characteristics – economic, political, sociological, and educational. After testing dozens of potential causal factors, we found only two that strongly predict these country-level coefficients. The share of a country's population whose ancestors hail originally from Europe is positively correlated, suggesting that the university's liberalizing effect is greatest in countries that share a European demographic heritage. This is perhaps unsurprising given that both the university and the worldview of liberalism might be regarded as outgrowths of the European experience. Additionally, the university effect is greater in democracies than in autocracies. This may be explained by the fact that in a free society students and teachers are free – or at any rate, free*er* – to develop a liberal curriculum and to openly display liberal perspectives.

Fifth, we examined the liberalizing effect of college through the life-cycle. Assuming that most respondents attended college as young adults, we treated age as a proxy for "years since university." We then estimated regression models (including the standard set of control variables and country dummies) separately for each of the seven indices. We found some evidence that effects increase with time, particularly for social capital and democratic values. For other outcomes, there is no apparent pattern, or a much subtler one. In any case, there is no evidence that the effects of university attendance attenuate as people grow older and become more removed from their university experience. As far as we can tell, attending a university produces a lifelong effect on social and political attitudes.

Sixth, we tested various moderators – background factors that might enhance or mitigate the impact of university on social and political attitudes. We found little evidence for moderators such as sex, urbanization, or social class.

Seventh, we explored the impact of university education on the stability of party identification. To address this question, we asked student-age respondents of our RNE survey about their own partisan preference and the preference of their parents. Our analysis suggests that a university education increases the probability of deviation from parents' partisanship by fourteen percentage points – a substantial effect.

Finally, we examined the aggregation problem. Do the individual-level effects of college presented in Chapter 4 scale up to societal levels? Our review of studies conducted on three outcomes measurable at country levels – participation, corruption, and democracy – suggests the affirmative. The impact of university education on social and political attitudes scales up. As levels of higher education increase, we should anticipate aggregate, societal effects.

Mechanisms

In Chapter 6 we took up the question of *why* university education might have a liberalizing effect on students. Since universities are complex organisms, it would not be surprising if the impact on social and political attitudes operated through multiple pathways. Our discussion focused on three frameworks that seem to have the most general purview.

The *empowerment* framework highlights the impact of a university education on knowledge, social networks, and overall competency – each of which enhances an individual's self-confidence and capacity. Although we do not doubt that a university education is empowering, we find little evidence that these effects serve as mediators in the adoption of a more liberal worldview.

The *allocation* framework highlights the impact of a university on economic achievement, as measured by occupational status or earnings. Our data suggests that this may serve as an important mediator with respect to opinions about redistribution and the welfare state, where university students and former students show greater reticence than those without university education. On other attitudinal dimensions, however, we find little evidence of an allocative effect.

The *socialization* framework, finally, highlights the role of the university as a purveyor of norms. A more liberal view of the world may arise from contact with professors, peers, the curriculum, programs in civic education, or some combination of the foregoing. Through these experiences, college students learn the sort of attitudes and behaviors that are considered appropriate for highly educated people.

In our view, this is the most plausible pathway from university education to liberal views. Regrettably, these are not easy matters to measure and test in a systematic fashion, though we do find some evidence that those who follow a humanities/social science track are more affected by a college education than those who follow a natural science/engineering track – confirming the importance of socialization at the level of disciplines.

HISTORY

In Part IV of the book we addressed historical questions. Chapter 7 shows that universities, where they existed, were bit players in society until the modern era. They could not possibly have influenced many people because there were so few of them and they were generally quite small.

During those early years, university communities may have embraced some core liberal values such as constitutionalism (rule of law), progress, law-abidingness, individualism, openness to new ideas, and, to be sure, education. But it was not until much later that university professors and students began to assume other liberal values such as freedom, secularism, equal rights, and democracy.

Moreover, the differentiation of the university from the rest of society along partisan-ideological lines seems to be a fairly recent development. In countries for which we possess longitudinal evidence of voting behavior, partisan affiliations, or left–right self-placement, it seems that the university was at least as conservative as society at large until the twentieth century. During this century, and particularly after World War II, a dramatic divergence begins in which university faculty – and, to a lesser extent, students and former students – move into the liberal-left camp. By the end of the twentieth century products of the university are *much* more liberal than the societies they inhabit, at least judging by partisan affiliations and overall ideology.

In Chapter 8, we explored variations across the disciplines that compose the modern university. Three factors seem to explain why faculty in some disciplines are more liberal in their party affiliation and overall ideology than others. First, there is the question of political relevance. Professors in disciplines whose focus embraces hotly debated subjects – race, sexuality, politics, and so forth – are apt to embrace more liberal views. Second, there is a question of methodology. Professors in disciplines with a less scientific approach have greater leeway for political commentary and engagement. Finally, there is a question we have framed as "human-ism." Professors in disciplines focused on the study of humans – including not only the humanities and social sciences but also biology and medicine – seem predisposed to more liberal views.

Disciplinary differences notwithstanding, the more important point is that virtually all academic fields congregate on the liberal-left end of the spectrum at the present time. Even the right wing of the academy, which according to most surveys is located in business and engineering schools, is to the left of the general public – a historic shift relative to the long history of the university (charted in Chapter 7).

Chapter 9 takes up the explanatory question: Why did universities trend in a liberal direction in the twentieth century? We argued that the most important *proximal* cause is self-selection. People with liberal sympathies are more inclined to pursue academic careers than those with centrist or conservative sympathies.

Why, then, is a university position so appealing to those with liberal sympathies? We argued that this is an outgrowth of the university's core mission. An institution organized to pursue general truths through rational inquiry is more likely to appeal to liberals than to conservatives. Just as those with a strong belief in God commit their lives to the church, those with a penchant for secular truths commit their lives to the university. Over time, under conditions of growing organizational autonomy, the influx of this type of person affects the configuration of the university, creating new disciplines and reshaping old ones. This, in turn, reinforces a process of recruitment in which those with liberal inclinations are more likely to enter the academy.

THE LONG VIEW

We are now in a position to put the various arguments of the book together into a single framework, illustrated in schematic fashion in Figure 10.1.

At the beginning of the causal chain is the founding of an institution devoted to rational inquiry – a university. We do not attempt to theorize why such institutions arise in some parts of the world earlier than others. However, the spread of universities throughout the world in the modern era suggests that the university performs some vital, and perhaps indispensable, functions.

We assume that, over time, this institution gains a degree of autonomy; that is, the ability to set its own curriculum, subject to demand from students as well as from firms and governments who employ those with university degrees. We

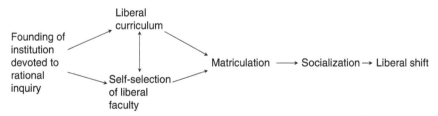

FIGURE 10.1 A long-range model of the university effect on students

also assume that inquiry takes an increasingly secular and rational course, establishing a liberal curriculum.

This, in turn, attracts persons of a liberal turn of mind. And they, in turn, shape the curriculum in a liberal direction. Faculty and curriculum interact over time, as indicated by the bidirectional line in Figure 10.1. The result is an increasingly liberal institution.

Students enter this milieu when they matriculate and are shaped by it through a complex process of socialization. This includes the influence of professors, peers, civic education programs, and the disciplines themselves – especially the social sciences and humanities, whose orientation is infused with normative concerns. The end-result is a liberal shift in social and political attitudes.

We believe the framework illustrated in Figure 10.1 is highly plausible. However, readers should bear in mind that the only portion of this causal model we are able to test in a rigorous empirical fashion is the link between matriculation and liberal social and political attitudes. Other posited links in this causal diagram are more difficult to ascertain, and thus remain speculative.

SOFT POWER

Thus far, this book has focused mostly on the impact of university education on students, their principal clientele. This choice of focus is strategic. Attendance at university comprises a recognizable treatment, allowing us to distinguish those who have been exposed to university life from those who have not. Causal estimates are possible.

However, this narrow approach to the question ignores spillover effects; that is, ways in which those in the treated group (students) might affect those in the control group (those who never attend an institution of higher education). It also neglects other mechanisms – other than formal degree programs, that is – by which universities impact politics and society. In this final section, we consider the university's impact on society *at large*.

It seems safe to assume that all citizens are affected by the existence of universities, even those who have never set foot in a dormitory or classroom. Some evidence of this societal effect was presented at the end of Chapter 5, where we looked at the question of "scaling up." Macro-level studies focused on the association between higher education and (a) political participation, (b) crime and corruption, and (c) democracy are encouraging. On these dimensions, there is a positive correlation between more educated populations and more desirable outcomes. However, questions may be raised about causal identification since there are many potential confounders as well as stochastic factors that make it difficult to distinguish signal from noise.

That said, the prima facie case for the university as a purveyor of facts and values in the modern era is quite strong. So far as we can tell, higher education exerts enormous "soft power."

Let us begin with the observation that although universities do not educate everyone, they do educate everyone who occupies an influential position in society. Virtually every chief executive officer, every top government official, and every civil society leader possesses a university degree. Even entertainment figures are likely to enter university at some point in their adult life.

Elites rule the world, and virtually all elites are highly educated. Insofar as universities matter, their indirect impact – through elites – may be more important than their direct influence. If universities socialize their students to a more liberal worldview, then this socialization effect is presumably magnified by the power that university graduates wield in societies around the world.

Granted, a smaller share of the population is highly educated in poorer societies, so fewer individuals are exposed to the direct impact of a university education. However, the influence of those elites who do obtain a college education may be greater. This is because education is usually accorded greater deference where it is in scarce supply. Having a college degree means a lot in a society where few can afford to attend college. Accordingly, in poorer societies the impact of college may flow primarily through indirect rather than direct channels. College socializes elites, and elites socialize non-elites.

Another factor to consider is the university's role as an organizational vehicle.[1] Universities bring together in one place individuals who are well positioned to bring about social change: namely, highly educated youths from privileged backgrounds. They have the skills and technology to mobilize; for example, to stage protests, to write political tracts, to give speeches, and to form alliances. Many of them have considerable free time on their hands, not to mention youthful energy and exuberance. Liebman, Walker, and Glazer (1972: 222) observe that "students are more readily mobilized than nonstudents, who are tied down by family and occupational responsibilities." By virtue of being thrown together at a liminal moment in their lives, group ties may form quickly and prove durable over the long haul. A good many influential firms, nongovernmental organizations, political parties, and revolutionary cells were formed by college classmates, growing from a handful of co-conspirators to national or international prominence. Universities are reliable incubators of novel ideas. Conveniently, leading universities are often located in cities, maximizing the visibility of actions undertaken and offering easy access to government, media, and other leading sectors.

More generally, universities have been instrumental in the professionalization of society. As economies become more complex, the demand for specialized skills grows. Universities have met that demand with courses and degree programs crafted to satisfy every occupational niche. As a result, more and more people are incentivized – and in some cases compelled by licensing laws – to attend

---

[1] For discussion, see Altbach (1984), Lipset (1967, 1972), and Lipset and Altbach (1969).

university and to complete a degree program of one sort or another. Over time, amateurs are displaced by professionals and a culture of expertise spreads. Because these forces transcend national boundaries, universities contribute to a unified, globalized world in which the same professional norms and standards apply everywhere.[2]

Relatedly, universities produce most of the base-level knowledge that informs decisions made by policymakers in all spheres of life – business, government, civil society, and individual households. We look to university faculty, or those with advanced degrees employed outside the hallowed halls of academe, to tell us where to dig for oil, how to address global warming, and how to raise our children.

There is no significant problem in society that has not been granted academic treatment. In a schooled society, David Baker (2014: 8) remarks, "dimensions of education reach into and define nearly every facet of human life." Although not everyone reads academic journals and monographs, this sort of basic research informs popular venues such as news reports, party platforms, television, Tweets, and Facebook postings. In addition, academics serve on special commissions, give expert testimony, write reports, and serve as consultants to a wide range of decisionmakers. Clark Kerr (2001 [1963]: xiv) notes, "The university's invisible product, knowledge, may be the most powerful single element in our culture, affecting the rise and fall of professions and even of social classes, of regions and even of nations."

To be sure, eggheads are rarely prominent in the public sphere. The general public pays little attention to the academy and its arcane forms of knowledge. Laypeople do not attend academic conferences, read academic journals, or follow what goes on in the ivory tower. It's dull.

However, what the public learns from popular sources – for example, from politicians, journalists, and entertainers – often derives from academic research. Consider the phenomenon of global warming. Most people believe it is real and that human activity has something to do with current climate trends. This is because scientists have been working on the problem for decades and have reached a strong consensus, and this consensus has filtered down to the general public through popular news sources.

Even on topics where academics do not reach consensus, popular debates tend to replicate academic debates. On questions of economic policy, for example, conservatives cite Milton Friedman and liberals cite John Maynard Keynes – an implicit acknowledgment of the power of the academy to shape public discourse. In Keynes's (1936: 383) much-quoted words, "The ideas of economists and political philosophers, both when they are right and when they are wrong are more powerful than is commonly understood. Indeed, the world is ruled by little else. Practical men, who believe themselves to be quite exempt from any intellectual influences, are usually slaves of some defunct economist."

---

[2] See Frank and Meyer (2007, 2020), Larson (1979), and Meyer (1977).

Insofar as ideas matter, universities matter, for that is where many of our most influential ideas come from.[3]

Modern universities are the high churches of secular society. They attract many of the brightest intellects. They train those who occupy the top rungs of virtually every institution, public or private. They help to professionalize occupations so that virtually every white-collar job now has its own academic discipline and professional association. They produce the practical knowledge that is increasingly important for running modern governments and economies. And they dispense that ineluctable elixir known as wisdom. In the words of Talcott Parsons and Gerald Platt (1973: vi), "Higher education, including the research complex, ha[s] become the most critical single feature of the developing structure of modern societies."

In this light, the influence of the university on modern life is ubiquitous. And the more complex society becomes, the more we are likely to depend upon the opinions of university-trained experts. Post-industrial societies are knowledge societies. Brain rules over brawn. This, in turn, bolsters the stature of the university, its degrees, its graduates, and its distinctive way of viewing the world. If we are correct in concluding that the university exerts a liberalizing effect on students, one may anticipate an even broader effect on society at large.

This effect is presumably expanding, given that enrollment in institutions of higher education is expanding at a steady rate throughout most of the world. If the rich world today offers a glimpse of the poor world tomorrow, we can reasonably expect that a fifth of the world's population will have a college degree at some point in the near future.

Of course, there are countervailing trends that challenge the hegemony of students, professors, and university-trained elites. In many countries, politics has taken a populist turn with a profoundly anti-intellectual bent. Universities have been targeted by leaders like Viktor Orbán in Hungary, Recep Tayyip Erdogan in Turkey, and Ron DeSantis (Republican hopeful) in the US.

Of equal importance is the proliferation of new media – blogs, niche cable television and radio shows (streamable on the web), Facebook, Twitter, and so forth. These venues do not privilege higher learning. People can say what they wish, and what they have to say is rarely informed by the latest academic research. Peer-reviewed publications are not the currency of social media. Here, bad information often seems to drive out good.

We cannot confidently predict how everything will shake out. Evidently, many factors are at work, and their purview extends far beyond the modest scope of this book. What we can predict, based on the evidence gathered here, is that the university will remain in the liberal corner.

---

[3] On the influence of ideas on politics and society, see Béland and Cox (2010), Grayling (2010), Jacobs (2009), Rueschemeyer (2006), and Wuthnow (1987).

Afterword

The American University

In recent years, higher education in the US has become a partisan battleground. Books and articles bemoaning the state of the university appear regularly and the issue has gained center stage in political rhetoric and news reportage. Outrage is especially keen on the right, where choice slogans like "woke," "politically correct," "cancel culture," "critical race theory," and "multiculturalism" suggest that higher education is out of step with the mainstream.[1]

In this Afterword, we reflect on the state of the American academy, drawing on results from the previous chapters. The first section explores the liberalizing effect of a college education in the US. The second section looks at the political views of the professoriate. The final section discusses the problem of ideological non-diversity and what might be done about it.

THE LIBERALIZING EFFECT OF COLLEGE

When comparing the overall impact of a college education on social and political attitudes across countries, we found that the US is exceptional. Table 5.3 suggests that the liberalizing effect of higher education may be greater for the US than for any other country in our global sample with the possible exception of France. (France has a higher score on the principal component index while the US has a higher score on the simple average index.) Although these results are based on observational data and hence do not have the same claims to causal identification as the Romanian Natural Experiment (RNE), the strength of the relationship between university

---

[1] This literature is cited copiously in Chapter 2. For recent treatments, see Binder and Kidder (2022) and Musto (2022).

education and liberalism appears to be especially strong in the US. If conservative commentators are upset, it is perhaps for good reason.

Let us take a closer look. In Figure 11.1, we present estimates for the US (depicted by a vertical line) along with estimates for all other countries ($N=78$) included in the latest wave of the World Values Survey (WVS)/European Values Survey (EVS), depicted by a histogram. As previously, our regression model includes background covariates measuring pretreatment characteristics of subjects including age, sex, father's educational attainment, mother's educational attainment, and father's job when the respondent was a child.

The estimated impact of university attendance in the US is indeed larger than the global average for every index considered, confirming that the liberalizing effect of university is distinctively strong. The US is exceptional along this dimension.

However, many of these university effects are nonpartisan in nature. In fact, the dimensions on which the impact of university education is strongest – relative to the global mean – are social capital, democracy, and law-abidingness. There would not appear to be any disagreement between Democrats and Republicans on the value of these classic-liberal virtues. Nothing here to jangle conservatives' nerves.

For outcomes that are more ideological in nature, the results for the US are only slightly stronger than the global mean. That is to say, the estimated effect of university attendance is still positive and substantively large, but estimates for the US are closer to estimates for other countries.

Importantly, attending college does *not* appear to make Americans less religious, a feature that matters a great deal to commentators who are critical of the American academy from a socially conservative perspective. Indeed, the impact of university education on church attendance, church membership, and belief in God is either positive or null. (This is similar to the results for the rest of the world, as portrayed in Figure 4.7.)

Economic conservatives should be pleased to discover that university attendance in the US is associated with greater hostility to the welfare state and to redistributive policies generally, as it is in other countries. (Recall that liberalism is defined in this book according to its historic meaning, which is skeptical of redistribution.) One possible explanation, vetted in Chapter 6, is that university education enhances future earnings, placing graduates in a higher income bracket and hence changing their perceived self-interest.

In summary, the impact of a university education on social and political attitudes in the US might be a little more profound than it is elsewhere. But the differences are most notable along non-ideological dimensions. We have characterized this impact as "liberal," a worldview that is in some respects aligned with the agenda of the Democratic Party and in some respects aligned with the agenda of the Republican Party.

With respect to party affiliation, Americans with university degrees have been moving away from the Republican Party for some time, with a marked acceleration

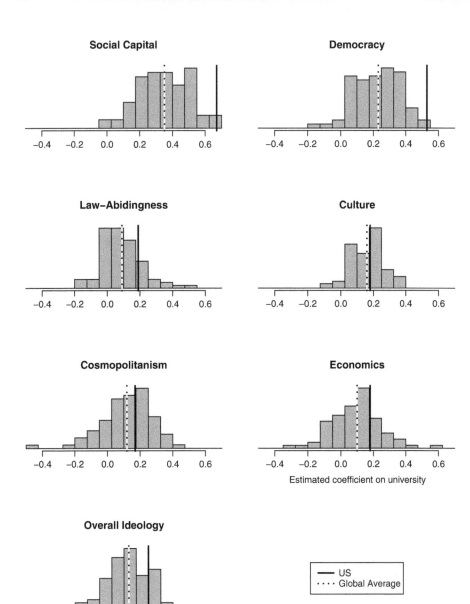

FIGURE 11.1 The impact of higher education in the US in comparative perspective
Histograms show distribution of coefficient estimates on university attendance from
separate regressions for each country predicting the specified index with background
covariates measuring age, sex, father's educational attainment, mother's educational
attainment, and father's occupation when the respondent was a child. Data drawn from
WVS/EVS surveys. Vertical solid and dashed lines show estimated coefficient on
university attendance using US subsample and the average coefficient estimate across
all countries.

in recent years. The same trend is evident in other Organisation for Economic Co-operation and Development (OECD) countries (see Figure 7.17). However, this may have more to do with changes in conservatism than with changes in the college experience. Where right-wing parties take on a populist hue, as the Republican Party has in recent years, we can expect highly educated voters to feel alienated, even if they agree with the party's stance on economic issues.

THE PROFESSORIATE

Conservative unease with the American university is not just about the university's impact on students. In Chapter 6, we discussed the complaint that conservative views are not welcome on university campuses. We also discussed the selection effect, according to which academic careers are more attractive to those with liberal views, leading to an ideologically skewed pattern of recruitment.

To measure this effect, we compared the views of the American professoriate with other Americans (see Table 7.5). Figure 11.2 extracts some of this information, comparing the attitudes of professors with members of the general population who do, and do not, have university degrees.

It will be seen that American university faculty hold views that are more liberal than the average citizen on most dimensions, especially when compared to citizens without a college degree (who, along most dimensions, offer the least liberal responses). Differences are especially stark on issues of a cultural nature; for example, capital punishment, abortion, gender, and sexual identity. Professors are much more likely to have voted and they are somewhat more likely to support the Democratic Party and to situate themselves on the left end of the political spectrum. There is no difference at all with respect to attendance at religious services.

In most respects, therefore, the views of American academics follow our understanding of liberalism. The one exception is their greater support for redistribution, which we have classified as leftist rather than liberal, and which sets university professors apart from the attitudes of those who have university degrees in the general public. However, the differences between these groups are not so great, and there is no difference whatsoever between professors and less educated members of the general public. It is the highly educated members of the general public who most strongly oppose redistributive policy measures, according to this survey. (This is in keeping with the general effect of a university education, noted earlier.)

Across most of the outcomes surveyed in Figure 11.2, contrasts between members of the general public with and without degrees are about as great as the contrast between professors and highly educated members of the general public. One possible interpretation is that this pattern reflects "degrees of education," with the professoriate being the most educated. In any case, across a broad range of outcomes the views of professors are a lot more

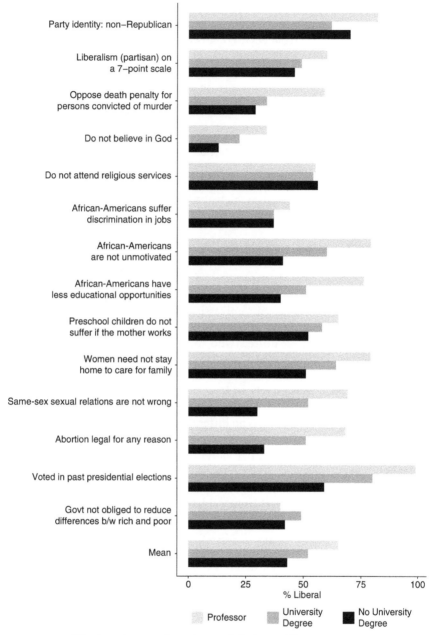

FIGURE 11.2 The American professoriate and the lay public
Share of respondents who offer "liberal" responses. Sources: Politics of the American
Professoriate survey (Gross and Simmons 2014b); General Social Survey (NORC 2019).
For further information, see Table 7.5.

liberal than the non-college-educated and slightly more liberal than the college-educated.

Of course, *some* faculty members hold views that are a lot more left wing than those held by most Americans (with or without college degrees). Lately, these ideas have been getting a lot of attention in the media and in conservative circles. For example, critical race theory, a concept that is difficult to define but highly critical of mainstream approaches to racial issues, is currently in the crosshairs of Republican politicians and media pundits.

This book does not take a position in these debates, which lie far from the authors' expertise. The point we want to stress is that kerfuffles of this sort may have more to do with partisan agendas than with the landscape of the American academy.

There are over 5,000 colleges and universities in the US, most of which are privately run. We have no way of estimating how many departments, programs, and special centers and institutes operate across these campuses. But we do know that they house roughly 800,000 college faculty, including tenure-track professors, instructors, and lecturers.[2] On a per-capita basis, the US probably possesses the largest and most diverse university sector in the world.

In this light, one should not be surprised that some colleges, some programs, and some university professors hold views that are out of the mainstream. Arguably, this is something to celebrate rather than to bemoan. After all, one purpose of the university is to explore new and controversial ideas and to expose students to a range of perspectives.

In any case, one should not confuse the tails of a distribution with the mean. If one wishes to know the views of American academics, one should consult surveys of the subject such as those reported in Table 8.1 and others discussed in Chapter 7. If these statistics do not produce stimulating fodder for Twitter or soundbites for cable news, so much the better. Americans should be pushing back against growing affective polarization.

A final point concerns the changing shape of the American university. Long-standing trends suggest that STEM (science, technology, engineering, mathematics) disciplines and professional schools (especially schools of business and management) will continue to expand in the coming decades. By contrast, disciplines within the humanities are likely to remain stable or shrink (Frank and Meyer 2020). These trends follow the changing demands, and increasingly technical nature, of the workforce.

As it happens, the expanding fields are those where the professoriate holds more centrist views while the contracting or static fields are those where the professoriate leans more to the left (see Table 8.1). Since technical and professional education is also less prone to politicization, these trends may moderate the tenor of the university experience over time. There is no Marxist school of engineering.

---

[2] See https://nces.ed.gov/programs/digest/d14/tables/dt14_315.20.asp.

THE DIVERSITY PROBLEM

Having said this, we do not wish to appear entirely complacent. It *is* a problem, in our view, that most of the ideological diversity found on American university campuses is on the left rather than the right. There are many flavors of left but there are hardly enough conservatives to offer variety on the right. We suspect that this imbalance impairs the quality of research, of teaching, and of debate – within the classroom and without[3] – and there is no doubt it makes campus conservatives uncomfortable (as discussed in Chapter 9).

We see no easy solution to this problem given the predominant patterns of recruitment into the humanities and social sciences. One cannot hire people who do not exist. Granted, one can find warm bodies with the requisite degrees and ideological views for any faculty position. However, one must be wary of prioritizing ideology over teaching and research. There is also an adverse selection problem. If affirmative action for conservatives is widely embraced, candidates desperate for employment would be incentivized to adopt, or feign, conservative views in order to get hired.

The more important point is that ideology is not a relevant criterion for a faculty position. Inquiring about a job candidate's political views is a bit like inquiring about their religion, country of origin, sexuality, or marital status. These personal attributes are not germane to most academic jobs, at least not in any obvious sense. Asking about them, or attempting to determine them (e.g., from social media sites), may be viewed as offensive and could be illegal.

Moreover, people who wear their ideology on their sleeve – who are clearly and demonstrably on the right or left – are often not very thoughtful observers and may have difficulty assuming a dispassionate view of the topics they are teaching and researching. This is especially problematic in the humanities and social sciences. Fields where we worry about the ideological predominance of liberals are also fields where we ought to worry about ideological hacks, on the left or the right.

To put it bluntly, hiring dogmatic rightists is not a good solution to the problem of dogmatic leftists. Doing so will undermine the practice of scholarly inquiry as well as its perceived legitimacy, encouraging the cynical view that "It's all politics." The American academy needs more ideological diversity but it does not need more ideologues.

Under the circumstances, the only sensible solution we can envision to the problem of liberal hegemony is a long-term one. We must work hard to make

---

[3] Critical discussions have focused on political science (Campbell 2019; Gray 2019; Maranto, Redding, and Hess 2009; Rom 2019; Wilson 2019; Zigerell 2017, 2019), psychology (Crawford and Jussim 2017; Duarte et al. 2015; Lukianoff and Haidt 2019; Tetlock 1994), sociology (Klein and Stern 2013; Martin 2016), economics (Klein and Stern 2009), English (Abrams 1997), philosophy (Peters et al. 2020), gender studies (Söderlund and Madison 2017), and the university at large (Parsons 2020; Redding 2013). For a more optimistic account of the social sciences, see Grossman (2021).

conservatives feel at home in the academy, overcoming the widely held perception that being a college professor is a lefty occupation. At the same time, we must motivate young people with conservative views to pursue academic careers. This will take time. And it will take work, on both sides of the aisle.

Leftists must stop presuming that everyone in the academy (and in their classroom) shares their worldview. Ridiculing the Republican Party is highly inappropriate and unprofessional when standing behind a classroom podium.

Conservatives must be careful about running down the academy. The more they caricature the university as a cockeyed liberal behemoth, the more they are likely to discourage thoughtful conservatives from pursuing academic careers.

CONCLUSIONS

The impact of college on students – of which there are roughly 20 million in any given year across the US – is much more important than its impact on academics or aspiring academics. Arguably, we should care about the views of the professoriate only insofar as they influence the views of students. Alas, we cannot separate out the impact of professors from the impact of other aspects of the college experience – empowerment, allocation, and other aspects of socialization, as discussed in Chapter 6.

What we can determine with some degree of confidence is the *overall* effect of going to college on social and political attitudes. We have shown that this impact is profound, especially in the US.

We characterized this effect as *liberal* – a wide-ranging moniker encompassing social capital (e.g., a greater propensity for political engagement), democracy (e.g., support for democratic freedoms), law-abidingness (e.g., intolerance for crime and corruption), culture (e.g., support for equal rights for women and minorities), cosmopolitanism (e.g., support for supranational organizations and identities), and economics (e.g., less support for redistribution).

Although American professors lean to the left on economic issues, those graduating with a college degree are evidently leery of taxing and spending, and of redistributive measures generally. Either leftist professors are not proselytizing or students are not listening. On *this* dimension, we suggested, the liberal impact of university is probably a product of economics: college graduates stand to make more money than those without a college degree and this may affect their view of redistribution.

We leave to readers to determine whether the liberalizing effect of college should be regarded in a positive or negative light. But we want to signal that many of these effects should be inoffensive – and perhaps even pleasing – to conservatives. In this respect, widespread suspicion of the American university from the right may be misplaced.

Romanian Natural Experiment Questionnaire

This is the text of the questionnaire, entitled "Views of Romanian Society and Politics," completed by survey respondents in Romania and described in Chapter 3. The Romanian translation is available upon request.

Most of these questions were drawn from the World Values Survey 6 (WVS 6) or the 2015 Comparative Study on the Phenomenon of Corruption in the Romanian Ministry of Interior (CSC),[1] as noted later.

The survey is designed to test a number of different outcomes that form the basis of four studies that we conducted, as indicated later. Each was pre-registered separately.

Study 1: Social Capital

Voting (V)
Other modes of political participation (P)
Membership (M)
Trust (T)

Study 2: Crime and Corruption

Crime/corruption (C)

Study 3: Cultural Values

Cultural values (CV) (labeled "traditional values" in the pre-registration document)

Study 4: Ideology

Ideology (I) (labeled "political liberalism" in the pre-registration document)

---

[1] See: www.mai-dga.ro/wp-content/uploads/2017/01/Studiu-comparativ-privind-fenomenul-coruptiei-in-MAI.pdf.

INTRODUCTION

This is a short survey of attitudes toward politics and society in Romania. It should take five to ten minutes to complete. It is entirely voluntary and you may exit the survey at any time.

Participants are eligible to win a free smartphone or tablet. The link to qualify for that offer is at the end of the survey.

All information provided in this survey is confidential.

If you have questions about the survey, or about any other aspect of this process, please contact one of the names below.

We appreciate your help!

Researchers:

- John Gerring, Professor, Department of Government, University of Texas at Austin, USA
- Emanuel Coman, Assistant Professor, Department of Political Science, Trinity College, Dublin, Ireland
- Stephen Jessee, Associate Professor, Department of Government, University of Texas at Austin, USA

QUESTIONS OF THEORETICAL INTEREST

Questions randomized within this section.

For each of the following actions indicate whether you think it can be justified in some circumstances.

10-point scale: 1 = Never justifiable ... 5 = Sometimes justifiable ... 10 = Always justifiable

- q1_1 – Claiming government benefits to which you are not entitled (C) – (WVS 6)
- q1_2 – Avoiding a fare on public transport (C) – (WVS 6)
- q1_3 – Stealing property (C) – (WVS 6)
- q1_4 – Cheating on taxes if you have a chance (C) – (WVS 6)
- q1_5 – Someone accepting a bribe in the course of their duties (C) – (WVS 6)
- q1_6 – Homosexuality (CV) – (WVS 6)
- q1_7 – Prostitution (CV) – (WVS 6)
- q1_8 – Abortion (CV) – (WVS 6)
- q1_9 – Divorce (CV) – (WVS 6)
- q1_10 – Sex before marriage (CV) – (WVS 6)
- q1_11 – For a man to beat his wife (CV) – (WVS 6)
- q1_12 – Parents beating children (CV) – (WVS 6)
- q1_13 – For a magistrate or policeman to accept a bribe to close a case (C) – (WVS 6)

- q1_14 – Providing information accessed or obtained as part of your job, to people to whom it may be of interest (C) – (CSC)
- q1_15 – To receive money (a police officer) to not fine someone while in traffic (C) – (CSC)
- q1_16 – To favor the firm of a friend to obtain funds/contracts from/with public institutions (C) – (CSC)
- q1_17 – For a bureaucrat to accept a present to hasten the issuing of a document (C) – (CSC)
- q1_18 – To help relatives or friends avoid sanctions or to be advantaged in solving some problems (C) – (CSC)
- q1_19 – To hire a relative in a public institution (C) – (CSC)
- q1_20 – For a public employee to receive a present AFTER they have favorably pursued your request, without breaking their work conduct (C) – (CSC)
- q1_21 – To offer money or presents to a doctor to treat you (C) – (CSC)
- q1_22 – To give money or presents to a doctor because you are happy with the way they treated you (C) – (CSC)
- q1_23 – To give presents to a teacher because you are pleased with the way they educated your children (C) – (CSC)

To what extent do you agree or disagree with the following statements?

Fully agree, Partially agree, Neither agree nor disagree, Partially disagree, Fully disagree

- q2_1 – Most people can be trusted (T) – (WVS 6)
- q2_2 – Political leaders can be trusted (T) – (WVS 6)
- q2_3 – Punishment for corruption is too mild (C) – (CSC)
- q2_4 – Corruption is inevitable, and has always been around (C) – (CSC)
- q2_5 – Corruption is forgivable if no alternative is available in order to get something done (C) – (CSC)
- q2_6 – If I witnessed an act of corruption, I would report it (C) – (CSC)

How common are the following practices among people you know (friends, family, business associates)?

Never, Occasionally, Every now and then, Regularly, All the time

- q3 – Giving or receiving bribes in exchange for favors or work conducted, or to get out of a jam (C) – (CSC)

q4 – In the 2019 European Union elections, did you vote? *(V)*

Yes, No, Don't remember, Not old enough to qualify

q5 – How interested are you in politics? *(P)*

Not at all interested, Not very interested, Somewhat interested, Very interested (WVS 6)

For each of the following organizations, indicate your current involvement.

Not a member, Inactive member, Active member

- q6_1 – Church or religious organization (CV) – (WVS 6)
- q6_2 – Sport or recreational organization (M) – (WVS 6)
- q6_3 – Art, music or educational organization (M) – (WVS 6)
- q6_4 – Labor union (M) – (WVS 6)
- q6_5 – Political party (P) – (WVS 6)
- q6_6 – Environmental organization (M) – (WVS 6)
- q6_7 – Professional association (M) – (WVS 6)
- q6_8 – Humanitarian or charitable organization (M) – (WVS 6)
- q6_9 – Consumer organization (M) – (WVS 6)
- q6_10 – Self-help group, mutual aid group (M) – (WVS 6)
- q6_11 – Other organization (M) – (WVS 6)

Here are some forms of political action that people can take. For each one, indicate your involvement ...

I would never under any circumstances do this, I might do this, I definitely would do this or have done this

- q7_1 – Voting (V) – (WVS 6)
- q7_2 – Signing a petition (P) – (WVS 6)
- q7_3 – Joining in boycotts (P) – (WVS 6)
- q7_4 – Attending peaceful demonstrations (P) – (WVS 6)
- q7_5 – Joining strikes (P) – (WVS 6)
- q7_6 – Any other act of protest (P) – (WVS 6)

How do you feel about the following statements?

Strongly agree, Agree, Neither agree nor disagree, Disagree, Strongly disagree

- q8_1 – When jobs are scarce, men should have more right to a job than women (CV) – (WVS 6)
- q8_2 – When jobs are scarce, employers should give priority to people of this country over immigrants (CV) – (WVS 6)
- q8_3 – If a woman earns more money than her husband, it's almost certain to cause problems (CV) – (WVS 6)
- q8_4 – Having a job is the best way for a woman to be an independent person (CV) – (WVS 6)

Apart from weddings and funerals, about how often do you attend religious services these days? (CV) – (WVS 6)

- q9_1 – More than once a week
- q9_2 – Once a week
- q9_3 – Once a month
- q9_4 – Only on special holy days
- q9_5 – Once a year
- q9_6 – Less often
- q9_7 – Never, practically never

q10 – How important is God in your life? *(CV) – (WVS 6)*

10-point scale: 1= "not at all important," 10 = "very important"

q_11 – All things considered, would you say that the world is better off, or worse off, because of science and technology? (CV) – (WVS 6)

10-point scale: 1 = "the world is a lot worse off" … 10 = "the world is a lot better off"

Below are various groups of people. Please indicate any that you would *not* like to have as neighbors …

- q12_1 – Drug addicts (CV) – (WVS 6)
- q12_2 – People of a different race (CV) – (WVS 6)
- q12_3 – People who have AIDS (CV) – (WVS 6)
- q12_4 – Immigrants/foreign workers (CV) – (WVS 6)
- q12_5 – Homosexuals (CV) – (WVS 6)
- q12_6 – People of a different religion (CV) – (WVS 6)
- q12_7 – Unmarried couples living together (CV) – (WVS 6)
- q12_8 – People who speak a different language (CV) – (WVS 6)

For each of the following statements, indicate your views.

Strongly agree, Agree, Neither agree nor disagree, Disagree, Strongly disagree

- q13_1 – One of my main goals in life has been to make my parents proud (CV) – (WVS 6)
- q13_2 – When a mother works for pay, the children suffer (CV) – (WVS 6)
- q13_3 – On the whole, men make better political leaders than women do (CV) – (WVS 6)
- q13_4 – A university education is more important for a boy than for a girl (CV) – (WVS 6)
- q13_5 – On the whole, men make better business executives than women do (CV) – (WVS 6)
- q13_6 – Being a housewife is just as fulfilling as working for pay (CV) – (WVS 6)

q14 – If there were a national election tomorrow, for which party on this list would you vote? (I) – (WVS 6)

- The Save Romania Union
- The Social-Democratic Party
- The National Liberal Party
- Democratic Alliance of Hungarians in Romania
- Alliance of Liberals and Democrats
- People's Movement Party
- Other

POST-SURVEY QUESTIONS

p1. What was the last high school that you attended?

- County [prepopulated menu]
- City [prepopulated menu]
- High school [prepopulated menu]

p2. Have you finished high school?

- No
- Yes, without Bac
- Yes, with Bac

[If the latter, then ask ...]

GRADYEAR. In what year did you finish high school?

[If high school finished in 2019, then ask ...]

p4. Which of the following best describes your current situation?

- In the process of applying for admission to university, with intention to start this fall
- Admitted to university but have not started yet
- Enrolled in university and attending
- None of the above

p5. Have you ever attended, or do you plan to attend, a vocational school (post-secondary)?

- I am planning to attend
- I am currently attending
- I have attended

p6. Have you ever – currently, or in the past – attended university (even for a short period of time)?

- No [skip the following questions on university education]
- Yes

p7. Are you currently enrolled in university?

- No
- Yes

p8. How many years of university education have you completed?

- Less than one year
- One year
- Two years
- Three years
- Four years
- Five years or more

p9. What is the name of the last university you attended, or the university you currently attend or plan to attend?

pre-populated list

p10. What is, or was, your major course of study for the BA?

pre-populated list

p11. Please indicate your sex

- Male
- Female

p12. Are you currently (answer one of the following) . . .

- Married
- Living together as married
- Divorced
- Separated
- Widowed
- Single

p13. Have you had any children?

- No children
- One child
- Two children
- Three children

- Four children
- Five children
- Six children
- Seven children
- Eight or more children

p14_1. Are you employed now or not?

- Yes
- No

[If answered yes on p14_1]]

p14_2. About how many hours a week?

- Full-time employee (30 hours a week or more)
- Part-time employee (less than 30 hours a week)
- Self-employed

[If answered no on p14_2]

p14_3. Which of the following fits your description

- Retired/pensioned
- Housewife not otherwise employed
- Student
- Unemployed
- Other (write in): _____

p15. Would you describe yourself as belonging to the

- Upper class
- Upper middle class
- Lower middle class
- Working class
- Lower class

p16. Imagine an income scale on which 1 indicates the lowest income group and 10 the highest income group in your country. Indicate in what group your household is, counting all wages, salaries, pensions, and other incomes that come in.

10-point scale: 1 = Lowest group ... 10 = Highest group

p17. Please indicate your year of birth

year

p18. In what country do you currently live?

pre-populated list

[Ask only if answer to previous question is Romania]

p19. What is the postal code of the town or city where you currently live?

p20. What is the highest educational level that your father attained?

- No formal education
- Incomplete primary school
- Complete primary school
- Incomplete secondary school: technical/vocational type
- Complete secondary school: technical/vocational type
- Incomplete secondary: university-preparatory type
- Complete secondary: university-preparatory type
- Some university-level education, without degree
- University-level education, with degree
- Master degree
- Doctoral (PhD)

p21. What party does your father support (to the best of your knowledge)? If your father is deceased or you have little contact with him, answer for your mother. *(I)*

- The Save Romania Union
- The Social-Democratic Party
- The National Liberal Party
- Democratic Alliance of Hungarians in Romania
- Alliance of Liberals and Democrats
- People's Movement Party
- Other

p22. Would you describe your family – when you were growing up – as belonging to the

- Upper class
- Upper middle class
- Lower middle class
- Working class
- Lower class

p23. If you wish, please tell us what ethnic group you identify with.

pre-populated list

APPENDIX B

World Values Survey/European Values Survey Questionnaire

These questions are reproduced (verbatim) from the merged World Values Survey (WVS)/European Values Survey (EVS), 2017. Note that some questions on the WVS are not included in the EVS, meaning they cover a smaller sample, as laid out in Table 3.3. For each question or answer option (constituting a separate variable in the dataset), we list the WVS code first (usually starting with "Q") followed by the EVS code (if included in the EVS survey).

On this list are various groups of people. Could you please mention any that you would not like to have as neighbors?

- Q18/A124_08 – Drug addicts
- Q19/A124_02 – People of a different race
- Q20 – People who have AIDS
- Q21/A124_06 – Immigrants/foreign workers
- Q22/A124_09 – Homosexuals
- Q23 – People of a different religion
- Q25 – Unmarried couples living together
- Q26 – People who speak a different language

For each of the following statements I read out, can you tell me how strongly you agree or disagree with each. Do you strongly agree (1), agree (2), disagree (3), or strongly disagree (4)?

- Q27/D054 – One of my main goals in life has been to make my parents proud
- Q28/D061 – When a mother works for pay, the children suffer
- Q29/D059 – On the whole, men make better political leaders than women do
- Q30/D060 – A university education is more important for a boy than for a girl
- Q31/D078 – On the whole, men make better business executives than women do

285

- Q32 – Being a housewife is just as fulfilling as working for pay
- Q33/C001_01 – When jobs are scarce, men should have more right to a job than women
- Q34/C002_01 – When jobs are scarce, employers should prioritize people of this country over immigrants
- Q35 – If a woman earns more money than her husband, it's almost certain to cause problems

Q57/A165. Generally speaking, would you say that most people can be trusted or that you need to be very careful in dealing with people?

1. Most people can be trusted
2. Need to be very careful

Please look at this card and tell me, for each item listed, how much confidence you have in them, is it a great deal, quite a lot, not very much or none at all?

- Q82/E069_18A – Main regional organization
- Q83/E069_20 – United Nations Organization

Now I am going to read off a list of voluntary organizations. For each organization, could you tell me whether you are an active member, an inactive member or not a member of that type of organization?

- Q94/A065 – Church or religious organization
- Q95/A074 – Sports or recreational organization
- Q96/A066 – Art, music or educational organization
- Q97/A067 – Labor union
- Q98/A068 – Political party
- Q99/A071 – Environmental organization
- Q100/A072 – Professional organization
- Q101/A080_01 – Humanitarian or charitable organization
- Q102/A078 – Consumer organization
- Q103/A080_02 – Self-help group, mutual aid group
- Q105/A079 – Other organization

Q111/B008. Here are two statements people sometimes make when discussing the environment and economic growth. Which of them comes closer to your own point of view? (*Read out and code one answer*):

1. Protecting the environment should be given priority, even if it causes slower economic growth and some loss of jobs.
2. Economic growth and creating jobs should be the top priority, even if the environment suffers to some extent.
3. Other answer (code if volunteered only!).

Q154/E003. If you had to choose, which of the things on this card would you say is most important?

1. Maintaining order in the nation
2. Giving people more say in important government decisions
3. Fighting rising prices
4. Protecting freedom of speech

Q163. All things considered, would you say that the world is better off, or worse off, because of science and technology? Please tell me which comes closest to your view on this scale: 1 means that "the world is a lot worse off," and 10 means that "the world is a lot better off."

Q164/F063. How important is God in your life? Please use this scale to indicate. 10 means "very important" and 1 means "not at all important."

Q171/F028. Apart from weddings and funerals, about how often do you attend religious services these days?

1. More than once a week
2. Once a week
3. Once a month
4. Only on special holy days
5. Once a year
6. Less often
7. Never, practically never

Please tell me for each of the following actions whether you think it can always be justified, never be justified, or somewhere in between, using this card (1= "Never justifiable"; 10= "Always justifiable").

- Q177/F114A – Claiming government benefits to which you are not entitled
- Q178/F115 – Avoiding a fare on public transport
- Q179 – Stealing property
- Q180/F116 – Cheating on taxes if you have a chance
- Q181/F117 – Someone accepting a bribe in the course of their duties
- Q182/F118 – Homosexuality
- Q183/F119 – Prostitution
- Q184/F120 – Abortion
- Q185/F121 – Divorce
- Q186 – Sex before marriage
- Q189 – For a man to beat his wife
- Q190 – Parents beating children

Do you think that your country's government should or should not have the right to do the following?

- Q196/H009 – Keep people under surveillance in public areas
- Q197/H010 – Monitor all emails and any other information exchanged on the Internet
- Q198/H011 – Collect information about anyone living in this country without their knowledge

Q199. How interested would you say you are in politics? Are you...

1. Very interested
2. Somehow interested
3. Not very interested
4. Not at all interested

Now I'd like you to look at this card. I'm going to read out some forms of political action that people can take, and I'd like you to tell me, for each one, whether you have done any of these things, whether you might do it or would never under any circumstances do it (1="Have done"; 2="Might do"; 3="Would never do").

- Q209/E025 – Signing a petition
- Q210/E026 – Joining in boycotts
- Q211/E027 – Attending peaceful demonstrations
- Q212/E028 – Joining strikes

When elections take place, do you vote always, usually or never? Please tell me separately for each of the following levels:

- Q222/E264 – National level

Q223/E179. If there were a national election tomorrow, for which party on this list would you vote? Just call out the number on this card.

I'm going to describe various types of political systems and ask what you think about each as a way of governing this country. For each one, would you say it is a very good, fairly good, fairly bad or very bad way of governing this country? (1="Very good"; 2="Fairly good"; 3="Fairly bad"; 4="Very bad")

- Q235/E114 – Having a strong leader who does not have to bother with parliament and elections
- Q236/E115 – Having experts, not government, make decisions according to what they think is best for the country
- Q237/E116 – Having the army rule
- Q238/E117 – Having a democratic political system

Q240/E033. In political matters, people talk of "the left" and "the right." How would you place your views on this scale, generally speaking? (*Code one number*) [Show scale 1 to 10]

Many things are desirable, but not all of them are essential characteristics of democracy. Please tell me for each of the following things how essential you think it is as a characteristic of democracy. Use this scale where 1 means "not at all an essential characteristic of democracy" and 10 means it definitely is "an essential characteristic of democracy"

- Q243/E226 – People choose their leaders in free elections
- Q245/E228 – The army takes over when the government is incompetent
- Q246/E229 – Civil rights protect people from government oppression
- Q248/E233B – People obey their rulers

Q250/E235. How important is it for you to live in a country that is governed democratically? On this scale where 1 means it is "not at all important" and 10 means "absolutely important" what position would you choose?

People have different views about themselves and how they relate to the world. Using this card, would you tell me how close do you feel to … ?

- Q258/G062 – your continent
- Q259/G063 – the world

References

Aarøe, Lene, Vivek Appadurai, Kasper M. Hansen et al. 2021. "Genetic predictors of educational attainment and intelligence test performance predict voter turnout." *Nature Human Behaviour* 5(2): 281–291.

Abramowitz, Alan I., Kyle L. Saunders. 2008. "Is polarization a myth?" *Journal of Politics* 70(2): 542–555.

Abrams, Meyer H. 1997. "The transformation of English studies: 1930–1995." *Daedalus* 126(1): 105–131.

Acemoglu, Daron, Simon Johnson, James A. Robinson, Pierre Yared. 2005. "From education to democracy?" *American Economic Review* 95(2) (May): 44–49.

Adcock, Robert. 2014. *Liberalism and the Emergence of American Political Science: A Transatlantic Tale*. Oxford: Oxford University Press.

Adcock, Robert, Mark Bevir, Shannon C. Stimson (eds.). 2009. *Modern Political Science: Anglo-American Exchanges since 1880*. Princeton, NJ: Princeton University Press.

Adegbuyi, Fadeki. 2021. "Caught in the study web: Exploring Gen Z's ambitious and anxiety-fuelled pursuit of straight A's across YouTube, TikTok, Discord, and Twitter." *Cybernaut* (May 24). https://every.to/cybernaut/caught-in-the-study-web.

Albornoz, Orlando. 1967. "Academic freedom and higher education in Latin America." In Seymour Martin Lipset (ed.), *Student Politics*. New York: Basic Books: 283–292.

al-Gharbi, Musa. 2019. "Seizing the means of knowledge production." Heterodox (October 4). https://heterodoxacademy.org/blog/seizing-means-knowledge-production.

Allport, Gordon W. 1929. "The composition of political attitudes." *American Journal of Sociology* 35(2): 220–238.

Almond, Gabriel Abraham, Sidney Verba. 1963. *The Civic Culture: Political Attitudes and Democracy in Five Nations*. Princeton, NJ: Princeton University Press.

Altbach, Edith H. 1969. "Vanguard of revolt: Students and politics in Central Europe, 1815–1848." In Seymour Martin Lipset and Philip G. Altbach (eds.), *Students in Revolt*. Boston, MA: Houghton Mifflin: 451–464.

Altbach, Philip G. 1967. "Students and politics." In Seymour Martin Lipset (ed.), *Student Politics*. New York: Basic Books: 74–93.

Altbach, Philip G. 1984. "Student politics in the Third World." *Asian Journal of Social Science* 12(2): 1–17.

Altbach, Philip G. (ed.). 1989. *Student Political Activism: An International Reference Handbook*. Westport, CT: Greenwood Press.

Altbach, Philip G. 1997. *Student Politics in America: A Historical Analysis*. Piscataway, NJ: Transaction Publishers.

Altbach, Philip G. 2007. "Student politics: Activism and culture." In James J. F. Forest and Philip G. Altbach (eds.), *International Handbook of Higher Education*. Dordrecht: Springer: 329–346.

Altbach, Philip G. (ed.). 2013. *The International Imperative in Higher Education*. New York: Springer.

Altbach, Philip G., Norman T. Uphoff. 1973. *The Student Internationals*. Metuchen, NJ: The Scarecrow Press.

Alwin, Duane Francis, Ronald Lee Cohen, Theodore Mead Newcomb. 1991. *Political Attitudes over the Life Span: The Bennington Women after Fifty Years*. Madison: University of Wisconsin Press.

Amaral, Alberto, Guy Neave, Christine Musselin, Peter Maassen (eds.). 2009. *European Integration and the Governance of Higher Education and Research*. New York: Springer.

Amin, Vikesh, Jere R. Behrman, Hans-Peter Kohler, Yanyan Xiong, Junsen Zhang. 2015. "Causal inferences: Identical twins help and clarity about necessary assumptions is critical." *Social Science & Medicine* 127(20): 1e202.

Angell, Robert Cooley. 1928. *The Campus: A Study of Contemporary Undergraduate Life in the American University*. New York: D. Appleton and Company.

Angrist, Joshua D. 2014. "The perils of peer effects." *Labour Economics* 30: 98–108.

Ansell, Ben W. 2008. "University challenges: Explaining institutional change in higher education." *World Politics* 60(2): 189–230.

Ansell, Ben W., Johannes Lindvall. 2013. "The political origins of primary education systems: Ideology, institutions, and interdenominational conflict in an era of nation-building." *American Political Science Review* 107(3): 505–522.

Ansolabehere, Stephen, Eitan Hersh. 2012. "Validation: What big data reveal about survey misreporting and the real electorate." *Political Analysis* 20: 437–459.

Antonovici, Valeriu. 2009. "Piaţa Universităţii-loc memorial?" *Sfera Politicii* 139: 94–99.

Apfeld, Brendan. 2019. "Spatial and temporal university database." Working paper. https://brendanapfeld.com/files/univ_database.pdf.

Apfeld, Brendan, Emanuel Coman, John Gerring, Stephen Jessee. 2022a. "Education and social capital." *Journal of Experimental Political Science* 9: 162–188.

Apfeld, Brendan, Emanuel Coman, John Gerring, Stephen Jessee. 2022b. "The impact of university attendance on partisanship." *Political Science Research and Methods* (first view): 1–14.

Apfeld, Brendan, Emanuel Coman, John Gerring, Stephen Jessee. 2022c. "Higher education and political corruption." SSRN, April 21. https://ssrn.com/abstract=4089817.

Apfeld, Brendan, Emanuel Coman, John Gerring, Stephen Jessee. 2023. "Higher education and cultural liberalism." *Journal of Politics* 85(1) (January): 34–48.

Appiah, Kwame A. 2006. *Cosmopolitanism: Ethics in a World of Strangers*. New York: W. W. Norton.

Aristotle. 1941. *The Basic Works of Aristotle*, ed. Richard McJoen. New York: Random House.

Aristotle. 1987. *Nicomachean Ethics*, trans. J. A. K. Thomson. New York: Penguin Books.

Aristotle. 1988. *The Politics*, ed. Stephen Everson. New York: Cambridge University Press.

Armstrong, Elizabeth A., Laura T. Hamilton. 2013. *Paying for the Party: How College Maintains Inequality*. Cambridge, MA: Harvard University Press.

Arnett, Jeffrey Jensen. 2014. *Emerging Adulthood: The Winding Road from the Late Teens through the Twenties*. New York: Oxford University Press.

Arnold, Matthew. 2006 [1869]. *Culture and Anarchy*. New Haven, CT: Yale University Press.

Arthur, James, Ian Davies, Carole Hahn (eds.). 2008. *Sage Handbook of Education for Citizenship and Democracy*. London: Sage.

Astin, Alexander W. 1978. *Four Critical Years*. San Francisco, CA: Jossey-Bass.

Astin, Alexander W. 1993. *What Matters in College: Four Critical Years Revisited*. San Francisco, CA: Jossey-Bass.

Astin, Alexander W. 1998. "The changing American college student: Thirty-year trends, 1966–1996." *The Review of Higher Education* 21(2): 115–135.

Astin, Alexander W., Linda J. Sax, Juan Avalos. 1999. "The long-term effects of volunteerism during the undergraduate years." *The Review of Higher Education* 21 (2): 187–202.

Aufderheide, Patricia (ed.). 1992. *Beyond PC: Toward a Politics of Understanding*. Minneapolis, MN: Graywolf Press.

Axtell, James. 1998. *The Pleasures of Academe: A Celebration and Defense of Higher Education*. Lincoln: University of Nebraska Press.

Axtell, James. 2016. *Wisdom's Workshop: The Rise of the Modern University*. Princeton, NJ: Princeton University Press.

Aydin, Hasan, Viktor Mak, Kristina Andrews. 2021. "Academic freedom and living in exile: Experiences of academics in Turkey." In Hasan Aydin and Winston Langley (eds.), *Human Rights in Turkey: Assaults on Human Dignity*. Cham: Springer: 339–363.

Babbitt, Irving. 1908. *Literature and the American College: Essays in Defense of the Humanities*. New York: Houghton Mifflin.

BAC. 2011, July 3. Editorial Board. "S-au afisat rezultatele la Bacalaureat. Cea mai slaba promovabilitate din istorie si licee in care toti elevii au picat examenul." www.hotnews .ro/stiri-esential-9250011-bac-2011-cea-mai-slaba-promovabilitate-din-istorie-licee-care-toti-elevii-picat-examenul.htm.

Baer, Douglas E., Ronald D. Lambert. 1982. "Education and support for the dominant ideology." *Canadian Review of Sociology and Anthropology* 19: 173–195.

Bailey, Mandi, Lee R. Williams. 2016. "Are college students really liberal? An exploration of student political ideology and attitudes toward policies impacting minorities." *Social Science Journal* 53(3): 309–317.

Baker, David. 2014. *The Schooled Society: The Educational Transformation of Global Culture*. Stanford, CA: Stanford University Press.

Bakker, Ryan, Catherine De Vries, Erica Edwards et al. 2015. "Measuring party positions in Europe: The Chapel Hill expert survey trend file, 1999–2010." *Party Politics* 21(1): 143–152.

Baldassarri, Delia, Andrew Gelman. 2008. "Partisans without constraint: Political polarization trends in American public opinion." *American Sociological Review* 114 (2): 408–446.

Baldick, Chris. 1996. *Criticism and Literary Theory 1890 to the Present*. New York: Routledge.

Barber, Benjamin. 1992. *Aristocracy of Everyone*. New York: Oxford University Press.

Bárd, Petra. 2020. "The rule of law and academic freedom or the lack of it in Hungary." *European Political Science* 19(1): 87–96.

Barro, Robert J., Jong-Wha Lee. 2013. "A new data set of educational attainment in the world, 1950–2010." *Journal of Development Economics* 104: 84–198.

Barro, Robert J., Jong-Wha Lee. 2015. *Education Matters: Global Schooling Gains from the 19th to the 21st Century*. Oxford: Oxford University Press.

Barrow, Clyde M. 1990. *Universities and the Capitalist State: Corporate Liberalism and the Reconstruction of American Higher Education, 1894–1928*. Madison: University of Wisconsin Press.

Barrow, Lisa, Ofer Malamud. 2015. "Is college a worthwhile investment?" *Annual Review of Economics* 7(1): 519–555.

Barton, Allen H. 1959. *Studying the Effects of College Education: A Methodological Examination of Changing Values in College*. New York: Edward W. Hazen Foundation.

Baud, Michiel, Rosanne Rutten (eds.). 2004. *Popular Intellectuals and Social Movements: Framing Protest in Asia, Africa, and Latin America*. Cambridge: Cambridge University Press.

Bayer, Alan E. 1970. *College and University Faculty: A Statistical Description*. A Report on a Collaborative Survey by The Carnegie Commission on the Future of Higher Education and The American Council on Education. Washington, DC: American Council on Education.

Beecher, Jonathan. 2021. *Writers and Revolution: Intellectuals and the French Revolution of 1848*. Cambridge: Cambridge University Press.

Béland, Daniel, Robert Henry Cox (eds.). 2010. *Ideas and Politics in Social Science Research*. Oxford: Oxford University Press.

Bell, Daniel. 1973. *The Coming of Post-Industrial Society: A Venture in Social Forecasting*. New York: Basic Books.

Bell, Duncan. 2014. "What is liberalism?" *Political Theory* 42(6): 682–715.

Bell, Edward, Julie Aitken Schermer, Philip A. Vernon. 2009. "The origins of political attitudes and behaviours: An analysis using twins." *Canadian Journal of Political Science/Revue canadienne de science politique* 42(4): 855–879.

Bellei, Cristián, Cristian Cabalín, Víctor Orellana. 2014. "The 2011 Chilean student movement against neoliberal educational policies." *Studies in Higher Education* 39 (3): 426–440.

Benavot, Aaron. 1996. "Education and political democratization: Cross-national and longitudinal findings." *Comparative Education Review* 40: 377–403.

Ben-David, Joseph. 1977. *Centers of Learning: Britain, France, Germany, United States*. New York: McGraw-Hill.

Benenson, Jodi, Inger Bergom. 2019. "Voter participation, socioeconomic status, and institutional contexts in higher education." *The Review of Higher Education* 42(4): 1665–1688.

Benewick, Robert, Philip Green (eds.). 1998. *The Routledge Dictionary of Twentieth-Century Political Thinkers*, 2nd ed. London: Routledge.

Bennett, William John. 1984. *To Reclaim a Legacy: A Report on the Humanities in Higher Education*. Washington, DC: National Endowment for the Humanities.

Berggren, Niclas, Henrik Jordahl, Charlotta Stern. 2007. "The political opinions of Swedish social scientists." 711. IFN Working Paper.

Bergman, Jay. 1998. "Was the Soviet Union totalitarian? The view of Soviet dissidents and the reformers of the Gorbachev era."*Studies in East European Thought* 50(4): 247–281.

Berinsky, Adam J., Gabriel S. Lenz. 2011. "Education and political participation: Exploring the causal link." *Political Behavior* 33(3): 357–373.

Berlin, Isaiah. 1969. *Four Essays on Liberty*. Oxford: Clarendon Press.

Berman, Paul (ed.). 2011. *Debating PC: The Controversy over Political Correctness on College Campuses*. London: Delta.

Bernasconi, Andrés. 2015. "El Gobierno de las Instituciones." In Andrés Bernasconi (ed.), *La Educación Superior de Chile: Transformación, Desarrollo, y Crisis*. Santiago: Ediciones UC: 259–294.

Bernhard, Michael H. 1993. *The Origins of Democratization in Poland: Workers, Intellectuals, and Oppositional Politics, 1976–1980*. New York: Columbia University Press.

Bernstein, Michael A. 2014. *A Perilous Progress*. Princeton, NJ: Princeton University Press.

Bernstein, Robert, Anita Chadha, Robert Montjoy. 2001. "Overreporting voting: Why it happens and why it matters." *Public Opinion Quarterly* 65(1): 22–44.

Bértoa, Fernando Casal. 2013. "Post-communist politics: On the divergence (and/or convergence) of East and West." *Government and Opposition* 48(3): 398–433. doi: 10.1017/gov.2013.9.

Bérubé, Michael. 2006. *What's Liberal about the Liberal Arts? Classroom Politics and "Bias" in Higher Education*. New York: W. W. Norton.

Bessant, Judith, Analicia Mejia Mesinas, Sarah Pickard (eds.). 2021a. *When Students Protest: Universities in the Global North*. Lanham, MD: Rowman & Littlefield.

Bessant, Judith, Analicia Mejia Mesinas, Sarah Pickard (eds.). 2021b. *When Students Protest: Universities in the Global South*. Lanham, MD: Rowman & Littlefield.

Binder, Amy J., Jeffrey L. Kidder. 2022. *The Channels of Student Activism: How the Left and Right Are Winning (and Losing) in Campus Politics Today*. Chicago, IL: University of Chicago Press.

Binder, Amy J., Kate Wood. 2012. *Becoming Right*. Princeton, NJ: Princeton University Press.

Bird, Kelli A., Benjamin L. Castleman, Jeffrey T. Denning et al. 2021. "Nudging at scale: Experimental evidence from FAFSA completion campaigns." *Journal of Economic Behavior & Organization* 183: 105–128.

Black, Jim Nelson. 2004. *Freefall of the American University: How Our Colleges Are Corrupting the Minds and Morals of the Next Generation*. Nashville, TN: WND Books.

Blau, Peter M. 1953. "Orientation of college students toward international relations." *American Journal of Sociology* 59(3): 205–214. https://doi.org/10.2307/2961376.

Blessinger, Patrick, John P. Anchan (eds.). 2015. *Democratizing Higher Education: International Comparative Perspectives*. London: Routledge.

Bloom, Allan. 1987. *Closing of the American Mind*. New York: Simon and Schuster.

Blossfeld, Hans-Peter, Andreas Timm (eds.). 2003. *Who Marries Whom? Educational Systems as Marriage Markets in Modern Societies*. Dordrecht: Kluwer Academic Publishers.

Boardman, Jason D., Jason M. Fletcher. 2015. "To cause or not to cause? That is the question, but identical twins might not have all of the answers." *Social Science & Medicine (1982)* 127: 198.

Bobba, Matteo, Decio Coviello. 2007. "Weak instruments and weak identification, in estimating the effects of education, on democracy." *Economics Letters* 96(3): 301–306.

Bobo, Lawrence, Frederick C. Licari. 1989. "Education and political tolerance: Testing the effects of cognitive sophistication and target group affect." *Public Opinion Quarterly* 53(3): 285–308.

Bod, Rens. 2013. *A New History of the Humanities: The Search for Principles and Patterns from Antiquity to the Present*. Oxford: Oxford University Press.

Bok, Derek. 1982. *Beyond the Ivory Tower: Social Responsibilities of the Modern University*. Cambridge, MA: Harvard University Press.

Bok, Derek. 2013. *Higher Education in America*, revised ed. Princeton, NJ: Princeton University Press.

Boldt, W. J. and J. B. Stroud. 1934. "Changes in the attitudes of college students." *Journal of Educational Psychology* 25(8): 611–619. https://doi.org/10.1037/h0073863.

Bonica, Adam. 2016. *Database on Ideology, Money in Politics, and Elections: Public version 2.0 [Computer file]*. Stanford, CA: Stanford University Libraries. https://data .stanford.edu/dime.

Bonilla, Frank. 1960. "The Student Federation of Chile: 50 years of political action." *Journal of Inter-American Studies* 2(3): 311–334.

Bonilla, Frank, Myron Glazer. 1970. *Student Politics in Chile*. New York: Basic Books.

Borcan, Oana, Mikael Lindahl, Andreea Mitrut. 2017. "Fighting corruption in education: What works and who benefits?" *American Economic Journal: Economic Policy* 9(1): 180–209.

Boren, Mark Edelman. 2001. *Student Resistance: A History of the Unruly Subject*. New York: Routledge.

Borgonovi, Francesca. 2012. "The relationship between education and levels of trust and tolerance in Europe." *British Journal of Sociology* 63(1): 146–167.

Bound, John, Gary Solon. 1999. "Double trouble: On the value of twins-based estimation of the return to schooling." *Economics of Education Review* 18(2): 169–182.

Bourdieu, Pierre. 1984. *Distinction: A Social Critique of the Judgement of Taste*. Cambridge, MA: Harvard University Press.

Bourdieu, Pierre. 1988. *Homo Academicus*, trans. P. Collier. Stanford, CA: Stanford University Press.

Bourdieu, Pierre. 1989. *The State Nobility: Elite Schools in the Field of Power*. Stanford, CA: Stanford University Press.

Bourdieu, Pierre, Jean-Claude Passeron. 1990. *Reproduction in Education, Society and Culture*. Thousand Oaks, CA: Sage.

Bovens, Mark, Anchrit Wille. 2017. *Diploma Democracy: The Rise of Political Meritocracy*. Oxford: Oxford University Press.

Bowen, William G., Derek Bok. 1998. *The Shape of the River: Long-Term Consequences of Considering Race in College and University Admissions*. Princeton, NJ: Princeton University Press.

Bowles, Samuel, Herbert Gintis. 1976. *Schooling in Capitalist America: Educational Reform and the Contradictions of Economic Life*. New York: Basic Books.

Boxer, Marilyn Jacoby. 2001. *When Women Ask the Questions: Creating Women's Studies in America*. Baltimore, MD: Johns Hopkins University Press.

Braben, Donald W. 2008. *Scientific Freedom: The Elixir of Civilization*. New York: John Wiley & Sons.

Brancati, Dawn. 2016. *Democracy Protests*. Cambridge: Cambridge University Press.

Brand, Jennie E. 2010. "Civic returns to higher education: A note on heterogeneous effects." *Social Forces* 89(2): 417–433.

Breemes, E. L., H. H. Remmers, C. L. Morgan. 1941. "Changes in liberalism-conservatism of college students since the depression." *Journal of Social Psychology* 14(1): 99–107. https://doi.org/10.1080/00224545.1941.9921497.

Brehm, John, Wendy Rahn. 1997. "Individual-level evidence for the causes and consequences of social capital." *American Journal of Political Science* 41(3): 999–1023.

Bridges, David (ed.). 1997. *Education, Autonomy, and Democratic Citizenship: Philosophy in a Changing World*. London: Routledge.

Brint, Steven. 1984. "New-class and cumulative trend explanations of the liberal political attitudes of professionals." *American Journal of Sociology* 90: 30–71.

Brint, Steven. 1994. *In an Age of Experts: The Changing Role of Professionals in Politics and Public Life*. Princeton, NJ: Princeton University Press.

Brint, Steven, Michaela Curran, Matthew C. Mahutga. 2022. "Are U.S. professionals and managers more left than blue-collar workers? An analysis of the general social survey, 1974 to 2018." *Socius* 8.

Brody, Richard A. 1978. "The puzzle of political participation in America." In A. King (ed.), *The New American Political System*. Washington, DC: American Enterprise Institute for Public Policy Research.

Brombert, Victor. 1961. *The Intellectual Hero*. Philadelphia, PA: Lippincott.

Brooks, Clem. 2014. "Nations, classes, and the politics of professors: A comparative perspective." In Neil Gross and Solon Simmons (eds.), *Professors and Their Politics*. Baltimore, MD: Johns Hopkins University Press: 82–109.

Brooks, David. 2010. *Bobos in Paradise: The New Upper Class and How They Got There*. New York: Simon and Schuster.

Brooks, Rachel (ed.). 2016. *Student Politics and Protest: International Perspectives*. London: Taylor & Francis.

Brower, Daniel R. 1970. "Reformers and rebels: Education in tsarist Russia." *History of Education Quarterly* 10(1) (Spring): 127–136.

Brower, Daniel R. 1975. *Training the Nihilists*. Ithaca, NY: Cornell University Press.

Brubacher, John S. 1967. "The autonomy of the university." *Journal of Higher Education* 38(5): 237–249.

Bruce, Steve. 2011. *Secularization: In Defence of an Unfashionable Theory*. Oxford: Oxford University Press.

Brusco, Valeria, Marcelo Nazareno, Susan C. Stokes. 2004. "Vote buying in Argentina." *Latin American Research Review* 39(2): 66–88.

Bryant, Alyssa N. 2003. "Changes in attitudes towards women's roles: Gender-role traditionalism among college students." *Sex Roles* 48: 131–142.

Buckley, William F. 1951. *God and Man at Yale: The Superstitions of "Academic Freedom."* Washington, DC: Regnery Publishing.

Budiman, Arief. 1978. "The student movement in Indonesia: A study of the relationship between culture and structure." *Asian Survey* 18(6): 609–625.

Buerkle, Karen, Alya Guseva. 2002. "What do you know, who do you know? School as a site for the production of social capital and its effects on income attainment in Poland and the Czech Republic." *American Journal of Economics and Sociology* 61(3): 657–680.

Bugelski, Richard, Olive P. Lester. 1940. "Changes in attitudes in a group of college students during their college course and after graduation." *Journal of Social Psychology* 12(2): 319–332. https://doi.org/10.1080/00224545.1940.9921476.

Bullock, John G. 2021. "Education and attitudes toward redistribution in the United States." *British Journal of Political Science* 51(3): 1230–1250.

Bülow, Marisa von, Germán Bidegain Ponte (2015). "It takes two to tango: Students, political parties, and protest in Chile (2005–2013)." In Paul Almeida and Allen Cordero Ulate (eds.), *Handbook of Social Movements across Latin America.* Dordrecht: Springer: 179–194.

Bunch, Will. 2022. *After the Ivory Tower Falls: How College Broke the American Dream and Blew Up Our Politics – And How to Fix It.* New York: William Morrow.

Burden, Barry C. 2009. "The dynamic effects of education on voter turnout." *Electoral Studies* 28: 540–549.

Burden, Barry C., Pamela Herd, Bradley M. Jones, Donald P. Moynihan. 2020. "Education, early life, and political participation: New evidence from a sibling model." *Research & Politics* 7(3).

Burean, Toma. 2019. "Democrats on the streets: Drivers of student protest participation in Romania." *Partecipazione e conflitto* 12(1): 22–42.

Busemeyer, Marius R., Julian L. Garritzmann, Erik Neimanns. 2020. *A Loud but Noisy Signal? Public Opinion and Education Reform in Western Europe.* Cambridge: Cambridge University Press.

Bush, Vannevar. 1945. *Science the Endless Frontier: A Report to the President, Director of the Office of Scientific Research and Development.* Washington, DC: United States Government Printing Office.

Butterfield, Herbert. 1965 [1931]. *The Whig Interpretation of History.* New York: W. W. Norton.

Calculator salarii. 2019. "Salariu mediu pe economie in anul 2019 este 5163 Lei." www.calculator-salarii.ro/salariu-mediu-pe-economie.

Calhoun, Craig (ed.). 2008. *Sociology in America: A History.* Chicago, IL: University of Chicago Press.

Callan, Eamonn. 1997. *Creating Citizens: Political Education and Liberal Democracy.* Oxford: Clarendon Press.

Campante, Filipe R., Davin Chor. 2012. "Why was the Arab world poised for revolution? Schooling, economic opportunities, and the Arab spring." *The Journal of Economic Perspectives* 26(2): 167–187.

Campbell, Angus, Philip E. Converse, Warren E. Miller, Donald E. Stokes. 1960. *The American Voter.* New York: John Wiley.

Campbell, Bradley, Jason Manning. 2014. "Microaggression and moral cultures." *Comparative Sociology* 13(6): 692–726.

Campbell, Bradley, Jason Manning. 2018. *The Rise of Victimhood Culture: Microaggressions, Safe Spaces, and the New Culture Wars.* New York: Springer.

Campbell, Colin, Jonathan Horowitz. 2016. "Does college influence sociopolitical attitudes?" *Sociology of Education* 89(1): 40–58.

Campbell, David E., Meira Levinson, Frederick M. Hess (eds.). 2012. *Making Civics Count: Citizenship Education for a New Generation.* Cambridge, MA: Harvard Education Press.

Campbell, James. 2019. "The trust is gone." *PS: Political Science & Politics* 52(4): 715–719.

Canaan, Serena, Pierre Mouganie. 2018. "Returns to education quality for low-skilled students: Evidence from a discontinuity." *Journal of Labor Economics* 36(2): 395–436.

Cantoni, Davide, Yuyu Chen, David Y. Yang, Noam Yuchtman, Y. Jane Zhang. 2017. "Curriculum and ideology." *Journal of Political Economy* 125(2): 338–392.

Caplan, Bryan. 2018. *The Case against Education: Why the Education System Is a Waste of Time and Money.* Princeton, NJ: Princeton University Press.

Cardiff, Christopher F., Daniel B. Klein. 2005. "Faculty partisan affiliations in all disciplines: A voter-registration study." *Critical Review* 17(3–4): 237–255.

Carey, Kevin. 2016. *The End of College: Creating the Future of Learning and the University of Everywhere.* New York: Riverhead Books.

Carl, Noah. 2015. "Can intelligence explain the overrepresentation of liberals and leftists in American academia?" *Intelligence* 53(2015): 181–193.

Carl, Noah. 2017. *Lackademia: Why Do Academics Lean Left?* London: Adam Smith Institute.

Carl, Noah. 2018. "The Political Attitudes of British Academics." *Open Quantitative Sociology & Political Science* 1(1).

Carnes, Nicholas, Noam Lupu. 2016. "What good is a college degree? Education and leader quality reconsidered." *The Journal of Politics* 78(1): 35–49.

Carney, Dana R., John T. Jost, Samuel D. Gosling, Jeff Potter. 2008. "The secret lives of liberals and conservatives: Personality profiles, interaction styles, and the things they leave behind." *Political Psychology* 29: 807–840.

Caron, Jean-Claude. 1991. *Générations romantiques. Les étudiants de Paris et le Quartier latin (1814–1851).* Paris: Armand Colin.

Cassel, Carol A., Celia C. Lo. 1997. "Theories of political literacy." *Political Behavior* 19 (4): 317–335.

Castiglione, Baldassare. 2003 [1528]. *The Book of the Courtier.* North Chelmsford, MA: Courier Corporation.

Cattaneo, Matias D., M. Jansson, X. Ma. 2018. "Simple local polynomial density estimators." *Journal of the American Statistical Association* 115(531): 1449–1455.

Cattaneo, Matias D., Nicolas Idrobo, Rocio Titiunik. 2020. *A Practical Introduction to Regression Discontinuity Designs.* Cambridge: Cambridge University Press.

Caute, David. 1964. *Communism and the French Intellectuals 1914–1960.* New York: Macmillan.

Chan, Roy Y. 2016. "Understanding the purpose of higher education: An analysis of the economic and social benefits for completing a college degree." *Journal of Education Policy, Planning and Administration* 6(5): 1–40.

Chang, Eric C. C., Nicholas N. Kerr. 2017. "An insider–outsider theory of popular tolerance for corrupt politicians." *Governance* 30(1): 67–84.

Charle, Christophe. 1993. "Academics or intellectuals? The professors of the University of Paris and political debate in France from the Dreyfus affair to the Algerian war." In Jeremy Jennings (ed.), *Intellectuals in Twentieth-Century France*. London: Palgrave Macmillan: 94–116.

Charle, Christophe. 2015. *Birth of the Intellectuals: 1880–1900*. New York: John Wiley & Sons.

Checkoway, Barry. 2001. "Renewing the civic mission of the American research university." *The Journal of Higher Education* 72(2): 125–147.

Cheung, Hoi Yan, Alex W. H. Chan. 2008. "Corruption across countries: Impacts from education and cultural dimensions." *Social Science Journal* 45(2): 223–239.

Chong, Alberto, Mark Gradstein. 2015. "On education and democratic preferences." *Economics & Politics* 27(3): 362–388.

Claeys, Gregory. 2004. *Encyclopedia of Nineteenth Century Thought*. London: Routledge.

Clark, Burton R., Martin Trow. 1966. "The organizational context." In Theodore Mead Newcomb and Everett Keith Wilson (eds.), *College Peer Groups: Problems and Prospects for Research*. Chicago, IL: Aldine: 17–70.

Close, Caroline. 2019. "The liberal party family ideology: Distinct, but diverse." In Caroline Close and Émilie Van Haute (eds.), *Liberal Parties in Europe*. London: Routledge: 326–347.

Close, Caroline, Émilie Van Haute (eds.). 2019. *Liberal Parties in Europe*. London: Routledge.

Clydesdale, Tim. 2008. *The First Year Out: Understanding American Teens after High School*. Chicago, IL: University of Chicago Press.

Cobban, Alan Balfour. 1975. *The Medieval Universities: Their Development and Organization*. London: Methuen.

Coenders, Marcel, Peer Scheepers. 2003. "The effect of education on nationalism and ethnic exclusionism: An international comparison." *Political Psychology* 24(2): 313–343.

Cohen, Robert. 1993. *When the Old Left Was Young: Student Radicals and America's First Mass Student Movement, 1929–1941*. Oxford: Oxford University Press.

Colby, Anne, Elizabeth Beaumont, Thomas Ehrlich, Jason Stephens. 2003. *Educating Citizens: Preparing America's Undergraduates for Lives of Moral and Civic Responsibility*. New York: John Wiley & Sons.

Cole, Julio H., Andrés Marroquín Gramajo. 2009. "Homicide rates in a cross-section of countries: Evidence and interpretations." *Population and Development Review* 35(4): 749–776.

Coleman, James Smoot (ed.). 1965. *Education and Political Development*. Princeton, NJ: Princeton University Press.

Collins, Allan, Richard Halverson. 2018. *Rethinking Education in the Age of Technology: The Digital Revolution and Schooling in America*. New York: Teachers College Press.

Collins, Randall. 1998. *The Sociology of Philosophies: A Global Theory of Intellectual Change*. Cambridge, MA: Harvard University Press.

Coman, Emanuel. 2017. "Dimensions of political conflict in West and East: An application of vote scaling to 22 European parliaments." *Party Politics* 23(3): 248–261.

Connelly, John, Michael Grüttner (eds.). 2010. *Universities under Dictatorship*. University Park, PA: Penn State Press.

Converse, Philip E. 1964. "The nature of belief systems in mass publics." In David E. Apter (ed.), *Ideology and Its Discontents*. New York: The Free Press of Glencoe.

Converse, Philip E. 1972. "Change in the American electorate." In Angus Campbell and Philip Converse (eds.), *The Human Meaning of Social Change*. New York: Russell Sage Foundation.

Coppedge, Michael, John Gerring, Carl Henrik Knutsen et al. 2020. "V-Dem Codebook v10." Varieties of Democracy (V-Dem) Project.

Cote, James, Anton L. Allahar. 2011. *Lowering Higher Education: The Rise of Corporate Universities and the Fall of Liberal Education*. Toronto: University of Toronto Press.

Courtenay, William J. 1989. "Inquiry and inquisition: Academic freedom in medieval universities." *Church History* 58(2): 168–181.

Crăciun, Oana. 2013, August 12. "Dosarele de corupție la BAC, pe masa DNA. Ministerul Educației a găsit 15 posibile fraude la Bacalaureatul din 2013." https://adevarul.ro/news/eveniment/ministerul-educatiei-1_52091281c7b855ff56ce603f/index.html.

Crawford, Jarret T., Lee J. Jussim (eds.). 2017. *The Politics of Social Psychology*. New York: Routledge.

Cremin, Lawrence A. (ed.). 1957. *The Republic and the School: Horace Mann on the Education of Free Men*. New York: Teachers College Press.

Cremin, Lawrence A. (ed.). 1961. *Crusade against Ignorance: Thomas Jefferson on Education*. New York: Teachers College Press.

Currid-Halkett, Elizabeth. 2017. *The Sum of Small Things: A Theory of the Aspirational Class*. Princeton, NJ: Princeton University Press.

Curry, Matthew, Jennie E. Brand. 2015. "Enduring effects of education." *Emerging Trends in the Social and Behavioral Sciences: An Interdisciplinary, Searchable, and Linkable Resource*, 1–14. https://doi.org/10.1002/9781118900772.etrds0115.

D'Souza, Dinesh. 1991. *Illiberal Education: The Politics of Race and Sex on Campus*. New York: Simon and Schuster.

Dahl, Robert A. 1961. *Who Governs? Democracy and Power in an American City*. New Haven, CT: Yale University Press.

Dahlum, Sirianne, Tore Wig. 2019. "Educating demonstrators: Education and mass protest in Africa." *Journal of Conflict Resolution* 63(1): 3–30.

Dahlum, Sirianne, Tore Wig. 2021. "Chaos on campus: Universities and mass political protest." *Comparative Political Studies* 54(1): 3–32.

Dalton, Russell J., David M. Farrell, Ian McAllister. 2011. *Political Parties and Democratic Linkage: How Parties Organize Democracy*. Oxford: Oxford University Press.

Daniels, Ronald J., Grant Shreve, Phillip Spector. 2021. *What Universities Owe Democracy*. Baltimore, MD: Johns Hopkins University Press.

Danziger, Kurt. 1994. *Constructing the Subject: Historical Origins of Psychological Research*. Cambridge: Cambridge University Press.

Davis, Nancy J., Robert V. Robinson. 1991. "Men's and women's consciousness of gender inequality: Austria, West Germany, Great Britain, and the United States." *American Sociological Review* 56(1): 72–84.

Dawes, Christopher T., Aysu Okbay, Sven Oskarsson, Aldo Rustichini. 2021. "A polygenic score for educational attainment partially predicts voter turnout." *Proceedings of the National Academy of Sciences of the United States of America* 118(50): e2022715118.

Dearden, Robert Frederick. 2011. *The Philosophy of Primary Education: An Introduction*. London: Routledge.

Deary, Ian J., G. David Batty, Catherine R. Gale. 2008. "Bright children become enlightened adults." *Psychological Science* 19: 1–6.

DeConde, Alexander (ed.). 1971. *Student Activism: Town and Gown in Historical Perspective*. New York: Scribner's.

Dee, Thomas S. 2004. "Are there civic returns to education?" *Journal of Public Economics* 88: 1697–1720.

De Groot, Gerard J. (ed.). 1998. *Student Protest: The Sixties and After*. London: Addison Wesley.

DellaPosta, Daniel, Yongren Shi, Michael Macy. 2015. "Why do liberals drink lattes?" *American Journal of Sociology*, 120(5): 1473–1511.

Deming, David J. 2022. "Four facts about human capital." *Journal of Economic Perspectives* 36(3): 75–102.

Deng, Peng, Xiaojia Hou, Ting Jiang et al. 2019. *A Century of Student Movements in China: The Mountain Movers, 1919–2019*. Blue Ridge Summit, PA:Lexington Books.

De Ruggiero, Guido. 1927. *The History of European Liberalism*. Oxford: Oxford University Press.

Dewey, John. 1897. *My Pedagogic Creed*. New York: E. L. Kellogg & Company.

Dewey, John. 1923. *Democracy and Education: An Introduction to the Philosophy of Education*. New York: Macmillan.

Dewey, John. 2013 [1899]. *The School and Society and the Child and the Curriculum*. Chicago, IL: University of Chicago Press.

De Witte, Hans. 1999. "'Everyday' racism in Belgium: An overview of the research and an interpretation of its link with education." In Louk Hagendoorn and Shervin Nekuee (eds.), *Education and Racism*. London: Routledge: 47–74.

Dey, Eric L. 1996. "Undergraduate political attitudes: An examination of peer, faculty, and social influences." *Research in Higher Education* 37: 535–554.

Dey, Eric L. 1997. "Undergraduate political attitudes: Peer influence in changing social contexts." *The Journal of Higher Education* 68(4): 398–413.

Dhondt, Pieter, Elizabethanne Boran (eds.). 2017. *Student Revolt, City, and Society in Europe: From the Middle Ages to the Present*. London: Taylor & Francis.

Dhondt, Pieter, Florea Ioncioaia. 2017. "Christmas carolling in Bucharest and campfire singing in Iași: Students as a specific social group in Ceaușescu's Romania 1." In Pieter Dhondt and Elizabethanne Boran (eds.), *Student Revolt, City, and Society in Europe*. London: Taylor & Francis: 203–216.

Dimulescu, Valentina. 2018, August 8. Personal communication.

Dinesen, Peter, Christopher T. Thisted, Magnus Johannesson Dawes et al. 2016. "Estimating the impact of education on political participation: Evidence from monozygotic twins in the United States, Denmark and Sweden." *Political Behavior* 38(3): 579–601.

Disi Pavlic, Rodolfo. 2017. Policies, politics, and protests: Explaining student mobilization in Latin America. PhD dissertation, Department of Government, University of Texas at Austin.

Disi Pavlic, Rodolfo. 2018. "Sentenced to debt: Explaining student mobilization in Chile." *Latin American Research Review* 53(3).

Dodson, Kyle. 2014. "The effect of college on social and political attitudes and civic participation." In Neil Gross and Solon Simmons (eds.), *Professors and Their Politics*. Baltimore, MD: Johns Hopkins University Press: 135–157.

Doherty, Daniel, Alan S. Gerber, Donald P. Green. 2006. "Personal income and attitudes toward redistribution: A study of lottery winners." *Political Psychology* 27(3): 441–458.

Dong, Bin, Benno Torgler. 2013. "Causes of corruption: Evidence from China." *China Economic Review* 26(1): 152–169.

Donoghue, Frank. 2008. *The Last Professors: The Corporate University and the Fate of the Humanities*. New York: Fordham University Press.

Donoso, Sofía. 2016. "When social movements become a democratizing force: The political impact of the student movement in Chile." In Thomas Davies, Holly Eva Ryan, and Alejandro Milcíades Peña (eds.), *Protest, Social Movements and Global Democracy since 2011: New Perspectives*. Bingley: Emerald Group Publishing Limited: 167–196.

Donoso, Sofía. 2017. "'Outsider' and 'insider' strategies: Chile's student movement, 1990–2014." In Sofia Donoso and Marisa Von Bülow (eds.), *Social Movements in Chile*. New York: Palgrave Macmillan: 65–97.

Dorling, Danny. 2012. *The Visualization of Spatial Social Structure*. New York: John Wiley & Sons.

Douglass, John Aubrey. 2021. *Neo-nationalism and Universities: Populists, Autocrats, and the Future of Higher Education*. Baltimore, MD: Johns Hopkins University Press.

Drake, David. 2005. *French Intellectuals and Politics from the Dreyfus Affair to the Occupation*. New York: Springer.

Duarte, José L., Jarret T. Crawford, Charlotta Stern et al. 2015. "Political diversity will improve social psychological science." *Behavioral and Brain Sciences* 38: 1–58.

Duch, Raymond M., Michaell A. Taylor. 1993. "Postmaterialism and the economic condition." *American Journal of Political Science* 37(3): 747–779.

Dumitru, Mircea. 2017, May 3. "Cuantumul taxei de studio (în lei) pentru anul universitar 2017–2018." https://drive.google.com/file/d/0B-WydKlC-sxCeE9kQnc3UDJWblE/view.

Dunn, Kris. 2011. "Left-right identification and education in Europe: A contingent relationship." *Comparative European Politics* 9(3): 292–316.

Dunning, Thad, Guy Grossman, Macartan Humphreys et al. (eds.). 2019. *Information, Accountability, and Cumulative Learning: Lessons from Metaketa I*. Cambridge: Cambridge University Press.

Durkheim, Émile. 1973 [1903]. *Moral Education*. Glencoe, IL: Free Press.

Dynes, Wayne R. 1995. "Queer studies: In search of a discipline." *Academic Questions* 8 (4): 34–52.

Eagan, Eileen. 1981. *Class, Culture, and the Classroom: The Student Peace Movement of the 1930s*. Philadelphia, PA: Temple University Press.

Eddy, Edward Danforth. 1959. *The College Influence on Student Character: An Exploratory Study in Selected Colleges and Universities Made for the Committee for the Study of Character Development in Education*. Washington, DC: American Council on Education.

Eftedal, Nikolai Haahjem, Thomas H. Kleppesto, Nikolai Olavi Czajkowski et al. 2020. "Causality and confounding between right wing authoritarianism, education, and socio-economic status: A twin study." https://doi.org/10.31234/osf.io/vws83.

Eitzen, D. Stanley, Gary M. Maranell. 1968. "The political party affiliation of college professors." *Social Forces* 47(2): 145–153.

Elchardus, Mark, Bram Spruyt. 2009. "The culture of academic disciplines and the sociopolitical attitudes of students: A test of selection and socialization effects." *Social Science Quarterly* 90(2): 446–460.

Elchardus, Mark, Bram Spruyt. 2010. "Does higher education influence the attitudes with regard to the extreme right?" *European Journal of Social Sciences* 18(2): 181–195.

Ellis, John M. 2020. *The Breakdown of Higher Education: How It Happened, the Damage It Does, and What Can Be Done.* New York: Encounter Books.

Elman, Colin, John Gerring, James Mahoney (eds.). 2020. *The Production of Knowledge: Enhancing Progress in Social Science.* Cambridge: Cambridge University Press.

Emler, Nicholas, Elizabeth Frazer. 1999. "Politics: The education effect." *Oxford Review of Education* 25(1–2): 251–273.

Emmerson, Donald K. (ed.). 1968. *Students and Politics in Developing Nations.* New York: Frederick A. Praeger.

Emsley, Richard, Hanhua Liu. 2013. "PARAMED: Stata module to perform causal mediation analysis using parametric regression models," Statistical Software Components S457581, Boston College Department of Economics, revised April 26, 2013.

Enamorado, Ted, Kosuke Imai. 2019. "Validating self-reported turnout by linking public opinion surveys with administrative records." *Public Opinion Quarterly* 83 (4): 723–748.

Enders, Craig K. 2010. *Applied Missing Data Analysis.* New York: The Guilford Press.

Erasmus. 1998 [1516]. *Erasmus: The Education of a Christian Prince with the Panegyric for Archduke Philip of Austria.* Cambridge: Cambridge University Press.

Erlingsson, Gissur Ólafur, Gunnar Helgi Kristinsson. 2019. "Exploring shades of corruption tolerance: Tentative lessons from Iceland and Sweden." *Kyiv-Mohyla Law & Politics Journal* 5: 141–164.

Etzioni-Halevy, Eva. 1986. "Radicals in the establishment: Towards an exploration of the political role of intellectuals in Western societies." *Journal of Political and Military Sociology* 14: 29–40.

Euben, J. Peter. 1997. *Corrupting Youth: Political Education, Democratic Culture, and Political Theory.* Princeton, NJ: Princeton University Press.

European Commission. 2006. *Monitoring Report on the State of Preparedness for EU Membership of Bulgaria and Romania.* https://ec.europa.eu/neighbourhood-enlargement /sites/near/files/pdf/key_documents/2006/sept/report_bg_ro_2006_en.pdf.

Faia, Michael A. 1974. "The myth of the liberal professor." *Sociology of Education* 47 (2): 171. https://doi.org/10.2307/2112104.

Fajnzylber, Pablo, Daniel Lederman, Norman Loayza. 2002. "What causes violent crime?" *European Economic Review* 46(7): 1323–1357.

Farnworth, Margaret, Dennis R. Longmire, Vincent M. West. 1998. "College students' views on criminal justice." *Journal of Criminal Justice Education* 21(1): 39–57.

Fass, Paula S. 1977. *The Damned and the Beautiful: American Youth in the 1920s: American Youth in the 1920s.* New York: Oxford University Press.

Fass, Paula S. 1991. *Outside In: Minorities and the Transformation of American Education.* New York: Oxford University Press.

Favors, Jelani M. 2019. *Shelter in a Time of Storm: How Black Colleges Fostered Generations of Leadership and Activism.* Chapel Hill: University of North Carolina Press.

Fawcett, Edmund. 2018. *Liberalism: The Life of an Idea.* Princeton, NJ: Princeton University Press.

Fay, Paul J., Warren C. Middleton. 1940. "Certain factors related to liberal and conservative attitudes of college students: Parental membership in certain organizations." *Journal of Social Psychology* 12(1): 55–69. https://doi.org/10.1080/00224545.1940.9713803.

Feldman, Jonathan. 1989. *Universities in the Business of Repression: The Academic-Military-Industrial Complex and Central America.* Boston, MA: South End Press.

Feldman, Kenneth A., Theodore M. Newcomb. 1969. *The Impact of College on Students.* London: Jossey-Bass.

Findley, Michael G., Kyosuke Kikuta, Michael Denly. 2021. "External validity." *Annual Review of Political Science* 24: 365–393.

Fink, Carole, Philipp Gasset, Getlef Junker. 1998. *1968: The World Transformed.* New York: Cambridge University Press.

Fischer, Didier. 2000. *L'histoire des étudiants en France de 1945 à nos jours.* Paris: Flammarion.

Fischer, Mira, Björn Kauder, Niklas Potrafke, Heinrich W. Ursprung. 2017. "Support for free-market policies and reforms: Does the field of study influence students' political attitudes?" *European Journal of Political Economy* 48: 180–197.

Flacks, Richard, Nelson Lichtenstein (eds.). 2015. *The Port Huron Statement: Sources and Legacies of the New Left's Founding Manifesto.* Philadelphia: University of Pennsylvania Press.

Ford, Robert, William Jennings. 2020. "The changing cleavage politics of Western Europe." *Annual Review of Political Science* 23: 295–314.

Fosse, Ethan, Jeremy Freese, Neil Gross. 2014. "Political liberalism and graduate school attendance: A longitudinal analysis." In Neil Gross and Solon Simmons (eds.), *Professors and Their Politics.* Baltimore, MD: Johns Hopkins University Press: 52–81.

Fosse, Ethan, Neil Gross, Joseph Ma. 2014. "Political bias in the graduate school admissions process: A field experiment." In Neil Gross and Solon Simmons (eds.), *Professors and Their Politics.* Baltimore, MD: Johns Hopkins University Press: 109–134.

Fowler, James H., Christopher T. Dawes. 2008. "Two genes predict voter turnout." *Journal of Politics* 70(3): 579–594.

Fowler, James H., Christopher T. Dawes. 2013. "In defense of genopolitics." *American Political Science Review* 107(2): 362–374.

Fowler, James H., Laura A. Baker, Christopher T. Dawes. 2008. "Genetic variation in political participation." *American Political Science Review* 102(2): 233–248.

François, Abel, Cal Le Gall, Raul Magni Berton. 2016. "Politics, economics, ethics and religion in French academia." *French Politics* 14(3): 363–379. https://doi.org/10.1057/s41253-016-0002-9.

Frank, David John, Jay Gabler. 2006. *Reconstructing the University: Worldwide Shifts in Academia in the 20th Century.* Stanford, CA: Stanford University Press.

Frank, David John, John W. Meyer. 2007. "University expansion and the knowledge society." *Theory and Society* 36(4): 287–311.

Frank, David John, John W. Meyer. 2020. *The University and the Global Knowledge Society*. Princeton, NJ: Princeton University Press.

Franklin, Mark N. 1992. "The decline of cleavage politics." In Mark N. Franklin, T. Machie, and H. Valen (eds.), *Electoral Change: Responses to Evolving Social and Attitudinal Structures in Western Countries*. Cambridge: Cambridge University Press: 324–356.

Franklin, Mark N. 2004. *Voter Turnout and the Dynamics of Electoral Competition in Established Democracies since 1945*. Cambridge: Cambridge University Press.

Freeden, Michael. 1986. *Liberalism Divided: A Study in British Political Thought 1914–1939*. Oxford: Oxford University Press.

Freeden, Michael. 2003. *Ideology: A Very Short Introduction*. Oxford: Oxford University Press.

Freeden, Michael, Javier Fernández-Sebastián, Jörn Leonhard (eds.). 2019. *In Search of European Liberalisms: Concepts, Languages, Ideologies*. New York: Berghahn Books.

Freedman, James O. 2001. *Idealism and Liberal Education*. Ann Arbor: University of Michigan Press.

Freire, Paulo. 1970. *Pedagogy of the Oppressed*. New York: Continuum.

Frisell, Thomas, Anna Sara Oberg, Ralf Kuja-Halkola, Arvid Sjolander. 2012. "Sibling comparison designs: Bias from non–shared confounders and measurement error." *Epidemiology* 23(5): 713–720.

Fukuyama, Francis. 2018. *Identity: Contemporary Identity Politics and the Struggle for Recognition*. London: Profile Books.

Fukuyama, Francis. 2022. *Liberalism and Its Discontents*. New York: Farrar, Straus & Giroux.

Furner, Mary O. 1975. *Advocacy and Objectivity: A Crisis in the Professionalization of American Social Science, 1865–1905*. Lexington: University Press of Kentucky.

Furqan, Maham, Haider Mahmood. 2020. "Does education reduce homicide? A panel data analysis of Asian region." *Quality & Quantity* 54(4): 1–13.

Gaasholt, Gystein, Lise Togeby. 1995. "Interethnic tolerance, education, and political orientation: Evidence from Denmark." *Political Behavior* 17(3): 265–285.

Gallego, Aina. 2010. "Understanding unequal turnout: Education and voting in comparative perspective." *Electoral Studies* 29(2): 239–248.

Galston, William A. 2001. "Political knowledge, political engagement, and civic education." *Annual Review of Political Science* 4(1): 217–234.

Ganzach, Yoav. 2020. "From intelligence to political ideology: Socioeconomic paths." *Personality and Individual Differences* 164(March): 1–4.

Gardner, Lee. 2018. "Want to kill tenure? Be careful what you wish for." *Chronicle of Higher Education* 20.

Garrison, K. C., Margaret Mann. 1931. "A study of the opinions of college students." *Journal of Social Psychology* 2(2): 168–178. https://doi.org/10.1080/00224545.1931.9918965.

Garritzmann, Julian L. 2017. "The partisan politics of higher education." *PS: Political Science & Politics* 50(2): 413–417.

Gavit, John Palmer. 1925. *College*. New York: Harcourt, Brace & Company.

Geiger, Roger L. 1986. *To Advance Knowledge: The Growth of American Research Universities, 1900–1940*. New York: Oxford University Press.

Geiger, Roger L. 2014. *The History of American Higher Education: Learning and Culture from the Founding to World War II*. Princeton, NJ: Princeton University Press.

Gelepithis, Margarita, Marco Giani. 2022. "Inclusion without solidarity: Education, economic security, and attitudes toward redistribution." *Political Studies* 70(1): 45–61.

Gelman, Andrew, Guido Imbens. 2019. "Why high-order polynomials should not be used in regression discontinuity designs." *Journal of Business & Economic Statistics* 37(3): 447–456.

Gerber, Larry G. 2014. *The Rise and Decline of Faculty Governance: Professionalization and the Modern American University*. Baltimore, MD: Johns Hopkins University Press.

Gerring, John. 1998. *Party Ideologies in America, 1828–1996*. Cambridge: Cambridge University Press.

Gerring, John. 2005. "Minor parties in plurality electoral systems." *Party Politics* 11(1): 79–107.

Gerring, John. 2010. "Causal mechanisms: Yes, but..." *Comparative Political Studies* 43(11) (November): 1499–1526.

Gerring, John, Brendan Apfeld, Tore Wig, Andreas Tollefsen. 2022. *The Deep Roots of Modern Democracy: Geography and the Diffusion of Political Institutions*. Cambridge: Cambridge University Press.

Gerring, John, Philip Bond, William Barndt, Carola Moreno. 2005. "Democracy and growth: A historical perspective." *World Politics* 57(3) (April): 323–364.

Gesthuizen, Maurice, Tom Van der Meer, Peer Scheepers. 2008. "Education and dimensions of social capital: Do educational effects differ due to educational expansion and social security expenditure?" *European Sociological Review* 24(5): 617–632.

Gethin, Amory, Clara Martínez-Toledano, Thomas Piketty (eds.). 2021. *Political Cleavages and Social Inequalities: A Study of Fifty Democracies, 1948–2020*. Cambridge, MA: Harvard University Press.

Gethin, Amory, Clara Martínez-Toledano, Thomas Piketty. 2022. "Brahmin left versus merchant right: Changing political cleavages in 21 Western democracies, 1948–2020." *The Quarterly Journal of Economics* 137(1): 1–48.

Gevers, Lieve, Louis Vos. 2004. "Student movements." In Walter Rüegg (ed.), *A History of the University in Europe: Volume 3, Universities in the Nineteenth and Early Twentieth Centuries (1800–1945)*. Cambridge: Cambridge University Press: 269–362.

Gibbs, Paul (ed.). 2017. *The Pedagogy of Compassion at the Heart of Higher Education*. New York: Springer.

Gibson, John. 2001. "Unobservable family effects and the apparent external benefits of education." *Economics of Education Review* 20(3): 225–233.

Gidengil, Elisabeth, Lasse Tarkiainen, Hanna Wass, Pekka Martikainen. 2019. "Turnout and education: Is education proxying for pre-adult experiences within the family?" *Political Science Research and Methods* 7(2): 349–365.

Gillespie, James M., Gordon W. Allport. 1955. *Youth's Outlook on the Future: A Cross-National Study*. New York: Doubleday & Co.

Gilliland, A. R. 1940. "The attitude of college students toward God and the church." *Journal of Social Psychology* 11(1): 11–18. https://doi.org/10.1080/00224545.1940.9918729.

Gilliland, A. R. 1953. "Changes in religious beliefs of college students." *Journal of Social Psychology* 37(1): 113–116. https://doi.org/10.1080/00224545.1953.9921875.

Giroux, Henry A. 1988. "Literacy and the pedagogy of voice and political empowerment." *Educational Theory* 38(1): 61–75.

Giroux, Henry A. 2014. *Neoliberalism's War on Higher Education*. New York: Haymarket Books.

Giroux, Henry A. 2015. *University in Chains: Confronting the Military-Industrial-Academic Complex*. London: Routledge.

Glaeser, Edward L., Raven E. Saks. 2006. "Corruption in America." *Journal of Public Economics* 90(6–7): 1053–1072.

Glaeser, Edward L., Bruce I. Sacerdote. 2008. "Education and religion." *Journal of Human Capital* 2(2): 188–215.

Glaeser, Edward L., Rafael La Porta, Florencio Lopez-de-Silanes, Andrei Shleifer. 2004. "Do institutions cause growth?" *Journal of Economic Growth* 9(3): 271–303.

Glaser, James M. 2001. "The preference puzzle: Educational differences in racial-political attitudes." *Political Behavior* 23(4): 313–334.

Gless, Darryl, Barbara Herrnstein Smith (eds.). 2020. *The Politics of Liberal Education*. Durham, NC: Duke University Press.

Gold, Steven J., Stephanie J. Nawyn (eds.). 2019. *Routledge International Handbook of Migration Studies*. London: Routledge.

Goldsen, Rose K., Morris Rosenberg, Robin M. Williams Jr, Edward A. Suchman. 1960. *What College Students Think*. Princeton, NJ: D Van Nostrand.

Golebiowska, Ewa A. 1995. "Individual value priorities, education, and political tolerance." *Political Behavior* 17(1): 23–48.

Goodman, Paul. 1962. *The Community of Scholars*. New York: Random House.

Goody, Jack (ed.). 1975. *Literacy in Traditional Societies*. Cambridge: Cambridge University Press.

Gordon, Peter, Denis Lawton. 2002. *A History of Western Educational Ideas*. London: Routledge.

Gouldner, Alvin W. 1979. *The Future of Intellectuals and the Rise of the New Class*. New York: Seabury.

Graff, Gerald. 1993. *Beyond the Culture Wars: How Teaching the Conflicts Can Revitalize American Education*. W. W. Norton & Company.

Grant, Gerald, David Riesman. 1978. *The Perpetual Dream: Reform and Experiment in the American College*. Chicago, IL: University of Chicago Press.

Gray, John. 1995. *Liberalism*, 2nd ed. Minneapolis: University of Minnesota Press.

Gray, Phillip W. 2019. "Diagnosis versus ideological diversity." *PS: Political Science & Politics* 52(4): 728–731.

Grayling, Anthony C. 2010. *Ideas That Matter: The Concepts That Shape the 21st Century*. New York: Basic Books.

Greer, Scott. 2017. *No Campus for White Men: The Transformation of Higher Education into Hateful Indoctrination*. Nashville, TN: WND Books.

Gross, Neil. 2013. *Why Are Professors Liberal and Why Do Conservatives Care?* Cambridge, MA: Harvard University Press.

Gross, Neil, Ethan Fosse. 2012. "Why are professors liberal?" *Theory and Society* 41(2): 127–168.

Gross, Neil, Solon Simmons. 2009. "The religiosity of American college and university professors." *Sociology of Religion: A Quarterly Review* 70(2): 101–129. https://doi.org/10.1093/socrel/srp026.

Gross, Neil, Solon Simmons (eds.). 2014a. *Professors and Their Politics*. Baltimore, MD: Johns Hopkins University Press.

Gross, Neil, Solon Simmons. 2014b. "The social and political views of American college and university professors." In Neil Gross and Solon Simmons (eds.), *Professors and Their Politics*. Baltimore, MD: Johns Hopkins University Press: 19–52.

Grossmann, Matt. 2021. *How Social Science Got Better: Overcoming Bias with More Evidence, Diversity, and Self-Reflection*. Oxford: Oxford University Press.

Guimond, Serge, Douglas L. Palmer. 1990. "Type of academic training and causal attributions for social problems." *European Journal of Social Psychology* 20: 61–75.

Guimond, Serge, Douglas L. Palmer. 1996. "The political socialization of commerce and social science students: Epistemic authority and attitude change." *Journal of Applied Social Psychology* 26: 1985–2013.

Gutmann, Amy. 1987. *Democratic Education*. Princeton, NJ: Princeton University Press.

Haber, Jonathan. 2014. *MOOCs*. Cambridge, MA: MIT Press.

Habermas, Jurgen. 1971. *Toward a Rational Society: Student Protest, Science, and Politics*. Chichester: John Wiley.

Haegel, Florence. 1999. "The effect of education on the expression of negative views towards immigrants in France: The influence of the Republican model put to the test." In Louk Hagendoorn and Shervin Nekuee (eds.), *Education and Racism*. London: Routledge: 33–46.

Haerpfer, C., Ronald Inglehart, A. Moreno et al. (eds.). 2020. *World Values Survey: Round Seven-Country-Pooled Datafile*. Madrid: JD Systems Institute & WVSA Secretariat. doi: 10.14281/18241.1.

Hagendoorn, Louk, Shervin Nekuee. 1999. *Education and Racism*. London: Routledge.

Hainmueller, Jens, Michael J. Hiscox. 2007. "Educated preferences: Explaining attitudes toward immigration in Europe." *International Organization* 61(2): 399–442.

Hakhverdian, Armen, Erika Van Elsas, Wouter Van der Brug, Theresa Kuhn. 2013. "Euroscepticism and education: A longitudinal study of 12 EU member states, 1973–2010." *European Union Politics* 14(4): 522–541.

Haley, Hillary, Jim Sidanius. 2005. "Person-organization congruence and the maintenance of group-based social hierarchy: A social dominance perspective." *Group Processes & Intergroup Relations* 8(2): 187–203.

Halsey, Albert H. 1992. *The Decline of Donnish Dominion: The British Academic Professions in the Twentieth Century*. Oxford: Oxford University Press.

Halsey, Albert H., Martin A. Trow. 1971. *The British Academics*. Cambridge, MA: Harvard University Press.

Halstead, J. Mark. 1996. "Values and values education in schools." In J. Mark Halstead and Monica J. Taylor (eds.), *Values in Education and Education in Values*. London: Taylor & Francis: 3–14.

Hamburger, Joseph. 1965. *Intellectuals in Politics: John Stuart Mill and the Philosophic Radicals*. New Haven, CT: Yale University Press.

Hamilton, Richard F., Lowell L. Hargens. 1993. "The politics of the professors: Self-identifications, 1969-1984." *Social Forces* 71: 603–627.

Hangartner, Dominik, Lukas Schmid, Dalston Ward, Stefan Boes. 2020. "Which political activities are caused by education? Evidence from school entry exams." https://ssrn.com/abstract=3707982 or http://dx.doi.org/10.2139/ssrn.3707982.

Hanson, Jana M., Dustin D. Weeden, Ernest T. Pascarella, Charles Blaich. 2012. "Do liberal arts colleges make students more liberal? Some initial evidence." *Higher Education* 64(3): 355–369.

Hao, Zhidong, Peter Zabielskis (eds.). 2020. *Academic Freedom under Siege: Higher Education in East Asia, the U.S., and Australia.* New York: Springer.

Harper, Manly H. 1927. *Social Beliefs and Attitudes of American Educators.* New York: Teachers College.

Harris, Albert J., Hermann H. Remmers, C. E. Ellison. 1932. "The relation between liberal and conservative attitudes in college students, and other factors." *Journal of Social Psychology* 3(3): 320–336. https://doi.org/10.1080/00224545.1932.9919155.

Hartz, Louis. 1955. *The Liberal Tradition in America: An Interpretation of American Political Thought since the Revolution.* Boston, MA: Houghton Mifflin Harcourt.

Hasegawa, Kenji. 2019. *Student Radicalism and the Formation of Postwar Japan.* London: Palgrave Macmillan.

Hastie, Brianne. 2007. "Higher education and sociopolitical orientation: The role of social influence in the liberalisation of students." *European Journal of Psychology of Education* 22(3): 259–274.

Hauser, Seth. 2000. "Education, ability, and civic engagement in the contemporary United States." *Social Science Research* 29(4): 556–582.

Havemann, Ernest, Patricia Salter West. 1952. *They Went to College: The College Graduate in America Today.* New York: Harcourt, Brace.

Heater, Derek. 1996.*World Citizenship and Government: Cosmopolitan Ideas in the History of Western Political Thought.* New York: St. Martin's.

Heater, Derek. 2003. *A History of Education for Citizenship.* London: Routledge.

Heerwig, Jennifer A., Brian J. McCabe. 2009. "Education and social desirability bias: The case of a Black presidential candidate." *Social Science Quarterly* 90(3): 674–686.

Hellenbrand, Harold. 1990. *The Unfinished Revolution: Education and Politics in the Thought of Thomas Jefferson.* Newark: University of Delaware Press.

Heller, Henry. 2016. *The Capitalist University: The Transformations of Higher Education in the United States since 1945.* London: Pluto Press.

Helliwell, John F., Robert D. Putnam. 2007. "Education and social capital." *Eastern Economic Journal* 33(1): 1–19.

Hello, Evelyn, Peer Scheepers, Mérove Gijsberts. 2002. "Education and ethnic prejudice in Europe: Explanations for cross-national variances in the educational effect on ethnic prejudice." *Scandinavian Journal of Educational Research* 46(1): 5–24.

Hello, Evelyn, Peer Scheepers, Ad Vermulst, Jan R. M. Gerris. 2004. "Association between educational attainment and ethnic distance in young adults: Socialization by schools or parents?" *Acta Sociologica* 47(3): 253–275.

Henderson, John, Sara Chatfield. 2011. "Who matches? Propensity scores and bias in the causal effects of education on participation." *Journal of Politics* 73(3): 646–658.

Henry, Douglas V., Michael D. Beaty (eds.). 2007. *The Schooled Heart: Moral Formation in American Higher Education.* Waco, TX: Baylor University Press.

Henry, P. J., Jaime L. Napier. 2017. "Education is related to greater ideological prejudice." *Public Opinion Quarterly* 81(4): 930–942.

Hertzog, Matthew J. 2017. *Protections of Tenure and Academic Freedom in the United States: Evolution and Interpretation.* New York: Springer.

Heywood, Paul M. (ed.). 2014. *Routledge Handbook of Political Corruption.* London: Routledge.

Highton, Benjamin. 2009. "Revisiting the relationship between educational attainment and political sophistication." *The Journal of Politics* 71(4): 1564–1576.

Hillygus, D. Sunshine. 2005. "The missing link: Exploring the relationship between higher education and political engagement." *Political Behavior* 27(1): 25–47.

Hirst, Paul H. 2010. *Knowledge and the Curriculum: A Collection of Philosophical Papers.* London: Routledge.

Hodson, Gordon, Michael A. Busseri. 2012. "Bright minds and dark attitudes: Lower cognitive ability predicts greater prejudice through right-wing ideology and low intergroup contact." *Psychological Science* 23(2012): 1–9.

Hofstadter, Richard. 1955. *Academic Freedom in the Age of the College.* New York: Columbia University Press.

Hofstadter, Richard. 1966. *Anti-Intellectualism in American Life.* New York: Vintage.

Hoge, Dean R., Irving E. Bender. 1974. "Factors influencing value change among college graduates in adult life." *Journal of Personality and Social Psychology* 29(4): 572–585. https://doi.org/10.1037/h0036220.

Holbein, John, D. Sunshine Hillygus, Christina Gibson-Davis, Matthew Lenard, Darryl Hill. 2018. "The development of students' engagement in school, community, and democracy." *British Journal of Political Science* 50(4): 1439–1457.

Holmes, Kim R. 2016. *The Closing of the Liberal Mind: How Groupthink and Intolerance Define the Left.* New York: Encounter Books.

Honaker, James, Gary King, Matthew Blackwell. 2011. "Amelia II: A program for missing data." *Journal of Statistical Software* 45(7): 1–47.

Honeywell, Roy J. 2011. *The Educational Work of Thomas Jefferson.* New York: Read Books.

Hooghe, Liesbet, Gary Marks, Carole J. Wilson. 2002. "Does left/right structure party positions on European integration?" *Comparative Political Studies* 35(8): 965–989.

Hooghe, Marc, Thomas de Vroome. 2015. "How does the majority public react to multiculturalist policies? A comparative analysis of European countries." *American Behavioral Scientist* 59(6): 747–768.

Horn, Gerd-Rainer. 2007. *The Spirit of '68: Rebellion in Western Europe and North America, 1956–1976.* Oxford: Oxford University Press.

Horn, Max. 1979. *The Intercollegiate Socialist Society, 1905–1921: Origins of the Modern American Student Movement.* Boulder, CO: Westview Press.

Horowitz, David. 2009. *Indoctrination U.: The Left's War against Academic Freedom.* New York: Encounter Books.

Horowitz, David. 2013. *The Professors: The 101 Most Dangerous Academics in America.* New York: Simon and Schuster.

Horowitz, David, Jacob Laksin. 2009. *One-Party Classroom: How Radical Professors at America's Top Colleges Indoctrinate Students and Undermine Our Democracy.* Washington, DC: Crown Forum.

Howard, Lawrence C. 1958. "The academic and the ballot." *School and Society* 86 (November 22): 415–419.

Huang, Jian, Henriette Maassen Van den Brink, Wim Groot. 2009. "A meta-analysis of the effect of education on social capital." *Economics of Education Review* 28(4): 454–464.

Humberstone, T. Lloyd. 1951. *University Representation*. London: Hutchinson.

Humphreys, Macartan, Alexandra Scacco. 2020. "The aggregation challenge." *World Development* 127.

Hunter, James Davison. 1991. *Culture Wars: The Struggle to Define America*. New York: Basic Books.

Huntington, Samuel P. 1968. *Political Order in Changing Societies*. New Haven, CT: Yale University Press.

Hutchins, Robert Maynard. 1936. *The Higher Learning in America*. New Haven, CT: Yale University Press.

Hyman, Herbert H. 1959. *Political Socialization: A Study in the Psychology of Political Behavior*. Glencoe, IL: Free Press.

Hyman, Herbert H., Charles R. Wright. 1979. *Education's Lasting Influence on Values*. Chicago, IL: University of Chicago Press.

Imai, Kosuke, Luke Keele, Dustin Tingley, Teppei Yamamoto. 2011. "Unpacking the black box of causality: Learning about causal mechanisms from experimental and observational studies." *American Political Science Review* 105(4) (November): 765–789.

Inglehart, Ronald. 2018. *Cultural Evolution: People's Motivations Are Changing, and Reshaping the World*. Cambridge: Cambridge University Press.

Ivarsflaten, E., Rune Stubager. 2013. "Voting for the populist radical right in Western Europe: The role of education." In J. Rydgren (ed.), *Class Politics and the Radical Right*. London: Routledge: 122–137.

Jackman, Mary. 1978. "General and applied tolerance: Does education increase commitment to racial integration?" *American Journal of Political Science* 22 (May): 302–334.

Jackman, Mary, Michael J. Mulha. 1984. "Education and intergroup attitudes: Moral enlightenment, superficial democratic commitment, or ideological refinement?" *American Sociological Review* 49 (August): 751–769.

Jacob, Margaret C. 1997. *Scientific Culture and the Making of the Industrial West*, 2nd ed. New York: Oxford University Press.

Jacob, Philip E. 1957. *Changing Values in College: An Exploratory Study of the Impact of College Teaching*. New York: Harper.

Jacobs, Alan M. 2009. "How do ideas matter? Mental models and attention in German pension politics." *Comparative Political Studies* 42(2): 252–279.

Jacobsen, Dag Ingvar. 2001. "Higher education as an arena for political socialisation: Myth or reality?" *Scandinavian Political Studies* 24(4): 351–368.

Jaksic, Sonia, Ivan Nazario. 1989. "Chile." In Philip G. Altbach (ed.), *Student Political Activism: An International Reference Handbook*. Westport, CT: Greenwood Press: 359–370.

Jarausch, Konrad H. 2014. *Students, Society and Politics in Imperial Germany: The Rise of Academic Illiberalism*. Princeton, NJ: Princeton University Press.

Jasinska-Kania, Aleksandra. 1999. "The impact of education on racism in Poland compared with other European countries." In Louk Hagendoorn and Shervin Nekuee (eds.), *Education and Racism*. London: Routledge: 75–92.

Jaspers, Karl. 1960 [1923]. *The Idea of the University*. London: Peter Owen.

Jennings, Jeremy, Tony Kemp-Welch (eds.). 1997. *Intellectuals in Politics: From the Dreyfus Affair to the Rushdie Affair*. London: Routledge.

Jennings, M. Kent, George Markus. 1984. "Partisan orientations over the long haul: Results from the three-wave political socialization panel study." *American Political Science Review* 78: 1000–1018.

Jennings, M. Kent, Laura Stoker. 2008. "Another and longer look at the impact of higher education on political involvement and attitudes." Paper delivered at the Midwest Political Science Association Meeting, Chicago, IL.

Jennings, M. Kent, Richard G. Niemi. 1981. *Generations and Politics*. Princeton, NJ: Princeton University Press,

Jenssen, Anders Todal, Heidi Engesbak. 1994. "The many faces of education: Why are people with lower education more hostile towards immigrants than people with higher education?" *Scandinavian Journal of Educational Research* 38(1): 33–50.

Jewett, Andrew. 2014. "Naturalizing liberalism in the 1950s." In Neil Gross and Solon Simmons (eds.), *Professors and Their Politics*. Baltimore, MD: Johns Hopkins University Press: 191–216.

Jewett, Andrew. 2020. *Science under Fire: Challenges to Scientific Authority in Modern America*. Cambridge, MA: Harvard University Press.

Jian, Chen, Martin Klimke, Masha Kirasirova et al. (eds.). 2018. *The Routledge Handbook of the Global Sixties: Between Protest and Nation-Building*. London: Routledge.

Johnson, Danette Ifert. 2004. "Relationships between college experiences and alumni participation in the community." *Review of Higher Education* 27(2): 169–185.

Johnston, Michael. 2005. *Syndromes of Corruption: Wealth, Power, and Democracy*. Cambridge: Cambridge University Press.

Jones, Edward S. 1926. "The opinion of college students." *Journal of Applied Psychology* 10(4): 427–436.

Jones, Vernon. 1938. "Attitudes of college students and the changes in such attitudes during four years in college." *Journal of Educational Psychology* 29(1): 14–25. https://doi.org/10.1037/h0055012.

Jost, John T. 2009. "'Elective affinities': On the psychological bases of left-right differences." *Psychological Inquiry* 20: 129–141.

Jost, John T., Orsolya Hunyady. 2005. "Antecedents and consequences of system-justifying ideologies." *Current Directions in Psychological Science* 14: 260–265.

Junes, Tom. 2015. *Student Politics in Communist Poland: Generations of Consent and Dissent*. Lanham, MD: Lexington Books.

Jung, Haeil, Jung ah Gil. 2019. "Does college education make people politically liberal? Evidence from a natural experiment in South Korea." *Social Science Research* 81 (August 2018): 209–220. https://doi.org/10.1016/j.ssresearch.2019.03.014.

Kam, Cindy D., Carl Palmer. 2008. "Reconsidering the effects of education on political participation." *Journal of Politics* 70(3): 612–631.

Kam, Cindy D., Carl Palmer. 2011. "Rejoinder: Reconsidering the effects of education on political participation." *Journal of Politics* 73(3): 659–663.

Kamenetz, Anya. 2010. *DIY U: Edupunks, Edupreneurs, and the Coming Transformation of Higher Education*. Chelsea, VT: Chelsea Green Publishing.

Kanazawa, Satoshi. 2010. "Why liberals and atheists are more intelligent." *Social Psychology Quarterly* 73: 33–57.

Kane, Emily W. 1995. "Education and beliefs about gender inequality." *Social Problems* 42(1): 74–90.

Kant, Immanuel. 1960 [1803]. *Lecture Notes on Pedagogy*, trans. Annette Churton and published as *Kant on Education*. Ann Arbor: University of Michigan Press.

Kaslovsky, Jaclyn. 2015. "The effect of education on ideological polarization in the U.S. Congress: An instrumental variable analysis." *The Journal of International Politics and Affairs* 16.

Kass, Leon. 1981. *The Aims of Liberal Education*. Chicago, IL: University of Chicago Publications Office.

Kassow, Samuel D. 1989. *Students, Professors, and the State in Tsarist Russia*. Berkeley: University of California Press.

Katznelson, Ira. 2021. "Measuring liberalism, confronting evil: A retrospective." *Annual Review of Political Science* 24: 1–19.

Kaufmann, Eric. 2021. "Academic freedom in crisis: Punishment, political discrimination, and self-censorship." *Center for the Study of Partisanship and Ideology* 2: 1–195.

Keller, Morton, Phyllis Keller. 2001. *Making Harvard Modern: The Rise of America's University*. Oxford: Oxford University Press.

Kelly-Woessner, April, Matthew Woessner. 2008. "Conflict in the classroom: Considering the effects of partisan difference on political education." *Journal of Political Science Education* 4(3): 265–285.

Keohane, Nannerl O. 2006. *Higher Ground: Ethics and Leadership in the Modern University*. Durham, NC: Duke University Press.

Kerckhoff, Alan C. 1976. "The status attainment process: Socialization or allocation?" *Social Forces* 55(2): 368–381.

Kerr, Clark. 2001 [1963]. *The Uses of the University*. Cambridge, MA: Harvard University Press.

Kerr, Clark, John T. Dunlop, Frederick H. Harbison, Charles A. Myers. 1960. *Industrialism and Industrial Man*. Cambridge, MA: Harvard University Press.

Key, Valdimar Orlando. 1961. *Public Opinion and American Democracy*. New York: Alfred A. Knopf.

Keynes, John Maynard. 1936. *The General Theory of Employment, Interest and Money*. London: Macmillan.

Kim, Quee Young. 1978. "Academic discipline and ideological spectrum: The Korean professoriate." *Asian Survey* 18(11): 1152–1167. https://doi.org/10.2307/2643298.

Kimball, Bruce A. 1986. *Orators and Philosophers: A History of the Idea of Liberal Education*. New York: Teachers College Press.

Kimball, Roger. 1990. *Tenured Radicals: How Politics Has Corrupted Our Higher Education*. New York: Harper & Row.

Kingston, Paul W., Ryan Hubbard, Brent Lapp, Paul Schroeder, Julia Wilson. 2003. "Why education matters." *Sociology of Education* 76(1) (January): 53–70.

Kirby, William C. 2022. *Empires of Ideas: Creating the Modern University from Germany to America to China*. Cambridge, MA: Harvard University Press.

Kirchgässner, Gebhard. 2005. "(Why) are economists different?" *European Journal of Political Economy* 21(3): 543–562.

Kitschelt, Herbert. 1994. *The Transformation of European Social Democracy*. Cambridge: Cambridge University Press.

Klein, Daniel B., Andrew Western. 2004–2005. "Voter registration of Berkeley and Stanford faculty." *Academic Questions* 18: 53–65.

Klein, Daniel B., Charlotta Stern. 2005a. "Political diversity in six disciplines." *Academic Questions* 18(1): 40–52.

Klein, Daniel B., Charlotta Stern. 2005b. "Professors and their politics: The policy views of social scientists." *Critical Review* 17: 257–303.

Klein, Daniel B., Charlotta Stern. 2007. "Is there a free-market economist in the house? The policy views of American Economic Association members." *American Journal of Economics and Sociology* 66(2) (April): 309–334.

Klein, Daniel B., Charlotta Stern. 2009. "Groupthink in academia: Majoritarian departmental politics and the professional pyramid." *The Independent Review* 13 (4): 585–600.

Klein, Daniel B., Charlotta Stern. 2018. "Sociology and classical liberalism." In Irving Horowitz (ed.), *Culture and Civilization*. London: Routledge: 130–148.

Klemenčič, Manja. 2014. "Student power in a global perspective and contemporary trends in student organising." *Studies in Higher Education* 39(3): 396–411.

Klemenčič, Manja, Sjur Bergan (eds.). 2015. *Student Engagement in Europe: Society, Higher Education and Student Governance*. Higher Education Series. Strasbourg: Council of Europe.

Kleppestø, Thomas Haarklau, Nikolai Olavi Czajkowski, Olav Vassend et al. 2019. "Correlations between social dominance orientation and political attitudes reflect common genetic underpinnings." *Proceedings of the National Academy of Sciences* 116(36): 17741–17746.

Klofstad, Casey A. 2007. "Talk leads to recruitment: How discussions about politics and current events increase civic participation." *Political Research Quarterly* 60(2f): 180–191.

Knode, Jay C. 1943. "Attitudes on state university campuses." *American Sociological Review* 8(6): 666. https://doi.org/10.2307/2085227.

Koblik, Steven, Stephen Richards Graubard (eds.). 2000. *Distinctively American: The Residential Liberal Arts Colleges*. Piscataway, NJ: Transaction Publishers.

Kochetkova, Inna. 2009. *The Myth of the Russian Intelligentsia: Old Intellectuals in the New Russia*. London: Routledge.

Kornhauser, Arthur W. 1938. "Attitudes of economic groups." *The Public Opinion Quarterly* 2(2): 260–268.

Kors, Alan Charles, Harvey Silverglate. 1999. *The Shadow University: The Betrayal of Liberty on America's Campuses*. New York: Simon and Schuster.

Kotschnig, Walter M. 1937. *Unemployment in the Learned Professions: An International Study of Occupational and Educational Planning*. London: Oxford University Press.

Kozlov, Dmitry. 2020. "'Do you dare to go to the square?': The legacy of Soviet dissidents in Russian public protests of the 2000s and 2010s." *Post-Soviet Affairs* 36 (3): 211–225.

Kriesi, Hanspeter, Edgar Grande, Romain Lachat, Martin Dolezal, Simon Bornschier, Timotheos Frey. 2006. "Globalization and the transformation of the national political space: Six European countries compared." *European Journal of Political Research* 45 (6): 921–956.

Kronman, Anthony T. 2007. *Education's End: Why Our Colleges and Universities Have Given Up on the Meaning of Life*. New Haven, CT: Yale University Press.

Kulp, Daniel H., Helen H. Davidson. 1933. "Sibling resemblance in social attitudes." *The Journal of Educational Sociology* 7(2): 133–140.

Kurzman, Charles. 2008. *Democracy Denied, 1905–1915*. Cambridge, MA: Harvard University Press.

Kurzman, Charles, Erin Leahey. 2004. "Intellectuals and democratization, 1905–1912 and 1989–1996." *American Journal of Sociology* 109(4): 937–986.

Kurzman, Charles, Lynn Owens. 2002. "The sociology of intellectuals." *Annual Review of Sociology* 28(1): 63–90.

Kuvvet, Emre. 2021. "Even finance professors lean left." *Academic Questions* 34(2). https://doi.org/10.51845/34su.2.3.

La Falce, David, Simon Peter Gomez. 2007. "Political attitudes in the classroom: Is academia the last bastion of liberalism?" *Journal of Political Science Education* 3 (1): 1–20.

la Roi, Chaim, Jornt Mandemakers. 2018. "Acceptance of homosexuality through education? Investigating the role of education, family background and individual characteristics in the United Kingdom." *Social Science Research* 71: 109–128.

Ladd, Everett Carl, Jr., Seymour Martin Lipset. 1971. "The politics of American political scientists." *PS: Political Science and Politics* 4(2) (Spring): 135–144.

Ladd, Everett Carl, Jr., Seymour Martin Lipset. 1975. *The Divided Academy: Professors and Politics*. New York: McGraw-Hill.

Ladd, Everett Carl, Jr., Seymour Martin Lipset. 2001. "Carnegie Commission National Survey of Higher Education: Technical report." Pittsburgh, PA: Carnegie Institute.

Lambert, Eric G., Lois A. Ventura, Daniel E. Hall, Terry Cluse-Tolar. 2006. "College students' views on gay and lesbian issues: Does education make a difference?" *Journal of Homosexuality* 50(4): 1–30.

Lamont, Michèle. 1987. "Cultural capital and the liberal political attitudes of professionals: Comment on Brint." *American Journal of Sociology* 92: 1501–1506.

Lancee, Bram, Oriane Sarrasin. 2015. "Educated preferences or selection effects? A longitudinal analysis of the impact of educational attainment on attitudes towards immigrants." *European Sociological Review* 31(4): 490–501.

Landes, David S. 1975. *The Unbound Prometheus: Technological Change and Industrial Development in Western Europe from 1750 to the Present*. Cambridge: Cambridge University Press.

Landes, David S. 2006. "Why Europe and the West? Why not China?" *Journal of Economic Perspectives* 20(2): 3–22.

Landreth, Harry, David C. Colander. 2001. *The History of Economic Thought*. Boston, MA: Houghton Mifflin.

Langbert, Mitchell. 2018. "Homogenous: The political affiliations of elite liberal arts college faculty." *Academic Questions* 31(2): 186–197.

Langbert, Mitchell, Anthony J. Quain, Daniel B. Klein. 2016. "Faculty voter registration in economics, history, journalism, law, and psychology." *Econ Journal Watch* 13(3): 422–451.

Langton, K., M. Kent Jennings. 1968. "Political socialization and the high school civics curriculum in the United States." *American Political Science Review* 62: 862–867.

Lanning, John Tate. 1940. *Academic Culture in the Spanish Colonies*. New York: Oxford University Press.

Laqueur, Walter. 1962. *Young Germany: A History of the German Youth Movement*. Piscataway, NJ: Transaction Publishers.

Larregue, Julien. 2018. "Conservative apostles of objectivity and the myth of a 'liberal bias' in science." *American Sociologist* 49(2): 312–327. https://doi.org/10.1007/s12108-017-9366-9.

Larson, Edward J., Larry Witham. 1998. "Leading scientists still reject God." *Nature* 394(6691): 313. https://doi.org/10.1038/28478.

Larson, Magali Sarfatti. 1979. *The Rise of Professionalism: A Sociological Analysis.* Berkeley: University of California Press.

Lazarsfeld, Paul. F. 1959. "Foreword." In Allen H. Barton, *Studying the Effects of College Education: A Methodological Examination of Changing Values in College.* New York: Edward W. Hazen Foundation: 5–10.

Lazarsfeld, Paul F., Wagner Thielens. 1958. *The Academic Mind: Social Scientists in a Time of Crisis.* Glencoe, IL: Free Press.

Lazarsfeld, Paul F., Bernard Berelson, Hazel Gaudet. 1944. *The People's Choice: How the Voter Makes Up His Mind in a Presidential Campaign.* New York: Columbia University Press.

Lederman, Daniel, Norman V. Loayza, Rodrigo R. Soares. 2005. "Accountability and corruption: Political institutions matter." *Economic & Politics* 7(1): 1–35.

Lehman, Edward C. 1975. "Who leaves the ivory tower? Academicians and radical politics." *Sociological Focus* 8(4): 359–374. https://doi.org/10.1080/00380237.1975.10570910.

Leslie, Stuart W. 1993. *The Cold War and American Science: The Military-Industrial-Academic Complex at MIT and Stanford.* New York: Columbia University Press.

Leuba, James Henry. 1921. *The Belief in God and Immortality: A Psychological, Anthropological and Statistical Study.* Chicago, IL: Open Court Publishing Company.

Levine, Lawrence W. 1996. *The Opening of the American Mind: Canons, Culture, and History.* Boston, MA: Beacon Press.

LeVine, Robert A. 1966. "American college experience as a socialization process." In Theodore M. Newcomb and Everett K. Wilson (eds.), *College Peer Groups: Problems and Prospects for Research.* Chicago, IL: Aldine.

Levinson, Meira. 1999. *The Demands of Liberal Education.* Oxford: Oxford University Press.

Levy, Daniel C. 1991. "The decline of Latin American student activism." *Higher Education* 22(2): 145–155.

Levy, Marion Joseph. 1966. *Modernization and the Structure of Societies: The Organizational Contexts of Societies.* Princeton, NJ: Princeton University Press.

Liebman, Arthur, Kenneth N. Walker, Myron Glazer. 1972. *Latin American University Students: A Six Nation Study.* Cambridge, MA: Harvard University Press.

Lipset, Seymour Martin. 1959. "Some social requisites of democracy: Economic development and political development." *American Political Science Review* 53 (March): 69–105.

Lipset, Seymour Martin (ed.). 1967. *Student Politics.* New York: Basic Books.

Lipset, Seymour Martin. 1972. *Rebellion in the University: A History of Student Activism in America.* London: Kegan Paul.

Lipset, Seymour Martin. 1982. "The academic mind at the top: The political behavior and values of faculty elites." *Public Opinion Quarterly* 46(2): 143–168. https://doi.org/10.1086/268710.

Lipset, Seymour Martin, Everett Carll Ladd, Jr. 1971. "College generations: From the 1930s to the 1960s." *The Public Interest* 25 (Fall).

Lipset, Seymour Martin, Everett Carll Ladd, Jr. 1972. "The politics of American sociologists." *American Journal of Sociology* 78(1) (July): 67–104.

Lipset, Seymour Martin, Gary Marks. 2000. *It Didn't Happen Here: Why Socialism Failed in the United States*. New York: W. W. Norton & Company.

Lipset, Seymour Martin, Philip G. Altbach (eds.). 1969. *Students in Revolt*. Boston, MA: Houghton Mifflin.

Literat, Ioana. 2012. "'Original democracy': A rhetorical analysis of Romanian post-revolutionary political discourse and the University Square protests of June 1990." *Central European Journal of Communication* 5(8): 25–39.

Locke, John. 1887 [1693]. *Some Thoughts Concerning Education*. Cambridge: Cambridge University Press.

Lockyer, Adam, Peter K. Hatemi, R. Hopcroft. 2018. *Genetics and Politics: A Review for the Social Scientist*. Oxford: Oxford University Press.

Loftus, Jeni. 2001. "America's liberalization in attitudes toward homosexuality, 1973 to 1998." *American Sociological Review* 66(5): 762–782.

Lott, John R., Jr. 1990. "An explanation for public provision of schooling: The importance of indoctrination." *Journal of Law & Economics* 33(1) (April): 199–232.

Lottes, Lisa L., Peter J. Kuriloff. 1994. "The impact of college experience on political and social attitudes." *Sex Roles* 31 (1/2): 31–54.

Lührmann, Anna, Nils Düpont, Masaaki Higashijima et al. 2020. Varieties of party identity and organization (V-Party) dataset vi. Varieties of Democracy (V-Dem) Project.

Lukianoff, Greg. 2014. *Unlearning Liberty: Campus Censorship and the End of American Debate*. New York: Encounter Books.

Lukianoff, Greg, Jonathan Haidt. 2019. *The Coddling of the American Mind: How Good Intentions and Bad Ideas Are Setting Up a Generation for Failure*. New York: Penguin Books.

Luna, Juan Pablo. 2010. "Segmented party-voter linkages in Latin America: The case of the UDI." *Journal of Latin American Studies* 42: 325–356.

Luskin, Robert C. 1987. "Measuring political sophistication." *American Journal of Political Science*, 31: 856–899.

Luskin, Robert C. 1990. "Explaining political sophistication." *Political Behavior* 12(4): 331–361.

Macedo, Stephen. 2009. *Diversity and Distrust: Civic Education in a Multicultural Democracy*. Cambridge, MA: Harvard University Press.

Maier, Joseph, Richard W. Weatherhead. 1979. *The Latin American University*. Albuquerque: University of New Mexico Press.

Makdisi, George. 1981. *The Rise of Colleges: Institutions of Learning in Islam and the West*. Edinburgh: Edinburgh University Press.

Ma-Kellams, Christine, Aida Rocci Ruiz, Jacqueline Lee, Andrea Madu. 2014. "Not all education is equally liberal: The effects of science education on political attitudes." *Journal of Social and Political Psychology* 2(1): 143–163.

Makowsky, Michael D., Stephen C. Miller. 2014. "Education, intelligence, and attitude extremity." *Public Opinion Quarterly* 78(4): 832–858.

Mandel, Ernest. 1969. "The new vanguard." In Tariq Ali (ed.), *The New Revolutionaries*. London: Peter Owen: 47–66.

Mannheim, Karl. 1936. *Ideology and Utopia*. New York: Harcourt, Brace & World.

Maranell, Gary M., D. Stanley Eitzen. 1970. "The effect of discipline, region, and rank on the political attitudes of college professors." *Sociological Quarterly* 11(1): 112–118. https://doi.org/10.1111/j.1533-8525.1970.tb02080.x.

Maranto, Robert, Fredrick M. Hess, Richard E. Redding (eds.). 2009. *The Politically Correct University: Problems, Scope, and Reforms.* Washington, DC: AEI Press.

Maranto, Robert, Richard E. Redding, Frederick M. Hess. 2009. "The PC academy debate: Questions not asked." In Robert Maranto, Richard E. Redding, and Frederick M. Hess (eds.), *The Politically Correct University: Problems, Scope, and Reforms.* Lanham, MD: Rowman & Littlefield: 3–14.

Mariani, Mack D., Gordon J. Hewitt. 2008. "Indoctrination U.? Faculty ideology and changes in student political orientation." *PS: Political Science and Politics* 41(4): 773–783.

Markovits, Andrei S., Philip S. Gorski. 1993. *The German Left: Red, Green and Beyond.* Cambridge: Polity Press.

Marquart-Pyatt, Sandra, Pamela Paxton. 2007. "In principle and in practice: Learning political tolerance in Eastern and Western Europe." *Political Behavior* 29(1): 89–113.

Marsden, George. 1994. *The Soul of the American University: From Protestant Establishment to Established Nonbelief.* New York: Oxford University Press.

Marshall, Byron K. 1992. *Academic Freedom and the Japanese Imperial University, 1868–1939.* Berkeley: University of California Press.

Martin, Chris C. 2016. "How ideology has hindered sociological insight." *The American Sociologist* 47(1): 115–130.

Mattson, Kevin. 2010. *Intellectuals in Action: The Origins of the New Left and Radical Liberalism, 1945–1970.* University Park, PA: Penn State Press.

Mayer, Alexander K. 2011. "Does education increase political participation?" *Journal of Politics* 73(3): 633–645.

Mayrl, Damon, Jeremy E. Uecker. 2011. "Higher education and religious liberalization among young adults." *Social Forces* 90(1): 181–208.

McClintock, Charles G., Charles B. Spaulding, Henry A. Turner. 1965. "Political orientations of academically affiliated psychologists." *American Psychologist* 20(3): 211.

McCloskey, Deirdre Nansen. 2019. *Why Liberalism Works: How True Liberal Values Produce a Freer, More Equal, Prosperous World for All.* New Haven, CT: Yale University Press.

McClosky, Herbert, Alida Brill. 1983. *Dimensions of Tolerance: What Americans Believe about Civil Liberties.* New York: Russell Sage Foundation.

McDonough, Kevin, Walter Feinberg (eds.). 2003. *Citizenship and Education in Liberal-Democratic Societies: Teaching for Cosmopolitan Values and Collective Identities.* Oxford: Oxford University Press.

McFalls, Joseph A., Michael J. Engle, Bernard J. Gallagher. 1999. "The American sociologist: Characteristics in the 1990s." *The American Sociologist* 30(3): 96–100.

McGinn, Noel F., Erwin H. Epstein (eds.). 1999. *Comparative Perspectives on the Role of Education in Democratization. Part I: Transitional States and States of Transition.* New York: Peter Lang.

McGinn, Noel F., Erwin H. Epstein (eds.). 2000. *Comparative Perspectives on the Role of Education in Democratization. Part II: Socialization, Identity, and the Politics of Control.* New York: Peter Lang.

McIlrath, Lorraine, Ann Lyons (eds.). 2012. *Higher Education and Civic Engagement: Comparative Perspectives*. New York: Springer.

Mead, Lawrence M. 2013. "The universities: Avatars of modernity." *Society* 50(2): 167–175.

Meeusen, Cecil, Thomas de Vroome, Marc Hooghe. 2013. "How does education have an impact on ethnocentrism? A structural equation analysis of cognitive, occupational status and network mechanisms." *International Journal of Intercultural Relations* 37 (5): 507–522. http://dx.doi.org/10.1016/j.ijintrel.2013.07.002.

Meiklejohn, Alexander. 1920. *The Liberal College*. Boston, MA: Marshall Jones.

Meyer, John W. 1977. "The effects of education as an institution." *American Journal of Sociology* 83(1): 55–77.

Mi, Park. 2005. "Organizing dissent against authoritarianism: The South Korean student movement in the 1980s." *Korea Journal* 45(3): 261–289.

Michel, Jean-Baptiste, Yuan Kui Shen, Aviva Presser Aiden et al. 2011. "Quantitative analysis of culture using millions of digitized books." *Science* 331(6014): 176–182.

Michels, Robert. 1915. *Political Parties*, trans. Eden and Cedar Paul. London: Jarrald & Sons.

Middleton, Russell, Snell Putney. 1963. "Student rebellion against parental political beliefs." *Social Forces* 45(3): 438–440. https://doi.org/10.1093/sf/45.3.438.

Milem, Jeffrey F. 1998. "Attitude change in college students: Examining the effect of college peer groups and faculty normative groups." *Journal of Higher Education* 69 (2): 117–140.

Mill, James. 1969. *James Mill on Education*, ed. Wyndham H. Burston. Cambridge: Cambridge University Press.

Ministerul Educației Naționale. "Învățământ postliceal." www.edu.ro/invatamant-postliceal.

Mocan, Naci H. 2008. "What determines corruption? International evidence from microdata." *Economic Inquiry* 46(4): 493–510.

Mocan, Naci H., Colin Cannonier. 2012. "Empowering women through education: Evidence from Sierra Leone." NBER Working Paper.

Mokyr, Joel. 2016. *A Culture of Growth*. Princeton, NJ: Princeton University Press.

Moore, Gwyn, Karl C. Garrison. 1932. "A comparative study of social and political attitudes of college students." *The Journal of Abnormal and Social Psychology* 27(2): 192–208.

Murtin, Fabrice, Romain Wacziarg. 2014. "The democratic transition." *Journal of Economic Growth* 19(2): 141–181.

Musto, Ronald. 2022. *The Attack on Higher Education: The Dissolution of the American University*. Cambridge: Cambridge University Press.

Nakhaie, M. Reza, Robert J Brym. 1999. "The political attitudes of Canadian professors." *The Canadian Journal of Sociology* 24(3): 329–353.

Nakhaie, M. Reza, Robert J. Brym. 2011. "The ideological orientations of Canadian university professors." *Canadian Journal of Higher Education* 41(1): 18–33. https://doi.org/10.47678/cjhe.v41i1.2181.

Narveson, Jan, James P. Sterba. 2010. *Are Liberty and Equality Compatible?* Cambridge: Cambridge University Press.

Neagu, Alina. 2010, July 5. "Bacalaureat 2010: Procent de promovabilitate de 67,4%, cel mai slab din ultimul deceniu. Funeriu explică: Toleranță-zero față de actele de fraudă." www

.hotnews.ro/stiri-esential-7531190-video-bacalaureat-2010-procent-promovabilitate-67-4-cel-mai-slab-din-ultimul-deceniu-funeriu-explica-toleranta-zero-fata-actele-frauda.htm.

Newcomb, Theodore Mead. 1943. *Personality and Social Change: Attitude and Social Formation in a Student Community.* New York: Dryden.

Newcomb, Theodore Mead. 1967. *Persistence and Change: Bennington College and Its Students after Twenty-Five Years.* New York: Wiley.

Newcomb, Theodore Mead, Everett K. Wilson (eds.). 1966. *College Peer Groups: Problems and Prospects for Research.* Chicago, IL: Aldine.

Newman, Frank, Lara Couturier, Jamie Scurry. 2010. *The Future of Higher Education: Rhetoric, Reality, and the Risks of the Market.* New York: John Wiley & Sons.

Newman, John Henry. 1976 [1852]. *The Idea of a University Defined and Illustrated*, edited with introduction and notes by Ian T. Ker. Oxford: Clarendon.

Newton, Arthur Percival. 1924. *The Universities and Educational Systems of the British Empire.* London: W. Collins.

Nie, Norman H., D. Sunshine Hillygus. 2001. "Education and democratic citizenship." In Diane Ravitch and Joseph Viteritti (eds.), *Making Good Citizens: Education and Civil Society.* New Haven, CT: Yale University Press.

Nie, Norman H., Jane Junn, Kenneth Stehlik-Barry. 1996. *Education and Democratic Citizenship in America.* Chicago, IL: University of Chicago Press.

Niemi, Richard G., Jonathan D. Klingler. 2012. "The development of political attitudes and behaviour among young adults." *Australian Journal of Political Science* 47(1): 31–54.

Nogee, Philip, Murray B. Levin. 1958. "Some determinants of political attitudes among college voters." *Public Opinion Quarterly* 22(4): 449–463. https://doi.org/10.1086/266819.

NORC. 2019. *General Social Surveys, 1972–2018: Cumulative Codebook.* Chicago, IL: National Data Program for the Social Sciences, University of Chicago.

Norris, Pippa, Ronald Inglehart. 2011. *Sacred and Secular: Religion and Politics Worldwide*, 2nd ed. Cambridge: Cambridge University Press.

Novak, Steven J. 1977. *The Rights of Youth.* Cambridge, MA: Harvard University Press.

Nunn, Clyde Z., Henry J. Crockett, J. Allen Williams, Jr. 1978. *Tolerance for Non-Conformity.* San Francisco, CA: Jossey-Bass.

Nussbaum, Martha Craven. 1998. *Cultivating Humanity.* Cambridge, MA: Harvard University Press.

Nussbaum, Martha Craven. 2010. *Not for Profit: Why Democracy Needs the Humanities.* Princeton, NJ: Princeton University Press.

Oakeshott, Michael. 1989. *The Voice of Liberal Learning.* New Haven, CT: Yale University Press.

Ocantos, Ezequiel Gonzalez, Chad Kiewiet de Jonge, David W. Nickerson. 2014. "The conditionality of vote-buying norms: Experimental evidence from Latin America." *American Journal of Political Science* 58(1): 197–211.

Ohlander, Julianne, Jeanne Batalova, Judith Treas. 2005. "Explaining educational influences on attitudes toward homosexual relations." *Social Science Research* 34 (4): 781–799.

Ohmann, Richard. 1997. "English and the Cold War." In Noam Chomsky, David Barsamian, and Howard Zinn (eds.), *The Cold War and the University.* New York: New Press: 73–105.

Ohmann, Richard. 2003. *Politics of Knowledge: The Commercialization of the University, the Professions, and Print Culture.* Middletown, CT: Wesleyan University Press.

Okbay, Aysu, Jonathan P. Beauchamp, Mark Alan Fontana et al. 2016. "Genome-wide association study identifies 74 loci associated with educational attainment." *Nature* 533(4604): 539–542.

Ordorika, Imanol. 2021. "Student movements and politics in Latin America: A historical reconceptualization." *Higher Education* 83(12): 1–19.

Ordorika, Imanol, Roberto Rodríguez-Gómez, M. Gil Antón. 2019. "Las luchas estudiantiles de 1918 a 2018." In Imanol Ordorika, Roberto Rodríguez-Gómez, and Manuel Gil Antón (eds.), *Cien años de movimientos estudiantiles.* Mexico City: Programa Universitario de Estudios sobre Educación Superior, UNAM: 9–23.

Ortmann, Stephan. 2015. "The umbrella movement and Hong Kong's protracted democratization process." *Asian Affairs* 46(1): 32–50.

Oskarsson, Sven, Peter Thisted Dinesen, Christopher T. Dawes, Magnus Johannesson, Patrik K. E. Magnusson. 2017. "Education and social trust: Testing a causal hypothesis using the discordant twin design." *Political Psychology* 38(3): 515–531.

Otsuka, Michael. 2003. *Libertarianism without Inequality.* Oxford: Clarendon Press.

Owen, Stephanie, Isabel Sawhill. 2013. *Should Everyone Go to College?* Washington, DC: Brookings Institution, Center on Children and Families.

Pace, C. Robert. 1939. "The relationship between liberalism and knowledge of current affairs." *Journal of Social Psychology* 10(2): 247–258. https://doi.org/10.1080/00224545.1939.9713363.

Pace, C. Robert. 1949. "What kind of citizens do college graduates become?" *The Journal of General Education* 3(3): 197–202.

Palacios-Valladares, Indira, Gabriel Ondetti (2018). "Student protest and the Nueva Mayoría reforms in Chile." *Bulletin of Latin American Research* 38(5): 638–653.

Paloczi-Horvath, George. 1971. *Youth Up in Arms: A Political and Social World Survey 1955–1970.* London: Weidenfeld & Nicolson.

Parker, Kim. 2019. "The growing partisan divide in views of higher education." *PEW Research Center: Social and Demographic Trends* 19.

Parsons, Jessica. 2020. "Political bias in America's universities." Dissertation, The Florida State University.

Parsons, Talcott. 1938. "The role of ideas in social action." *American Sociological Review* 3: 652–664.

Parsons, Talcott, Gerald M. Platt. 1973. *The American University.* Cambridge, MA: Harvard University Press.

Pascarella, Ernest T., Patrick T. Terenzini. 1991. *How College Affects Students: Findings and Insights from Twenty Years of Research.* San Francisco, CA: Jossey-Bass.

Pascarella, Ernest T., Patrick T. Terenzini. 2005. *How College Affects Students: A Third Decade of Research.* San Francisco, CA: Jossey-Bass.

Peri, Pierangelo. 1999. "Education and prejudice against immigrants." In Louk Hagendoorn and Shervin Nekuee (eds.), *Education and Racism.* London: Routledge: 21–32.

Persson, Mikael. 2015. "Education and political participation." *British Journal of Political Science* 45(3): 689–703.

Persson, Mikael, Karl-Oskar Lindgren, Sven Oskarsson. 2016. "How does education affect adolescents' political development?" *Economics of Education Review* 53: 182–193.

Peters, R. S. 1968. *Ethics and Education*, 5th ed. London: George Allen & Unwin Ltd.

Peters, Uwe, Nathan Honeycutt, Andreas De Block, Lee Jussim. 2020. "Ideological diversity, hostility, and discrimination in philosophy." *Philosophical Psychology* 33 (4): 511–548.

Peterson, Patti McGill. 1972. "Student organizations and the antiwar movement in America, 1900–1960." *American Studies* 13(1): 131–147.

Peterson, Steven A., Albert Somit (eds.). 2017. *Handbook of Biology and Politics*. Cheltenham: Edward Elgar Publishing.

Phelan, Jo, Bruce G. Link, Ann Stueve, Robert E. Moore. 1995. "Education, social liberalism, and economic conservatism: attitudes toward homeless people." *American Sociological Review* 60(1): 126–140.

Pietsch, Tamson. 2015. *Empire of Scholars: Universities, Networks and the British Academic World 1850–1939*. Manchester: Manchester University Press.

Piketty, Thomas. 2020. *Capital and Ideology*. Cambridge, MA: Harvard University Press.

Pipes, Richard. 1961. "The historical evolution of the Russian intelligentsia." In *The Russian Intelligentsia*. New York: Columbia University Press.

Plato. 1992 [ca. 375 BCE]. *Republic*, trans. G. M. A. Grube and C. D. C. Reeve. Indianapolis, IN: Hackett.

Post, Robert C. 2012. *Democracy, Expertise, and Academic Freedom: A First Amendment Jurisprudence for the Modern State*. New Haven, CT: Yale University Press.

Pradhanawati, Ari, George Towar Ikbal Tawakkal, Andrew D. Garner. 2019. "Voting their conscience: Poverty, education, social pressure and vote buying in Indonesia." *Journal of East Asian Studies* 19(1): 19–38.

Pratto, Felicia, Jim Sidanius, Lisa M. Stallworth, Bertram F. Malle. 1994. "Social dominance orientation: A personality variable predicting social and political attitudes." *Journal of Personality and Social Psychology* 67: 742.

Prentice, Deborah A. 2012. "Liberal norms and their discontents." *Perspectives on Psychological Science* 7(5): 516–518.

Pressey, Sidney L. 1946. "Changes from 1923 to 1943 in the attitudes of public school and university students." *Journal of Psychology: Interdisciplinary and Applied* 21(1): 173–188. https://doi.org/10.1080/00223980.1946.9917279.

Pridemore, William Alex. 2008. "A methodological addition to the cross-national empirical literature on social structure and homicide: A first test of the poverty-homicide thesis." *Criminology* 46: 133–154.

Pritchard, Keith W., Sing-Nan Fen, Thomas H. Buxton. 1971. "The political leanings of college teachers of education in eight selected universities and colleges." *The Western Political Quarterly* 24(3): 549. https://doi.org/10.2307/446923.

Pritchett, Lant. 2013. *The Rebirth of Education: Schooling Ain't Learning*. Washington, DC: CGD Books.

Putnam, Robert D. 1995. "Tuning in, tuning out: The strange disappearance of social capital in America." *Political Science and Politics* 28(4): 664–683.

Quintilian. 1892 [ca. 95 CE]. *Institutes of Oratory*, trans. John Selby Watson. London: George Bell & Sons.

Rados, Leonidas, Pieter Dhondt. 2017. "The first student strike in 1880: Socialist influences in the city of Iași 1." In Pieter Dhondt and Elizabethanne Boran (eds.), *Student Revolt, City, and Society in Europe*. London: Routledge: 323–337.

Rama, Shinasi A. (ed.). 2019. *The End of Communist Rule in Albania: Political Change and the Role of the Student Movement*. London: Routledge.

Rauch, Jonathan. 2021. *The Constitution of Knowledge: A Defense of Truth*. Washington, DC: Brookings.

Rauf, Tamkinat. 2021. "How college makes liberals (or conservatives)." *Socius* 7.

Ravitch, Diane. 2000. *Left Back: A Century of Battles over School Reform*. New York: Simon and Schuster.

Ravitch, Diane. 2001. "Education and democracy." In Diane Ravitch and Joseph P. Viteritti (eds.), *Making Good Citizens: Education and Civil Society*. New Haven, CT: Yale University Press: 15–29.

Ravitch, Diane, Joseph P. Viteritti (eds.). 2001. *Making Good Citizens: Education and Civil Society*. New Haven, CT: Yale University Press.

Reader, Keith A. 1987. *Intellectuals and the Left in France since 1968*. New York: Springer.

Redding, Richard E. 2013. "Politicized science." *Society* 50(5): 439–446.

Reimer, Sam. 2010. "Higher education and theological liberalism: Revisiting the old issue." *Sociology of Religion: A Quarterly Review* 71(4): 393–408.

Reuben, Julie A. 1996. *The Making of the Modern University: Intellectual Transformation and the Marginalization of Morality*. Chicago, IL: University of Chicago Press.

Rex, Millicent B. 1946. "The university constituencies in the recent British election." *Journal of Politics* 8(2) (May): 201–211.

Reyes, Daisy Verduzco. 2018. *Learning to Be Latino: How Colleges Shape Identity Politics*. New Brunswick, NJ: Rutgers University Press.

Rich, Harvey E. 1977. "The liberalizing influence of college: Some new evidence." *Adolescence* 12(46): 199.

Ridder-Symoens, Hilde de (ed.). 2003a. *A History of the University in Europe. Volume 1: Universities in the Middle Ages*. Cambridge: Cambridge University Press.

Ridder-Symoens, Hilde de (ed.). 2003b. *A History of the University in Europe. Volume 2: Universities in Early Modern Europe (1500–1800)*. Cambridge: Cambridge University Press.

Riffer, Roger L. 1972. "Determinants of university students' political attitudes or demythologizing campus political activism." *Review of Educational Research* 42(4): 561–571.

Rindermann, Heiner, Carmen Flores-Mendoza, Michael A. Woodley. 2012. "Political orientations, intelligence and education." *Intelligence* 40(2): 217–225.

Ringer, Fritz K. 1969. *The Decline of the German Mandarins: The German Academic Community, 1890–1933*. Middletown, CT: Wesleyan University Press.

Rojas, Fabio. 2007. *From Black Power to Black Studies: How a Radical Social Movement Became an Academic Discipline*. Baltimore, MD: Johns Hopkins University Press.

Rojas, Fabio. 2014. "Activism and the academy: Lessons from the rise of ethnic studies." In Neil Gross and Solon Simmons (eds.), *Professors and Their Politics*. Baltimore, MD: Johns Hopkins University Press: 243–266.

Rollin, Charles. 1872 [1731]. *Traite des Etudes*. Paris: Librairie de Firmin Didot.

Rom, Mark Carl. 2019. "A liberal polity: Ideological homogeneity in political science." *PS: Political Science & Politics* 52(4): 701–705.

Rorty, Amélie Oksenberg (ed.). 1998. *Philosophers on Education: Historical Perspectives*. London: Routledge.

Rorty, Richard. 1998. *Achieving Our Country: Leftist Thought in Twentieth-Century America*. Cambridge, MA: Harvard University Press.

Rosenberg, Morris. 1956. "Misanthropy and political ideology." *American Sociological Review* 21(6): 690–695. www.jstor.org/stable/2088419.

Ross, Dorothy. 1992. *The Origins of American Social Science*. Cambridge: Cambridge University Press.

Roth, Michael S. 2014. *Beyond the University: Why Liberal Education Matters*. New Haven, CT: Yale University Press.

Rothblatt, Sheldon. 1976. *Tradition and Change in English Liberal Education: An Essay in History and Culture*. London: Faber and Faber.

Rothman, Stanley. 2017. *The End of the Experiment: The Rise of Cultural Elites and the Decline of America's Civic Culture*. London: Routledge.

Rothman, Stanley., S. Robert Lichter. 2009. "The vanishing conservative: Is there a glass ceiling?" In Robert Maranto, Richard E. Redding, and Frederick M. Hess (eds.), *The Politically Correct University: Problems, Scope, and Reform*. Washington, DC: AEI Press: 60–76.

Rothman, Stanley, April Kelly-Woessner, Matthew Woessner. 2011. *The Still Divided Academy: How Competing Visions of Power, Politics, and Diversity Complicate the Mission of Higher Education*. Lanham, MD: Rowman and Littlefield.

Rothman, Stanley, Neil Nevitte, S. Robert Lichter. 2005. "Politics and professional advancement." *Academic Questions* 18(2): 71–84.

Rousseau, Jean-Jacques. 2007 [1762]. *Emile, or On Education*, trans. Barbara Foxley. London: Penguin.

Rüegg, Walter (ed.). 2004. *A History of the University in Europe. Volume 3: Universities in the Nineteenth and Early Twentieth Centuries (1800–1945)*. Cambridge: Cambridge University Press.

Rüegg, Walter (ed.). 2011. *A History of the University in Europe. Volume 4: Universities since 1945*. Cambridge: Cambridge University Press.

Rueschemeyer, Dietrich. 2006. "Why and how ideas matter." In Robert E. Goodin and Charles Tilly (eds.), *The Oxford Handbook of Contextual Political Analysis*. Oxford: Oxford University Press: 227–251.

Ruiter, Stijn, Tubergen Van Frank. 2009. "Religious attendance in cross-national perspective: A multilevel analysis of 60 countries." *American Journal of Sociology* 115(3): 863–895.

Sacerdote, Bruce. 2011. "Peer effects in education: How might they work, how big are they and how much do we know thus far?" In Eric Hanushek, Stephen Machin, and Ludger Woessmann (eds.), *Handbook of the Economics of Education*, 1st ed., vol. 3. New York: Elsevier: 249–277.

Saltmarsh, John, Edward Zlotkowski (eds.). 2011. *Higher Education and Democracy: Essays on Service-Learning and Civic Engagement*. Philadelphia, PA: Temple University Press.

Sanborn, Howard, Clayton L. Thyne. 2014. "Learning democracy: Education and the fall of authoritarian regimes." *British Journal of Political Science* 44(4): 773–797.

Scheepers, Peer, Manfred Te Grotenhuis, Frans Van Der Slik. 2002. "Education, religiosity and moral attitudes: Explaining cross-national effect differences." *Sociology of Religion* 63(2): 157–176.

Schnabel, Landon. 2018. "Education and attitudes toward interpersonal and state-sanctioned violence." *PS – Political Science and Politics* 51(3): 505–511.

Schnittker, Jason, Jere R. Behrman. 2012. "Learning to do well or learning to do good? Estimating the effects of schooling on civic engagement, social cohesion, and labor market outcomes in the presence of endowments." *Social Science Research* 41(2): 306–320. http://dx.doi.org/10.1016/j.ssresearch.2011.11.010.

Schochet, Peter Z. 2008. "Technical methods report: Statistical power for regression discontinuity designs in education evaluations." Washington, DC: National Center for Education Evaluation and Regional Assistance, Institute of Education Sciences, US Department of Education.

Schofer, Evan, John W. Meyer. 2005. "The worldwide expansion of higher education in the twentieth century." *American Sociological Review* 70(6): 898–920.

Schofer, Evan, Wesley Longhofer. 2011. "The structural sources of association." *American Journal of Sociology* 117(2): 539–585.

Schofer, Evan, Francisco O. Ramirez, John W. Meyer. 2020. "The societal consequences of higher education." *Sociology of Education* 94(1): 1–19.

Schonberg, William B. 1974. "Modification of attitudes of college students over time: 1923–1970." *Journal of Genetic Psychology* 125(2): 107–117. https://doi.org/10.1080/00221325.1974.10532308.

Schoon, Ingrid, Helen Cheng, Catharine R. Gale et al. 2010. "Social status, cognitive ability, and educational attainment as predictors of liberal social attitudes and political trust." *Intelligence* 38: 144–150.

Schrecker, Ellen W. 1986. *No Ivory Tower: McCarthyism and the Universities.* New York: Oxford University Press.

Schrecker, Ellen W. 2010. *The Lost Soul of Higher Education: Corporatization, the Assault on Academic Freedom, and the End of the American University.* New York: The New Press.

Schuller, Tom, John Preston, Cathie Hammond et al. 2004. *The Benefits of Learning: The Impact of Education on Health, Family Life and Social Capital.* London: RoutledgeFalmer.

Schwadel, Philip. 2011. "The effects of education on Americans' religious practices, beliefs, and affiliations." *Review of Religious Research* 53(2): 161–182.

Schwadel, Philip, Christopher R. H. Garneau. 2017. "The diffusion of tolerance: Birth cohort changes in the effects of education and income on political tolerance." *Sociological Forum* 32(4): 748–769.

Schwarcz, Vera. 1986. *The Chinese Enlightenment: Intellectuals and the Legacy of the May Fourth Movement of 1919.* Berkeley: University of California Press.

Scott, Joan Wallach. 2019. *Knowledge, Power, and Academic Freedom.* New York: Columbia University Press.

Scott, Ralph. 2022. "Does university make you more liberal? Estimating the within-individual effects of higher education on political values." *Electoral Studies* 77: 102471.

Seigel, Jerrold. 1999. *Bohemian Paris: Culture, Politics, and the Boundaries of Bourgeois Life, 1830–1930.* Baltimore, MD: Johns Hopkins University Press.

Shapira, Rina, Eva Etzioni-Halevy, Anat Barak. 1986. "Political attitudes of Israeli students: A comparative perspective." *Higher Education* 15(3): 231–246. www.jstor.org/stable/3446687.

Shapiro, Ben. 2004. *Brainwashed: How Universities Indoctrinate America's Youth.* Nashville, TN: WND Press.

Shapiro, Harold T. 2009. *A Larger Sense of Purpose: Higher Education and Society.* Princeton, NJ: Princeton University Press.

Shatz, Marshall. 1980. *Soviet Dissent in Historical Perspective.* Cambridge: Cambridge University Press.

Sheldon, Garrett Ward. 2001. *Encyclopedia of Political Thought.* New York: Infobase Publishing.

Shields, Jon A., Joshua M. Dunn, Sr. 2016. *Passing on the Right: Conservative Professors in the Progressive University.* Oxford: Oxford University Press.

Shils, Edward. 1989. "The modern university and liberal democracy." *Minerva* 27(4): 425–460.

Shimbori, Michiya. 1963. "Comparison between pre-and post-war student movements in Japan." *Sociology of Education* 37(1): 59–70.

Shumar, W. 1997. *College for Sale: A Critique of the Commodification of Higher Education.* London: Falmer Press.

Sidanius, James, Felicia Pratto, Michael Martin, Lisa Stallworth. 1991. "Consensual racism and career track: Some implications of social dominance theory." *Political Psychology* 12: 691–721.

Sidanius, James, Shana Levin, Colette Van Laar, David O. Sears. 2008. *The Diversity Challenge: Social Identity and Intergroup Relations on the College Campus.* New York: Russell Sage Foundation.

Sides, John, Daniel J. Hopkins (eds.). 2015. *Political Polarization in American Politics.* New York: Bloomsbury Publishing USA.

Sieben, Inge, Paul M. de Graaf. 2004. "Schooling or social origin? The bias in the effect of educational attainment on social orientations." *European Sociological Review* 20 (2): 107–122.

Sinclair, Upton. 1923. *The Goose-Step: A Study of American Education,* vol. 1. Pasadena, CA: Upton Sinclair.

Singer, Peter. 1972. "Famine, affluence, and morality." *Philosophy and Public Affairs* 229: 229–239.

Slaughter, Sheila. 2014. *Academic Capitalism in the Age of Globalization.* Baltimore, MD: Johns Hopkins University Press.

Smith, Bruce L. R., Jeremy D. Mayer, A. Lee Fritschler. 2008. *Closed Minds? Politics and Ideology in American Universities.* Washington, DC: Brookings Institution Press.

Smith, Christian. 2014. *The Sacred Project of American Sociology.* Oxford: Oxford University Press.

Smith, Henry DeWitt. 1970. "The origins of student radicalism in Japan." *Journal of Contemporary History* 5(1): 87–103.

Smith, Henry DeWitt. 1972. *Japan's First Student Radicals.* Cambridge, MA: Harvard University Press.

Smith, Kevin, John R. Alford, Peter K. Hatemi et al. 2012. "Biology, ideology, and epistemology: How do we know political attitudes are inherited and why should we care?" *American Journal of Political Science* 56(1): 17–33.

Soares, Glaucio A. D. 1967a. "The active few." In Seymour Martin Lipset (ed.), *Student Politics.* New York: Basic Books: 124–147.

Soares, Glaucio A. D. 1967b. "Intellectual identity and political ideology among university students." In Seymour M. Lipset and Aldo Solari (eds.), *Elites in Latin America*. New York: Oxford University Press: 431–434.

Söderlund, Therese, Guy Madison. 2017. "Objectivity and realms of explanation in academic journal articles concerning sex/gender: A comparison of gender studies and the other social sciences." *Scientometrics* 112(2): 1093–1109.

Sondheimer, Rachel Milstein, Donald P. Green. 2010. "Using experiments to estimate the effects of education on voter turnout." *American Journal of Political Science* 54(1): 174–189.

Spaulding, Charles B., Henry A. Turner. 1968. "Political orientation and field of specialization among college professors." *Sociology of Education* 41(3): 247. https://doi.org/10.2307/2111874.

Spruyt, Bram. 2014. "An asymmetric group relation? An investigation into public perceptions of education-based groups and the support for populism." *Acta Politica* 49(2): 123–143.

Stan, Ana-Maria. 2017. "The 1922–1923 student revolts at the University of Cluj, Romania: From local anti-Semitic academic protests to national events." In Pieter Dhondt and Elizabethanne Boran (eds.), *Student Revolt, City, and Society in Europe*. London: Routledge: 286–303.

Starr, Paul. 2007. *Freedom's Power: The True Force of Liberalism*. New York: Basic Books.

Statera, Gianni. 1975. *Death of a Utopia: The Development and Decline of Student Movements in Europe*. New York: Oxford University Press.

Stember, Herbert. 1953. "Student opinion on issues of academic freedom." *Journal of Social Issues* 9(3): 43–47. https://doi.org/10.1111/j.1540-4560.1953.tb00935.x.

Stephens, William N., C. Stephen Long. 1970. "Education and political behavior." *Political Science Annual* 2(1): 3–33.

Stern, Ludmila. 2006. *Western Intellectuals and the Soviet Union, 1920–40: From Red Square to the Left Bank*. London: Routledge.

Stolzenberg, Ellen Bara, Kevin Eagan, Hilary B. Zimmerman et al. 2019. *Undergraduate Teaching Faculty: The HERI Faculty Survey 2016–2017*. Los Angeles, CA: Higher Education Research Institute Graduate School of Education & Information Studies, University of California, Los Angeles.

Stone, Lawrence. 1964. "The educational revolution in England, 1560–1640." *Past & Present* 28: 41–80.

Stouffer, Samuel A. 1955. *Communism, Conformity, and Civil Liberties*. New York: John Wiley and Sons.

Strauss, Leo. 2004 [1959]. "What is liberal education?" *Academic Questions* 17(1): 31–36.

Strother, Logan, Spencer Piston, Ezra Golberstein, Sarah E. Gollust, Daniel Eisenberg. 2020. "College roommates have a modest but significant influence on each other's political ideology." *Proceedings of the National Academy of Sciences* (December): 1–5.

Stubager, Rune. 2008. "Education effects on authoritarian–libertarian values: A question of socialization." *The British Journal of Sociology* 59(2): 327–350.

Stubager, Rune. 2010. "The development of the education cleavage: Denmark as a critical case." *West European Politics* 33(3): 505–533.

Stubager, Rune. 2013. "The changing basis of party competition: Education, authoritarian–libertarian values and voting." *Government and Opposition* 48(3): 372–397.

Sullivan, David. 2020. *Education, Liberal Democracy and Populism: Arguments from Plato, Locke, Rousseau and Mill.* London: Routledge.

Surridge, Paula. 2016. "Education and liberalism: Pursuing the link." *Oxford Review of Education* 42(2): 146–164.

Svallfors, S. 2004. "Class, attitudes and the welfare state: Sweden in comparative perspective." *Social Policy and Administration* 38: 119–138.

Symonds, Percival M. 1925. "A social attitude questionnaire." *Journal of Educational Psychology* 16(5): 316.

Teorell, Jan, Michael Coppedge, Staffan Lindberg, Svend-Erik Skaaning. 2019. "Measuring polyarchy across the globe, 1900–2017." *Studies in Comparative International Development* 54(1): 71–95.

Tetlock, Philip E. 1994. "Political psychology or politicized psychology: Is the road to scientific hell paved with good moral intentions?" *Political Psychology* 15(3): 509–529.

Thompson, Robert J., Jr. 2014. *Beyond Reason and Tolerance: The Purpose and Practice of Higher Education.* Oxford: Oxford University Press.

Torstendahl, Rolf. 1993. "The transformation of professional education in the nineteenth century." In Sheldon Rothblatt and Bjorn Wittrock (eds.), *The European and American University since 1800.* Cambridge: Cambridge University Press: 109–141.

Transparency International. 2013. *Global Corruption Report: Education.* Abingdon: Earthscan by Routledge.

Treas, Judith. 2002. "How cohorts, education, and ideology shaped a new sexual revolution on American attitudes toward nonmarital sex, 1972–1998." *Sociological Perspectives* 45(3): 267–283.

Tromly, Benjamin. 2013. *Making the Soviet Intelligentsia: Universities and Intellectual Life under Stalin and Khrushchev.* Cambridge: Cambridge University Press.

Truex, Rory. 2011. "Corruption, attitudes, and education: Survey evidence from Nepal." *World Development* 39(7): 1133–1142.

Turnbull, George. 1742. *Observations upon Liberal Education, in All Its Branches.* London: Millar.

Turner, Henry A., Carl Hetrick. 1970. "Political attitudes and participation of American academics, 1970." ICPSR 7371. https://doi.org/10.3886/ICPSR07371.v1.

Turner, Henry A., Charles B. Spaulding. 1969. "Political attitudes and behavior of selected academically-affiliated professional groups." *Polity* 1(3): 309–336. https://doi.org/10.2307/3233943.

Turner, Henry A., Charles G. McClintock, Charles B. Spaulding. 1963. "The political party affiliation of American political scientists." *Western Political Quarterly* 16(3): 650–665.

Turner, R. Steven. 1974. "University reformers and professorial scholarship in Germany 1760–1806." In Lawrence Stone (ed), *The University in Society, Volume II: Europe, Scotland, and the United States from the 16th to the 20th Century.* Princeton, NJ: Princeton University Press: 495–532.

Turner, Stephen. 2014. *American Sociology: From Pre-Disciplinary to Post-Normal.* London: Palgrave Macmillan.

UNESCO Institute for Statistics. 2012. *International Standard Classification of Education: ISCED 2011*. Montreal: UNESCO Institute for Statistics.

Uslaner, Eric M., Bo Rothstein. 2016. "The historical roots of corruption: State building, economic inequality, and mass education." *Comparative Politics* 48(2): 227–248.

van de Werfhorst, Herman G. 2020. "Are universities left-wing bastions? The political orientation of professors, professionals, and managers in Europe." *The British Journal of Sociology* 71(1): 47–73.

van de Werfhorst, Herman G., Nan Dirk de Graaf. 2004. "The sources of political orientations in post-industrial society: Social class and education revisited." *The British Journal of Sociology* 55(2): 211–235.

van de Werfhorst, Herman G., Gerbert Kraaykamp. 2001. "Four field-related educational resources and their impact on labor, consumption, and sociopolitical orientation." *Sociology of Education* 74(4): 296–317.

Van der Waal, Jeroen, Peter Achterberg, Dick Houtman. 2007. "Class is not dead – It has been buried alive: Class voting and cultural voting in postwar Western societies (1956–1990)." *Politics & Society* 35(3): 403–426.

Van Dyke, Nella. 1999. "The dynamics of college student protest, 1930–1990." PhD dissertation, Department of Sociology, University of Arizona.

Van Dyke, Nella. 2003. "Crossing movement boundaries: Factors that facilitate coalition protest by American college students, 1930–1990." *Social Problems* 50(2): 226–250.

Verba, Sidney, Kay L. Schlozman, Henry E. Brady. 1995. *Voice and Equality: Civic Volunteerism in American Politics*. Cambridge, MA: Harvard University Press.

Voas, David, Mark Chaves. 2016. "Is the United States a counterexample to the secularization thesis?" *American Journal of Sociology* 121(5): 1517–1556.

Von Dirke, Sabine. 1997. *All Power to the Imagination! The West German Counterculture from the Student Movement to the Greens*. Lincoln: University of Nebraska Press.

Wagner, Ulrich, Andreas Zick. 1995. "The relation of formal education to ethnic prejudice: Its reliability, validity and explanation." *European Journal of Social Psychology* 25(1): 41–56.

Wallerstein, Immanuel, Paul Starr (eds.). 1971. *The University Crisis Reader. Volume I: The Liberal University under Attack; Volume II: Confrontation and Counterattack*. New York: Random House.

Walter, Richard J. 1968. *Student Politics in Argentina: The University Reform and Its Effects, 1918–1964*. New York: Basic Books.

Walton, Grant W., Caryn Peiffer. 2017. "The impacts of education and institutional trust on citizens' willingness to report corruption: Lessons from Papua New Guinea." *Australian Journal of Political Science* 52(4): 517–536.

Wasburn, Philo C., Tawnya J. Adkins Covert. 2017. *Making Citizens: Political Socialization Research and Beyond*. New York: Springer.

Washburn, Jennifer. 2005. *University, Inc.: The Corporate Corruption of American Higher Education*. New York: Basic Books.

Wasserstrom, Jeffrey. 1991. *Student Protests in Twentieth-Century China: The View from Shanghai*. Stanford, CA: Stanford University Press.

Weakliem, David L. 2002. "The effects of education on political opinions: An international study." *International Journal of Opinion Research* 13(2): 141–157.

Webster, Noah. 1787. "Education." *American Magazine* (December).

Weidman, John. 1989. "Undergraduate socialization: A conceptual approach." *Higher Education: Handbook of Theory and Research*, vol. 5. New York: Agathon: 289–322.

Weil, Frederick D. 1985. "The variable effects of education on liberal attitudes: A comparative historical analysis of anti-Semitism using public opinion survey data." *American Sociological Review* 50: 458–474.

Weisenfeld, Ursula, Ingrid Ott. 2011. "Academic discipline and risk perception of technologies: An empirical study." *Research Policy* 40(3): 487–499.

Weiss, Meredith Leigh, Edward Aspinall (eds.). 2012. *Student Activism in Asia: Between Protest and Powerlessness*. Minneapolis: University of Minnesota Press.

Weisz, George. 1983. *The Emergence of Modern Universities in France, 1863–1914*. Princeton, NJ: Princeton University Press.

Weitz-Shapiro, Rebecca, Matthew S. Winters. 2017. "Can citizens discern? Information credibility, political sophistication, and the punishment of corruption in Brazil." *The Journal of Politics* 79(1): 60–74.

Whewell, William. 1838. *On the Principles of English University Education*. London: J. W. Parker.

Whitehead, Alfred North. 1967. *The Aims of Education*. New York: Free Press.

Wilson, John K. 1995. *The Myth of Political Correctness: The Conservative Attack on Higher Education*. Durham, NC: Duke University Press.

Wilson, J. Matthew. 2019. "The nature and consequences of ideological hegemony in American political science." *PS: Political Science & Politics* 52(4): 724–727.

Wodtke, Geoffrey T. 2012. "The impact of education on intergroup attitudes: A multiracial analysis." *Social Psychology Quarterly* 75(1): 80–106.

Woessner, Matthew, April Kelly-Woessner. 2009a. "I think my professor is a Democrat: Considering whether students recognize and react to faculty politics." *PS: Political Science and Politics* 42(2): 343–352.

Woessner, Matthew, April Kelly-Woessner. 2009b. "Left pipeline: Why conservatives don't get doctorates." In Robert Maranto, Fredrick Hess, and Richard Redding (eds.), *The Politically Correct University: Problems, Scope, and Reforms*. Washington, DC: AEI Press: 38–59.

Woessner, Matthew, April Kelly-Woessner. 2020. "Why college students drift left: The stability of political identity and relative malleability of issue positions among college students." *PS: Political Science & Politics* 53(4): 657–664.

Wolff, Robert Paul. 1969. *The Ideal of the University*. Boston, MA: Beacon Press.

Wolfinger, Raymond, Steven J. Rosenstone. 1980. *Who Votes?* New Haven, CT: Yale University Press.

Wren, J. Thomas, Ronald Riggio (eds.). 2009. *Leadership and the Liberal Arts: Achieving the Promise of a Liberal Education*. New York: Springer.

Wright, James D. 1975. "The socio-political attitudes of White, college-educated youth." *Youth & Society* 6(3): 251–296. https://doi.org/10.1177/0044118X7500600301.

Wright, John Paul, Ryan T. Motz, Timothy S. Nixon. 2019. "Political disparities in the academy: It's more than self-selection." *Academic Questions* 32(3): 402–411.

Wright, Teresa. 2001. *The Perils of Protest: State Repression and Student Activism in China and Taiwan*. Honolulu: University of Hawaii Press.

Wuthnow, Robert. 1987. *Meaning and Moral Order: Explorations in Cultural Analysis*. Berkeley: University of California Press.

Yang, Jinyu, Bryony Hoskins. 2020. "Does university have an effect on young people's active citizenship in England?" *Higher Education* 80: 839–856.

Yeh, Wen-hsin. 1992. "Educating young radicals: Shanghai University, 1922–1927." *Republican China* 17(1): 71–77.

Zeilig, Leo. 2007. *Revolt and Protest: Student Politics and Activism in Sub-Saharan Africa*. New York: Bloomsbury Publishing.

Zhang, Tony Huiquan, Robert Brym. 2019. "Tolerance of homosexuality in 88 countries: Education, political freedom, and liberalism." *Sociological Forum* 34(2).

Zhao, Dingxin. 2001. *The Power of Tiananmen: State-Society Relations and the 1989 Beijing Student Movement*. Chicago, IL: University of Chicago Press.

Zigerell, Lawrence J. 2017. "Reducing political bias in political science estimates." *PS: Political Science & Politics* 50(1): 179–183.

Zigerell, Lawrence J. 2019. "Left unchecked: Political hegemony in political science and the flaws it can cause." *PS: Political Science & Politics* 52(4): 720–723.

Zimmerman, Seth D. 2014. "The returns to college admission for academically marginal students." *Journal of Labor Economics* 32(4): 711–754.

Zipp, John F., Rudy Fenwick. 2006. "Is the academy a liberal hegemony? The political orientations and educational values of professors." *International Journal of Public Opinion Quarterly* 70(3): 304–326.

Index

Aboaf, Isabelle Mireille, 197
academic disciplines. *See* disciplines
activism. *See also* student activists and protests
  liberalism and, 9
admissions processes, for universities, in
  Romanian Natural Experiment,
  61–62
Altbach, Philip, 160
American Social Science Association
  (ASSA), 228
Aristotle, 13
Arnold, Matthew, 13
as-if random assignment, in Romanian Natural
  Experiment, 58–61
ASSA. *See* American Social Science Association
autonomy, of universities, 243–244
  in Europe, 243–244
  in Latin America, 244
  in US, 244
Al-Azhar University, 168

bac exam, for Romanian Natural Experiment,
  52, 53, 56
  cheating issues for, 57–58
    in-exam, 57
    post-exam, 58
  ex ante evaluations, 58–61
  manipulations of, 57–58
  nonparametric density estimates for, 60
  pass/fail variables, 61
  pretreatment covariates, 73
  scores for, 70–72
    student average score histograms, 59,
    60–61
  test effects, 74–75

treatment thresholds for, 63
Baker, David, 266
Barton, Allen, 20
Bennett, William, 15
Bensel, Richard, 197
Bentham, Jeremy, 8
bias
  in causal-effects studies, 27–28, 30
    publication bias, 32
    research bias, 32
    social desirability bias, 82–84
Bildung, in higher education, 15, 149
Bloom, Alan, 15
Bok, Derek, 14
"Bologna Process." *See* European Higher
  Education Area
Bolsonaro, Jair, 233
Bourdieu, Pierre, 234–235
Bowen, William, 14
Brombert, Victor, 177
Bush, Vannevar, 243

cancel culture, 9, 18, 216–217
capital. *See* cultural capital; social capital
Caplan, Bryan, 15
Castiglione, Baldassare, 13
causal-effects studies, of education, 21–32,
  34–46
  analysis of, 32, 139–140
  bias in, 27–28, 30
    publication, 32
    research, 32
  characteristics of, 22–24
  exogenous shocks in, 29
  findings of, 24–25

United Kingdom (UK) (cont.)
   political ideology of (from 1900 to
     1997), 196
United States (US). *See also specific topics*
  academic disciplines in
   contemporary comparisons between,
     223–226, 227
   historical evolution of, 224–225
   by party affiliation, 226
  comparative views of universities in, 203,
    204, 209
  social and political attitudes in (1996–2016),
    210–211
  student activists and protests in, 189–190
  universities in, 268–275
   autonomy of, 244
   comparative perspectives of, 270
   diversity issues in, 274–275
   liberalizing effect of, 268–271
   professoriate in, 271–273
  university constituencies in
   Cornell University, 196–198
   flagship university counties in, 199–201
   Harvard University, 198–199
Universal Declaration of Human Rights, 51
universities, university education and, 50–52.
    See also liberal universities; Romanian
    Natural Experiment; student activists
    and protests
  autonomy of, 243–244
   in Europe, 243–244
   in Latin America, 244
   in US, 244
  comparative views by group, 202–209
   Romanian Natural Experiment and,
    205–209
   through surveys, 203
   in US, 203, 204, 209
  core mission of, 242
  faculty at, 179–182
   conservative, 240–241
   International Social Survey of, 181
   studies and surveys of, 180, 183–184
   in Sweden, 182
  freedom of, 246–247
  frequency of term in Google Books, 174
  functionalist approach to liberalism
    influenced by, 242–246
  gestalt of, 161–162
  global expansion of, 170, 173
  graduates of, 201
  history of, 168–175

   during colonial era, 169
   in modern era, 169
   studia generalia ideal in, 168
  intellectuals and, 175–179
  International Standard Classification of
    Education, 50
  massive open online courses as
    supplement, 175
  methodological approaches to, 50–51
  in Organisation for Economic Co-operation
    and Development, 202
  overview of, 209–213
  partisanship influenced by, 133, 202
  perceptions of, 214
  political ideology on, 213–215
   historical turning points for, 216
  political indoctrination in, 51
  regional accessibility to, 169
  soft power and, 264–267
  tertiary educational attainment and
   from 1950 to 2015, 171
   in 2015, 172
  time-series data on, 182–185
   campaign contributions by academics in,
    182–185, 186
   political affiliations of academics in,
    182, 185
  under Universal Declaration of Human
    Rights, 51
  in US, 268–275
   autonomy of, 244
   comparative perspectives of, 270
   diversity issues in, 274–275
   liberalizing effect of, 268–271
   professoriate in, 271–273
university as weathervane theory, 233–234
university effect, 253–255, 263
  social capital index, 256–259
US. *See* United States

Van Dyke, Nella, 189–190
Varieties of Democracy project, 124–129, 138
Veblen, Thorstein, 248
victimhood, 18

Wallace, Henry, 221
Walter, Richard, 187–188
Washington, George, 177
Weber, Max, 177
Webster, Noah, 15
Whewell, William, 13
White privilege, 18

For EU product safety concerns, contact us at Calle de José Abascal, 56–1°,
28003 Madrid, Spain or eugpsr@cambridge.org.

www.ingramcontent.com/pod-product-compliance
Ingram Content Group UK Ltd.
Pitfield, Milton Keynes, MK11 3LW, UK
UKHW010249140625
459647UK00013BA/1740